A History of War Crimes Trials in Post 1945 Asia-Pacific

Zhaoqi Cheng

A History of War Crimes Trials in Post 1945 Asia-Pacific

Zhaoqi Cheng
Shanghai Jiao Tong University
Shanghai, China

Translated by

Jun He
East China University of Science and Technology
Shanghai, China

Fangbin Yang
East China University of Political Science and Law
Shanghai, China

ISBN 978-981-13-6699-4 ISBN 978-981-13-6697-0 (eBook)
https://doi.org/10.1007/978-981-13-6697-0

Jointly published with Shanghai Jiao Tong University Press
The print edition is not for sale in China Mainland. Customers from China Mainland please order the print book from: Shanghai Jiao Tong University Press.
ISBN of the China Mainland edition: 978-7-313-16041-6

Library of Congress Control Number: 2019936149

Translation from the Chinese language edition: 东京审判——为了世界和平 by Zhaoqi Cheng, © Shanghai Jiao Tong University Press 2017. Published by Shanghai Jiao Tong University Press. All Rights Reserved.

This Palgrave Macmillan imprint is published by the registered company Springer Nature Singapore Pte Ltd.
The registered company address is: 152 Beach Road, #21-01/04 Gateway East, Singapore 189721, Singapore

Preface

Since ancient times, the greatest disasters that mankind have experienced have been wars. During the twentieth century, two World Wars broke out. Advancements in science and technology mean that mountains and rivers can no longer serve as a barrier to block attacks, and the destructive nature of war has reached an almost unprecedented level whereby human civilization could be outright destroyed. Investigating the responsibility of those who wage war, and preventing further war crimes from taking place by punishing the perpetrators have become critical issues that need to be solved urgently. Since the late nineteenth century, war crimes have attracted the attention of the international community.

The "Convention with Respect to the Laws and Customs of War on Land" was established at the International Peace Conference at The Hague in 1899. The conventions of the Second Hague Conference in 1907 saw only a few major advancements from the 1899 convention. As early as 1864, the International Committee of the Red Cross has settled treaties on the treatment of sick and wounded prisoners. After several amendments, the Treaty on the Treatment of Prisoners of War was promulgated in 1929. These treaties and provisions specify the treatment of prisoners, and what assistance should be provided to the wounded and the sick. It assesses the use of weapons and the means of war, and explicitly prohibits excessive harm to military personnel and civilians. It plays a positive role in limiting the vicious outcome of war and punishing the violators.

The enactment of laws and regulations on war marks a great improvement in the rationality of mankind. But preventing war is obviously much more important than limiting the crimes committed during the war. This is because the catastrophe caused by war itself is far more serious and massive than the crimes committed during the war. It is also much more difficult to create legislation to limit war activities than it is to regulate general war crimes. For instance: what is aggression? What is the difference between aggression and self-defense? Is there any limit to self-defense? And if so, what is the limit? How can you determine one party in the war as an aggressor? So far these questions have not found satisfactory answers. This proves that legislation, while it might seem easy, is actually extremely difficult.

It was the tremendous losses caused by the First World War that made the international community realize that legislation—albeit difficult to achieve—would be necessary. After World War I, the preparatory committee of the Paris Peace Conference's "Liability and Punishment Commission for War Initiators" put forward a report proposing that heads of state should be prosecuted for launching war. The report was ultimately not approved by the Peace Conference. However, the Allies still persevered with the prosecution of Wilhelm II, the last German Emperor, by virtue of Section 227 of the Vienna Convention: "The highest crime in violation of international morality and treaties". Once again, the Allies failed because of the Netherlands's refusal to extradite the accused. This well-known abortion trial was not about Wilhelm II dodging a bullet, but about missing an opportunity to place responsibility with those who started the war. The case can serve as a symbol of how difficult it is to punish those responsible for starting a war.

The most important act by the international community to limit war crimes was during the 1928 International Convention, commonly known as the "Kellogg-Briand Pact". As its real name, the Pact of Paris, indicates, signatory states promised not to use war to resolve "disputes or conflicts of whatever nature or of whatever origin they may be, which may arise among them". It was signed on 27 August 1928 by what were then the 15 strongest countries, including the United States, Britain, France, Germany, Japan and Italy. Soon after, a further 63 countries signed it including the Soviet Union. Consequently, it was signed by almost all of the world's great families.

The "non-war" idea advocated by the Pact of Paris had almost universal acceptance and marked an important milestone in history. We cannot blame later generations for criticizing the convention by not being explicit about "invasion"; the defect did exist. However, just because the convention avoided the difficult by choosing the easy, it was at the time possible for all countries to reach a "non-war" consensus.

Of course, the ideals of a "non-war" agreement fell apart when there was breach of contract, and the pact was merely a scrap of paper. Since then, the Eurasian bells and fires have fueled one other and eventually led to much further destruction in World War II. This shows that we cannot avoid a war without proper legal enforcement, and we cannot trust in mere unfettered promises.

In view of this, when rebuilding the postwar international order, the allied countries, having learnt painful lessons, had to overcome all kinds of difficulties, and finally build the foundation for protecting civilizations from further destruction. Seventy years after the war, though war had not ceased to exist, there were no uncontrollable battles between powerful nations, much less a world war. Although world peace could not be fully guaranteed, the process to focus on peace had seen momentum. The two military trials in Tokyo and Nuremberg became important cornerstones for the postwar foundation of peace.

"Anti-peace crimes" were viewed to be as serious as "crimes against humanity" during the Nuremberg trials, and were of even greater significance during the Tokyo Trials. Anti-peace crimes were the most severe crimes in Tokyo, and all defendants appeared in court on these charges. The importance of anti-peace crimes in Tokyo trials remains unparalleled. The Tokyo Trials were also known as the Class A Trials, "anti-peace crime trials", and "Class A anti-pacifist crimes" in the International Military Tribunal for the Far East Charter. The defendants in the Tokyo Trial were known as "Class A war criminals". During the Nuremberg trials, "Class C humanitarian crimes" were not lighter but even heavier than "Class A anti-peace crimes"; so there was no such thing as Class A trials or Class A war criminals.

In a court speech, Keenan, the chief prosecutor of the Tokyo trial, made many references to "humanity", "civilization" and "peace", reaffirming that "we are not conducting ordinary trials today, but the battle to save human civilization from destruction". When the defense questioned jurisdiction prior to the opening of the court session, Keenan made it clear that "safeguarding peace" was the "mission" of the Tokyo Trials. Safeguarding world peace was the Allies' fundamental purpose in conducting the Tokyo Trials. Even so, jurisdiction was a contentious issue during the trial, and after, it was the protracted offensive and defensive. The prosecutors (like the judge's corps) still adhered to the "procedural justice" of the "ordinary trial". During postwar trial discussions, the allies highlighted that they were fully aware of difficulties they might face in complying with existing judicial fairness (such as the so-called "ex post facto law"). They opted not to carry out speedy executions or establish a simple military court, but instead adopted a cautious approach in the allied courts. This showed the allied countries' firm determination not only to win trust, but to set an example for future generations to defend peace.

Today, Japan's Prime Minister Shinzo Abe publicly stated in the House of Representatives that "the Tokyo Trial was victor's justice"; the Japanese Liberal Democratic Party set up a special agency to "review" the Tokyo Trial; and the Japanese government frequently accuse others of "changing the status quo" while constantly trying to overthrow the basic "status quo" postwar order in East Asia, which is based on the Tokyo Trial. Reviewing these great trials from 70 years ago is of great importance to human history. It helps us revisit the significance of the Tokyo Trial and confirm our confidence in upholding their results.

Shanghai, China Zhaoqi Cheng

Contents

Part I

1 The Road to the Tokyo Trials 3
- *1 Major Allies' Stances on Trials Against Japan* 3
- *2 The United Nation's War Crimes Commission and the Development of the Laws of War* 14
- *3 Preparatory Work Ahead of the Tokyo Trials* 21
- *4 Summary* 40
- *Bibliography* 41

2 The Dispute Over Jurisdiction Prior to the Court Opening 43
- *1 Questions from the Defense* 43
- *2 The Prosecution's Reply* 49
- *3 Debate Continues* 54
- *4 Related Continuing Debates* 57
- *5 Summary* 67
- *Bibliography* 67

3 The Trials 71
- *1 Trial Procedures* 71
- *2 The Crimes Against Peace Trials* 80
- *3 The Trial Proceedings for War Crimes* 90

4 *Summary* 102
Bibliography 103

4 The Declaration of Judgment 105
1 *Disagreements Among Judges and the Formation of the Verdict* 105
2 *Interpretations of the Verdict and the Individual Opinions* 112
3 *Reactions to the Verdict and How It Was Evaluated* 123
4 *Summary* 126
Bibliography 126

5 Other Asian Trials for Japanese War Crimes 127
1 *The Allies' Trials* 127
2 *The "Quasi-Class A" Trial* 133
3 *Class B and C Trials Conducted Within the Allied Nations* 140
4 *After the Trials* 157
5 *Summary* 160
Bibliography 160

Part II

6 A Reevaluation of the Tokyo Trial Argument 165
1 *Following Discussions on the Issues of the "Ex Post Facto" Law* 165
2 *The Issue of Conspiracy* 167
3 *The Issue of Crimes Against Humanity* 172
4 *The Reevaluation of the War Responsibility of the Showa Emperor* 176
5 *Summary* 187
Bibliography 191

7 Evidence-Take Nanjing Massacre as Example 195
1 *The Reevaluation of the Testimony of Matsui Iwane* 196
2 *A Review of the Testimony of Ogawa Sekijiro* 214
3 *Summary* 242
Bibliography 242

8 Tokyo Trials and International Rules of Law 245
1 The Origin and Formation of the Views of Illegal War 245
2 Aggressive War Is an International Crime 249
3 The Establishment of Individual Criminal Responsibility 254
4 Strengthening the Concept of Humanity and Human Rights 261
5 The Demonstration of Judicial Justice 265
6 Summary 275
Bibliography 276

9 Tokyo Trials and World Peace 279
1 Deny Japan's National Aggressive Policy, Reject Militarism 279
2 Open Up International Judicial Precedent, Prosecute War Criminal Responsibility 285
3 Promote Popularization of Democracy and Establish a Peaceful Order 294
4 Summary 302
Bibliography 303

Appendix 307

Postscript 357

List of Figures

Chapter 1

Fig. 1 Foreign Ministers' Meeting in Moscow (Above: From left to right, front row: Chinese Ambassador to the Soviet Union Fu Bingchang, US Secretary of State Hull, Representative Molotov of the Soviet People's Association for Foreign Affairs, British Foreign Minister Eden) Below: Hull suggested that China should participate later, because the Chinese national flag was not prepared for the meeting. Therefore, the United States, Soviet Union and British flags were removed 5

Fig. 2 Three leaders at the Cairo Conference (From left: President of the Chinese National Government Chiang Kai-shek, US President Roosevelt, British Prime Minister Winston Churchill, and Madame Chiang Soong Mei-ling) 6

Fig. 3 Mao Zedong and Zhu De meet with Hurley (In November 1944, the leaders of the Chinese Communist Party Mao Zedong and Zhu De met in Yan'an with Hurley, the private representative of President Roosevelt) 6

Fig. 4 The Yalta Conference (From left to right, front row: British Prime Minister Churchill, US President Roosevelt, Soviet Union leader Stalin) 7

Fig. 5 The Potsdam Conference (1) (From left: Soviet Union leader Stalin, U.S. President Truman, British Prime Minister Churchill) 7

Fig. 6 The Potsdam Conference (2) (The British general election results were announced during the Potsdam Conference. Attlee replaced Churchill as prime minister, and subsequently signed later documents and participated in meetings) 8
Fig. 7 The original draft of the Potsdam Proclamation (The leaders' signatures were originally ordered United States, UK, then China. They were later changed to United States, China, UK, when the document was officially released on July 26, 1945) 8
Fig. 8 Japan's Surrender (On September 2, 1945, aboard the US "Missouri" battleship, Meiji Michijiro signed a surrender on behalf of Japan) 31
Fig. 9 IMTFE prosecutors 32
Fig. 10 IMTFE judges 33
Fig. 11 Judge Mei Ju-ao and President Webb 35
Fig. 12 IMTFE Class A war crimes defendants (1) 36
Fig. 13 IMTFE Class A war crimes defendants (2) 37
Fig. 14 The IMTFE courtroom 39
Fig. 15 The IMTFE seating chart 40

Chapter 2

Fig. 1 The courtroom and national flags (1) (The judges of India and the Philippines had not arrived before the opening of the Tokyo Trials, so there were only nine national flags) 45
Fig. 2 The courtroom and national flags (2) (The national flags of France and the Netherlands look similar, and were once misplaced) 45
Fig. 3 The courtroom and national flags (3) (All the judges present at the court. From left to right: India, Netherlands, Canada, United Kingdom, United States, Australia, China, Soviet Union, France, New Zealand, Philippines) 46
Fig. 4 The courtroom and national flags (4) (After India gained independence in August 1947, the Tokyo tribunal changed the Indian flag) 46
Fig. 5 The defense team at the trials 48
Fig. 6 Deputy Director of the defense team Kiyose Ichiro (first from the right, front row) 48
Fig. 7 Chief Prosecutor Joseph B. Keenan (on the podium) 49
Fig. 8 Defense counsel Major Blakeney (the speaker on the podium) 56
Fig. 9 The Japanese government researched the documents of the Tokyo Trials (1) (The Japanese government held

a countermeasure meeting two days before the Tokyo Trials were announced) 64
Fig. 10 The Japanese government researched the documents of Tokyo Trials (2) (The Japanese government authorized scholars to study "urgent" Tokyo Trial documents) 65
Fig. 11 The Japanese government researched the documents of Tokyo Trials (3) (Kaya Okinori, an A-class war criminal who was released and returned to politics, commissioned scholars to research the Tokyo Trials) 66

Chapter 3

Fig. 1 Interpreters at the Tokyo Trials 79
Fig. 2 Emperor of Manchukuo Puyi and the prosecutors (Puyi, called as a witness, testified in court for eight days. From left to right, front row: Prosecutor Golunsky from the Soviet Uninon, Puyi and Chief Prosecutor Keenan. Puyi and Henry Chiu were looking at each other. Qiu was the prosecutors' secretary of China standing in the back row) 84
Fig. 3 Puyi testified in court (On August 26, 1946, when the defense counsel Okamoto cross-examined Puyi, he presented to the court a book. The book had a picture of a fan on which was a Chinese poem written by Puyi. Okamoto requested the court to use the picture for the purposes of handwriting identification. And the court finally accepted the fan as evidence) 85
Fig. 4 Chinese prosecutor Judson Nyi (Chief adviser of the prosecution team, podium speaker) 86
Fig. 5 Chinese prosecution team (From left to right, front row: Yu Kwei—adviser, Judson Nyi—adviser, Hsiang Che-chun, Wu Xueyi—adviser, Zheng Luda—translator, Zhang Peiji—translator. From left to right, back row: Zhou Xiqin—translator, James Liu—secretary, Yang Qinglin—secretary to the judge, Daniel S. Ao—adviser. Photographer: Gao Wenbin) 88
Fig. 6 Prosecutors (From left to right, back row: Quilliam from New Zealand, Henry Chiu from China, Oneto from France, Lopez from the Philippines, Nolan from Canada. From left to right, front row: Comyns from the UK, Keenan from the US, Borgerhoff Mulder from the Netherlands, Mansfield from Australia) 95

Fig. 7 Chinese prosecutor Hsiang Che-chun 96
Fig. 8 Female prosecutors in the Tokyo Trials (Prosecutor Llewellyn participated in the presentation phase of China) 97
Fig. 9 Female prosecutors in the Tokyo Trials (Prosecutor Lambert read the summation in the case of Hoshino) 98
Fig. 10 Reverend John Magee, a member of the International Committee for the Nanking Safety Zone provided evidence for the Rape of Nanking (The court played a video clip shot by him that recorded the atrocities committed by the Japanese troops) 100

Chapter 4

Fig. 1 Judges and national flags (President Webb was absent between November and December 1947. The court placed the Australian flag to the far left. Deputy of the President Cramer sat in the middle of the bench) 108
Fig. 2 Defendants during the trials 118
Fig. 3 Seven defendants who were sentenced to death by hanging (Itagaki Seishiro, Tojo Hideki, Doihara Kenji, Hoshino Naoki, Matsui Iwane, Muto Akira, and Kimura Heitaro) 119

Chapter 5

Fig. 1 Distribution of courts (Drawn by Zhao Yuhui) 129
Fig. 2 GHQ Trial/Marunouchi Trial 136
Fig. 3 Defendant Tamura was at the trial 137
Fig. 4 Defendant Toyoda was walking into the courtroom 138
Fig. 5 Manila tribunal 139
Fig. 6 US Army's Manila trials of Yamashita Tomoyuki 140
Fig. 7 US Army's Manila trials of Honma Masaharu 141
Fig. 8 US Army's Yokohama trial (The photo was taken on May 7, 1948. Five Japanese defendants were charged with killing 62 US military pilots in 1945) 142
Fig. 9 US Army's Yokohama trial (The photo was taken on March 11, 1948. Chief Counsel Frank Seidel was speaking) 143
Fig. 10 Some defendants and defense counsels at the Yokohama trial 144
Fig. 11 Photocopy of the defendant Takehiko held by the Peiping court 149
Fig. 12 Courtroom of the Special Military Court of Shenyang, People's Republic of China 154

Fig. 13 Related documents of Rokusashi Takebe at the Fushun War Criminals Management Office (The receipt for the indictment and other documents that was served to the suspected Rokusashi Takebe at the Fushun War Criminals Management Office by the Supreme Court of the People's Republic of China. Rokusashi Takebe was sentenced to 20 years in prison by the New China Shenyang Court in July 1956, but then released and returned to Japan due to encephalopathy) 155
Fig. 14 Special Military Court of Taiyuan, People's Republic of China (June 12–20, 1956, eight Japanese war criminals were tried at the Taiyuan Special Military Court) 156

Chapter 6

Fig. 1 MacArthur and Emperor Hirohito 180

Chapter 7

Fig. 1 The affidavit of Ogawa Sekijiro (Ogawa Sekijiro stated in his affidavit that he was asked to strictly deal with the crimes when meeting general Matsui in Shanghai on January 4, 1938) 219
Fig. 2 The diary of Ogawa Sekijiro (The diary of January 4, 1938 recorded Ogawa's activities in detail that he did not leave the headquarters of the tenth army in Hangzhou. It also recorded in detail that when Ogawa met Matsui on the January 15, 1938, Matsui's long speech did not mention a single word about the crimes and the bearing and discipline of the army) 220

Chapter 8

Fig. 1 The defense councils (The US defense councils in the Tokyo trial mostly were soldiers and wore military uniforms at the beginning of the trial. After presentation of the prosecution case, they all wore suits) (**a**) UMEZU Yoshijiro's defense council Major Blakeney in military uniform and MUTO Akira's defense council senior captain Furness (Later he was promoted as major) (**b**) Blakeney in suits (**c**) the defendant HATA Shunroku's US defense council in military uniforms (**d**) Lazarus in suits 274

Chapter 9

Fig. 1 Yamashita Tomoyuki 290
Fig. 2 Hirota Koki 291
Fig. 3 The whole scene of the Tokyo trial court 302

List of Tables

Chapter 1

Table 1 The list of suspects arrested for Class A war crimes 22
Table 2 List of IMTFE prosecutors 30
Table 3 List of IMTFE judges 34
Table 4 List of Class A war criminals 38

Chapter 3

Table 1 55 counts in the indictment 73

Chapter 4

Table 1 Convictions and where judges voted on the death penalty (speculation) 111
Table 2 Defendants' conviction and sentencing at the IMTFE 116

Chapter 5

Table 1 33 acts identified by the UNWCC as war crimes in May 1944 131
Table 2 Outline of the trials against Japan in Asia 133
Table 3 Outline of British Army's trials 145
Table 4 Outline of Australia's trials 147
Table 5 Outline of the trials in China 149
Table 6 Outline of the Netherlands' trials 152

Part I

CHAPTER 1

The Road to the Tokyo Trials

World War I caused unprecedented damage and the whole world reacted with great and grave concern. Despite the establishment of international organizations and group efforts to sign relevant treaties, these failed to put a stop to the war. World War II spread throughout almost the entire civilized world except North America; from the bitterest northern regions to the hottest equatorial rainforests, and from the most isolated islands in the far east Pacific to continents out in the far west. It evolved from a spate of brutal killings to well-planned and "scientific" genocide. Human civilization was threatened with destruction, both in breadth and depth. The postwar trials, especially the two major international military trials by the East and the West, occurred while these concerns brewed.

1 Major Allies' Stances on Trials Against Japan

1.1 Declarations Issued by the Allies' Leaders

After the war broke out, governments and people from all walks of life strongly condemned the aggression and atrocities.

In November 1940, the Polish and Czechoslovak governments in exile issued an unprecedented joint statement condemning Germany's atrocities. This was the first statement of its kind from any Western country since the outbreak of World War II. On October 25, 1941, British Prime Minister Winston S. Churchill followed in their footsteps, and issued a declaration saying that the war would only serve a purpose if the

Z. Cheng, *A History of War Crimes Trials in Post 1945 Asia-Pacific*,
https://doi.org/10.1007/978-981-13-6697-0_1

Nazis were to be punished. On November 25, Soviet Foreign Minister Vyacheslav Molotov similarly issued a statement condemning the Nazi atrocities.

On January 13, 1942, nine countries in exile (Belgium, Czechoslovakia, France, Greece, Luxembourg, the Netherlands, Norway, Poland and Yugoslavia) held a joint meeting to discuss war crimes at the St. James Palace in London. Other countries, including China, Britain, the United States, the Soviet Union and India were also invited. The nine nations issued a decree for war crimes to be punishable, and demanded that it be a key outcome of the war.

On August 1, US President Franklin D. Roosevelt issued a statement saying—for the first time—that "the Eurasian aggressors" would eventually be brought to justice. On November 6, during the 25th anniversary of the Russian revolution, Marshal Joseph Stalin announced at a Moscow rally that one of the goals of war would be to "destroy the abhorrent European 'new order', and punish those who established it".

In October 1943, the foreign ministers of the United States, Britain and the Soviet Union held a joint meeting in Moscow. On November 1, the "Declaration on Cruelty" was issued in the names of the heads of these three countries. As with the Moscow declaration, this declaration had special significance, specifically, that it was the first time the United States, Britain and the Soviet Union had collectively reached an agreement on how to punish wartime atrocities (Figs. 1, 2, 3, 4, 5, 6, and 7).

The declaration set out two key principles. First, that perpetrators of atrocities should be repatriated in the aftermath of the war, and made to enforce the legal sanctions of their host country. Secondly, that major criminals should be punished collectively by the allied countries, and that those outside of a clear and specific geographical region should not be subject to the principle of bondage.

The second principle made clear that the objects it dealt with were not traditional war criminals that violated ordinary war crimes, but leaders of axis countries that have never been put to trial in the past, so-called "principal war criminals". When this principle was announced, the Soviet Union and Japan were still bound by the "Soviet–Japanese neutral treaty" and therefore it was ostensibly directed at Nazi Germany, without mentioning Japan. What this meant, however, was that Class A and B/C crimes could be initially distinguished, and used in the future trials against Japan.

Fig. 1 Foreign Ministers' Meeting in Moscow (Above: From left to right, front row: Chinese Ambassador to the Soviet Union Fu Bingchang, US Secretary of State Hull, Representative Molotov of the Soviet People's Association for Foreign Affairs, British Foreign Minister Eden) Below: Hull suggested that China should participate later, because the Chinese national flag was not prepared for the meeting. Therefore, the United States, Soviet Union and British flags were removed

Fig. 2 Three leaders at the Cairo Conference (From left: President of the Chinese National Government Chiang Kai-shek, US President Roosevelt, British Prime Minister Winston Churchill, and Madame Chiang Soong Mei-ling)

Fig. 3 Mao Zedong and Zhu De meet with Hurley (In November 1944, the leaders of the Chinese Communist Party Mao Zedong and Zhu De met in Yan'an with Hurley, the private representative of President Roosevelt)

Fig. 4 The Yalta Conference (From left to right, front row: British Prime Minister Churchill, US President Roosevelt, Soviet Union leader Stalin)

Fig. 5 The Potsdam Conference (1) (From left: Soviet Union leader Stalin, U.S. President Truman, British Prime Minister Churchill)

Fig. 6 The Potsdam Conference (2) (The British general election results were announced during the Potsdam Conference. Attlee replaced Churchill as prime minister, and subsequently signed later documents and participated in meetings)

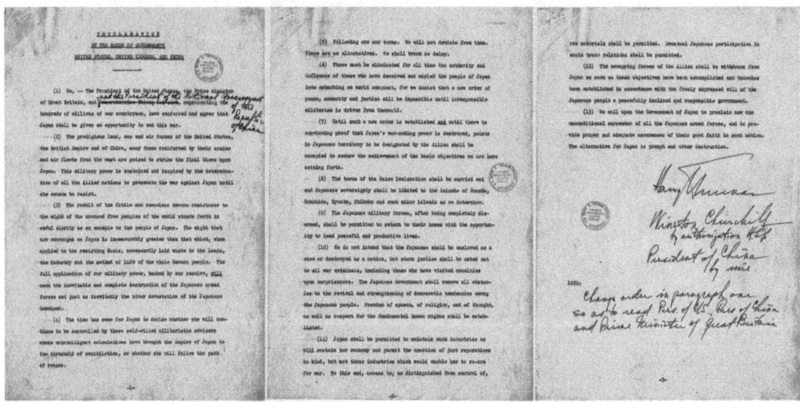

Fig. 7 The original draft of the Potsdam Proclamation (The leaders' signatures were originally ordered United States, UK, then China. They were later changed to United States, China, UK, when the document was officially released on July 26, 1945)

On December 1, 1943, the heads of the United States, China and Britain collectively issued the "Cairo Declaration", which stated that "the purpose of this war is for the three major allies to stop and punish Japanese aggression". On July 26, 1945, the heads of the United States, the Soviet Union and the United Kingdom signed the "Potsdam Proclamation" on behalf of the heads of the United States, China and the UK. In Article 10, it clearly stated that war criminals "would be brought to justice".

In China, leaders of the KMT, the CPC and other factions repeatedly censured the Japanese atrocities. Although they did not explicitly state the need for trials, they sternly proposed "punishment", "redress" and "rehabilitation".

1.2 America's Stance on Trials Against Japan

There were many different opinions on America's draft policies concerning war criminal trials. The most contentious debate about the trials arose between US Army Secretary Henry Lewis Stimson and US Treasury Secretary Henry Morgenthau.

Morgenthau asserted that the list of major war criminals should be handed over to the local military authority, and that they should be executed immediately after their arrest. He said that the allies should organize military tribunals to try ordinary war criminals. His view was that anybody found guilty of war crime convictions should be executed. Many felt that Morgenthau had such extreme views given his Jewish background, and he had earlier expressed his outrage at the Nazi Holocaust. During his visit to the United States, Churchill proposed that convicted war criminals should be sent to the firing range, and Morgenthau approved. He believed that extended trials could lead to inevitable protractions and uncertainties, and that many would lead to abortion, such as the trial of William II after World War I. Crucially, Morgenthau believed that the people of Germany and Japan should be held responsible for the war. He felt that a trial could lead to much bureaucracy, whereas only a few people needed to take responsibility.

Stimson, on the contrary, believed that harsh punishments would not help in eliminating war, but would only deepen resentments. Stimson firmly believed that civilized means such as "trials" were the only way to truly prevent the revival of warrior madmen. He felt it was better to trial them, using nonmilitary "civilians", instead of simply killing them to get "revenge".

Before trials were officially approved, the U.S. State Department had some trepidations. Secretary of State Cordell Hull advocated for some expeditious executions. But unlike Morgenthau, he said that executions should be carried out by the military courts. Speaking at the foreign ministers' meeting in Moscow, he said: If Hitler, Mussolini and Hideki Tojo were seized, they should immediately be handed over to the Provisional Military Tribunal and executed the next day. For some time, President Roosevelt favored the idea as well. But after Morgenthau's views were fiercely criticized by the media, Roosevelt spoke in favor of the trials.

By the end of 1944 and with victory approaching, the U.S. State Department, the War Department and the Navy collectively formed the State-War-Navy Coordinating Committee (SWNCC) to review their policies concerning Japan. In January 1945, the Subcommittee for the Far East (SFE) was established, and it accelerated the committee's pace of work and led to the Potsdam Proclamation being released.

On August 9, the day after the "Charter of the International Military Tribunal" (also known as Nuremberg Tribunal's Charter) was approved, the SFE asserted that the time limit for prosecuting Japan would be extended from "The Manchurian Incident", according to "common conspiracy" by the International Military Tribunal on the German Judgment. On August 13, the committee decided to hold Japan's leaders accountable for "crimes against peace" and "crimes against humanity". On August 24, the SFE submitted a report to the SWNCC, arguing that occupational forces should arrest Japanese suspects, and prevent them from committing suicide as "martyrs". The report stressed that, as with international military tribunals, all countries participating would be allowed to appoint prosecutors, and would be equal under international agreements. MacArthur, the Commander-in-Chief of Japan's Allied Forces, was granted international rights to recognize or change the verdict.

Following this decision, the U.S. State Department, the War Department and the Navy debated multiple times whether the trial was dominated by the United States, or was sufficiently coordinated by the allied nations. Finally, they decided that the trials should be conducted by the allied nations, and that the US representative would take the lead. On October 2, the Joint Chiefs of Staff (JCS) and the SWNCC ordered Commander-in-Chief MacArthur to begin preparations for the Tokyo Trial.

1.3 Britain's Stance on Trials Against Japan

For a long time, Britain advocated the execution of the Axis leaders, rather than putting them to trial. In the summer of 1944, when the Allied forces landed in Normandy, they decided that they needed to set the record straight over what measures should be taken over the Axis. The British Cabinet commissioned Justice John Simon to draft documents approving war criminals' immediate execution. Later, Churchill changed his mind, partly because the Soviet Union and other countries advocated trials instead of executions.

Since the battlefield in East Asia was only a secondary battlefield for Britain (with Nazi Germany being the primary concern), Britain mainly focused on Japan's ordinary war criminals. On October 16, 1945, the Commonwealth countries held a meeting to discuss the atrocities committed by the Japanese army—that is, their Class B/C crimes. The committee decided that they would complete the trials of 500 Class B/C war criminals by July 31, 1946. The British government and the Foreign Ministry decided that countries which detained major war criminals should be free to carry out their own judgement.

After the United States decided to adopt the Allies' trials (especially after John M. Weir, the war crimes commission Joint Chiefs of Staff, visited Britain), the United Kingdom accepted the United States' proposal. On November 16, 1945, the British Foreign Ministry held a meeting to finalize its agreement with the Allies. It troubled the UK that the United States' dominance would weaken the influence of Britain, however, Britain could not afford to assume more responsibility in the Far East. The United Kingdom accepted the United States' proposal because it was pressured by Australia and other Commonwealth countries. Influential people, including Britain's Chief Prosecutor Hartley William Shawcross of the Nuremberg Trials, believed that British participation in the Tokyo Trial would have be conducive to the promotion of national prestige, and this also had an impact.

1.4 China's Stance on Trials Against Japan

Japan's invasion of China was much earlier than its invasion of other countries in the Asia-Pacific region and Nazi Germany's invasion of European countries. China, therefore, has always taken an unswerving stance on punishing Japanese war criminals. On January 13, 1942, the

Chinese government declared that "all grievances and grief suffered by the Chinese people" must be "redressed and rehabilitated"; and "all criminals that committed such crimes" must be "punished according to laws" when 9 countries, once occupied by Nazi Germany, declared the *Joint Declaration on Punishment for Enemy Atrocities.*

In August 1943, China's top leaders cabled the Ministry of Foreign Affairs to claim that the trial against Japanese war criminals should be brought before an international court, organized by the Allies under international laws available. China proposed that small-scale actions were started as a result of Japanese aggression in northeast China, even if some countries considered it an outbreak of Pacific War. The Chinese government explicitly announced that the crimes committed by Japanese troops against the Chinese people, in particular the Nanking Massacre, could not be forgiven; although China officially declared war against Japan after the attack on Pearl Harbor.

China submitted a primary list of Japanese war criminals headed by Emperor Hirohito in June 1945. This list consisted of 173 war criminals in the army and 13 in the navy, as well as 50 political criminals and 20 special war criminals. In September, 12 major war criminals were picked up from primary list: Shigeru Honjō, Doihara Kenji, Hisao Tani, Hashimoto Kingoro, Itagaki Seishiro, Hata Shunroku, Tojo Hideki, Takaji Wachi, Eisa Aki, Takashi Sakai, Rensuke Isogai and Seiichi Kita. In January 1946, China submitted another list of 21 major war criminals: Jirō Minami, Araki Sadao, Hiranuma Kiichiro, Nobuyuki Abe, Mitsumasa Yonai, Koiso Kuniaki, Shimada Shigetaro, Hirota Koki, Matsuoka Yosuke, Togo Shigenori, Umezu Yoshijiro, Matsui Iwane, Hisaichi Terauchi, Renya Mutaguchi, Masakazu Kawabe, Masayuki Tani, Otozō Yamada, Hachirō Arita, Kazuo Aoki, Nobumasa Suetsugu and Toshizō Nishio. These two lists containing the names of 33 war criminals were presented to the Allied General Headquarters in Japan. China gave up on insisting the accountability of Emperor Hirohito after America's decision. The Chinese government named 2523 war criminals of the total 3147 given to the UNWCC Subcommittee for the Far East in late March, 1947.

1.5 The Soviet Union's Stance on Trials Against Japan

The Soviet Union's stance on Japan was distinctively different from that on the Germans due to the signature of Non-Aggression Pact with Japan. The Soviet Union was active during the trials against Germany and proposed "strict punishment" because it sacrificed a lot in the war against Germany. On October 14, 1942, the Soviet Union sent the nine governments in exile letters to support the punishments proposed by Roosevelt against the named war criminals, and it appealed to set up the "Special International Court" to punish Nazi leaders in the war. The Soviet Union was unsatisfied with Britain's reluctance to punish Rudolf Walter Richard Hess, who admitted his crimes. As a result, it independently set up the National Special Committee for the research of Nazi criminals on November 2, 1942. On November 6, 1943, the date of the revolutionary anniversary, Stalin said he wanted "strict punishments" for "all fascist perpetrators responsible for this war". On November 29, 1943, during the dinner party of the Tehran Conference, Stalin advanced his intentions of wiping out 50–100,000 people. Toward the end of 1942, the Soviet Union began trialing war criminals in Kiev and Kharkov in Ukraine. In mid-August 1944, the Soviet Union established the "Poland Soviet Union Special Committee" and searched the German army stationed at the Majdanek concentration camp in Lublin, east Poland. When the Soviet Union launched a counteroffensive in Eastern Europe, it captured German officers and diplomats and carried out a "public trial" on leaders and artists affiliated with Axis.

In contrast, the Soviet Union was inactive during the trials in Japan. The Nomonhan and Lake Khasan battles were settled through diplomatic channels and the Soviet Union almost did not involve itself against Japan during the Second World War. After it was determined that the Central Powers Court would make the policy of trialing Japanese war criminals, judges were respectively selected by the Supreme Commander of countries assigned in the Japanese Instrument of Surrender. Until early January 1946, China, Britain, Australia, New Zealand, France, and the Netherlands would present nominations—yet the Soviet Union made no remarks on it. On January 18, the Soviet Union recognized the judges and procurators who presented themselves at the International Military Tribunal for the Far East. It was approaching the date of trial when the Soviet Union's delegation arrived at Tokyo. During this trial, the Soviet Union focused on the border conflicts in Nomonhan and Lake Khasan.

After the Tokyo trial, the Soviet Union independently judged Japanese criminals on biologic warfare crimes in Khabarovsk.

1.6 *Australia's Stance on Trials Against Japan*

Australia's location in the South Pacific, far away from the other great powers, meant that it was able to maintain peace for a very long time. Japan's southern advancement was the first time its people had encountered a powerful foreign enemy, and the result was a horror that the Australians would never be able to forget. In the Asia-Pacific region, especially the South Pacific, resistance against Japanese aggression led to great sacrifice and Australia paid dearly. Therefore, Australia's attitude toward the postwar trials was very firm. On September 10, 1945, Australian Foreign Minister Herbert Vere Evatt said that it was Australia's "responsibility" to "extinguish" all Japanese war criminals. Some Japanese scholars argued that Australia—as a member of the Commonwealth—was a subsidiary of Britain, and wasn't qualified to voice its own view. However, Australia enhanced its international status and voice by also attaching importance to the trials, albeit causing some confusion in the process.

Unlike Britain, Australia never changed in its stance on its policies or lost enthusiasm for them. Instead, it always remained consistent, and was especially firm in its pursuit of the Emperor of Japan. Britain believed that Hitler emerged after World War I because of the abandonment of the constitutional monarchy, and that Japan needed an emperor to feel "safe". Australia, however, had the opposite view and believed that it was impossible for Japan to undergo fundamental changes unless the responsibility of the Emperor Showa was pursued. It felt that the Emperor needed to be held responsible for the eradication of Japan's old system.

William Flood Webb became the President of the Far East International Military Tribunal. He was elected into this important position because of his extensive experience serving as President of the Queensland Court of Justice and Director of the Australian Japanese Criminal Investigation Commission. His position meant that Australia played a positive and influential role in the postwar trials against Japan.

2 The United Nation's War Crimes Commission and the Development of the Laws of War

2.1 *The Commission's Responsibilities*

As early as June 1942, British Prime Minister Winston Churchill proposed the establishment of a commission for the investigation of war crimes. During his visit to the United States, it gained the approval of

US President Roosevelt, and Churchill subsequently made this proposal to the British Cabinet upon his return to the UK. Later, British Lord Chancellor and Chief Justice of the Supreme Court John Simon was appointed head of the Commission. In the same year, on October 7, Roosevelt and Simon issued statements in the American and British capitals about setting up the investigation commission. In his statement, Roosevelt stressed: "it is not the intention of this Government or of the Governments associated with us to resort to mass reprisals. It is our intention that just and sure punishment shall be meted out to the ringleaders..."

On October 14, 1942, the Soviet Union sent a letter to the nine governments in exile, saying that they supported Roosevelt's statement and that they advocated for the establishment of a "Special International Court of Justice". On November 2, the Soviets took the lead in setting up a "special national committee" to investigate Nazi war crimes.

In March 1943, the British government consulted the US, Soviet and Chinese governments about setting up the Commission. Britain hoped that a United States representative would assume the post of chairman, and that the Commission would include the four major allied powers, the British dominions, and all of the governments in exile. On October 20, at a meeting hosted by the British Foreign Ministry, seventeen nations and governments in exile (Britain, Australia, Belgium, Canada, China, Czechoslovakia, Greece, India, Luxembourg, the Netherlands, New Zealand, Norway, Poland, South Africa, the United States, Yugoslavia and France) made an agreement that the United Nations War Crimes Commission and the Development of the Laws of War (UNWCC) would soon be established in London.

The aim of the Commission was to serve as a body which gathered evidence of war crimes and lists of criminals, which could then be relayed back to regional governments. The Commission was based in London because the main task at the time was investigating evidence of Nazi war crimes. The first chairman was a British representative, Cecil Hurst, who was also a judge at the permanent International Court of Justice. The Soviet Union refused to participate, partly because their proposal was not unanimously approved. It was a requirement of the Soviet Union for Ukraine and other republics to participate in the commission, much as India and the other Commonwealth dominions did. At the end of the year, the United States persuaded Britain to allow republics of the Soviet Union to participate as advisers to the Soviet representative, but the Soviet Union rejected this offer.

On January 18, 1944, the UNWCC was officially established. During its first meeting, which took place on the 20th, many members said that the Commission should not be limited to collecting criminal evidence and compiling lists of war criminals, but should expand to address the overall issue of war prisoners. After, the Commission decided to set up three committees. The first committee (Committee I) was dedicated to collecting and reviewing evidence and making catalogs. The participating countries were Belgium, the United Kingdom, the United States, Czechoslovakia, Australia and Norway. The second committee (Committee II) was in charge of developing an integrated approach to apprehending and punishing Axis war criminals. The participating countries included the United States, China, India, Free France,[1] Norway, Yugoslavia, Australia, Libya, Belgium, Luxembourg, Czechoslovakia and the Netherlands. The third committee (Committee III) handled legal affairs. The participating countries included China, Czechoslovakia, Greece, the United States, Poland, the United Kingdom, Luxembourg, Yugoslavia, Norway, Denmark, the Netherlands, India and Australia.

2.2 *Restrictions on the Commission from Britain and the United States*

The United States and Britain expected the UNWCC to be a consultative organization, whereas other participating countries wanted it to be a decision-making body.

As the Commission came into operation, various proposals took it beyond what was originally envisioned. In March 1943, the US representative to the UNWCC, Herbert Pell, proposed to the UNWCC's legal committee that the body open up its investigations to "crimes against humanity" and that Nazi criminals be prosecuted. Most UNWCC members approved this move, although their opinions on the various crimes may have differed.

The U.S. State Department and military were concerned about retaliation of the Axis Powers. Although they believed that crimes against the Jewish community should be punished, they did not approve of penalties being extended to the Axis Powers' prewar crimes in their own countries. Bohuslav Ečer, the representative of Czechoslovakia, felt not only that cruelty in war was a crime in itself, but that the war of aggression was

[1] Refers to the government in exile at that time.

as well. On January 18, 1944, the committee held its first formal meeting, and most members advocated expanding the commission to address the overall war criminal issue. The entrusting clause was expanded, and the Commission began to actively advise all governments on legal issues, approaches to apprehending and extraditing war criminals, and decisions related to policy. Neither the United States nor Britain had been willing to see this happen.

On September 26, 1944, Committee II drew up a draft treaty for the United Nations war crimes court (known as "the Treaty Tribunal"). It suggested that all members of the UNWCC should participate, and that the Tribunal should include civil servants who did not belong to military courts. It also suggested that not only "major war criminals", but minor war criminals should be tried. In addition, given that time was required to establish the Treaty Tribunal, members urged that a mixed military tribunal should be created beforehand. On October 6, Chairman of the UNWCC Sir Cecil Hurst sent a letter to British Foreign Secretary Robert Anthony Eden, in which he told him the proposals for the two tribunals. On January 4, 1945, the British Foreign Office agreed to the setting up of a mixed tribunal, but it rejected the treaty tribunal.

Toward the end of February 1946, the United States began working on disbanding the UNWCC. On February 26, the Assistant Secretary of State wrote to the three Coordinating Committees, saying: "there is no value in the Commission". Then, in March, the United States began to cut the committee's funding and personnel, and then only provided formal support.

On April 24, 1947, at a commission meeting in London, British representative Robert Craigie proposed that the UNWCC should be closed by the end of the year. The proposal, however, was strongly opposed by the new UNWCC Chairman, Australian Lord Robert Wright.

Britain and the United States wanted to restrict and disband the UNWCC in order to expand their power. Smaller countries in the 17 member states, however, began making use of their collective strength against the two nations. On June 24, 1946, the newly appointed US legal advisor Charles H. Fahy, complained: "Small nations that make up the majority forced or tried to force the passage of the resolution". He also said: "The UNWCC has been abused by the Allies; they will put those they want to punish on the war criminal lists just for political reasons".

Owing to the United States' and Britain's dissatisfaction, and with the trials of Tokyo and other major countries coming to an end, the UNWCC officially closed in March 1948. During its operation, the UNWCC held a total of 135 meetings.

2.3 *China's Persistence*

Eurocentrism and the United States' and Britain's fear at Japanese retaliation meant that at first the Allies didn't discuss how to punish Japanese war criminals. However, the Chinese government's attitude was completely different. After learning that the Allies would punish Nazi German criminals after the war, China began actively appealing for an international law on punishing war crimes. They repeatedly stressed that "the same principle should be applied to punishing the atrocities of the Japancsc army", and launched a tireless diplomatic mediation.

There were clear differences between China and Western countries in both the time and scope for investigation of Japanese war crimes. Britain and the United States agreed that the principle of punishing Japanese atrocities should be similar to that of German crimes. However, they argued that the starting point of the investigation should be when China officially declared war on Japan after the attack on Pearl Harbor. Australia agreed with them on this. But the Chinese government insisted that war crimes committed by the Japanese should be investigated as far back as September 18, 1931, when Japan invaded Mukden. They were concerned that crimes committed during the Nanking Massacre might not be brought to justice, and that would be unacceptable for the Chinese people.

The Chinese Foreign Ministry said in a statement to the British government: "The scope of the war crimes should include all atrocities committed within Chinese territory since the 'Mukden Incident of 1931'". Since then, no matter what propositions other countries put forward—at the UNWCC's preparatory or formal meetings—Chinese representatives have taken an unswerving stance on this statement. It was the Chinese representatives' insistence that related documents, such as the "Draft Convention on UN War Crimes Tribunal", should not set a time limit for prosecution after the "Pearl Harbor Incident".

2.4 The Far Eastern and Pacific Subcommittee

There were two reasons why the UNWCC was unable to start investigating Japanese war crimes as soon as possible. The UNWCC was afraid of Japanese retaliation on American and British prisoners. Also, because Japan is far away from the West, it made it difficult for the Allies to collect evidence and conduct an investigation. Therefore, Australia and the Netherlands proposed the establishment of the South Pacific Commission to investigate Japanese atrocities. On April 25, 1944, at the 15th UNWCC meeting, the Chinese ambassador to Britain Wellington Koo put forward a proposal for setting up the Far Eastern and Pacific Subcommittee. On May 16, the UNWCC decided to set up the subcommittee in the Chinese municipality of Chongqing.

After six months of preparation, the subcommittee held its inaugural meeting on November 29, 1944. It was chaired by former Chinese foreign minister Wang Chonghui, and members included China, Australia, Belgium, Czechoslovakia, France, India, Luxembourg (however, Luxembourg representatives didn't attend), the Netherlands, the United Kingdom, the United States and Poland.

The principal mission of the subcommittee was to gather evidence and provide a list of war criminals. China repeatedly insisted on setting the starting date of the subcommittee's temporal jurisdiction as the "Mukden Incident of 1931", or at least the "July 7 Incident of 1937", when Japanese forces launched attacks on Beijing's suburbs. France, the United States and Australia all submitted lists of war criminals and witnesses to the subcommittee. China's list was the longest; it was prepared, verified, translated by relevant departments, and then signed by top leaders. The subcommittee received 26 lists, which included a total 3147 war criminals. These lists were transferred to the General Headquarters through the UNWCC.

In May 1945, Committee II began discussing the Japan issue. It was generally accepted that the principle for Germany's trials would apply equally to Japan. UNWCC Chairman, Australian Lord Robert Wright, proposed an advisory policy on Japanese war criminals after the Potsdam Proclamation. On August 8, the day the "Charter of the International Military Tribunal" was approved, the Far East and Pacific Special Commission was set up in London. It had nine members: the United States, Britain, China, France, the Netherlands, Canada, Australia, New Zealand and India. The same day, the UNWCC approved the Moscow

Declaration, the Jackson Report, the Potsdam Proclamation, and the London Accord.

On August 29, the UNWCC approved an advisory policy on Japanese war criminals. The original document was drawn up by special commission chairman Wellington Koo. U.S. Representative Joseph V. Hodgson made some changes so that the document would apply to US policy. The revised points were as follows:

- First, that major war criminals should be judged by an international tribunal which governs "crimes against peace", "war crimes" and "crimes against humanity".
- Second, the United States was in favor of prosecuting the Japanese leadership as "a criminal conspiracy".
- Third, that there should be the election of prosecutors. (This was originally suggested by Wellington Koo. As with the Nuremberg Tribunal, which had four chief prosecutors appointed by the United States, Britain, France and the Soviet Union, it was proposed that this international tribunal should consist of Far East and Pacific Special Commission members and chief prosecutors appointed by each of the ten member countries.)
- Fourth, that it should be determined whether the "Supreme Commander for the Allied Powers" or the "governing council" should be the main body of the International Tribunal. This had yet to be determined, but it was decided that judges were to be appointed by the above ten nations. Hodgson rejected a more detailed policy drafted by Wellington Koo, in order to give the Supreme Commander (an American) greater discretion.

Following these amendments, the UNWCC introduced a number of policies on Japan that had previously just applied to Germany. However, while the policies on Germany were jointly established by four countries, the policies on Japan were actually decided by the United States. Therefore, the policies toward Japan and Germany were not identical.

3 Preparatory Work Ahead of the Tokyo Trials

3.1 The Arrest of War Criminal Suspects

Before the International Prosecution Bureau was established, the General Headquarters (GHQ) began arresting Japanese war criminal suspects. On the night of August 30, 1945, MacArthur arrived in Japan and ordered the head of the CIC Elliot Thorpe to arrest Tojo Hideki and prepare the list of major war criminals (Class A war criminals). On September 11, the GHQ began issuing warrants. When the US Attorney General's delegation led by Joseph B. Keenan arrived in Tokyo on December 6, the last batch of Class A war criminals had been arrested.

MacArthur proposed that the United States should conduct a separate trial that looked specifically at Japanese atrocities in the Pacific Ocean and soldiers' abuse of US war prisoners. But the United States had also set guidelines for the timely arrest of suspects. On August 16, JCS Chairman Marshall called MacArthur, and instructed him to follow the precedent of apprehending German war criminals before following the official directive. The first few arrests included the Tojo cabinet, which had launched war against the United States, and a number of war criminals named by the Allies. Important Japanese figures in politics, military, finance, and literature were also arrested, as well as politicians from other countries, ambassadors to Japan who had aided Japan during the war, and even Japanese broadcasters, who had implemented psychological tactics that led to the arrest of Allied troops. By September 11, four arrest operations had been conducted, which led to the total apprehension of 127 Class A war criminals (Table 1).

3.2 The International Prosecution Section

The day after Keenan arrived in Japan, MacArthur called for a meeting and the immediate trial of a number of Japanese war criminals. By December 8, the International Prosecution Section (IPS) was established and Keenan was appointed Director. The IPS was a subdivision of the General Headquarters and the prosecutorial organ of the International Military Tribunal for the Far East (IMTFE). It dealt with evidence collection, and the investigation and prosecution of Japanese war criminals. (In theory, that made Keenan the Procurator-General of the IMTFE. However, this was not officially announced until January 19, 1946, when

Table 1 The list of suspects arrested for Class A war crimes

Time	*Name*	*Title/position*	*Time*	*Name*	*Title/position*
First arrest (42 suspects)					
September 11, 1945	**Tojo Hideki**[a]	Prime Minister		Tobita Tokio	Supervisor, Affiliated Hospital of Tokyo Captives Shelter
(Out of 39 suspects, 2 committed	**Togo Shigenori**	Foreign Minister		Tokuda Hisakichi	Became a Class B and C war criminal due to the human test of the Tokyo Captive Shelter
suicide, 37 were arrested)	**Shimada Shigetaro**	Navy Minister		Ueda Yoshitake	Vice Admiral
	Kaya Okinori	Finance Minister		Khin Maung Thein	Burmese Ambassador to Japan
	Suzuki Teiichi	President of Planning Board		Aung San	Deputy Military Officer of Myanmar Embassy in Japan and founder of Burma Independence Army
	Hashida Kunihiko (suicide)	Minister of Education		Jose Laolaier	President of the Philippines during the Japanese occupation
	Honma Masaharu	Commander of the Japanese 14th Army		Benigno Aquino	Senator of the Philippines
	Ino Hiroya	Minister of Agriculture and Forestry		Jorge Vargas	Philippines Ambassador to Japan
	Iwamura Michiyo	Finance Minister		Luang Wichitwathakan	Thai Ambassador to Japan
	Kishi Nobusuke	Minister of Commerce and Industry		Mahendra Pratap	Indian freedom fighter

(continued)

Table 1 (continued)

Time	*Name*	*Title/position*	*Time*	*Name*	*Title/position*
	Chikahiko Koizumi (suicide)	Minister of Health and Welfare		Heinrich Stahmer	German Ambassador to Japan
	Shigenori Kuroda	Commander of the Japanese 14th Army		Alfred Kretschmer	Deputy Military Officer of German Ambassador to Japan
	Shozo Murata	Ambassador to the Philippines		Josef Meisinger	Deputy Police Officer of German Ambassador to Japan
	Nagahama Akira	Gendarmerie Commander of the Japanese 14th Army		Josias Van Dienst	Dutch Announcer at the Tokyo Broadcasting
	Terashima Ken	Minister of Communications		Lily Abegg	German Announcer at the Tokyo Broadcasting
	Miura Soichi			Charles Cousins	Australian Announcer at the Tokyo Broadcasting
	Shigeru			Streeter	US Staff at the Manuscript Department of Tokyo Broadcasting
	Ota Shinichi			John Poland	Australian Announcer at the Shanghai Broadcasting
	James W.		September 21, 1945 (2 suspects)	Doihara Kenji	Inspector General of Military Education
	Sasaki Kunichi				
	Suzuki Kaorini			Nobuyuki Abe	Prime Minister
	Takeuchi		October 22, 1945 (1 suspect)	Abe Genki	Minister of Internal Affairs

Second arrest (11 suspects)

(continued)

Table 1 (continued)

Time	*Name*	*Title/position*	*Time*	*Name*	*Title/position*
November 19, 1945 (11 suspects)	**Araki Sadao**	Army Minister		Honjo Shigeru	Commander of Kwantung Army
	Koiso Kuniak	Prime Minister		Kanokogi Kazunobu	Managing Director of Public Expression Patriotic Association
	Matsuoka Yosuke	Foreign Minister		Kuhara Fusanosuke	Secretary-general of the Rikken Seiyūkai
	Matsui Iwane	Commander-in-chief of the Central China Area Army		Kuzuo Yoshihisa	Director of General Affairs of the Imperial Rule Assistance Association
	Minami Jiro	Commander of the Kwantung Army		Masaki Jinzaburō	Inspector General of Military Education
	Shiratori Toshio	Ambassador to Italy			
Third arrest (59 suspects)					
December 2, 1945 (59 suspects)	**Hata Shunroku**	Commanding General of the Central China Expeditionary Army		Mizuno Rentaro	Minister of Education
	Hiranuma Kiichiro	Prime Minister		Renya Mutaguchi	Commander of the Japanese 15th Army
	Hoshino Naoki	Prime Minister		Nagatomo Tsugio	Commander of the central gendarmerie
	Hirota Koki	President of the Planning Board		Nakajima Chikura	Minister of Munitions
	Okawa Shumei	Right-wing activist		Aketo Nakamura	General Officer in Thailand

(continued)

Table 1 (continued)

Time	*Name*	*Title/position*	*Time*	*Name*	*Title/position*
	Sato Kenryo	Chief of the Military Affairs Bureau		Nashimoto Morimasa (Prince Nashimoto Morimasa)	Lieutenant general and the only member of the Imperial Family arrested for Class A war crimes
	Aikawa Yoshisuke	President of the Manchurian Heavy Industry Company		Nishio Toshizō	Commanding General of the Central China Expeditionary Army
	Amo Eiji	Chief of the Intelligence Section		Nami Toshiro	Head of the Japanese 28th Division
	Ando Kisaburo	Minister of Internal Affairs		Okabe Nagakage	Minister of Education
	Aoki Kazuo	Minister of Greater East Asia		Okura Kunihiko	President of Toyo University
	Arima Yoriyasu	Secretary-General of the Imperial Rule Assistance Association		Ono Hirohito	Commanding General of the Central China Expeditionary Army
	Ginjiro Fujiwara	Minister of Munitions		Ota Kozo	Minister of Education
	Furuno Inosuke	President of Domei News Agency		Ota Masataka	Policy Director of General Affairs of the Imperial Rule Assistance Association
	Goko Kiyoshi	President of Mitsubishi Corporation		Sakurai Hyogoro	Minister of State

(continued)

Table 1 (continued)

Time	*Name*	*Title/position*	*Time*	*Name*	*Title/position*
	Goto Fumio	Minister of State		Ryoichi Sasakawa	Political activist
	Hata Hikosaburo	Chief of Staff of the Kwantung Army		Shimomura Hirosh	Chief of the Intelligence Section
	Honda Kumataro	Japanese Ambassador to Reorganized National Government of China		Shindo Kazuma	Head of the Right-wing Group
	Ida Iwakusu	Permanent Director of General Affairs of the Imperial Rule Assistance Association		Shiono Suehiko	Minister of Justice
	Ikeda Seihin	Finance Minister		Shioten Nobutaka	Head of the Anti-Semitism Association
	Ikezaki Chuko	Right-wing critic		Shoriki Matsutaro	Head of the Yomiuri Shimbun
	Ishida Otogoro	Head of gendarmerie		Tada Hayao	Commander of the North China Army
	Ishihara Hiroichiro	Right-wing entrepreneur		Takahashi Miyoshi	Commanding Officer of Combined Fleet
	Kamisago Masashichi	Commanding Officer of Taiwan Military Police Corps		Takachi Shigeto	Commanding Officer of Korea Military Police Corps
	Kawabe Shozo	Chief of Staff Central China Expeditionary Army		Tani Masayuki	Foreign Minister
	Kikuchi Takeo	Head of Mukden Espionage Service		Tokutomi Iichiro	Right-wing activist

(continued)

Table 1 (continued)

Time	*Name*	*Title/position*	*Time*	*Name*	*Title/position*
	Kinoshita Eiichi	Principal of the school of Military Police Corps		Toyoda Soemu	Commander of Combined Fleet
	Kobayashi Junichiro	Director of General Affairs of the Imperial Rule Assistance Association		Tsuda Shingo	Entrepreneur
	Kobayashi Seizo	Governor-General of Taiwan		Ushiroku Jun	Chief of Staff Central China Expeditionary Army
	Yoshio Kodama	Head of Yoshio Secret Agency		Yokoyama Yui	Civil intelligence
	Matsuzaka Hiromasa	Finance Minister			
Fourth arrest (14 suspects)					
December 6, 1945 (9 suspects)	**Kido Koichi**	Minister of Internal Affairs		Godo Takuo	Minister of Commerce and Industry
	Oshima Hiroshi	Ambassador to Germany		Yakichiro Suma	Minister of Intelligence of Foreign Affairs Ministry
	Fumimaro Konoe	Prime Minister	March 16, 1946 (1 suspect)	Osami Nagano	Minister of Military Orders
	Sakai Tadamasa	Minister of Agriculture and Forestry	April 7, 1946 (1 suspect)	Oka Takazumi	Chief of the Navy Affairs Bureau
	Okochi Masatoshi	Physicist	April 29, 1946 (2 suspects)	Umezu Yoshijiro	Chief of the Japanese Army General Staff Office
	Ogata Taketora	Chief of the Intelligence Section		Foreign Minister	Foreign Minister
	Odate Shigeo	Chief of Tokyo Metropolitan Area	November 5, 1946 (1 suspect)	Hasegawa Kiyoshi	Governor-General of Taiwan

[a]Names in bold are Class A war criminals

the IMTFE Charter was approved, despite US President Truman signing his approval for the appointment of a Procurator-General as early as November 29, 1945.)

Keenan becoming Procurator-General made the Tokyo Trials different from the Nuremberg trials, as previously four countries (the United States, Britain, France and the Soviet Union) had had equal powers of adjudication. During the Tokyo Trials, Keenan's position as Procurator-General (or chief prosecutor) meant that he assumed overall responsibility and could override associate prosecutors (or deputy prosecutors) from other participating countries.

The number of US prosecutors far exceeded that of other countries. There were nearly 200 total prosecutors, translators, interpreters, and shorthand and administrative members of staff. This large team meant that the United States was seen to play a leading role in the Tokyo Trials.

The IPS had offices for administration, investigation and documentation. It also had country offices for China, the Soviet Union, Britain, France and other nations. After the IPS was formally established, it began investigating and collecting evidence, drawing up a list of war criminals and preparing evidence for prosecution. It interrogated suspects, questioned insiders, conducted field investigations and scrutinized literature.

1. **Interrogation and inquiry**. Confessions were extremely important because Japan had destroyed a large number of official documents by the end of the war. Before the IPS was officially created, the Procurator's Office of the General Headquarters began interrogating prisoners and questioning relevant people in custody. After it was launched, the IPS sought to obtain written confessions, which could be used in the trials.
2. **Collection of written evidence**. The destruction of many important files made this work especially hard. What's more, it was difficult to find sufficient evidence in the files that remained, and there were language obstacles. Without the collective assistance of all member nations, and the efforts of the IPS, this mission would never have been completed. Surprise discoveries were made during imperial meetings, cabinet meetings, the five prime ministers' meeting, and in impromptu meetings. They were also found in detailed records of the ministerial meetings. Many important, confidential documents were found when the allied military police searched a Japanese company. They found files describing how

Japan's aggressive policies took shape, how the aggression led to war and were instrumental in determining many defendants' individual responsibilities.

3. **Field investigation and evidence collection**. Throughout the investigation of Japanese atrocities across Asia, which included massacre, torture and rape, the IPS obtained statements from victims and insiders, and secured witnesses who were willing to testify in court. The IPS sent representatives to China, the Philippines, Indonesia and Myanmar, and it investigated atrocities committed by the Japanese army, such as those in Nanjing and Manila, acts committed during the Bataan Death March, forced labor along the Myanmar-Thailand Railway, and the abuse of prisoners at concentration camps in Southeast Asia. The collective evidence proved to be extremely important, though at the time, it seemed to be insufficient.

A list of defendants was also drawn up.

Another important task for the IPS was the drafting up of indictments. On March 2, 1946, Keenan set up a four-member committee that dealt with drafting indictments. It was under the sole responsibility of British prosecutor Arthur S. Comyns-Carr. On April 17, a draft indictment was submitted to the Prosecutor's Meeting for approval. On the 29th, Keenan submitted this indictment to the tribunal and defendants on behalf of the IPS. The Tokyo Trials' indictment was similar to that used during the Nuremberg tribunal, but many alleged charges were formally prosecuted.

The indictments in the Nuremberg trials included participation in a common plan or conspiracy, crimes against peace, conventional war crimes, and crimes against humanity. The Tokyo indictments included crimes against peace, murder crimes, conventional war crimes, and crimes against humanity. There were as many as 55 counts in three groups of the Tokyo indictments.

One striking feature of the Nuremberg indictments was that, as well as prosecuting individual German war criminals, they prosecuted important Nazi organizations and institutions. However, when IPS prosecutors carried out investigations during the Japanese trials, many organizations were not indicted. This was the case for far-right organizations such as the Black Dragon Militia, the Sakura Society, the Japan State Society, the Great Japan Youth Party, Japan's political party, and the Imperial Rule

Table 2 List of IMTFE prosecutors

Country	*Position*	*Name*
United States	Chief Prosecutor	Joseph Berry Keenan
China	Prosecutor	Hsiang Che-chun
United Kingdom	Prosecutor	Arthur. S. Comyns-Carr
Soviet Union	Prosecutor	Sergei Alexandrovich Golunsky
Australia	Prosecutor	Alan James Mansfield
Canada	Prosecutor	Henry Grattan Nolan
France	Prosecutor	Robert L. Oneto
Netherlands	Prosecutor	W. G. Frederick Borgerhoff Mulder
New Zealand	Prosecutor	Ronald Henry Quilliam
India	Prosecutor	P. P. Govinda Menon
Philippines	Prosecutor	Pedro Lopez

Assistance Association. Furthermore, the prosecutors determined that the starting point of prosecution should be as early as 1928, the year when the "Kellogg–Briand Pact" was signed (Table 2).

3.3 Issuance of the Charter and the Creation of the Tribunal

In December 1945, the foreign ministers of the Soviet Union, the United States and Britain passed a resolution in Moscow. It stated: "The Supreme Commander shall issue all orders for the implementation of the Terms of Surrender, the occupation and control of Japan, and directives supplementary thereto". The resolution granted the Supreme Commander of the Allied Powers extensive powers. Unlike the IMT Charter, which was drawn up and signed by the United States, Britain, the Soviet Union and France (London, August 8, 1945), the IMTFE Charter was formulated by the Supreme Commander. It was drawn up in accordance with the indirect authorization of the three foreign ministerial resolutions, and a series of international documents.

On January 19, 1946, the Supreme Commander of the Allied Powers MacArthur issued a special proclamation, ordering the establishment of an International Military Tribunal for the Far East (IMTFE). On April 26, the content of the charter was slightly adjusted. The amendments were as follows: (1) To increase the number of judges from nine to eleven. In addition to the nine judges who signed Japan's instrument of surrender, two more judges were introduced from India and the

Philippines. (2) To delete the term "civilian populations" in the description of crimes against humanity.

The IMTFE Charter was drawn up by the IPS with reference to the IMT Charter used in the Nuremberg Trials, and consisted of seventeen articles in five sections. It laid out the framework for tribunals, such as the powers of tribunals and trial conduct, fair trials for the accused and the procedure for fair trials. It also specified relevant jurisdictions and the general rules for evidence, penalties, judgment and reviews. It became a guiding principle for judgment and an important document in guiding trials (Figs. 8, 9, and 10 and Table 3).

The Indian and Philippine judges joined the IMTFE after the charter was amended on April 26, 1946. Three months after the trials, American Judge Higgins resigned for unknown reasons and returned home, with General Cramer replacing him through succession. The other judges remained in office until the court closed. Of the eleven judges, all were

Fig. 8 Japan's Surrender (On September 2, 1945, aboard the US "Missouri" battleship, Meiji Michijiro signed a surrender on behalf of Japan)

Fig. 9 IMTFE prosecutors

civil servants except Soviet Major-General Zaryanov and US Major-General Cramer. All of the judges had their own strengths and were well-respected in their own countries.

Unlike the Nuremberg Tribunal, the Tokyo Tribunal did not arrange for an alternative judge to appear before court when the head judge was absent. According to the charter: "When as many as six members of the Tribunal are present, they may convene the Tribunal in formal session. The presence of a majority of all members shall be necessary to constitute a quorum. In case the votes are evenly divided, the vote of the President shall be decisive". During the Tokyo Trials, the attendance

Fig. 10 IMTFE judges

rate was very high, apart from when the President and the Indian judge returned after a leave of absence. Before the hearing, Dutch judge Bert Roling proposed a confidentiality agreement. He argued that no matter how much the jurists might disagree with each other, the delegation should present a united front outside of the court. His proposal was approved by most of the judges. However, Indian judge Pal, who had arrived in Tokyo after the court hearing, refused to go along with this, saying that he hadn't signed the agreement.

Table 3 List of IMTFE judges

Country	*Name*	*Background*
Australia	Sir William Flood Webb	President of the Supreme Court of Queensland
Canada	Edward Stuart McDougall	Judge of the Court of King's Bench of Quebec
China	Mei Ju-Ao	Legislator of the Legislative Yuan
France	Henry Bernard	Chief Prosecutor of the Military Tribunal in Paris
Netherlands	Bernard Victor A. Röling	Judge of the Utrecht Court
Soviet Union	Ivan Mikheevich Zaryanov	Judge of the Military Collegium of the Supreme Court
United Kingdom	Lord William Donald	Judge of the Supreme Court of Scotland
United States	John P. Higgins	Judge of the Superior Court of Massachusetts
United States	Myron C. Cramer	Judge Advocate General of the United States Army
India	Radhabinod Pal	Judge of the Superior Court of Calcutta
New Zealand	Erima Harvey Northcroft	Judge of the Superior Court of New Zealand
Philippines	Delfin Jaranilla	Attorney General

Note Higgins resigned in June 1946, and the US government appointed Cramer to replace him

3.4 Determining a List for the Trials

Between autumn 1945 and early 1946, many countries including China, Australia and Britain submitted lists of Class A war criminals. Australia not only made a long list, but also insisted on including the Japanese Emperor as a war criminal. After a long period of discussion, on April 4, 1946, the IPS selected 29 people for trial. On the 8th, the committee removed Masaki Jinzaburo, Hiroshi Tamura, and Ishihara Seoul from the list, and the final list was submitted to Supreme Commander MacArthur by the 10th.

On the 13th, a 70-member Soviet delegation arrived in Japan, demanding that more war criminals be listed. On the 17th, after a heated debate, the prosecutors voted on whether to include Shigemitsu Mamoru, Umezu Yoshijiro, Aikawa Yoshisuke, Ginjiro Fujiwara and Kyoji Tominaga. After two rounds of voting, Shigemitsu Mamoru (6:4) and Umezu Yoshijiro (5:3) were added to the list. Therefore, 28

Japanese military and political leaders were charged with Class A war crimes (Figs. 11, 12, 13, and Table 4).

Fig. 11 Judge Mei Ju-ao and President Webb

Fig. 12 IMTFE Class A war crimes defendants (1)

Fig. 13 IMTFE Class A war crimes defendants (2)

Table 4 List of Class A war criminals

War criminals	*Charges*	*War criminals*	*Charges*
Araki Sadao	Invasion of Manchuria	Minami Jiro	Manchurian Incident
Doihara Kenji	Invasion of Manchuria, inhumane treatment of Prisoners of War	Muto Akira	Inhumane acts committed in Nanking, Sumatra, Philippines
Hashimoto Kingoro	Invasion of Manchuria, political propaganda	Oka Takazumi	Chief of the Navy Affairs Bureau, inhumane treatment of Prisoners of War
Hata Shunroku	Field Marshal, the Imperial Rule Assistance Association, the Rape of Nanking	Oshima Hiroshi	Diplomatic relationship between Japan and Germany
Hiranuma Kiichiro	Japanese Prime Minister during wartime	Sato Kenryo	Inhumane treatment of Prisoners of War
Hoshino Naoki	The rape of Nanking	**Okawa Shumei**	
Hirota Koki	Invasion of Manchuria, Planning Board	Shigemitsu Mamoru	The Pacific War
Itagaki Seishiro	War Minister, Invasion of Manchuria, the Lugouqiao Incident, inhumane treatment of prisoners of war	Shimada Shigetaro	Minister of the Navy, inhumane treatment of prisoners of war
Kaya Okinori	Minister of Finance	Shiratori Toshio	Diplomatic relationship between Japan and Italy, political propaganda
Kido Koichi	Recommendation of Tojo as prime minister	Suzuki Teiichi	President of Planning Board
Kimura Heitaro	Vice Minister of War, Burma atrocities	Togo Shigenori	The Pacific War
Koiso Kuniaki	Manchurian Incident, atrocities	Tojo Hideki	Prime Minister, The Pacific War
Matsuoka Yosuke		Umezu Yoshijiro	Invasion of Northeast China
Matsui Iwane	Nanjing atrocities	**Nagano Osami**	

3.5 *An Introduction to the Far East's International Military Tribunal*

The Tribunal was based at the former Army Academy in Tokyo, which had served as the Japanese staff headquarters during wartime. The building had three floors, and on the first floor, there was a trial hall, a lounge (for defendants, witnesses, defense lawyers, reporters, and observers), a lawyers' conference room and a reporters' telegraph room. The offices and an additional lounge (for court clerks, court stenographers, translators, printers, security guards, mailmen, and handymen) were also on the first floor. On the second floor, there were offices, lounges and conference rooms for the judges. The third floor had offices and conference rooms for IPS representatives (Figs. 14, and 15).

The trial hall was the center point of the IMTFE. It was converted from an auditorium, with the judge's bench at the head of the hall. The defendant's seat was located at the bottom of the hall, and in the middle,

Fig. 14 The IMTFE courtroom

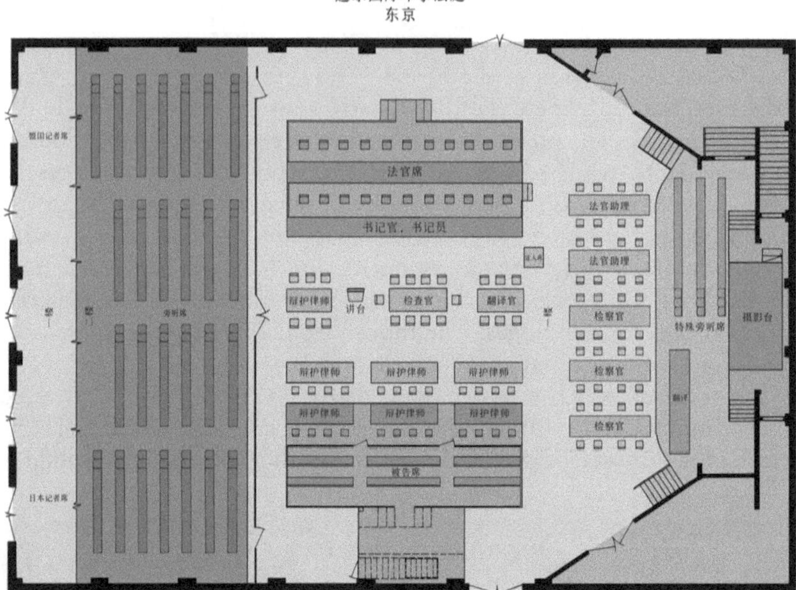

Fig. 15 The IMTFE seating chart

there were witness stands, and seats for the prosecution, the defense, and translators. On either side of the hall, there was a VIP and press gallery. In front of the press gallery, there were recording studios and a public gallery, which could accommodate up to 700 people. Since the trials were widely anticipated by the Japanese public, it was hard to get public gallery tickets. Many of those who attended were relatives of the defendants.

4 Summary

As the Tokyo Trials were historically unprecedented, prosecutors faced many difficult problems. There were questions over how to form a court, what laws to introduce, and which defendants to choose from. The most difficult part was coordinating the demands of different countries, which often involved tough negotiations. Ultimately, however, they achieved common ground in spite of their differences. The prime reason for this was Asia had never before seen such a catastrophe brought on by Japanese aggression. Whether the motives were to punish or prevent further crimes, prosecution was seen by the international community as a necessity.

Bibliography

1. Awaya, K., Nagai, H., & Toyoda, M. (Eds). (1999). *Tokyo saiban e no michi--Kokusai kensatsukyoku seisaku kettei kankei bunsho* [Road to the Tokyo Trials—Documents Related to the International Prosecution Section and Policy Decisions]. Tokyo: Gendai Shiryo Shuppan.
2. Bix, H. P., Toyoda, M., & Awaya, K. (Eds). (2000). *Tokyo saiban to kokusai kensatsukyoku: Kaitei kara hanketsu made* [The Tokyo Trials and International Prosecution Section: From the Trial to the Judgment]. Tokyo: Gendai Shiryo Shuppan.
3. Higurashi, Y. (2002). *Tokyo saiban no kokusai kankei--Kokusai seiji ni okeru kenryoku to kihan* [The International Relations of the Tokyo Trials—Power and Norms in International Politics]. Tokyo: Bokutakusha.
4. Awaya, K. (2006). *Tokyo saiban e no michi* [Road to the Tokyo Trials] (Vols. 1 and 2). Tokyo: Kodansha.
5. Higurashi, Y. (2008). *Tokyo saiban* [The Tokyo Trials]. Tokyo: Kodansha.
6. Mei, X., & Mei, X. (2013). *Mei Ru'ao dongjing shenpan wengao* [The Tokyo Trial Manuscripts of Mei Ru'ao]. Shanghai: Shanghai Jiao Tong University Press.
7. Cheng, Z., Gong, Z., & Zhao, Y. (2013). *Dongjian shenpan yanjiu shouce* [Handbook of the Tokyo Trial Studies]. Shanghai: Shanghai Jiao Tong University Press.
8. Yang, X. (2015). *Dongjing shenpan:zhanfan de daibu yu shifang* [Tokyo Trial: Arrest and Release of War Criminals]. Center for the Tokyo Trial Studies: Dongjing shenpan zai taolun [The Restudy on the Tokyo Trial]. Shanghai: Shanghai Jiao Tong University Press.
9. Wang, Z. (2015). *Dongjing shenpan zhong de guoji jianchaju-yi shenpan choubei jieduan wei zhongxin* [The International Prosecutorial Bureau in the Tokyo Trial—Focusing on the Preparatory Stage of the Trial]. Center for the Tokyo Trial Studies: *Dongjing shenpan zai taolun* [The Restudy on the Tokyo Trial]. Shanghai: Shanghai Jiao Tong University Press.
10. Liu, P. (2015). *Lianheguo zhanzheng zuixing weiyuanhui de sheli yu yunxing-yi taibei "guoshiguan"dangan wei zhongxin de tantao* [The Establishment and Operation of the UN War Crimes Committee—A Discussion Centered on the Archives of National History Museum in Taipei]. Beijing: Historical Research.
11. Yu, X., He Q., & Cai, D. (2015). *Dongjing shenpan* [Tokyo Trial]. Beijing: The Commercial Press.

CHAPTER 2

The Dispute Over Jurisdiction Prior to the Court Opening

The Tokyo Trials have caused ongoing and wide-ranging debate outside China, especially in Japan. Nearly all of the controversies attached to them can be traced back to the court debate, and the one on jurisdiction dates back to even before the opening of the court session.

1 Questions from the Defense

There were many debates over the Tokyo Trials: over their jurisprudence, evidence and procedures. Of all the disputes, the issue of jurisdiction, especially the "ex post facto" law proved to be the most contentious.

The IMTFE Charter was based on the Potsdam Proclamation and the Japanese surrender concerning the trial of Japanese war criminals. The jurisdiction of Class A crimes against peace, Class B conventional war crimes and Class C crimes against humanity were deliberated after the IMT Charter. When the court session opened, the defense team raised two "motions". The defense asked court president Webb and the other judges to "evade" the proceedings and they also denied the court's jurisdiction. The tribunal dismissed the first motion; however, the prosecution and the defense had a heated and far-reaching argument over the issue of jurisdiction.

Z. Cheng, *A History of War Crimes Trials in Post 1945 Asia-Pacific*,
https://doi.org/10.1007/978-981-13-6697-0_2

1.1 *The "Ex Post Facto" Law*

On May 13 (the fourth court day), the representative of the defense team Kiyose Ichiro delivered a long speech challenging the court's jurisdiction. He argued that:

1. The Tribunal was set up on the basis of Article 10 of the Potsdam Declaration of July 26, 1945, which states that "stern justice shall be meted out to all war criminals, including those who have visited cruelties upon our prisoners". On September 2, Japanese and Allied forces assembled along the USS Missouri in Tokyo Bay to sign the Japanese Instrument of Surrender, therefore both of them were bound by its terms.
2. The Tribunal did not have jurisdiction over "crimes against peace" and "crimes against humanity" because they had not existed in the Potsdam Declaration.
3. The generally accepted meaning of "war crimes" by nations of the world was crimes related to the violation of laws and rules of war—rules and conventions of war. With this in mind, there were only four typical crimes: violations of belligerents; violations by non-belligerents; plunder and espionage and war treason.
4. The Potsdam Declaration was accepted as a means of putting an end to the war that existed between Japan and the Allies, known in Japan as "The War of Greater East Asia". What the Allies called "The Pacific War" and the war in "the State of Manchukuo" were unrelated to the War of Greater East Asia, and it was deemed they should be ruled out.
5. The Changkufeng Incident and the Nomonhan Incident were already settled between Japan and the Soviet Union. Therefore, it was argued that they should be outside the scope of the tribunal.
6. When the Potsdam Declaration was issued, Japan and Thailand (Siam) were wartime allies, and therefore they were unconcerned with war crimes (Figs. 1, 2, 3, and 4).

All of Kiyose's questions were meant to prove that "crimes against peace" and "crimes against humanity" were "ex post facto" laws, laws that violated the legal principle of what a crime was deemed to be.

Fig. 1 The courtroom and national flags (1) (The judges of India and the Philippines had not arrived before the opening of the Tokyo Trials, so there were only nine national flags)

Fig. 2 The courtroom and national flags (2) (The national flags of France and the Netherlands look similar, and were once misplaced)

Fig. 3 The courtroom and national flags (3) (All the judges present at the court. From left to right: India, Netherlands, Canada, United Kingdom, United States, Australia, China, Soviet Union, France, New Zealand, Philippines)

Fig. 4 The courtroom and national flags (4) (After India gained independence in August 1947, the Tokyo tribunal changed the Indian flag)

1.2 The Unconditional Surrender

After challenging the jurisdiction of the tribunal, Kiyose cited from the British Manual of the Laws of War. He stressed that there were differences between the way Germany surrendered and Japan surrendered. He said that Germany resisted to the very end; Hitler committed suicide and only then did the capital ultimately collapsed. In that case, it was an unconditional surrender. However, the forces of the Allied Powers had not yet landed in Japan when the Potsdam Declaration was proclaimed. In Article 5 of that Declaration, it said that the "following are our terms", terms that ran from Article 6 to Article 13. Kiyose argued that the term "unconditional surrender", listed in Article 13, referred to the armed Japanese forces alone.

Kiyose raised the issue of "conditional surrender" because he wanted to question the interpretation of war criminals in the Declaration of Potsdam (as listed in Article 10: "stern justice shall be meted out to all war criminals"). He argued that war crimes should not extend to "crimes against peace" and "crimes against humanity"—terms that were adopted at the London Conference on August 8, 1945—because Japan had already signed the Declaration on July 26.

In *Hiroku: Tōkyō Saiban (The Secret Records of the Tokyo Trials)* published shortly before he died, Kiyose described in detail the "truth" about Japan's so-called "conditional surrender". He claimed that content on the Japanese Emperor appeared in Article 13 of the US-drafted Declaration of Potsdam, but it was deleted just before the Potsdam Conference, around the time that US Secretary of State James Francis Byrnes handed the text over to British Prime Minister Winston Churchill. In spite of these records, Kiyose insisted that the official text specified a "conditional surrender" (Figs. 5, 6, and 7).

Fig. 5 The defense team at the trials

Fig. 6 Deputy Director of the defense team Kiyose Ichiro (first from the right, front row)

Fig. 7 Chief Prosecutor Joseph B. Keenan (on the podium)

1.3 Trials by Neutral Nations

George A. Furness, the American counsel for the accused Shigemitsu Mamoru, contended that fair verdicts could only be found through trials by "representatives of neutral nations", in order that they would not become the "victor's justice". Opposing sides debated for a long time over whether the Tokyo Trials were the "victor's justice" or "civilization's justice", as Chief Prosecutor Joseph Keena had said in his opening statement. At the time, his statement did not cause controversy in the courtroom.

2 The Prosecution's Reply

The issue over jurisdiction was not completely unexpected. During the course of the postwar trials, representatives of China, the US and Great Britain had shown some doubt over the applicable law. According to Keenan, MacArthur had suggested that the "ex post facto" law should be avoided when they had met for the first time on December 7, 1945 (the day after Keenan had arrived in Japan with 38 US inspectors). It became clear that the prosecution was prepared and ready for the defense's questions over this.

The defense claimed that Keenan was overwhelmed and emotional, and that the remarks made by Comyns Carr were redundant. Keenan's remarks were indeed somewhat sentimental; he started his speech asking "Can it be that…?" and "…without the reach of any lawful punishment whatsoever?" The President Sir William Webb had to interrupt: "Mr. Chief Prosecutor, do you think those rhetorical phrases are fitting at this juncture?" At any rate, Keenan remained focused during his speech over the grounds of jurisdiction and the historical facts of Japan's unconditional surrender. Comyns Carr supplemented Keenan's argument by elaborating on the provisions of waging a war, and on war crimes citing authoritative works on international laws and international treaties.

There seemed to be a consensus among the IPS that the reply to the defense's arguments should be consistent, or that "we are not making new laws here". Chinese Judge Hsiang Che-chun said on May 14, "We are not making new laws to contradict members of the defense. The charter simply embodies the law and principles that are already in existence".

While the defense's doubts about the Tokyo Trials can be easily found in various Japanese and Western publications, it is necessary to elaborate on the prosecution's proposition, since it has rarely been mentioned.

2.1 Objections to the Argument of "Unconditional Surrender"

First, Keenan stressed that those responsible for "worldwide calamity" should be brought to trial and punished. He refuted attempts from the accused to restrict the jurisdiction of the court, pointing out that: (1) The Allies assessed via the Swiss government that the surrender of the Japanese government was without condition. (2) The Special Proclamation showed with abundant clarity that the Supreme Commander for the Allied Powers "is authorized to take such steps as he deems proper to effectuate the terms of surrender". (3) Apart from Article 10 of the Potsdam Declaration, other Articles were called to the Court's attention. Article 6 read as follows: "a new order of peace, security and justice will be impossible until irresponsible militarism is driven from the world", and Article 13 calls upon the government of Japan to proclaim unconditional surrender, and "the alternative for Japan is prompt and utter destruction". (4) Paragraphs 2, 3, 5 and 6 of the Instrument of Surrender state that there was "unconditional surrender", and that "the Emperor, the Japanese Government" would "take whatever action may be required by the Supreme Commander for the Allied Powers". All of these arguments served as solid proof of Japan's "unconditional surrender".

British Prosecutor Comyns Carr added that an attempt by the Japanese government to introduce a condition to the communication on August 10, 1945 was promptly rejected on August 11. He said that in the Instrument of Surrender itself, the Japanese Government had proclaimed unconditional surrender.

2.2 *Objections to the "Ex Post Facto" Law*

Keenan pointed out to the court that the defense had "conveniently omitted some very important and relevant" statements and declarations on "the generally accepted war crimes" before the Potsdam Declaration of July 1945. They were as follows:

1. In 1919, the signatories of the Treaty of Versailles, including Japan, made provisions for the trial of William II "for a supreme offense against international morality and the sanctity of the treaty".
2. In 1920, The Geneva Protocol for the Pacific Settlement of International Disputes—which was signed by forty-eight nations, including Japan—specifically stated that "a war of aggression constitutes an international crime". In almost the same language, a unanimous resolution followed during the Eighth Assembly of the League of Nations in 1927.
3. The Sixth Pan-American Conference of 1928 adopted a resolution on aggression, the preamble of which specifically stated that "a war of aggression constitutes an international crime against the human species".
4. As early as 1907, during the Hague Convention, a paragraph can be found in the "Convention Respecting the Laws and Customs of War on Land". It states that "Until a more complete code of laws of war has been issued, the high contracting parties deem it expedient to declare that - in cases not included in the regulations

adopted by them - the inhabitants and the belligerents remain under the protection and rule of the principle of the law of nations".

5. The very important Kellogg-Briand Pact, signed in August 27, 1928 by the contracting parties, brought together "all the civilized nations in the world". Its official title, the "Pact of Paris", indicated that nations would be condemned if they used war to resolve disputes. Keenan stressed that by 1928 "all the civilized nations in the world, by solemn commitments and agreements, should recognize and pronounce wars of aggression to be international crimes, and thus establish the illegality of war as a positive rule of international law". He added that "there was a superimposed contractual obligation not to wage war in violation of specific treaties". He hoped that "neither in points asserted in support of this motion nor any other time during this proceeding would there be the claim made by anyone that treaties have no significance".
6. On November 6, 1942, during a meeting of the Moscow Soviets on the 25th anniversary of the Revolution, Marshal Stalin announced that one of the objectives of war would be "to destroy the hated New Order in Europe and to punish those who established it". A year later, the same authority publicly reiterated their intention to punish criminals that were responsible for war crimes.
7. On November 1, 1943, the "Declaration on Cruelty" was issued in the names of US President Roosevelt, British Prime Minister Churchill and Moscow's Soviet Marshal Stalin. This declaration not only indicated what the consensus should be on how to punish war criminals, but it also made plain that those who waged war were "major war criminals".
8. On October 12, 1942, US President Roosevelt made a radio broadcast to the American nation, declaring that "the ringleaders and their brutal henchmen must be named, and apprehended, and tried in accordance with the judicial processes of criminal law". This broadcast was heard all over the world, and on February 12, 1943, on the birthday of Lincoln, President Roosevelt said that nations should "impose punishment and retribution in full upon their guilty and barbaric leaders".
9. During the Cairo Conference, the leaders of the US, China and the UK issued the Cairo Declaration, which clearly stated that "the

three Great Allies are fighting this war to restrain and punish the aggression of Japan".

Keenan became so emotional when replying to the defense's soundless proposition that he was interrupted several times by President Webb.

His associate Comyns Carr, who represented the United Kingdom, addressed the court on the same subject, arguing that:

1. "As [it] appears in the opening paragraph of the special proclamation that was established during this tribunal, the right of the Allied Nations to bring war criminals to justice is not based solely upon the assent of the Japanese Government, [either] by the Instrument of Surrender, the terms of the Potsdam Declaration or any other documents incorporated therewith. On the contrary, any nation or group of nations has an inherent right to bring war criminals to justice whenever and wherever they have the opportunity to do so, unless they have by treaty debarred themselves from that right". He quoted a passage from Stowell's "International Law", which was published in 1931.
2. Saying that the words "war criminals" in Paragraph 10 of the Potsdam Declaration had a narrow meaning was groundless, because Article 227 in the Treaty of Versailles had already made clear that William II of Hohenzollern, the former German Emperor, would be put on trial. This was a precedent for similar lawsuits.
3. The Hague Convention III of 1907 stipulated that hostilities between the contracting powers must not commence "without previous and explicit warning". In fact, this principle had long been recognized among the international society, and this was why Japan was condemned, after it treacherously begun an attack on the Russian fleet in 1904.
4. The Hague Convention IV of 1907 dealt not only with crimes committed against prisoners of war, but with many other war crimes. The defense's objection to "crimes against humanity" was without legal justification.
5. The practice of punishing war crimes had been a part of customary law long before war laws were drawn up in treaties and conventions. According to paragraph 44 of the Lieber Code: "all

wanton violence committed against persons in the invaded country… may seem adequate for the gravity of the offence".

6. Those who broke signed treaties were all war criminals and equally punishable according to the gravity of their offense.
7. Neither the Potsdam Declaration, the Instrument of Surrender nor the Charter made restricted provisions, and the Cairo Declaration made it clear that the territories Japan had stolen from the Chinese should be restored to China, as far back as 1914. There was nothing in the Charter, the Terms of Surrender or the Potsdam Declaration to prevent the tribunal from exercising jurisdiction with regards to crimes committed in China and the Soviet Union.
8. There was no limit as to which countries could commit war crimes against whom in paragraph 10 of the Potsdam Declaration. The mention of Korea in the Cairo Declaration helped to clear up some ambiguities.
9. Oppenheim's International Law was as comprehensive as it could be. The term "war crime" was a technical expression given to refer to acts of capture and punishment by enemy soldiers and enemy civilians.
10. It was necessary for defendants to show that they had signed for surrender in the belief that they were not among 28 listed war criminals. That is, they surrendered so that they should not be put to trial, in order to show that they would not continue to subject the population of Japan to what Article 13 of the Potsdam Declaration described as "prompt and utter destruction".

3 Debate Continues

What Keenan and Carr addressed in the court did not change the defense's proposition. Kiyose reiterated that the term "unconditional surrender" referred to the armed forces alone. He said that Japan recognized the necessity to obey the orders and directives of the Supreme Commander for the Allied Powers. However, this obedience went only as far as to be "in accordance with the terms of the Potsdam Declaration and does not mean that we should obey every single thing that the Supreme Commander should command". This quote became so famous that anyone against the Tokyo Trials would cite it. Kiyose argued that

Class A crimes (crimes against peace) and Class C crimes (crimes against humanity) were not crimes that fell under the scope of the Potsdam Declaration, so “the Japanese people are not bound to obey this order”. In spite of statements, speeches, laws and historical facts that Keenan and Comyns Carr referred to, Kiyose said that they had nothing to do with Japan.

After this, American defense counsel George A. Furness, Ben Bruce Blakeney and Samuel J. Kleiman addressed the court to support the motions raised by Kiyose. Furness raised several points. He said that the defendant Muto, chief of staff of the 14th Area Army of the Japanese Imperial Forces, had surrendered to the US armed forces; and defendants Itagaki (commanding general of the 7th Area Army), and Kimura (commanding general of the Burma Area Army, Sato and commanding general of the 27th Division of the Imperial Japanese Empire), had surrendered to the British Commonwealth of Nations. Once they had surrendered, each of the said defendants became prisoners of war. Therefore, Furness argued that “this tribunal is not a court authorized to impose sentences upon any of them according to Article 63 of the Geneva Convention”. Furness referred to the Convention Relative to the Treatment of Prisoners of War adopted in 1929. Article 63 reads: “A sentence shall only be pronounced on a prisoner of war by the same tribunals and in accordance with the same procedure as in the case of persons belonging to the armed forces of the detaining power”.

Major Blakeney, the counsel for Umezu Yoshijiro, was the “bravest” defendant counsel in the eyes of the defense team. He started his argument by questioning the distinction made by Comyns Carr between a lawful and unlawful war. He asked whether it was true “that all killing on the victorious side is lawful, and all killing on the losing side is murderous”. He added that “the powers by The Hague Conventions, and by the Geneva Protocol, have provided for the regulation of war without addressing this moral judgment”. He quoted Oppenheim in saying that “the rules of international law apply to war from whatever cause it originates” (Fig. 8).

Blakeney was so vehement in his opposition speech that he was interrupted by President Webb during his speech on the atomic bomb over Hiroshima. Blakeney said that “crimes against peace” fell under “the rule of caprice, autocracy and absolutism”. He said that he thought what Japan had done was no different from what the US had. Blakeney

Fig. 8 Defense counsel Major Blakeney (the speaker on the podium)

questioned several points on the indictment: whether the charges and facts were relevant; whether the indictment clearly and fully described the facts that constituted the essential elements of a crime; and whether war was the act of individuals, and not of Japan. All he wanted was to dismiss the conspiracy counts of the indictment, which were listed as "crimes against peace".

It seemed as though the defense team would not stop arguing. To ensure that the trials were effective, on May 17, President Webb announced that the three motions filed by the defense would be "dismissed for reasons to be given later". The "reasons" Webb mentioned here were that: the tribunal was established in virtue of and to implement the December 1, 1943 Cairo Declaration, the July 26, 1945 Declaration of Potsdam, the September 2, 1945 Instrument of Surrender, and the December 26, 1945 Moscow Conference.

However, neither the defense team nor critics today find this an acceptable answer to the issue of jurisdiction. According to *Judging the*

Tokyo Trial, an early work written by Masajirō Takikawa, an associate defense counsel for Shimada Shigetaro:

> The court did not state the reasons for dismissing the jurisdictional motion until the verdict day. This important issue during the Tokyo Trials was thus put on hold until the very end. The defense team regarded this as absurd. It's like a police officer investigating taxes and when asked whether he has the right to do it, not answering, but forcing the other party to take out their account book, and questioning their turnover and expenses regardless. It was extremely mean for the court not to state their reasons for dismissing this motion. If the court did not know how to respond, then it should have announced an adjournment until they knew how. For the above reasons, the trial should have been conducted rationally rather than by force.

This opinion from the defense later spread widely across Japan.

It was true that the dispute over jurisdiction was stopped by Webb. However, as we can see from the strong statements made by the prosecution, the argument that "the court did not know how to respond" was flawed. The defense team themselves disregarded facts and in many instances, intentionally concealed the truth.

4 Related Continuing Debates

During the trials, nearly all of the prosecution's propositions and the defendants' charges were refuted by the defense. This is one way in which the Tokyo Trials became protracted. Jurisdiction was hotly debated by the offensive and defensive within the courtroom; however, debate over it never went beyond the courtroom at the time.

4.1 Early Attitudes Toward the Tokyo Trials Were Quite Positive

Although attitudes are massively negative today, early Japanese society viewed the trials extremely positively. It is well-known that professor Yokota Kisaburô of the University of Tokyo spoke highly of the trials. The eight-volume *Tokyo Trials*, a collection of court correspondence, gave lengthy details of the trial proceedings and was published simultaneously with the trials by the *Asahi Shimbun* newspaper. The foreword of its first volume showed Japan's prevailing view over the Tokyo Trials. It was published shortly after the court sessions opened:

> Some people question whether it is appropriate to judge defeated countries by the victors. This is often misunderstood as revenge, because it is indeed easy for victors to overuse their power.
>
> Are the Tokyo Trials based on vengeance? Historically, it is hard to believe that the thought of retribution - which has been gradually abandoned in the criminal law of various countries - would revive among civilized countries. We must accept it as a defense mechanism that the international community has to take, in order to prevent war from expanding, and to prevent future wars. What the defense mechanisms of the trials will bring to the new world will also determine the future of mankind, as well as the future of Japan, who is now standing on this experimental platform.
>
> The Tokyo Trials are open, to the Japanese people and to the world – so that history may be their judge. In Japan, no major incidents have received a public hearing since the February 26 Incident, the Spy Richard Sorge Incident, and the Kotoku Shusui Incident. Public hearings are the basic guarantee of human rights and it takes courage for human beings to conduct these self-examinations.
>
> From a historical point of view, we must admit that the Allies have shown collective courage, even though they have different backgrounds and military strengths.
>
> The Tokyo Trials lashed out at our past sins. Judgement will inevitably bring unbearable suffering. But if we did not look into the past, how could we move forward and regenerate? Only the end of a militant Japan can bring about a new Japan. If we did not cross this threshold and quash what exists at present, the light of the future will never shine on the right path.

As *Asahi Shimbun* was the most influential media in Japan, this foreword not only portrayed the idea of the left-to-neutral activists, but that of the mainstream at the time.

The "*Public Trial Records of the International Military in the Far East*", which included indictments and early trial records and hearings, was published in September 1948 before a verdict was delivered. The preface, written by Sasamori Junzō (later the president of the House of Representatives in the Liberal Democratic Party), states as follows:

> The "Public Trial Records of the International Military in the Far East" is a great piece of literature on human history's comprehensive innovation. It

> can be seen as a great guiding charter on leading human society towards a happier, cultural life, out of barbarism and towards civilisation, hypocrisy to reality, injustice to justice, partiality to justice, obedience to freedom, revenge to blessings, insult to love and respect, struggles to peace, splits to collaborations.

In November 1946, a trial society was established in the Waseda University Law Department. The university's minister of law and the later president Ryuichi Oda wrote in the foreword of the *Far-Eastern International Military Judicial Study* (published by the society):

> (Not only experts should recognise the trials), everyone in Japan should testify at the trials; as bystanders of international justice, they should face all the crime evidence filed in court, listen to every prosecutor's argument and defender's debate, and fully reflect on it. We must challenge our understandings of the trials and make new judgements. Only by doing so can we, Japanese nationals, be reborn as new internationals, and be accepted into the newly conceived international community. It is not an exaggeration to say that the records of the international military trials are a must-read for Japanese citizens.

Sasamori Junzō and Nobuharu Oda are not political leftists. Their comments show how positive Japanese attitudes were toward the Tokyo Trials at the time.

4.2 The Opinion of "Victor's Trial" Prevails in Japan

On April 21, 1950, head of the IPS Keenan wrote to MacArthur:

> It is financially impractical to publish the massive trial records; I am only concerned about publishing the opinions of every judge, and the opening statements [of the prosecution and the defense].
>
> I am not satisfied with this decision for several reasons. I feel that care should be taken with the publication of the indictments, opening statements, rulings, the opinions of the judges, and the trial summations. Most rulings include limited citation from the detailed court testimony, except for the dissenting opinion of Judge Pal. Under these circumstances, "the dissenting opinion of Judge Pal will be given undue emphasis and could be extremely misleading and could well cause reviewers to conclude that the majority decisions were unwarranted, and subject the entire prosecution

> to misconception." But, if the publication includes a more complete set of trial transcripts and testimony summations, I believe that the majority judgments will be seen as appropriate. I really hope that you understand what I have outlined here.

Keenan did not worry unduly. Japanese society became increasingly less enthusiastic about the Tokyo Trials because signs of the Cold War coming became palpable. By the time Keenan wrote his letter, the Cold War at the Korean Peninsula was turning into a hot war. Negative attitudes toward the trials rapidly spread, and Pal, whom Keenan had mentioned in his letter, was sent to Japan to act as a judge. He had been in frequent communication with the defense during the trials. More than one judge disagreed with the majority, but Pal was the only one who argued that the defendants should all be found "not guilty", thus fundamentally disproving of the Tokyo Trials.

Pal's proposition was sent to the defendant by the defense counsel before the verdict. On April 28, 1952, the same day that the United States ended its occupation of Japan, "*Justice Pal: On Japan's Innocence: The Verdict of Truth*" was published (edited by Tanaka Masaaki). The full transcript of Pal's dissenting opinion was also published in the same year. After that, negative attitudes toward the trials began to gradually prevail. And the Tokyo trials became further stigmatized as they became associated with the negative label: "A Tokyo Trial view of history".

According to Yoshinobu Higurashi, the most accomplished Japanese specialist on the Tokyo trials, a crucial points still being debated to the present day is how the trials should be characterized: as justice for the victor or for civilisation. He states that both views make valuable arguments, containing complicated nationalist sentiments, political ideologies, emotional views and a moral view of responsibility in wartime. As we see it, some of these "crucial points being debated to the present day" no longer exist. Those who stick to the view that the trials are civilisation's justice have become minorities since the 1980s. At the turn of the century, these minority views became even less visible in public discourse. Nowadays, when people examine the trials, they look beyond this argument. We cannot simply say that minorities have given up on their original stance, but many have shifted their focus and have become reflective. That being said, the view that the trials were the victors' justice has been met with increasing support.

Whether it was a highly positive reaction or remained debatable, Japanese mainstream attitudes toward the Tokyo Trials have changed. Nowadays, the general attitude toward the trials in Japanese society is that they were a bad idea, and positive views are only shared among academics.

4.3 *Criticism from Japanese Leftists*

The Tokyo Trials were completely supported by Japanese leftists. Today, this group still praises them for exposing Japanese invasion and violence. However, their praise is more muted than it was in the past. Leftists point out that the trials had the following problems and defects:

1. Western countries occupied 70% of the seats in the tribunal, although their war victims only accounted for some 10% of all war victims. A tribunal dominated by such colonial sovereign states is unlikely to fully investigate the crimes committed by Japanese troops against the invaded Asian countries and their people. Such tribunals were even considered "a winning ground for European and US colonial systems to continue exerting power over Asia".
2. The tribunal did not prosecute Japan for crimes against humanity. These had a negative impact on postwar Japan and led to many unresolved issues including the issue of compensation.
3. The early closure of the Tokyo Trials meant that a large number of war criminal suspects, who should have been tried, escaped sanctions and returned to politics. The early closure also meant, historically, that the vein of wartime militarism was not cut off.
4. "Only those responsible for military administration rather than command were chosen as defendants", therefore the Emperor was not included.
5. The Western colonial sovereign states led by America only conducted select trials, meaning that many serious crimes were left untried, such as Japan's bombing of Chinese cities, its bacterial warfare and chemical warfare against China, and America's violent bombing of Japanese cities like Tokyo. Leftists only specifically cite the atrocities committed by the US postwar: against North Korea, Vietnam and Iraq.

Criticism of the leftists has some justification. Apart from the reasons listed above, there are other issues, such as Japan's colonization of North

Korea and Taiwan, which should have been included in the Tokyo Trials. But these problems are seen as small and insignificant. Such things were not conducive in supporting the view that the Tokyo Trials had positive significance.

4.4 *Further Negation Over the Tokyo Trials in Japan*

In recent years, Japanese right-wing activists have refocused their view of history from the Nanjing Massacre to the Tokyo Trials. The first chapter of *The Tokyo Trial was Fabricated*, written by Toshiaki Kitaoka, is entitled "Why do we study the Tokyo Trial?" and is split into two sections. The first section argues that "The trauma of the Tokyo Trials is the fundamental reason for a loss of self-confidence among the Japanese people". The second section argues that "Abolishing the Tokyo Trials should have been the highest priority". Critics of the Tokyo Trial viewed that the proceedings of the trials were unjust, their legal basis was insufficient, and the evidence that was presented in them was problematic. In 1995, fifty years after the war, *The Defense Evidence That Was Rejected and Not Submitted by the IMTFE* was published in eight volumes in Japan. Later, *How the Nanking Massacre Was Manufactured: The Deception of the Tokyo Trials* was published. In this book, writer Fuji Nobuo, who claimed to be present at most of the trials, states:

> Neither the defense's evidence nor their final statement played a role in the trials. Judgements were made based on the evidence and the final statement of the prosecution's alone.
>
> I don't mean that all of the prosecution's evidence was wrong and the defense's was true. What I am trying to say is that, when I, a Japanese person with common sense, was reading evidence from both sides, I found that much of the evidence submitted by the prosecution was twisted, exaggerated and fabricated, while the defense's was perfectly plausible.

Unlike the early opposition of the trials—that mostly questioned jurisprudence—those who hold negative views of them nowadays have found their views via in-depth study of the literature on the prosecution and the tribunals.

Influenced by general mainstream suspicion, neutral scholars have also begun to question the Tokyo Trials. For instance, while refuting the Japanese war criminals' "dwarfisation" argument that Maruyama Masao raised in his famous article "The Spiritual State of the Militarism Rulers",

Keimura Kai discovered speeches made by Keenan and Matsui Iwane on the Tokyo tribunals in historical documents, and by Gorlin on the Nuremberg Tribunals, to find relevant, yet "out-of-context" evidence.

Academic works often conclude by outlining the so-called "problems" of the Tokyo Trials. In Yoshinobu Higurashi's significant work, *International Relations at the Tokyo Trials*, Yoshinobu outlines the complex relationships among different countries, and argues that the trials represented a compromise between various interests. No matter what the motive, Yoshinobu's study shows the "political personalities" of the trials and adds weakness to its idea of justice. The non-fiction TV series "The Tokyo Trials", which recently aired on NHK, was mainly based on Yoshinobu's findings. It was filmed eight years ago and showed the serious disagreement that existed between the judges on the applicable law.

Scholars that fully support the significance of the Tokyo Trials still often point out their various "problems". These result long-term in amplifying the defects and weakening the positive significance of the Tokyo Trials.

Now that the Japanese archives are declassified, we can see that the Japanese government was an organized behind-the-scenes facilitator in trying to overturn the trials. On January 17, 1946, the Japanese government held a countermeasure meeting, which was attended by Admirals Oikawa Koshiro, Shogo Yoshida, Shodaro Ushida, Kondo Nobutake, Narumi Inoue, along with many lieutenant and major generals. This date is worth noting because it was two days before MacArthur issued the IMTFE Charter on behalf of the Allies, and formally announced that it would conduct the Tokyo Trials. Looking through the archives, it is surprising to find that even during the 1950s and 1960s, long after the Tokyo Trials, "URGENT" is often imprinted on Japanese government documents detailing Tokyo's judicial affairs. Ironically, Kaya Okinori, an A-class war criminal who was released early on in the proceedings, and returned to politics as a "law minister", commissioned scholars to "research" the Tokyo Trials from a "legal" perspective.

Therefore, in March 2013, when Prime Minister Shinzo Abe addressed the House of Representatives, saying: "the Tokyo Trials were the victor's trial", this was not just a slip of the tongue. He specifically told the Japanese House of Representatives' budget committee that these problems should be judged by "specialists". Clearly he thought that the Tokyo Trials would be verturned. Although the Japanese government hasn't publicly denied the Tokyo Trials, it is not far from doing so (Figs. 9, 10, and 11).

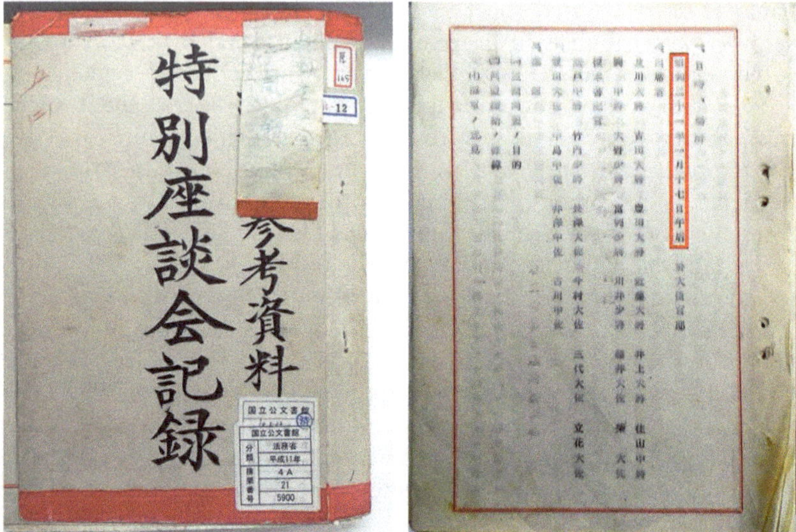

Fig. 9 The Japanese government researched the documents of the Tokyo Trials (1) (The Japanese government held a countermeasure meeting two days before the Tokyo Trials were announced)

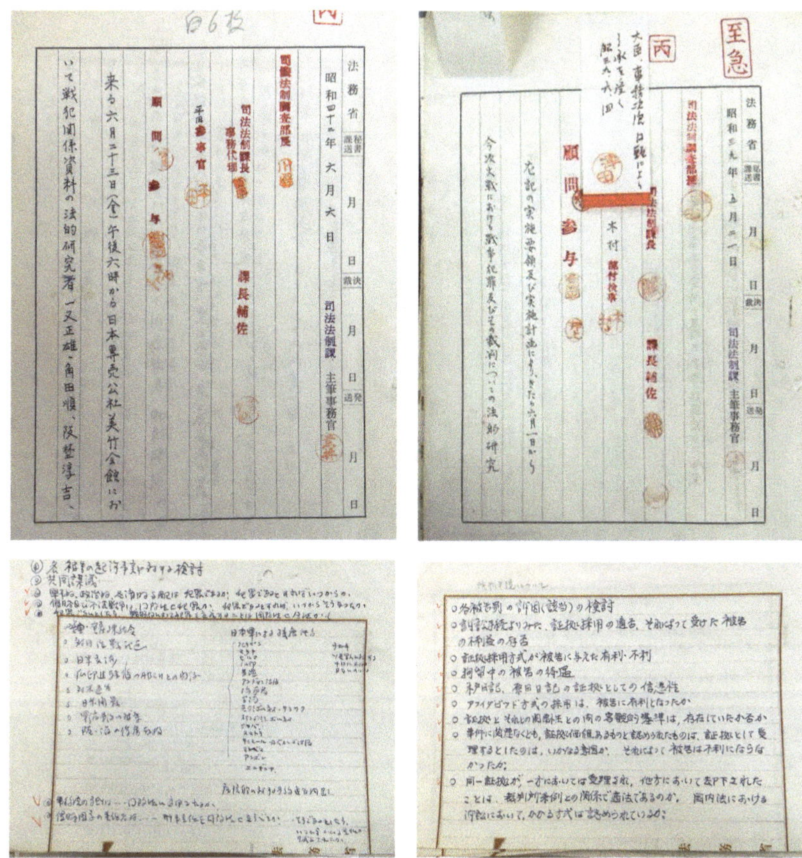

Fig. 10 The Japanese government researched the documents of Tokyo Trials (2) (The Japanese government authorized scholars to study "urgent" Tokyo Trial documents)

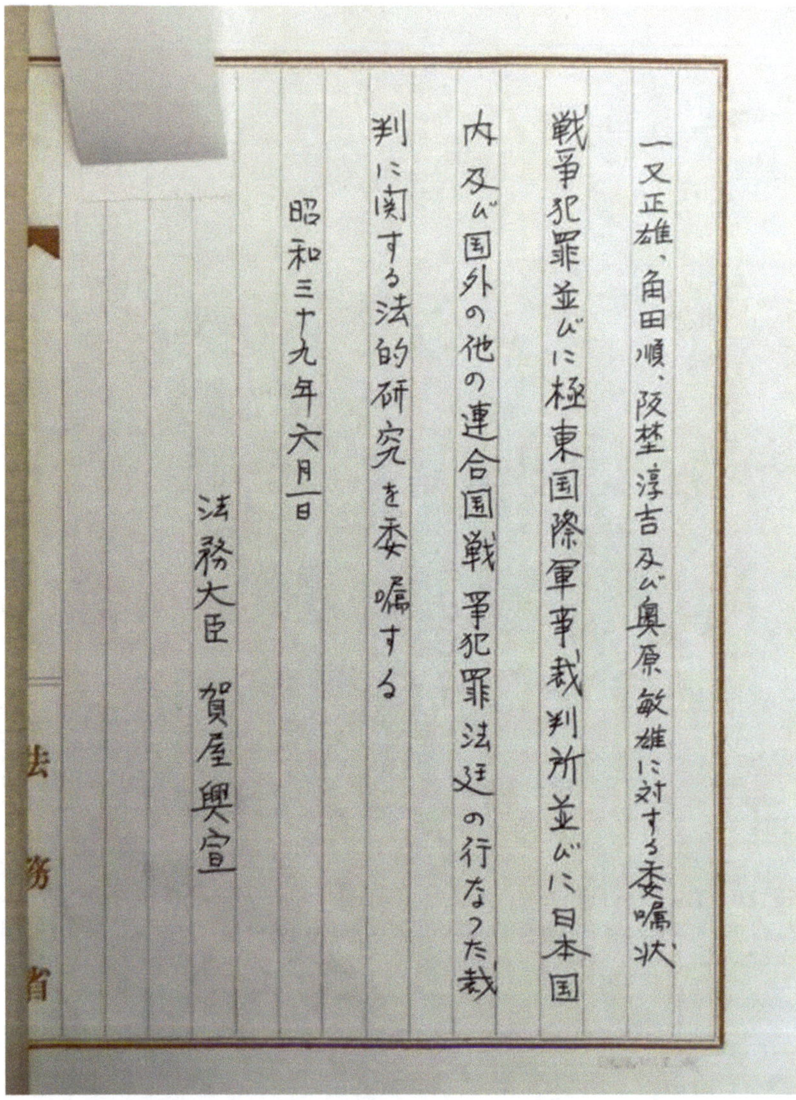

一又正雄、角田順、阪埜淳吉及び奥原敏雄に対する委嘱状

戦争犯罪並びに極東国際軍事裁判所並びに日本国内及び国外の他の連合国戦争犯罪法廷の行なった裁判に関する法的研究を委嘱する

昭和三十九年六月一日

法務大臣　賀屋興宣

法務省

Fig. 11 The Japanese government researched the documents of Tokyo Trials (3) (Kaya Okinori, an A-class war criminal who was released and returned to politics, commissioned scholars to research the Tokyo Trials)

5 Summary

In modern times, with war proving ever-increasingly destructive and powerful, the question over how to prevent it has been a major issue facing human society. Continuous efforts have been made over the years to address the concept of illegality in the wars after WWI, and this has gradually become the consensus of the international community. Articles on how to punish those who wage wars and destroy peace have been included in various international treaties. The prosecution of Kaiser Wilhelm was a significant precedent in judicial practice.

For various reasons, a number of works on the Tokyo Trials, especially Japanese ones, have become a microphone for the defense. The voice of the prosecution, as Keenan was worried about, has not only disappeared, but has been received negatively. Opposing parties continue to claim that the prosecution did not know how to respond when it came to the issue of jurisdiction. But studying original documents from the Tokyo Trials, it can be clearly seen that representatives of the prosecution, among them Keenan, Comyns Carr and Hsiang Che-chun, all made convincing arguments.

Bibliography

1. Kyokuto Kokusai Gunji Saiban Kohan Kankokai. (Ed.). (1948). *Kyokuto kokusai gunji saiban kohan kiroku* [Trial Records of the International Military Tribunal for the Far East]. Tokyo: Fuzanbo.
2. Nitta, M. (Ed.). (1968). *Kyokuto kokusai gunji saiban sokkiroku* [Stenographic Records of the International Military Tribunal for the Far East] (Vol. 1). Tokyo: Yushodo Shoten.
3. Tokyo Saiban Shiryo Kankokai. (Ed.). (1995). *Tokyo saiban kyakka miteishutsu bengogawa shiryo* [Rejected and Unsubmitted Documents of the Defense Side in the Tokyo Trials] (Vol. 8). Tokyo: Kokusho Kankokai.
4. Asahi Shinbun Hotei Kishadan. (Ed.). (1946). *Tokyo saiban* [The Tokyo Trials] (Vol. 1). Tokyo, Japan: Nyususha.
5. Kyokuto Kokusai Gunji Saiban Kenkyukai. (Ed.). (1947). *Kyokuto kokusai gunji saiban kenkyu* [Research on the Trials of the International Military Tribunal for the Far East] (Vol. 1). Tokyo: Heiwa Shobo.
6. Kyokuto Kokusai Gunji Saiban Kenkyukai. (Ed.). (1948). *Kyokuto kokusai gunji saiban kenkyu* [Research on the Trials of the International Military Tribunal for the Far East] (Vol. 2). Tokyo: Heiwa Shobo.
7. Takayanagi, K. (1948). *Kyokuto saiban to kokusaiho* [The Far East Trials and International Law]. Tokyo: Yuhikaku.

8. Stimson, H. L. (1947, January). The Nuremberg Trial: Landmark in Law Foreign Affair. *Foreign Affairs, 25*, 182.
9. Tanaka, M. (1952). *Paru hakasejutsu, shinri no sabaki, nihon muzairon* [Justice Dr. Pal's Statement, Judging Truth, and the Theory That Japan Was Not Guilty]. Tokyo, Japan: Taiheiyo Shuppansha.
10. Takikawa, M. (1952–1953). *Tokyo saiban o sabaku* [Judging the Tokyo Trials] (Vols. 1 and 2). Tokyo: Towasha.
11. Hayashi, I. (1962). *Kyokuto kokusai gunji saiban* [Trials of the International Military Tribunal for the Far East]. Tokyo: Jinbutsu Oraisha.
12. Kiyose, I. (1967). *Hiroku Tokyo saiban* [Confidential Documents and the Tokyo Trials]. Tokyo: Yomiuri Shinbunsha.
13. Minear, R. H. (1985). *Tokyo saiban: shosha no sabaki* [Victors' Justice: The Tokyo War Crimes Trial] (N. Ando, Trans.). Tokyo: Fukumura Shuppan Kabushiki Kaisha.
14. Fuji, N. (1995). *"Nankin daigyakusatsu" wa ko shite tsukurareta--Tokyo saiban teki giman* [This Is How the Rape of Nanking Was Created—Deception in the Tokyo Trials]. Tokyo: Tendensha.
15. Röling, B. V. A., Cassese, A., & Kurihara, K. (Commentary). (1996). *Rerinku hanji no Tokyo saiban* [Justice Röling's Tokyo Trials] (N. Kosuge, Trans.). Tokyo: Shinchosha.
16. *Maboroshiha, chukanha, daigyakusatsuha godo daianketo* [The Fiction Faction, the Middle Ground Faction, and the Massacre Faction: Major Joint Study of Three Factions]. (2001). *Shokun!* Tokyo: Bungei Shunjusha.
17. Higurashi, Y. (2002). *Tokyo saiban no kokusai kankei* [International Relations of the Tokyo Trials]. Tokyo: Bokutakusha.
18. Chaen, Y. (2003). *Senpan saiban no hoteki datosei o tou* [Questioning the Legal Validity of War Crime Trials]. In Taiheiyo Senso Kenkyukai (Ed.), *Tokyo saiban* [Tokyo Trials]. Tokyo: Shinjinbutsu Oraisha.
19. Ushimura, K. (2005). *Bunmei no sabaki o koeru--Tainichi senpan saiban dokkai no yomi* [Beyond the Judgment of Civilization: The Intellectual Legacy of the Japanese War Crimes Trials]. Tokyo: Chuo Koron Shinsha.
20. Yang, X. (2005). *Nanjing datusha shiliao ji: 7 dongjing shenpan* [A Collection of Historical Materials Relating to Nanjing Massacre: 7 Tokyo Trial]. Nanjing: Jiangsu People's Publishing Ltd and Phoenix Publishing House.
21. Awaya, K. (2006). *Tokyo saiban e no michi* [Road to the Tokyo Trials]. Tokyo: Kodansha.
22. Yomiuri Shinbun Senso Sekinin Kensho Iinkai. (Ed.). (2006). *Kensho senso sekinin* [Verifying Responsibility for War] (Vol. I). Tokyo: Chuo Koron Shinsha.
23. Kitaoka, T. (2006). *Tokyo saiban wa dechiage datta* [The Tokyo Trials Were a Fabrication]. Tokyo: Sogo Horei Shuppan Kabushiki Kaisha.

24. Onuma, Y. (2007). *Tokyo saiban, senso sekinin, sengo sekinin* [The Tokyo Trials, Responsibility for the War, and Responsibility After the War]. Tokyo: Toshindo.
25. Higurashi, Y. (2008). *Tokyo saiban* [The Tokyo Trials]. Tokyo: Kodansha.
26. Hosaka, M. (2008). *Tokyo saiban no kyokun* [Lessons of the Tokyo Trials]. Tokyo: Asahi Shinbun Shuppan.
27. Totani, Y. (2008). *Tokyo saiban: Dainiji sekai taisengo no ho to seigi no tsuikyu* [The Tokyo War Crimes Trial: The Pursuit of Justice in the Wake of World War II]. Tokyo: Misuzu Shobo.
28. Boister, N., & Cryer, R. (2012). *Tokyo saiban o saihyoka suru* [Tokyo International Military Tribunal: A Reappraisal] (K. Awaya, H. Fujita, Y. Takatori, & R. Okada, Trans.). Tokyo: Nippon Hyoron Sha.
29. Xiang, L. (2014). *Xiang zherui dongjing shenpan handian ji fatingxushu* [Hsiang Che-Chun's Letters, Telegrams and Statements at the Tokyo Trial]. Shanghai: Shanghai Jiao Tong University Press.

CHAPTER 3

The Trials

On April 29, 1946, Chief Prosecutor Joseph B. Keenan submitted an indictment to the court on behalf of the Allied Nations' prosecutors. On May 3, the court sessions were officially opened by the IMTFE.

1 Trial Procedures

1.1 Indictments and Arraignments

The IMTFE was based on both US and British common law. Before the actual trials began, there were several judicial procedures that needed to be implemented. It was required that parties read the indictment, which took as long as two days. As mentioned in the previous chapter, the indictment that was prepared by the IPS against the defendants contained 55 counts, and fell into three groups.

Group One (Counts 1–36) comprised of crimes against peace. The defendants of these crimes either fully or in part planned, prepared or waged wars of aggression against Asian countries (and allied colonies) that violated international law. The indictment stated: "the internal and foreign policies of Japan were dominated and directed by a criminal militaristic clique, and such policies were the cause of serious world troubles, aggressive wars and great damage to the interests of peace-loving peoples, as well as the interests of the Japanese people themselves… The main object of [the defendants in] this conspiracy was to secure by domination, exploitation or aggression, the states of the rest of the world; and

Z. Cheng, *A History of War Crimes Trials in Post 1945 Asia-Pacific*,
https://doi.org/10.1007/978-981-13-6697-0_3

to this end to commit, or encourage the commission of crimes against peace, war crimes and crimes against humanity as defined in the Charter of this Tribunal, thus threatening and injuring the basic principles of liberty and respect for the human personality".

Group Two (Counts 37–52) all involved crimes of murder, and were roughly divided into four categories by timeframe:

1. Between Japanese troops invading Southeast Asia in the 1940s and the "Pearl Harbor incident", when defendants formulated conspiracies to kill and murder members of the armed forces and civilians in Europe, America and Southeast Asia.
2. During the 14 years between the "Mukden Incident" and the surrender of Japan, when defendants conspired to kill prisoners of war from various nations.
3. During the "Pearl Harbor incident" and immediately after, when defendants ordered the Japanese army to launch military strikes against the Allied troops on both sides of the Pacific. Members of the armed forces and civilians from the Allied nations were killed—even though Japan was then at peace with them—in the regions of Nomenkan and Lake Khasan.
4. During six battles in China, when Japanese invaders killed unarmed Chinese soldiers and civilians.

Group Three (Counts 53–55) referred to conventional war crimes and crimes against humanity. Nineteen defendants of military commanders (including Dohihara, Hata, Hoshino and Itagaki) were accused of breaching the laws and customs of war, and abusing prisoners of war and civilians. Count 53 charged the accused with conspiring to commit crimes. Count 54 charged them with committing offenses. Count 55 charged the accused with conspiracy as far as failing to prevent subordinates from committing such crimes. All of the crimes in this group were committed between the outbreak of the "Pearl Harbor incident" and Japan's signing of surrender. However, in the case of China, crimes started as early as September 18, 1931 (Table 1).

The indictments of the Tokyo Trials were quite different to those of the Nuremberg Trials. While the Tokyo indictments listed 55 counts of crimes, the Nuremberg indictments only listed four. They also differed in that the Nuremberg Trials did not list crimes against humanity as a

Table 1 55 counts in the indictment

Group one: crimes against peace	
Count 1	Between January 1, 1928 and September 2, 1945, conspired to wage wars against East Asia and the Pacific and Indian Oceans
Count 2	Between January 1, 1928 and September 2, 1945, conspired to wage wars against (Manchuria) China
Count 3	Between January 1, 1928 and September 2, 1945, conspired to wage wars against whole China
Count 4	Between January 1, 1928 and September 2, 1945, conspired to wage wars against the United States, the British Commonwealth of Nations, France, the Netherlands, China, Portugal, Thailand, the Philippines, and the Soviet Union
Count 5	Between January 1, 1928 and September 2, 1945, Japan conspired with Germany and Italy to wage wars against nations and regions listed in counts 1 and 4
Count 6	Between January 1, 1928 and September 2, 1945, planned and prepared wars against China
Count 7	Between January 1, 1928 and September 2, 1945, planned and prepared wars against the United States
Count 8	Between January 1, 1928 and September 2, 1945, planned and prepared wars against the British Commonwealth of Nations
Count 9	Between January 1, 1928 and September 2, 1945, planned and prepared wars against Australia
Count 10	Between January 1, 1928 and September 2, 1945, planned and prepared wars against New Zealand
Count 11	Between January 1, 1928 and September 2, 1945, planned and prepared wars against Canada
Count 12	Between January 1, 1928 and September 2, 1945, planned and prepared wars against India
Count 13	Between January 1, 1928 and September 2, 1945, planned and prepared wars against the Philippines
Count 14	Between January 1, 1928 and September 2, 1945, planned and prepared wars against the Netherlands.
Count 15	Between January 1, 1928 and September 2, 1945, planned and prepared wars against France
Count 16	Between January 1, 1928 and September 2, 1945, planned and prepared wars against Thailand
Count 17	Between January 1, 1928 and September 2, 1945, planned and prepared wars against the Soviet Union
Count 18	On September 18, 1931, initiated wars against (Manchuria) China
Count 19	On July 7, 1937, initiated wars against China
Count 20	On December 7, 1941, initiated wars against the United States
Count 21	On December 7, 1941, initiated wars against the Philippines

(continued)

Table 1 (continued)

Count 22	On December 7, 1941, initiated wars against the British Commonwealth of Nations
Count 23	On September 22, 1940, initiated wars against France
Count 24	On December 7, 1941, initiated wars against Thailand
Count 25	During July and August, 1938, initiated wars against the Soviet Union in the regions of Lake Khasan
Count 26	During the summer of 1939, initiated wars against Outer Mongolia in the area of Khackhin-Gol River
Count 27	Between September 18, 1931 and September 2, 1945, waged wars against (Manchuria) China
Count 28	Between July 7, 1937 and September 2, 1945, waged wars against China.
Count 29	Between September 18, 1931 and September 2, 1945, waged wars against the United States
Count 30	Between September 18, 1931 and September 2, 1945, waged wars against the Philippines
Count 31	Between September 18, 1931 and September 2, 1945, waged wars against the British Commonwealth of Nations
Count 32	Between September 18, 1931 and September 2, 1945, waged wars against the Netherlands
Count 33	Between September 18, 1931 and September 2, 1945, waged wars against France
Count 34	Between September 18, 1931 and September 2, 1945, waged wars against Thailand
Count 35	Between September 18, 1931 and September 2, 1945, waged wars against the Soviet Union in the regions of Lake Khasan
Count 36	Between September 18, 1931 and September 2, 1945, waged wars against Outer Mongolia and the Soviet Union in the area of Khackhin-Gol River
Group two: crimes of murder	
Count 37	Between June 1, 1940 and December 8, 1941, conspired to murder soldiers and civilians by initiating unlawful hostilities against the United States, the Philippines, the British Commonwealth of Nations, the Netherlands and Thailand
Count 38	Between June 1, 1940 and December 8, 1941, conspired to murder soldiers and civilians by initiating unlawful hostilities against the United States, the Philippines, the British Commonwealth of Nations, the Netherlands and Thailand. (slightly different to Count 37 in articles)
Count 39	On December 7, 1941, attacked Pearl Harbour and murdered soldiers and civilians of the United States
Count 40	On December 8, 1941, murdered members of armed forces of the British Commonwealth of Nations at Kota Bahru, Kelantan
Count 41	On December 8, 1941, murdered members of armed forces of the British Commonwealth of Nations in Hong Kong

(continued)

Table 1 (continued)

Count 42	On December 8, 1941, murdered three members on the Petrel ship of the British Commonwealth of Nations in Shanghai
Count 43	On December 8, 1941, murdered soldiers and civilians of the United States and the Philippines in Davao
Count 44	Between September 18, 1931 and September 2, 1945, conspired to slaughter prisoners of war
Count 45	On December 12, 1937 and succeeding days, murdered civilians and disarmed soldiers of China in Nanking battles
Count 46	On October 21, 1938 and succeeding days, murdered civilians and disarmed soldiers of China in Guangzhou battles
Count 47	Around October 27, 1938, murdered civilians and disarmed soldiers of China in Wuhan battles
Count 48	Around June 18, 1944, murdered civilians and disarmed soldiers of China in Changsha battles
Count 49	Around August 8, 1944, murdered civilians and disarmed soldiers of China in Hengyang battles
Count 50	Around November 10, 1944, murdered civilians and disarmed soldiers of China in Guilin and Liuzhou battles
Count 51	During the summer of 1939, murdered soldiers of Outer Mongolia and the Soviet Union in the area of Khackhin-Gol River
Count 52	Murdered members of armed forces of the Soviet Union
Group three: conventional war crimes and crimes against humanity	
Count 53	Between December 7, 1941 and September 2, 1945, conspired to commit the breaches of the Laws and Customs of War against prisoners of war and civilians of the United States, the British Commonwealth of Nations, France, the Netherlands, the Philippines, China, Portugal and the Soviet Union
Count 54	Between December 7, 1941 and September 2, 1945, committed offenses violated the laws of war
Count 55	Between December 7, 1941 and September 2, 1945, deliberately and recklessly disregarded the legal duty to take adequate steps to prevent breaches

separate crime, but a conventional war crime. In addition, the group of crimes listed as murders were put forward by the United States, to explicitly investigate Japan's responsibility for Pearl Harbor. They were not explicitly separated during the Nuremberg trials.

After the reading of the indictments, there was a phase of arraignment, a stipulation of British and American law and a prerequisite for formal trials. On May 3, after the defendants were summoned to the court and their identity was verified, the marshal of court read out the indictments. On May 6, the court called on the accused to plead, and the 27 defendants from Araki to Umezu pleaded not guilty, all except for Okawa Shumei. The court had him removed for mental examination because they had judged his behavior unusual during the indictment hearing on May 4. The court allowed Okawa to make his plea when he was able to appear in court. However, on June 4, the court dropped charges against Okawa based on his psychiatric results. There was speculation from the outside world that Okawa had deliberately pretended to be mad in order to escape the trial.

After the indictment hearing and the pleas, the court dismissed a motion filed by defense counsel Kiyose that President Webb should evade the trial. They then discussed and made decisions related to objections that had been raised by either party (mainly the defense) concerning jurisdiction and translation issues. On June 4, the defendants were formally tried for the crimes they were accused of.

First, the prosecution introduced evidence, which included 15 stages: the Japanese Constitution; conspiracies to guide the public opinion of war; military aggression in Manchuria; military aggression throughout China; atrocities and trafficking of the opium drug in China; the formation of the so-called State of Manchukuo, affecting China's economy and politics; the allies of Germany, Italy and Japan, and separately France, French Indo-China and Thailand, and the Soviet Union; Japan's preparation for war; incidents in the U.S., Great Britain, and British Commonwealth countries; incidents in the Netherlands, Dutch East India and Portugal, and atrocities against prisoners of war and civilians (in separate stages). By January 27, 1947, the prosecution had completed its presentation of this evidence. The defense then presented a number of motions to dismiss the charges brought against the accused. After fierce debate on both sides, the court eventually rejected all motions.

By February 24, 1947, the trials had entered a phase of rebuttal for the defendants. These included general problems; matters concerning Manchuria, Manchukuo, China, the Soviet Union and the Pacific War; reservations, individual defense statements and additional evidence.

The prosecution provided its evidence in accordance with the 1928 laws of war, with atrocities making up a separate segment. The defense assessed where there were rebuttals, which in most cases, were where crimes were attached to individual defendants. The defense team were meant to prioritize their policies by considering how far they went in providing defense for the nation. But as the trials progressed, disagreements between the defendants gradually emerged. What's more, some defense counsels did not approve of the Japanese government. Therefore, many defendants' defenses ended up taking the form of individual defense.

1.2 Evidence and Witness

The rules regarding evidence during the Tokyo Trials were much less strict than those outlined in general Anglo-American law. The latter stipulated that the court should not accept hearsay or evidence that cannot be cross-examined. However, the IMTFT allowed for exceptions, saying: "the Tribunal shall not be bound by technical rules of evidence. It shall adopt and apply to the greatest possibilities, extend beyond expeditious and non-technical procedure, and shall admit any evidence which it deems to have probative value. All purported admissions or statements of the accused are admissible". This provision was convenient for time-pressed prosecutors during the evidence collecting stage. At the end of the war, the Japanese archives had largely been destroyed, and it was difficult for the prosecution to obtain sufficient government and military files in order to prove the individual responsibility of a defendant. This legal provision meant that written certificates, personal diaries, and additional documents could be submitted as evidence. However, it also meant that when any party objected to evidence, the judges had to vote on whether the document was of evidential value, which created countless side issues during the trials.

Prosecutors largely relied on the submitted investigation reports of Japanese atrocities committed on various battlefields. The Philippine prosecutor Pedro Lopez made many references to a 15,000-page report produced by the Legal Affairs Bureau of General Headquarters (GHQ). Some prosecutors even went to the battlefield themselves to investigate. Dutch associate prosecutor J. S. Sinninghe Damste spent six weeks before the trials collecting evidence in the Dutch East India. Chinese prosecutor Hsiang Che-chun also returned to China several times to collect evidence. The early Class B and Class C trial records from Asia-Pacific regions along with related materials were also frequently cited as evidence by the prosecution, such as the military trials conducted by the US army in Manila, Guam and Kwajalein, those by the British Army in Burma, and by France in Saigon. Out of all the prosecution's evidence, the court attached much importance to two voluminous personal diaries:

"Kido's Diary" and the "Saionji-Harada Memoirs". These records were the subject of severe criticism by the defense. As shown in the verdict: "they contain passages the defense considers embarrassing… the extent to which they are relevant, the Tribunal considers them helpful and reliable contemporary evidence of the matters recorded".

On the whole, the court was dissatisfied with the overall evidence submitted by both parties, especially by the defense. The court ruled: "Much of the evidence tendered by the defense was rejected, principally because it had too little or no probative value… many of the witnesses for the defense have not attempted to face up to their difficulties. They have met them with prolix equivocations and evasions, which only arouse distrust".

1.3 Translation

In order for a fair trial, the court provided to the accused with translation and interpreting services. Article 9, Section III of the IMTFE Charter states: "The trial and related proceedings shall be conducted in English and in the language of the accused. Translations of documents and other papers shall be provided as needed and requested". In spite of this, during the trials, the English-Japanese two-way translation often proved a challenge. There were similar translation problems during the Nuremberg Trials with the official languages English, French, German and Russian. But translation was more problematic during the Tokyo Trials, given that English and Japanese belong to different language families. Translation between English and Japanese could not be as fast or accurate as when translating between two Western languages; and this sentiment was very much conveyed during the translation of internal IPS documents and during the final verdict. In most cases, interpreters had to translate freely. Additional problems arose in that witnesses testified in Chinese, French, Mongolian and Russian. The French and Soviet prosecutors also insisted on speaking in their mother tongue. Obviously, the court did not anticipate and had not prepared for all of these situations.

Translation problems were often criticized by the defense. On May 6, 1946, defense counsel Takayanagi refused to make a plea, saying that there were differences between the English and Japanese translations of the indictment. On June 24, defense counsel Donihi listed 27 major errors in the English commentary of the film "Critical Period of Japan", which put the accused at a disadvantage. On October 4, defense counsel William Logan questioned the English translation of "Kido's Diary",

Fig. 1 Interpreters at the Tokyo Trials

and asked for it to be reviewed. During the first half of the trials, disputes over translations happened all the time. The head of the language department Lardner Moore was often involved in debates with the defense about alleged inaccurate or unfair translations.

The court subsequently took measures to improve the situation. It hired Chinese and Russian translators and insisted on the language department preparing its translation of documents for trial use in advance. On-the-spot translation was only carried out where there was evidence to be cross-examined. An effective translation inspection system was also established, which served as a three-tiered language arbitration board. Arbiters were Europeans and Americans, monitors were Americans of Japanese descent; and interpreters were Japanese nationals. Translators were Foreign Ministry staff, university teachers and even students. Some researchers believed that this system ran effectively during the trials, and that there was no clear evidence that translation errors could have seriously affected the overall verdict (Fig. 1).

2 The Crimes Against Peace Trials

Crimes against peace were at the core of the whole Tokyo Trials. The first 36 of the total 55 counts in the indictment were crimes against peace. Out of them, five counts were conspiracy charges and the remaining 31 counts were to do with the planning, preparation, initiation or waging of a war of aggression.

2.1 Conspiring to Wage Wars

All of the 28 accused of Count 1 were charged with conspiracy: to wage wars of aggression or wars in violation of international treaties after 1928, in order to dominate Asian or Pacific regions. Count 1 was the most important charge in the indictment.

The concept of "conspiracy" came from US judicial practice. The prosecution expressed that in criminal law, conspirators could either join together or withdraw. They either could or could not communicate with each other. Conspirators could also cooperate in the same crime, or engage in their own crimes. With this definition in mind, it can be seen that the conditions for identifying conspirators in a conspiracy were very loose.

As the Nuremberg Trials served as a precedent, the IMTFE Charter also charged people with crimes of conspiracy. But instead of giving it independent status, the Charter set it as a supplement to Crimes against Peace, Conventional War Crimes and Crimes against Humanity. Later on, the prosecution introduced conspiracy as an additional supplement to murder in the indictment.

Conspiracy was not a separate crime in the Tokyo Trials. The prosecution mainly used it as a tool to attach individual responsibility to defendants charged with Crimes against Peace. The prosecution could overcome the difficulties they had in lacking direct evidence, by using indirect evidence to charge defendants with conspiracy offenses. This was of great value during the Tokyo Trials.

Of course, the defense objected to this, saying that conspiracy, while special in US law, did not comply with the principles of international law. They saw it as a convenient legal weapon for prosecutors who were bent on punishing defendants. But their objections were dismissed by the court. After that, the argument between the prosecution and the defense shifted from conspiracy to the confirmation of historical facts, i.e., did

Japan commit conspiracy between 1928 and 1945? If so, shouldn't all the defendants (or just some of the defendants) be charged with conspiracy?

The defense argued that it was groundless to charge all 28 defendants with conspiracy to wage wars after 1928. The defense said: under the prosecution's logic, you could equally say that the expansion of England, France and Holland, the growth of the Russian Empire, and the gradual expansion of the original thirteen American states into the great American Republic, were "progressive conspiracies". Therefore, their foremost statesmen and generals should be held criminally responsible, whether they were imperialistic or anti-imperialistic in their personal convictions.

Finally, the court ruled that all of the accused be charged with conspiracies, from the perspective of Japanese political history at the time. It ruled that since 1928, Japanese troops had continued to invade neighboring countries. The court had the crucial task of determining the individual responsibility of these illegal attacks. However, it deemed that these decisions would not just be based on the observations of Japan's invasion history overseas. To find answers to such questions as: "why these things happened?" and "who should bear responsibility?" the history of Japan's domestic politics needed to be clarified. Based on various testimonies and evidence put forward by the prosecution and the defense, the court rendered the following verdict on conspiracy and the participation of co-conspirators.

In June 1928, certain members of the Kwantung Army murdered Chang Tso-lin, the Commander-in-Chief of the Chinese armies in Manchuria during the Tanaka Cabinet era. Tanaka's efforts to discipline the Army officers responsible for this murder were resisted by the Army General Staff, and had the War Minister's support. The government had been gravely weakened as a result of the Army's supporters becoming alienated. This led to a series of military coups in the early 1930s: the March Incident of 1931, the Assassination of Inukai in May 1932, and the February 26, 1936 Incident.

Defendants Okawa Shumei, Hashimoto Kinoro and Araki Sadao were energetic proponents of both political domination at home and military aggression abroad. They urged territorial expansion under the "Kodo (the imperial way)" and "Hakko Ichiu (the creation of a single world family)" principles, which appealed to many activists in political and military circles. The outbreak of the "Manchuria Incident" and "China Incident" meant that Japan's aggression abroad had an impact on its domestic politics. Its internal affairs, diplomatic, economic, industrial and military strategies changed to go along with the government's expansion plans, and more and more people, including navy officers and civilian cabinet officials, voluntarily joined or were forced into war. All of these people could be charged with conspiracy to wage wars of aggression in violation of international agreements.

On September 27, 1940, the conspirators were influential in Japan forming alliances with Germany and Italy. They not only launched the war of aggression against China, but also planned and prepared for the Pacific War that broke out a year later. The conspirators eventually controlled the political situation in Japan.

It can be seen from the overall ruling that the court was basically in favor of the prosecution's allegations. It also recognized the definition of conspiracy that was proposed by the prosecution. However, the court stipulated that "conspiracy" only applied to crimes against peace, not conventional war crimes, crimes against humanity or murder. The tribunal drew some conclusions that were different from the prosecution's: among the 25 defendants, it found Matsui Iwane and Shigemitsu Mamoru not guilty under Count 1 due to the lack of evidence. And although Matsui was found not guilty of crimes against peace, he was sentenced to death.

2.2 *The War of Aggression Against China*

Out of all of the World War II battlefields, China suffered the most and endured the longest, so most of the trials were focused on the war of aggression against China. While assessing the September 18 Incident (often referred to as the Liu Tiao-kow Incident or Mukden Incident) and the July 7 Incident (mostly referred to as the Lukuochiao Incident or the China Incident), the prosecution divided the 1931 and 1945 Japanese wars of aggression against China into two historical phases: the "Invasion of Manchuria" and the "Invasion of China". In July and August, the prosecution respectively submitted evidence for these two phases. In March 1947, the defense began their rebuttal.

The prosecution and the defense mainly debated the crimes of peace that Japan had allegedly committed against China. They assessed whether relevant defendants had planned and instigated war of aggressions, their inside stories regarding the outbreak of war, detailed accounts of various battles, and Japan's economic control and resource plundering of occupied territories. The prosecution believed that Japan not only invaded and occupied China—as well as other countries—during its war of aggression, but it also violated international agreements such as the 1919 Covenant of the League of Nations, the 1922 Nine-Power Treaty and the 1928 Pact of Paris. These constituted crimes against peace.

During the first phase, the prosecution contended, and later introduced evidence to prove, that between the 1927 Tanaka Positive Policy and the 1935 North China Autonomous Movement, Japanese military officials and Kwantung Army officers conspired to plan and commit extensive military aggression against China. This resulted in the occupation of three northeastern provinces: Jehol, Outer Mongolia and North China, and ultimately in the setting up of the puppet regime and state of Manchukuo. The defense rebutted the above charges. They asserted that the three powers' intervention[1] stopped Japan legitimately acquiring sovereignty over the Liaotung Peninsula. After that, Japan tried to defend its rights in Northeast China even though it recognized China's sovereignty. Japan's core interests in Northeast China were threatened by turbulence in the country, surging nationalism, the Northern Expedition's anti-Japanese movements and the Soviet Union's dominance being threatened. The "Liu Tiao-kow Incident" happened by accident, and was not deliberately caused by Japan. After this, the Japanese government and the Kwantung Army tried very hard to control the situation. However, it became uncontrollable, mainly because of Marshal Chang Hsueh-liang. The defense argued that the state of Manchukuo was established by locals, therefore it was neither the puppet regime and nor the Japanese base for invading China.

During the second phase, the evidence presented by the prosecution was focused on the Lukuochiao Incident, and the major battles between China and Japan during the Pacific War. The prosecution said

[1]Refers to April 23, 1895, six days after the signing of the "Shimonoseki Treaty". This was when Russia, Germany and France "advised" Japan to return the Liaotung Peninsula to China through diplomatic mediation.

Fig. 2 Emperor of Manchukuo Puyi and the prosecutors (Puyi, called as a witness, testified in court for eight days. From left to right, front row: Prosecutor Golunsky from the Soviet Uninon, Puyi and Chief Prosecutor Keenan. Puyi and Henry Chiu were looking at each other. Qiu was the prosecutors' secretary of China standing in the back row)

that Japan occupied most eastern China territories, and both planned and implemented the battles there. The defense argued that the Anti-Japanese Movement instigated by the Chinese Communist Party had caused large-scale hostilities. They claimed that the Japanese army had adhered to the no-aggravation policy long after the Lukuochiao Incident, and that China had aggravated and escalated the incident. After the Battle of Shanghai broke out on August 13, Japan persisted in saying that it tried to prevent the situation from deteriorating. The defense said that Japan had created several "new regimes" in China because they wanted to maintain peace and order there. The defense tried to prove to the court that the tensions between China and Japan had become gradually strained, but that it was China that was mainly responsible (Figs. 2, 3, and 4).

Fig. 3 Puyi testified in court (On August 26, 1946, when the defense counsel Okamoto cross-examined Puyi, he presented to the court a book. The book had a picture of a fan on which was a Chinese poem written by Puyi. Okamoto requested the court to use the picture for the purposes of handwriting identification. And the court finally accepted the fan as evidence)

Fig. 3 (continued)

Fig. 4 Chinese prosecutor Judson Nyi (Chief adviser of the prosecution team, podium speaker)

The court rejected the defense's statement and accepted the prosecution's. It ruled that: "The evidence is abundant and convincing that the Mukden Incident was carefully planned beforehand by officers of the Army General Staff, officers of the Kwantung Army, members of the Cherry Society, and others. Several participators in the plan, including Hashimoto, have on various occasions admitted their part in the plot and have stated that the objective of the Incident was to afford an excuse for occupation of Manchuria... and the establishment of a New State there... subservient to Japan".

The court ruled that Japan had further provoked the Lukuochiao Incident, and had also caused long-term conspiracies in China. It identified that the Japanese leaders' so-called "China Incident" or "China Affair" was in fact a war of aggression on China, running from September 18, 1931 to September 2, 1945. Japan organized and carried out battles, conflicts and separation activities in China. Its occupation of Chinese territory over fourteen years had one ultimate goal. High-ranking Japanese officials from political and military circles, commanders of troops and heads of spy agencies made plans and resolutions, or took action to invade China, and consequently were guilty of conspiracies to commit crimes against peace.

2.3 Crimes During the Pacific War

On December 7, 1941, Japan began its military attack, and its occupation of European colonies, the United States, and Asia-Pacific regions. This was when the Japanese fleet unexpectedly attacked Pearl Harbor (although Japan had started operations in Southeast Asia much earlier). There was no doubt that Japan had launched the Pacific War. The debate between the prosecution and the defense focused on what specific factors had led to the outbreak of war. Did the Japanese people act willingly or under pressure? The court tried the accused for conspiracy, and the organization and instigation of a war of aggression. All of those involved committed major events before the Pearl Harbor Incident (Fig. 5).

The prosecution looked at three ways in which the Pacific War had been facilitated: by Japan's signing of the Tri-Partite Pact with Germany and Italy; by Japan's relations with the United States and Commonwealth countries prior to the war—with a special emphasis on Japanese–US relations in 1941; and by Japan's pre-war relations with other European powers such as France and the Netherlands. The

Fig. 5 Chinese prosecution team (From left to right, front row: Yu Kwei—adviser, Judson Nyi—adviser, Hsiang Che-chun, Wu Xueyi—adviser, Zheng Luda—translator, Zhang Peiji—translator. From left to right, back row: Zhou Xiqin—translator, James Liu—secretary, Yang Qinglin—secretary to the judge, Daniel S. Ao—adviser. Photographer: Gao Wenbin)

prosecution contended that military and diplomatic actions committed by Germany and Japan against Britain, France and their colonies not only showed the trend of East and West echoing each other, but that there was a conspiracy between the two countries. The Non-Aggression Pact reached in August 1939 by Germany and the USSR, and the Kwantung Army's suffering during the Soviet Red Army's defeat in the Battle of Nomenkan, meant that Japan's advance to the North was not deferred until a better opportunity presented itself. It was intended to be the first step in the realization of Japan's national policy.

Germany's victory on the European battlefields stimulated Japan. It was interested in Germany's attitude toward it proposing military activity in French Indo-China and the Netherlands' East Indies. On July 1, 1940, Japan refused the US' agreement to preserve the status quo in the Pacific during the European War. During 1941, while negotiating with the United States, Japan was busy preparing for war, and attacked Pearl Harbor unannounced. The prosecution believed that these historical events were Japan's prelude to the Pacific War. They were long-term plans conspired by the Japanese government and the defendants.

The defense claimed that Japan was so indignant about the Non-Aggression Pact between Germany and the USSR that it terminated the Tri-Partite Pact with Germany and Italy. Therefore, Japan's action against French Indo-China and the Netherlands' East Indies had nothing to do with Nazi Germany. Both the Abe and Yonai Cabinet sought to improve relations between Japan and the United States. What they got was a unilateral blunt response. The defense argued that Japan's attacks on Great Britain and the United States were justifiable measures of self-defense. They said that these powers took measures in restricting the economy of Japan, meaning that it had no way of preserving its welfare and prosperity but by declaring war. The so-called new order in East Asia did not mean aggression or the violation of international treaties. Japan proposed this concept to show it wanted to maintain peace.

The court rejected the defense's argument and accepted the prosecution's. It said: "the acts of aggression against France, Britain, the United States and the Netherlands were prompted by the desire to deprive China of aid in the struggle against Japanese aggression… the attacks which Japan launched on December 7, 1941 against Britain, the United States and the Netherlands were wars of aggression." They were unprovoked attacks, prompted by the desire to seize possession of these nations.

2.4 Trials on Aggression Against the Soviet Union

Japan's military aggression against the Soviet Union and Outer Mongolia was recognized in the court as crimes against peace. Compared to the war of aggression against China and the Pacific War, these instances were simpler, so it took less time for the court to assess them.

The prosecution stressed that Japan's aggression against the Soviet Union was an integral part of its foreign aggression plan. Although seizing three northeast China provinces was attractive for natural resources, expansion and colonization, it was desirable also as an opportunity to antagonize the USSR. After the September 18 Incident, invading the Soviet Union's Far East through the north became a plan or motion for certain defendants. In November 1936, Japan and Germany signed the "Anti-Comintern Pact". The Pact, along with the Tripartite Alliance, targeted the USSR primarily. In 1938 and 1939, Japan launched offensive operations in Lake Khassan and Nomonhan. These battles suggested that Japan considered itself a participant in a conspiracy against the USSR.

The defense argued that Japan and relevant defendants had never had the subjective intention to invade the Soviet Union. They believed that the "Anti-Comintern Pact" (concluded between Japan and Nazi Germany in November 1936) and the Tripartite Alliance (formally established in September 1940) were only self-defense measures against the Soviet Union. Japan and its relevant defendants did not premeditate aggression against the Soviet Union. The two battles in Lake Khassan and Nomonhan were "border conflicts".

The defense's argument was easily proven false by the prosecution. It presented evidence of detailed plans instigated by the accused against the Soviets, and the court ruled in favor of them.

3 The Trial Proceedings for War Crimes

The atrocities committed during war were an important part of the prosecution and subsequent trial proceedings. Of the 15 stages of allegations, four were commonly associated with conventional war crimes.

3.1 Conventional War Crimes and Crimes Against Humanity During the Tokyo Trials

The IMTFE Charter stipulated that the tribunal had jurisdiction over the A-Class crimes against peace, B-Class conventional war crimes and C-Class crimes against humanity. Before World War II, conventional war crimes were uncommon in international criminal law, but long-term development and evolution led to changes in their core connotations. "Crimes against humanity" became new legal terminology. The Allied Nations formulated this charge in order to try and punish Nazi Germany for genocide. In addition to the Tokyo Trials, 51 tribunals for crimes were established in the Asia-Pacific region post-war, to try war criminals for Class-B and Class-C crimes.

According to the Charter of the International Military Tribunal (also known as the Charter of the Nuremberg Tribunal), "War crimes are namely, violations of the laws or customs of war. Such violations shall include, but not be limited to: murder, ill-treatment or the deportation of slave labor, or any other purpose of bringing a civilian population into occupied territory; murder or the ill-treatment of prisoners of war or persons at sea; the killing of hostages; the plunder of public or private property; wanton destruction of cities, towns or villages or devastation that is not justified by military necessity". The Tokyo Trial Charter removed these details and simply defined conventional war crimes as "violations of the laws or customs of war". But the prosecution's allegations against the defendants, which listed acts of murder, the ill-treatment of prisoners of war and civilians, as well as slave labor, show that these details still constituted the main ideas about what conventional war crimes were.

Since the nineteenth century, the international community has increasingly improved the provisions for the treatment of war prisoners and civilians. The 1907 Hague Convention No. IV, also known as the Regulations Concerning the Laws and Customs of War on Land, details the fundamental principles and laws concerning the concrete norms of war. What was especially important was the Geneva Convention, which was signed on July 27, 1929. As its full name, the Geneva Convention relative to the Treatment of Prisoners of War suggests, the convention stipulates the treatment of war prisoners by warring parties. There are over 97 articles detailing all of the provisions.

Japan sent representatives to attend the meeting and sign the convention. However, the Japanese government didn't ratify the Geneva Convention until the Pacific War broke out on December 7, 1941. Shortly after, the United States, Britain and a number of other Western countries demanded that Japan abide by the convention. Japan rejected it, but agreed to apply "mutatis mutandis": provisions of the said agreement toward prisoners of war in the United States and the Commonwealth countries.

Consequently, although the Japanese government had not ratified the convention, it was still bound by it. After signing the Geneva Convention, a number of countries including Japan also signed the Red Cross Convention, which stipulated that warring parties should provide aid to other injured persons in accordance with international law and international practice. As a matter of fact, the provisions for the treatment of prisoners of war, captured civilians and wounded persons under international law were highly sophisticated even before Japan launched its war of aggression. These three conventions became the legal foundation for two international military tribunals in Europe and Asia after World War II.

The defense had doubts that Japan was bound by these conventions, especially the 1929 Geneva Convention. They said that although the Japanese government had signed the convention, they had not ratified it and hence were not bound by the terms of it. Although the Japanese government ensured that they would respect the spirit of the convention, after they declared war on the US and UK on December 7, 1941, their guarantee became just another provision, which they applied only when it suited them.

The prosecution pointed out that the Japanese government had signed and ratified the 1907 Hague Convention IV on Respecting the Laws and Customs of War on Land, which ensured the humane treatment of prisoners of war. So even without ratifying the 1929 Geneva Conventions, Japan was obligated to "treat prisoners in a humane manner", and the prosecution could hold defendants criminally responsible for mistreating prisoners.

After hearing both parties' statements, the tribunal ruled that Japan was obligated to abide by the treaties, including the Geneva Convention, and to look after its prisoners. They stated: "The general principles of the law exist independently of the said conventions. The conventions merely reaffirm the pre-existing law and prescribe detailed provisions for its application".

The debate over conventional war crimes also saw consideration over whether internationally accepted laws and regulations were applied during the Sino-Japanese wars. While the war of aggression escalated against China, the Japanese authorities used the word "incident" rather than "war", to diminish the scale of formal fighting between both sides, such as with the "Manchuria Incident" and the "China Incident". Therefore, it can be said that the Japanese authorities did not recognize the need to follow internationally accepted laws and regulations during the Sino-Japanese "incident".

Since the Liu Tiao-Kow Incident, the Japanese army called captured Chinese soldiers nasty names such as "bandits". Many were captured during earlier crackdowns of anti-Japanese forces in northeastern China, and they were not given the treatment that prisoners of war deserve. It was common for Chinese soldiers to be killed, and Japan ignored wartime laws and regulations by claiming that the fighting was an “incident”. This was the defense that they adopted in court. Although the court acknowledged that China and Japan had not formally declared war on each other until the “Pearl Harbor incident”, it did not accept the argument that the fighting was simply an “incident”. It ruled that the Sino-Japanese War that followed the September 18th Incident should have abided by international war regulations and practices. The mistreatment and murder of prisoners of war was clearly an illegal act.

The term “crimes against humanity” first appeared in 1915. It was used in a statement to condemn the “Armenian massacre” perpetrated by the Allies on the Ottoman Turkish Empire. The concept became synonymous with genocide and extermination. In the summer of 1945, the Charter of the International Military Tribunal formally brought charges of “crimes against humanity” against defendants in London, and they gave these crimes this specific definition:

> Crimes against humanity, namely, murder, extermination, enslavement, deportation, and other inhumane acts committed against any civilian population, before or during the war; or persecutions on political, racial or religious grounds in execution of or in connection with any crime within the jurisdiction of the Tribunal.

In September 1939, Nazi Germany raided Poland and World War II began. However, the Nazis had already persecuted Jews before WWII, including a large number of German nationals. The Charter took this into consideration, which is why it included the words “before the war” and “civilian population”.

The Tokyo tribunals intended to continue following this definition, but the prosecution realized that Japan’s acts of murder, enslavement and persecution of civilians from other countries were different from those in Nazi Germany and so this definition was not a good fit. Therefore, “crimes against humanity” became attached to conventional war crimes during the Tokyo Trials, and the prosecution tried to testify to mostly typical war crimes, namely, the inhumane treatment of soldiers and civilians in wartime.

At any rate, the Nuremberg and Tokyo trials demanded that people follow the legal principles for granting humane treatment to prisoners, and crimes against humanity were officially recognized. They were adopted in twelve subsequent trials, and set the foundation for the international humanitarian law that exists today. Genocide and crimes against humanity were recognized during the 1990s International Criminal Tribunal for the Former Yugoslavia and the International Criminal Tribunal for Rwanda. They were also included in The Hague's 1998 Rome Statute of the International Court of Justice.[2] These tribunals not only adopted the definition of "crimes against humanity" set by the major Nuremberg and Tokyo trials half a century ago; they also supplemented other definitions to include sexual violence, torture, and imprisonment. They did this on the basis of the two trial constitutions, thereby enriching the idea about what constituted a crime against humanity.

3.2 The Prosecution's Evidence and Strategy for Conventional War Crimes

During the Tokyo Trials, prosecutors faced many difficulties presenting evidence of war crimes. The Japanese government destroyed its wartime archives on a mass scale, which caused complications during investigation and the collection of evidence. The prosecution thus decided to expose this shameful act in court, and present it as evidence. The Chief of Archives at the First Demobilization Bureau, Miyama Yazo, stated in his affidavit: "a notification was issued by the Adjutant General under the order of the War Minister on August 14, 1945 of the 20th year of Showa, to all Army troops saying to the effect that confidential documents held by each troop should be destroyed by fire immediately. The above notification was given by telephone to the troops in Tokyo and by telegram to other troops. This telegram and its draft were also destroyed by fire".

However, during the trials, the prosecution disputed among itself over whether to prosecute people for conventional war crimes and crimes against humanity. At the end of 1946, the trials were still at the prosecution stage. Chief prosecutor Keenan, proposed that the IPS drop the charges for these two crimes. He said that prosecuting people for conventional war crimes was not the main objective of the Tokyo Trials,

[2]The Statute of the International Criminal Court was adopted in Rome in 1998, and is commonly referred to as the Rome Statute. The Statute came into effect in 2002 and the International Criminal Court was formally established (in The Hague). The court is not a UN agency but an independent international criminal justice agency.

and that it would take a long time to present evidence, which was not conducive to the trials. His proposal was widely opposed. The prosecution argued among themselves and refused to reach a consensus. Finally, the Dutch prosecutor Damste suggested a compromise—that prosecutors from various countries provide a simple abstract for each piece of evidence and read it in court instead of the evidence itself. This would greatly reduce time spent proofreading everything.

As a result, the prosecution was able to submit large-scale evidence of conventional war crimes within just six weeks. Related atrocities included: killing, torture, rape, and other abuses of prisoners of war, military doctors, the wounded, patients and detained allies; requiring

Fig. 6 Prosecutors (From left to right, back row: Quilliam from New Zealand, Henry Chiu from China, Oneto from France, Lopez from the Philippines, Nolan from Canada. From left to right, front row: Comyns from the UK, Keenan from the US, Borgerhoff Mulder from the Netherlands, Mansfield from Australia)

Fig. 7 Chinese prosecutor Hsiang Che-chun

prisoners to perform military operations in inhumane environments, and refusing to provide proper food, water, clothing, and containment facilities; illegal and excessive punishment; ignoring the basic rights of the wounded, sick, military doctors and nurses; failing to fulfill international obligations to convey information about captives to the countries concerned; using poisonous gas in China; military raids and sabotage without justification; killing survivors from sinking ships; ignoring the rights of military medical ship merchants under international law, and attacking ships from neutral countries (Figs. 6, 7, 8, and 9).

Obviously, there was a serious problem with providing fast outline-based summaries of crimes. The full evidence, which revealed the atrocities of the Japanese army, was not demonstrated in the courtroom. Such details were supposed to be an important way for the court to educate the world on the full extent of war. It's regrettable that ordinary people have lost the opportunity to learn about this history.

Fig. 8 Female prosecutors in the Tokyo Trials (Prosecutor Llewellyn participated in the presentation phase of China)

Regardless of the pros or cons, the prosecution's presentation of war crimes evidence was well thought out. Unlike with crimes against peace, which were focused on the planning and launching of wars, it was difficult to directly pin conventional war crimes, crimes against humanity and even murder on 28 high-ranking defendants. There was little evidence to prove that they had personally committed crimes or had issued specific orders. The prosecutions' tactic was to submit huge piles of evidence proving that there had been widespread, prolonged and high-frequency Japanese atrocities across Asia and the Pacific. This proved that such atrocities had been normalized and could not have been arbitrarily raging within local armies. Instead, they had been guided by a unified policy that had come from the top of the Japanese government, and they argued that such a policy must have come from the defendants.

Fig. 9 Female prosecutors in the Tokyo Trials (Prosecutor Lambert read the summation in the case of Hoshino)

3.3 Atrocities Committed by the Japanese Army During 1928 and 1945

Despite difficulties in submitting evidence, the prosecution succeeded in connecting the atrocities committed by the Japanese army with the accused. Meanwhile, the prosecution intended to highlight a number of especially serious atrocities, to demonstrate to the world the appalling atrocities committed by the Japanese military and the government during the war.

The Rape of Nanking saw the Japanese army massacring, looting and raping Chinese citizens weeks after the 1937 Battle of Nanjing. It was a manifestation of murder, conventional war crimes, and crimes against humanity. It was also the most important case for the court in trying Japanese war atrocities.

The prosecution submitted to the court a telegram as evidence, which had been sent in early 1938 by Nanjing's US embassy to Washington.

The telegram described recent atrocities and attached a number of documents, one of which was a letter to China's American ambassador written by third secretary of embassy John M. Allison. John wrote that he had heard from 14 Americans who had witnessed atrocities that: "the city has fallen into the hands of the Japanese as captured prey, not merely taken in the course of organized warfare but seized by an invading army whose members seemed to have set upon the prize to commit unlimited acts of depredation and violence. Fuller data and our (embassy's) own observations have not brought out facts to discredit their (the 14 Americans') information. The civilian Chinese population remaining in the city crowded the streets of the so-called 'safety zone' as refugees, many of whom are destitute. Physical evidence is almost everywhere of the killing of men, women and children, of the breaking into and looting of property and of the burning and destruction of houses and buildings... over twenty thousand Chinese soldiers were systematically shot".

Witnesses and evidence exposed the Japanese army's sexual violence against Chinese women, as well as its massacre of civilians and unarmed soldiers. Chairman of the International Committee John Rabe reported to the German authorities that he and his colleagues believed there to have been some 20,000 incidents of rape. The U.S.' Miner Searle Bates, a founding member of the International Committee for the Safety Zone in Nanjing, testified for the prosecution. He estimated that there were at least 8000 incidents just based on reports he had heard from the Safety Zone.

China and the West submitted oral testimony and documentary evidence, and the prosecution proved to the court that the Japanese army had committed mass atrocities, such as carnage and rape, for at least six weeks after the fall of Nanjing. It was difficult for the defense to argue against the hellish scene painted by the prosecution. In other cases, defense lawyers hung on to the slightest of ambiguities and persisted in repeated and lengthy cross-examination of prosecution witnesses. However, they basically gave up arguing the Nanjing case, which meant that they acknowledged what the Japanese army had done after the Battle of Nanjing (Fig. 10).

The defense turned their focus toward where there was individual responsibility, in the cases of Matsui Iwane (Commander of the Central China Expeditionary Army); Muto Akira (Adjutant of General Staff in the Central China Expeditionary Army) and Hirota Koki (Minister of State). The defense tried to prove to the court that the defendants

Fig. 10 Reverend John Magee, a member of the International Committee for the Nanking Safety Zone provided evidence for the Rape of Nanking (The court played a video clip shot by him that recorded the atrocities committed by the Japanese troops)

neither ordered violence/slaughter, nor knew about their soldiers' appalling behavior. So this is why they did not take responsibility for not immediately putting a stop to their subordinates' behavior.

The Bataan Death March. The Japanese Army did not observe the laws of war when carrying out The Bataan Death March, which saw prisoners of war being moved from one place to another. They were forced to march long distances, and those who fell behind were beaten, tortured and murdered. The 1942 Bataan March of April saw American and Filipino soldiers marched from Bataan to San Fernando without sufficient food, water or rest. They were tortured and killed along the way. Evidence indicates that approximately 8000 prisoners died during the six-day movement. Tojo admitted that he had heard of this march from many different sources.

The Burma-Siam Railway Incident. Between 1942 and 1943, the Burma-Siam Railway Incident saw Japan furthering its strategic plans and linking its railroad in Bangkok, Siam to that in Moulmein, Burma. The Japanese army forced Western prisoners of war and locals to become builders in order that it be constructed. Thousands of enslaved workers died as a result of harsh conditions and inhumane enslavement. The court found that the death toll was approximately 16,000. Tojo told the tribunal that he had received reports that the prisoners employed for this project were in poor condition, and so he had relieved the Commanding General of Railway Construction from duty. However, the court also found other evidence that Tojo was lying, and could even have played a role in making the situation worse.

The execution of the Doolittle fliers. On April 18, 1942, as retaliation for Japan's attack on Pearl Harbor and in order to shock the Japanese military and civilians, US bombers led by James Harold Doolittle bombed major Japanese cities including Tokyo, Kobe and Osaka. Most American pilots landed in mainland China after completing their missions, but eight pilots were captured by the Japanese. In October, the China Expeditionary Army held a Japanese military tribunal executed three prisoners. The other five prisoners were mistreated, and one ended up dead in prison. On April 21, 1943, the White House protested to Japan about these incidents. The White House warned that it would try relevant Japanese officials, after the Allies had earlier made a statement saying that they would use judicial means to try Japanese war criminals. Later, the Tokyo tribunal ruled that this incident was typical in showing that Japan had committed conventional war crimes. This was not only because the victims were American military pilots, but because Prime Minister Tojo and Commander of the China Expeditionary Army Hata Shunroku were involved.

Before the bombing, there were no corresponding provisions listed in Japanese legislation. However, in order to impose the death penalty on the Doolittle pilots, Prime Minister Tojo ordered the creation of a new decree, and set the effective date of this "decree" from when the air strikes occurred. On August 13, 1942, Tojo issued the Military Regulations for the Punishment of Enemy Flyers, stating: "these military regulations shall be applicable to enemy flyers who have raided Japanese Manchukuo territories, or our operational areas, and have come within the jurisdiction of the Japanese Expedition Forces in China". In his testimony, Tojo stated that he had adopted the "legislation" and "trials" to intimidate the Allied Forces against other possible air strikes. His intention was to convince the court that he had used "civilized" conduct. He even said that he had "absolved" five of the pilots, saying that they had originally been sentenced to death. But such testimony just proved that he bore direct responsibility for the execution of the Doolittle fliers. Hata Shunroku took orders from Tojo and commanded Japanese soldiers in Shanghai to "try" and execute three American pilots. Thus, the prosecution charged him and Matsui Iwane on Count 55.

In addition to the important above-mentioned cases, the prosecution attached great importance to how prisoners of war and civilians from

China, the West and Southeast Asia had been treated by Japan during wartime. They looked at the implementation of corporal punishment, forced labor, accommodation, medical care and food hygiene. The prosecution intended to unveil how various atrocities had systematically been operated from grassroots level. They showed that not only Japanese soldiers at grassroots level had committed crimes, but that defendants who had not seemed directly responsible for the soldiers were responsible as well.

The defense were unable to provide strong proof to refute the large amount of evidence presented by the prosecution. As the final verdict shows, the court fully endorsed the prosecution.

4 Summary

The IMTFE Charter stated in its foreword that "there shall be established a Tribunal for the just and prompt trial and punishment of the major war criminals in the Far East". However, after the session began, it became clear that it would be difficult for the tribunal to close the trials within a short period of time (such as the half year that the Nuremberg trials took). Many issues prevented the trials from being expeditious. The prosecution and the defense had to prepare and submit large amounts of evidence, which they seldom reached a consensus on and often disputed. The defense submitted a lot of repetitive evidence, which was prolix and caused delays. This resulted in a tendency for the counsel to deem witnesses irrelevant. Translation issues were another challenge. Literal translation from Japanese into English or the reverse was often impossible. Even with the establishment of the Language Arbitration Board, fluent speakers of both languages often differed in opinion as to how to correctly paraphrase. As for the tribunal, they had to determine the value of a lot of evidence, and handle various motions that were constantly being generated.

The Allies carried out the Tokyo Trials mainly in the hope that later generations would learn from them and realize their positive significance. However, the judges understood that there was a risk long-term trials would do harm to this. The court charter also made clear that this was their original intention, therefore various provisions were included in the first place. According to the judgment, "neither these nor any other of the rules imposed by the Tribunal were applied with rigidity. Indulgences were granted from time to time, having regard of the paramount need for the Tribunal to do justice to the accused, and to possess itself of all facts relevant and material to the issues". All the rules, discussions and disputes over procedure, evidence and translation were for the court to conduct a fair and just trial with a modern legal spirit. What was most impressive was the unprecedented protection of defendants' rights. The tribunal chose a rougher road, because they were more focused on just and fair trials, rather than swift ones. There were criticisms that the Tokyo Trials were not completed as quickly as the Nuremberg Trials, leading to the world forgetting or having a negative opinion of them. However, some people acknowledge the court's efforts in ensuring fairness in the face of difficulties.

Bibliography

1. Totani, Y. (2008). *The Tokyo War Crimes Trial: The Pursuit of Justice in the Wake of World War II.* Cambridge: Harvard University Asia Center and Harvard University Press.
2. Boister, N., & Cryer, R. (2008). *The Tokyo International Military Tribunal: A Reappraisal.* Oxford University Press.
3. Higurashi, Y. (2002). *Tokyo saiban no kokusai kankei--Kokusai seiji ni okeru kenryoku to kihan* [The International Relations of the Tokyo Trials—Power and Norms in International Politics]. Tokyo: Bokutakusha.
4. Zhang, X., Xiang, L., & Xu, X. (Trans). (2015). *Yuandong guoji junshi fating panjueshu* [The Judgment of the International Military Tribunal for The Far East]. Shanghai: Shanghai Jiao Tong University Press.
5. Shanghai Jiao Tong University and National Library of China. (2013). *Yuandong guoji junshi fating tingshen jilu (80juan)* [Transcripts of the Proceedings of the International Military Tribunal for the Far East (80 vols.)]. Shanghai and Beijing: Shanghai Jiao Tong University Press and National Library of China Publishing House.
6. Shanghai Jiao Tong University and National Library of China. (2013). *Yuandong guoji junshi fating zhengju wenxian (50juan)* [A Collection of Court Evidence of the International Military Tribunal for the Far East (50 vols.)]. Shanghai and Beijing: Shanghai Jiao Tong University Press and National Library of China Publishing House.
7. Horwitz, S. (1950). The Tokyo Trial. *International Conciliation, 465*, 478–480.
8. Jaudel, E. (2013). *Dongjing shenpan-bei wangque de niulunbao* [Le proces de Tokyo: un Nuremberg oublie]. Shanghai: Shanghai Jiao Tong University Press.

CHAPTER 4

The Declaration of Judgment

The International Military Tribunal for the Far East (IMTFE) closed its sessions on April 16, 1948. After a six-month adjournment to write the verdict, the court reopened. The presiding president declared the court's judgment on the 25 defendants. Seven were executed on December 23, and 17 accused of Class A war crimes were acquitted and released on December 24. The two and a half year long Tokyo Trials eventually finished in late 1948. This chapter will provide an overview of the verdict, the trials' influence and several of the judges' minority opinions.

1 Disagreements Among Judges and the Formation of the Verdict

1.1 Judges' Different Opinions

In late January 1946, the United States contacted its allies (British, French, Soviet, Chinese, Canadian and Dutch) and asked them to nominate candidates to judge the trials in Tokyo. A special international tribunal was set up by Supreme Commander Douglas MacArthur, under the authority of the Allied Powers to assess Class A war crimes. On January 19, the IMTFE was established. A month later, nine judges including the one from the United States were appointed. The Philippines and India did not confirm whether they would participate until the Far Eastern Commission meeting on April 3, 1946. During this meeting, the US

Z. Cheng, *A History of War Crimes Trials in Post 1945 Asia-Pacific*,
https://doi.org/10.1007/978-981-13-6697-0_4

proposal was discussed, and India and the Philippines joined the trials as participating countries. Consequently, there were eleven participating countries in the Tokyo Trials, far more than the four countries (Britain, France, the Soviet Union and the United States) during the Nuremberg trials.

The Nuremberg trials' four judges were from Britain, France, the Soviet Union and the United States. They worked successfully together in the first-ever international criminal court, and reached a unified verdict on the trials. But the Tokyo Trials were totally different. Shortly after the sessions opened, different opinions emerged among the judges, and were divided as majority and minority opinions. Even the president was in the minority camp. This was mainly due to different understandings and positions on crimes against peace.

As mentioned in the previous chapter, crimes against peace were only proposed for the first time by the international community after WWII. They were applicable to wars of aggression and the Nuremberg and Tokyo courts both had jurisdiction. The defense team consistently questioned whether crimes against peace were "ex post facto" laws, and the judges argued about it as well.

On May 15, 1946, the defense challenged the tribunal's jurisdiction while it was hearing and adjudicating crimes against peace and humanity. A majority faction of judges headed by British judge Patrick supported the Charter, particularly regarding crimes against peace. However, the voice of opposition was very strong and the court was unable to reach an agreement immediately. Four days later, the tribunal dismissed the defense's motion, saying: "the reasons for this decision would be given later". On May 17, when Indian judge Radhabinod Pal arrived, he said that crimes against peace were illegitimate. This fueled dispute among the judges. Nine nations had already agreed that if there was disagreement among themselves, they would keep it from going public. However, this pact was broken by Pal because he refused to sign the earlier written agreement about minority opinion, which the other judges had signed.

The majority were distinguished from the minority in their positions on crimes against peace. The judges who supported them attached great importance to their universality and the pioneering value of having international military trials. They believed that the war of aggression was already a criminal act under international law when Japan surrendered. Therefore, those judges involved in determining facts had no right to comment on the Charter. Out of the eleven total judges, those from the United Kingdom, Canada, New Zealand, China, the Soviet Union, the United States and the Philippines held this position. The main three were William Donald Patrick from the UK, Edward Stuart McDougall from Canada and Erima Harvey Northcroft from New Zealand. The majority of the court held the same view of the Nuremberg Trials rules, as was eventually reflected in the verdict of the Tokyo Trials. But the judges from Australia, the Netherlands, France and India had doubts or even objections to issues, as they held different theoretical perspectives. Their opinions were influenced by their background, home trial system and even their relationships with various countries.

On January 30, 1947, the dissenting judges finally reached an agreement on one matter: jurisdiction once the final verdict was reached. However, disagreements amongs judges continued until the end of the trials. The minority judges ended up writing up their individual opinions, to be submitted alongside the verdict.

1.2 *Writing the Verdict: The Split, and Cooperating*

Since the judges couldn't agree with each other on several basic legal issues, it became more and more difficult for them to write a unified verdict. Once they knew that the Indian and Dutch judges held dissenting opinions, Judges Patrick and Northcroft reported to London. They did this in March–April 1947, and implied that any objections meant that the Tokyo Trials would not be taken seriously, and it would also affect people's views of the Nuremberg Trials. On May 14, the UK's Supreme Court of the House of Lords invited MacArthur to mediate. It also asked UNWCC chairman Sir William Wright to go to Tokyo and persuade dissenting judges. However, neither of these plans were ultimately implemented.

On November 10, President William F. Webb was called back to the bar by the Australian government and he was absent for over a month. Some scholars believe that Webb was called back because of his opposing stance to the UK, and therefore was a hindrance to the unified verdict. Judge Pal, who was the largest opposing figure, left court and returned home. In the absence of these two important figures, in March 1948, a "majority drafting committee" was established, and they started to prepare for the Tokyo Trials verdict.

Many years later, Dutch judge Bernard Victor A. Röling said: "as a general principle, the verdict should have been discussed in a chamber meeting attended by all of the judges… but this was not the case". Judge Mei Ju-ao also mentioned in a June letter to the Ministry of Foreign Affairs that the verdict would be drafted by the majority of the eleven judges. Seven departments were responsible for drafting the: (1) Introduction; (2) Invasion of China's Four Eastern Provinces (Manchuria); (3) Full Aggression against China; (4) Relationship between Japan and the Soviet Union; (5) Preparation for Full Aggression; (6) Launching and Expenditure of the Pacific War; (7) Atrocities Committed by the Japanese Troops (Fig. 1).

Fig. 1 Judges and national flags (President Webb was absent between November and December 1947. The court placed the Australian flag to the far left. Deputy of the President Cramer sat in the middle of the bench)

The judges in charge of those departments needed to "direct the court's assistants, and get the department ready for preparing drafts based on evidence and records of Japanese aggression against various countries". After the draft was written, it was revised and approved by the majority drafting committee. A month later, Judge Mei Ju-ao called the Ministry of Foreign Affairs, and said that he was responsible for confirming some of "Japan's aggression against China as historical fact", and that parts had been approved by the majority of judges.

The minority were not completely excluded from the drafting of the verdict. The majority's draft was distributed to them, and if they had a dissenting opinion, this could be informed in writing. Some minority judges—besides Pal—were not completely opposed. Judge Mei Ju-ao even told the Ministry of Foreign Affairs: "the president's opinion was not that different to mine. He said that he would still participate in the meeting (majority). France and the Netherlands are also likely to participate". Of course, Mei was somewhat optimistic because both the judges from France and the Netherlands were not in the majority. Although the majority was responsible for agreeing on the main, factual contents of the verdict, another important part of the verdict involved discussing and determining the individual responsibility of the defendants, and deliberating their penalties. This part involved "a long period of discussion and heated debate among the eleven judges, and was determined by vote" (Mei Ju-ao). Therefore, the verdicts of the Tokyo Trials cannot be simply seen as being given by "majority opinion", they should be regarded as a result of overall "cooperation".

In late July 1948, after some of the verdicts had been agreed, translators began to turn them into Japanese. The translation team was led by famous jurists Yoshiro Yokota, and Cheung Chau Ichiji, as well as Japanese Foreign Ministry official Kanazawa Hideaki. The translation work was closely monitored by the allied forces at the Hattori watch store president's private residence. Meanwhile, those judges holding minority opinions continued writing up their own individual assessments. Judge Pal's dissenting opinions were translated at the Japanese allied headquarters in Japan as early as June. About a month before the official verdict, all of the contents in the ruling were completed and approved. The trial proceedings therefore took two years, even the ruling took six months.

1.3 The Verdict, Executions and Release

On November 4, 1948, the Tokyo Trials reopened. It took seven days to read the total verdicts. Seven of the 25 defendants were sentenced to death by hanging, 16 defendants to life imprisonment, one defendant to 20 years' imprisonment and one defendant to seven years' imprisonment. See Tables 1 and 2 for the specific convictions and where judges voted on the death penalty. President Webb decided that the minority opinions of other judges would not be read out in court, but would be kept on file.

On November 24, the American counsel for Doihara and Hoshino appealed to the US Supreme Court to release their defendants. Later, the counsel for Kido Koichi, Oka Takazumi, Sato Kenryo, Shigemitsu Mamoru and Togo Shigenori lodged the same appeal. The US Supreme Court initially accepted appeals by a narrow majority, but later, owing to the pressure of American government and widespread public opinion, the court announced that the appeals were no longer in its jurisdiction and it would not hear them. On December 23, seven defendants were hanged in the Sugamo Prison.

Many people suspected of Class-A war crimes were being held in Sugamo while the Allies' policies on war crimes were changing. On December 24, 1948, the general headquarters released all of the remaining 17 Class-A war criminal suspects and said that they would no longer stand trial. One of the 17, Kishi Nobusuke, returned to Japan and later became Prime Minister in 1957. After Japan and the Allies signed the "San Francisco Peace Treaty" in 1951, movements for the release and amnesty of war criminals began to arise. In 1952, the Japanese House of Representatives passed a majority vote on the "Resolution on the Release of War Criminals". By late March, 1956, all of the detainees in the Sugamo Prison had been released.

Table 1 Convictions and where judges voted on the death penalty (speculation)

Defendants	*Araki*	*Oshima*	*Kido*	*Shimada*	*Hoshino*	*Tojo*	*Doihara*	*Matsui*	*Sato*	*Itagaki*	*Kimura*
Nationality of judges											
The US	√	√	×	×	√	√	√	√	√	√	√
The UK	√	√	√	√	√	√	√	√	√	√	√
China	√	√	√	√	√	√	√	√	√	√	√
The Philippines	√	√	√	√	√	√	√	√	√	√	√
New Zealand	√	√	√	√	√	√	√	√	√	√	√
Canada	×	×	√	×	√	√	√	√	√	√	√
The Netherlands	×	×	×	√	×	√	√	√	√	√	√
Australia	×	×	×	×	×	×	×	×	×	×	×
The Soviet Union	×	×	×	×	×	×	×	×	×	×	×
France	×	×	×	×	×	×	×	×	×	×	×
India	×	×	×	×	×	×	×	×	×	×	×

Note "√" is for death sentence, "×" is against death sentence. *Source* The Tokyo Trials, Vol. 2 published by Chuokoron-Shinsha in 1971

2 Interpretations of the Verdict and the Individual Opinions

This section will provide a brief introduction on the interpretations of the verdict and the individual opinions of other judges, in order to help the reader understand what views the judges held during these pioneering trials.

2.1 The Verdict

On November 4, 1948, President Webb began to read the 1444-page Verdict in English. It was also read at the same time by Japanese interpreters. The Verdict was made up of three parts, Part A (Chapters 1–3), Part B (Chapters 4–8), and Part C (Chapters 9–10).

2.1.1 The Tribunal and the Law

This part restated the legal basis for the establishment of the IMTFE, as well as the treaties that proved Japan's actions. It explained why the trials were so time-consuming and stated that the judges had unanimously agreed to simplify the indictment, because the original 55 counts were cumbersome and illogical. In one instance, it read: "as all of the accused are charged with conspiracy, we do not consider it necessary to add additional convictions for planning and preparation". Similarly, there was "no reason to register convictions for initiating as well as waging a war of aggression". And many murder charges overlapped with conventional war crimes and crimes against humanity, since the killing of prisoners of war/civilians belonged to the latter categories. So the tribunal dismissed all of these counts proposed by the prosecution; but it did not mean that these crimes would escape sanctions. In the charters of the Nuremberg Tribunal and the Tokyo Tribunal, crimes against humanity included "murders committed against any civilian population, before or during the war". Therefore, those defendants that committed murder could also be charged with crimes against humanity.

Finally, the tribunal ruled that there should be one charge for conspiracy, seven charges for the waging of wars, and two charges for conventional war crimes. They considered the charges against individual defendants for the following counts: 1, 27, 29, 31, 32, 33, 35, 36, 54 and 55.

The tribunal responded to the defense's two-year-old challenge over jurisdiction in Part A of the Verdict.[1] In fact, the Nuremberg tribunal earlier had faced almost the exact same challenge. So, the Tokyo tribunal made mention of Nuremberg. It said: "With the foregoing opinions of the Nuremberg tribunal and the reasoning by which they are reached, this tribunal is in complete accord... in view of the fact that all of the material in this tribunal respects the charter—much as the Nuremberg tribunal's did—this tribunal prefers to express its adherence to the relevant opinions of the Nuremberg tribunal rather than reason matters anew in a somewhat different language, which might open the door to controversy and give conflicting interpretations of the two schools of opinion". This was the most appropriate and best explanation the court could give.

2.1.2 Statements of Fact

Over half of the ruling, based on accounts and facts, was about how Japan had planned and launched wars of aggression against Asian countries between 1928 and 1945. It was split into five chapters: The military domination of Japan and its preparation for war; Japanese aggression against China; Japan's policy toward the USSR; the Pacific War, and conventional war crimes (atrocities). Out of these chapters, Japan's foothold in China was the most detailed, and it was separated into a further seven parts: Japan's invasion and occupation of Manchuria; the exploitation of Manchuria and subsequent consolidation of Manchukuo; the plan to advance further into China; events between the Marco Polo Bridge incident (July 7, 1937) and the Konoye Declaration (January 16, 1938); the provisional government in North China; the greater coprosperity sphere in East Asia, and Japan's economic domination of Manchuria/other parts of China.

[1]The seven grounds that the defense challenged in the tribunal were as follows: (1) The tribunal have no authority to try "crimes against peace"; (2) Wars of aggression do not, per se, constitute war crimes; (3) War is the act of a nation, for which there is no individual responsibility; (4) The charter only states "ex post facto" legislation; (5) Conventional war crimes would only be recognized by international law after the Declaration of Potsdam; (6) Wartime killings during belligerent operations only constitute violations of the law and are not acts of murder; (7) Accused prisoners of war are not triable by this tribunal, but by a court martial under the 1929 Geneva Convention. For more on the jurisdiction of the tribunal, please see Chapter 2 of this book.

Japanese leaders were charged with crimes against peace for conspiring to secure the domination (military, political and economic) of East Asia, the Pacific and the Indian Ocean. All of the defendants were charged with waging wars of aggression against China (count 27), the United States (count 29), the Philippines (count 30), the British Commonwealth (count 31) and the Netherlands (count 32). Some were charged with waging wars of aggression against France (count 33), the Mongolian Republic and the Soviet Union (count 35).

It was ruled that the encroachment on Northeast China was a result of Japan being increasingly dominated by political militarists. These conspirators dominated Japan. They decided on their own policies and were determined to implement them. While plotting acts of aggression against China, they were also preparing to invade other countries. While the Japanese military were carrying out their occupation of northeastern China, they were also preparing a northward attack on the Soviet Union. In 1933, the Saito Cabinet refused to withdraw from northern China, and it pulled out of the League of Nations, who opposed its invasion. Japan was free from foreign surveillance, and its preparations for war in the Pacific breached treaty obligations. Shiratori said in his lecture, "The Trend of the Great War" (published in June 1940): "It is not too much to say that the China Incident was the fuse that led to the European War". Looking back over history, these crimes of aggression began some 14 or 17 years after that. Some of the defendants were active from the very beginning, while some became active participants as war progressed. They were both conspirators and executors of a war of aggression.

Finally, the judges ruled that conspiracy only applied to crimes against peace, and not to conventional war crimes, crimes against humanity or murders. Based on this decision, the tribunal retained counts 54 and 55 for conventional war crimes and crimes against peace. It was ruled that numerous atrocities were committed by the Japanese army, and that many victims suffered. It was also ruled that the army adopted the same method of destruction in the wider Asia-Pacific region. There could only be one kind of atrocity, and it was carried out by the Japanese government, or individual officials and commanders. The ruling also stated that Japan's prisoner-of-war agencies functioned poorly. At the beginning of the Pacific War, the Japanese government set up institutions for prisoners of war and formulated relevant rules and regulations. However, the court ruled that they did not sufficiently prevent against atrocities. These systems did not abide by the standards of prevailing international treaties or practices. In the end, several defendants were found to be liable for a number of major Japanese atrocities, either by being "directly responsible" or by "neglect".

The Tokyo Trials verdict confirmed Japan's wartime responsibility, as well as its role in the Sino-Japanese War and the Pacific War.

2.1.3 Findings in the Indictment Counts

The tribunal proposed additional charges against individual defendants for the following ten counts: Count 1: Conspiracy to wage wars of aggression against regions in East Asia, the Pacific and the Indian Ocean (1928–1945); Count 27: Waging a war of aggression against China (September 18, 1931–September 2, 1945); Count 29: Waging a war of aggression against the United States (December 7, 1941–September 2, 1945); Count 31: Waging a war of aggression against the British Commonwealth (December 7, 1941–September 2, 1945); Count 32: Waging a war of aggression against the Netherlands (December 7, 1941–September 2, 1945); Count 33: Waging a war of aggression against France (after September 22, 1940); Count 35: Waging a war of aggression against the Soviet Union (July–August 1938); Count 36: Waging a war of aggression against the Mongolian People's Republic and the Soviet Union Socialist Republics (summer of 1939); Count 54: Ordering, authorizing or committing offenses that violate the laws of war (December 7, 1941–September 2, 1945); Count 55: Disregarding legal obligations to properly observe the rights and respect of prisoners of war and civilians (between December 7, 1941 and September 2, 1945).

Table 2 shows the 25 defendants' verdicts and what counts they were charged with under the indictment.

All of the defendants were found guilty of conspiracy except for Shigemitsu and Matsui. Oshima and Shiratori were found guilty of count 1 and Matsui was found guilty of count 55. Matsui was found guilty of "conventional war crimes" and was sentenced to death for neglect of duty. Oshima and Shiratori were sentenced to life imprisonment. If the Tokyo tribunal convicted the accused of conventional war crimes, they would be given the death sentence. No defendants were sentenced to death for "crimes against peace". The most severe sentence, arguably, was life imprisonment, and this was handed down after the court's careful consideration (Figs. 2 and 3).

Table 2 Defendants' conviction and sentencing at the IMTFE

		Crimes against peace								*Conventional war crimes Crimes against humanity*		*Sentencing*
	Defendants \ *Counts accused*	*1*	*27*	*29*	*31*	*32*	*33*	*35*	*36*	*54*	*55*	
1.	Araki Sadao	•	•	○	○	○	○	○	○	○	○	Life imprisonment
2.	Doihara Kenji	•	•	•	•	•	○	•	•	•	△	Death sentence
3.	桥本欣五郎	•	•	○	○	○				○	○	Life imprisonment
4.	Hata Shunroku	•	•	•	•	•		○	○	○	•	Life imprisonment
5.	Hiranuma Kiichiro	•	•	•	•	•	○	○	•	○	○	Life imprisonment
6.	Hoshino Naoki	•	•	○	○	○	○	○		○	•	Death sentence
7.	Hirota Koki	•	•	•	•	•	○	○		○	○	Life imprisonment
8.	板垣征四郎	•	•	•	•	•	○	•	•	•	△	Death sentence
9.	Kaya Okinori	•	•	•	•	•				○	○	Life imprisonment
10.	Kido Koichi	•	•	•	•	•	○	○	○	○	○	Life imprisonment
11.	木村兵太郎	•	•	•	•	•				•	•	Death sentence
12.	Koiso Kuniaki	•	•	•	•	•			○	○	•	Life imprisonment
13.	Matsui Iwane	○	○	○	○	○		○	○	○	•	Death sentence
14.	Minami Jiro	•	•	○	○	○				○	○	Life imprisonment
15.	武藤章	•	•	•	•	•	○		○	•	•	Death sentence
16.	Oka Takazumi	•	•	•	•	•				○	○	Life imprisonment
17.	Oshima Hiroshi	•	○	○	○	○				○	○	Life imprisonment
18.	Sato Kenryo	•	•	•	•	•				○	○	Life imprisonment
19.	Shigemitsu Mamoru	○	•	•	•	•	•	○		○	•	7 years' imprisonment
20.	Shimada Shigetaro	•	•	•	•	•				○	○	Life imprisonment
21.	Shiratori Toshio	•	○	○	○	○						Life imprisonment

(continued)

Table 2 (continued)

		Crimes against peace								Conventional war crimes Crimes against humanity		Sentencing
	Defendants / Counts accused	1	27	29	31	32	33	35	36	54	55	
22.	Suzuki Teiichi	•	•	•	•	•		○	○	○	○	Life imprisonment
23.	Togo Shigenori	•	•	•	•	•			○	○	○	20 years' imprisonment
24.	Tojo Hideki	•	•	•	•	•	•		○	•	Δ	Death sentence
25.	Umezu Yoshijiro	•	•	•	•	•			○	○	○	Life imprisonment

Note The original 28 defendants were reduced to 25 because Nagano Osami and Matsuoka Yosuke died of illness during the trials, and Okawa Shumei was found mentally unfit for the trials and the charges were dropped

○prosecuted—not guilty; •prosecuted—guilty; Δprosecuted—no judgment; blank—not being prosecuted

Fig. 2 Defendants during the trials

Some scholars believe that the Tokyo tribunal gave different verdicts (much as the Nuremberg tribunal did) because they viewed war atrocities as more serious and having a bigger international impact than crimes against peace. However, it is also possible that they felt capital punishment should be avoided because crimes against peace were not widely recognized at the time. In the case of Tojo Hideki, despite being charged with multiple crimes, he was only sentenced to death for his role in the atrocities committed by Japanese forces—the court found that in his role as prime minister and war minister, he permitted and even encouraged the inhuman and illegal employment of captives. The civil official Hoshino Naoki (who was Minister of Foreign Affairs), followed the same fate as Tojo. The judges voted six against five for his death sentence, which was dramatic and controversial at the time. However, given the court's heavy sentencing for those found guilty of conventional war crimes, it's not difficult to understand their verdict.

Fig. 3 Seven defendants who were sentenced to death by hanging (Itagaki Seishiro, Tojo Hideki, Doihara Kenji, Hoshino Naoki, Matsui Iwane, Muto Akira, and Kimura Heitaro)

2.2 *The Presiding President's Individual Opinion*

President Webb disagreed with the majority judges, and so he wrote a 21-page Separate Opinion on the crimes the defendants were convicted of. Webb also produced a 637-page judgment, in which he described in more detail his legal opinions. But it was never published and the public had limited knowledge of it. It is common practice in Anglo-American law for the head judge to write a "pilot ruling" as the basis for the final verdict, and the IMTFE followed suit.

From November 27, 1946 to January 20, 1947, Webb conveyed his judgment to his fellow judges. In his judgment, he questioned the inclusion of "conspiracies" in the tribunal. The majority tended to generalize accounts of conspiracy to wage wars of aggression, thereby reducing the role of individuals. But Webb was focused on the role of everyone, and the complex events that led to Japan attacking China and other countries. Approximately 60% of his judgment was focused on this.

Webb decided that all of the defendants should be convicted of war crimes, but he held different views to the majority on who was responsible. He surmised that all of the Japanese leaders must have known about the numerous and vicious war crimes troops were committing. These defendants must have clearly known about these crimes, yet had not taken any effective measures to stop them. Webb emphasized that the defendants had a responsibility to submit complaints to the cabinet. If the cabinet could not resolve the issue, they should have submitted complaints to the emperor. Webb also objected to the death penalty, which was given to defendants convicted of conventional war crimes and crimes against humanity. He thought a more suitable punishment should be a lifelong overseas exile. He felt the death penalty was inappropriate as that meant the Japanese Emperor was exempt from war responsibility.

David Cohen, a War Crime Studies scholar, felt that the president's judgment helped paint a complete picture of the trials, and provide further information about the defendants' legal responsibilities. However, there were two completely different schools of thought on Webb's assessment. Cohen believed that it "provided something that the majority had seriously lost: a logically reasonable explanation consistent with the facts and conclusions". He added that "if Webb's judgment was adopted by the court as the majority opinion, many criticisms of the tribunal might have been avoided".

Yoshinobu Higurashi said in his book that Webb was "impatient", "neurotic" and disliked by other judges. He said that his judgment was even criticized by the "prudent Chinese judge". New Zealand judge Northcroft sarcastically called his ruling "a bad dissertation on international law". However, Cohen clearly stated in his essay that Webb was a senior legal specialist on war crimes, and much more experienced than the other judges in the tribunal. The autocracy that he demonstrated in court demonstrated his control over the trial proceedings and his efforts to achieve a fair trial. The trial records showed that Webb repeatedly advised both the prosecution and the defense on some of the more effective examination methods. Webb's judgment and his legal opinions should be studied further and objectively by law researchers.

2.3 *The Indian Judge's Dissenting Opinion*

India's Judge Pal was the only judge who asserted that all of the Japanese Class A defendants were innocent of their crimes. Pal was often absent during the later stage of the trials, but still wrote up his individual assessment of them. He submitted his 1241-page opinion in June 1948, and then the relevant translation started. The trial records show that his main opinions were as follows: (1) "Crimes of conspiracy" do not exist; (2) Acts of aggression are illegal; (3) "Crimes against Peace" are the result of the court's ex post facto law; (4) Individuals cannot bear criminal responsibility; (5) Neglect does not necessarily constitute a crime; (6) The Japanese attack on Pearl Harbor was self-defense rather than aggression. Pal didn't deny that the Japanese Army had committed atrocities on multiple battlefields in his verdict. He agreed with the prosecution that the atrocities recurred and were widespread, but he firmly held that the defendants should not bear individual responsibility. In summary, Pal held the view that "the International Prosecution Sector had made the wrong charges against the wrong individuals, and had done so on the basis of inapplicable laws and inadequate evidence".

The reason why Pal's opinions were different to those of the other judges is possibly related to his experience of growing up in the colonies. He never firmly believed that such a stage would come to exist, where one could entrust an international court to dispense justice in the name of world peace. Reality, as he understood it, was what the great powers—or "pure opportunist Have and Holders" in his words—concerned themselves with, and they had developed such a law to protect their expansionist claims and gains at the expense of the weak. The Netherlands' judge said: "When he (Pal) justified the Japanese criminals, it seems to come from a legal view, but what really guided him was anti-imperialist political logic". David Cohen said that the biggest problem was that "Pal did not provide a reasonable ruling for each defendant he considered innocent". This made Pal's Dissenting Opinion read more like a political document.

After the United States ended its occupation of Japan in 1952, Pal's Dissenting Opinion was published. The Japanese were gradually made aware of it and it was used as a guideline by critics of the Tokyo Trials. It helped form the narrative of "the majority verdict of guilt vs Pal's verdict of acquittal". Pal had a lot of prestige in Japan, and a "Dr. Pal" monument can even be found near the Yasukuni Shrine in Tokyo. All of this is significant and provocative.

2.4 The Individual Opinions of the Dutch, French and the Filipino Judges

The Dutch judge's minority view: The Netherlands' Lord Justice Roling submitted a 343-page minority opinion. Roling acknowledged that the war of aggression was a criminal act under international law, but he believed that it should have been assessed according to the London Agreement of August 1945, rather than the Kellogg–Briand Pact of 1928. Roling also thought that the tribunal should not follow the charter so rigorously, yet he felt that their jurisdiction should be restricted to Pacific War incidents, and Japan–Russia border conflicts (the Changgufeng event and the Nuomenkan event) should be excluded. Roling held the same view as Sir Webb on sentencing: that it should follow international law. He thought that "joint conspiracy crimes" fell under Common Law, and that defendants who committed "crime against peace" should only be sentenced to death if they had committed conventional war crimes. He thought that it was inappropriate to convict Koki Hirota of crimes against peace and conventional war crimes and thought that he should be exonerated and released. He also thought that Shunroku Hata, Koichi Kido, Mamoru Shigemitsu and Shigenori Togo should be exonerated and released. However, he thought that Takasumi Oka, Kenryo Sato and Shigetaro Shimada—who were sentenced to life imprisonment—should be sentenced to death.

The French judge's minority Opinion France's Lord Justice Bernard submitted a 23-page dissenting opinion, which argued: (1) That there were significant deficiencies in the IMTFE trial proceedings. He said that the defendants were not properly defended, and argued against the verdict being drawn up by the majority. (2) He felt that wars of aggression should be illegal based on the principles of natural law, rather than the international conventions cited by the prosecution. (3) He felt that the prosecution did not present valid evidence of a "conspiracy", and so could not accuse the defense of crimes against peace. (4) He felt that it was inappropriate to attach the responsibility of "inactive" defendants to "conventional war crimes". (5) He ruled that the Japanese Emperor should be convicted.

The Filipino judge's verdict: Filipino judge Jaranilla did not disagree with the majority. However, he presented a 35-page concurring opinion which detailed his views on: "joint conspiracy crimes"; "inaction during the planning and preparation of war"; "motives for murder and other atrocities"; "the joint conspiracies of Japan and Germany"; "objections by the defense regarding jurisdiction"; "individual responsibilities"; "atomic bomb issues"; "the dissenting opinions of the Indian Lord Justice", and "inappropriate penalties". Jaranilla fully agreed with the charter and the jurisdiction of the Tokyo Trials, and felt that the United States used its atomic bomb legitimately. He thought that the verdicts of the Tokyo Trials were too lenient, and that all of the defendants should have been sentenced to death. We can see that Jaranilla's opinions were totally different from Pal's. This is partly because Jaranilla was one of the few survivors of the Bataan Death March—a famous incident carried out by the Japanese Army in the Philippines, during which many prisoners were abused.

3 Reactions to the Verdict and How It Was Evaluated

3.1 Initial Reactions to the Verdict

Before the trials began, British prosecutor Arthur Comyns Carr told the IPS: "The trials need to show the world that Japan is guilty of crimes of aggression; they should start quickly, to avoid them regarding the defendants as martyrs, whom at present they wish to see condemned. Furthermore, once the Nuremberg Trials are over, international concerns about the trials will disappear". His remarks proved to be extremely accurate. Once the verdict was delivered, the Allies changed their allegiance quietly, and there were no longer any attitudes toward the trial outcome being positive. However, the authorities did not publish the trial records or other relevant documents after the verdict, meaning that Keenan wrote a letter of complaint.

Former Prime Minister Hitoshi Ashida said that the verdicts did not cause much of a stir in Japan, but they aroused intense emotions within the defendants' families. Yoshinobu believed that the war atrocities that the trials exposed came as a huge shock to the Japanese people and were regarded with shame. Even if they thought that the defendants were victims of war, they could only accept the verdict of the trials. War-averse intellectuals were supportive of the trials. Politicians were unwilling to talk about them because of their sensitivities. Soon, however, they went from being placid to mounting a large-scale campaign, and protesting for the release of war criminals. Arthur Comyns Carr saw this coming, and said in 1949 that most Japanese still regarded the trials as "the victor's revenge".

3.2 *Different Perspectives and Evaluations*

After the trial, public attention gradually subsided, but academic research continued. People discussed the verdicts from different perspectives, criticizing or endorsing them. Criticism mainly focused on the following:

Contradictions in historic narratives: The heaviest criticism of the verdict was toward people being charged with "conspiracy". The court held that the defendants, Japan's leaders, actively conspired over an 18 year period to establish Japan's dominant position in the Asia-Pacific region. Most scholars believed that this verdict painted an overly simplistic view of history. They noted that the Japanese government had not been consistent in carrying out their war plans. Consequently, there were debates about the contradictory pictures of "Tokyo Trial view of history" given within the final verdict, and questions about why these had not been properly resolved. Yuma Totani believed that contradictory narratives are one of the reasons why disputes about the trials repeatedly arose.

Parts of the verdict also lacked sufficient detail or evidence. Cohen pointed out that the verdict tended not to refer back to evidence, even where there were large bodies of evidence that were unfavorable to the defendants. Some critics were not familiar with the 50,000-page trial records, or the 5000 pieces of supporting evidence that had been submitted by the prosecution. Therefore, many decided that the verdict was based on "the victor's justice". Neil Boister said: "The charter granted the Tokyo tribunal very broad, discretionary powers during sentencing, and the failure of the Tokyo tribunal to provide reasons for their sentences serves as a precedent in international criminal law… Not following the sentencing guidelines means that there are risks that people will be inattentive, and it is not a positively regarded precedent".

Some people hold different opinions on whether the verdict was "a positively regarded precedent". Supporters point out that several rulings in the Tokyo Trials have been subsequently cited as valid precedents in today's international tribunals. For example, the 1998 International Criminal Tribunal for Rwanda ruled that Rwanda's civil officers were responsible for genocide in 1994, and they referenced the case of Hoshino Naoki in the Tokyo Trials.

> It is only since the Tokyo Trials that the practice of prosecuting civil officers who violate international humanitarian law has been established. Former Japanese Foreign Minister Hoshino Naoki was convicted by the Tokyo tribunal for "the Rape of Nanking".

When Hoshino's verdict was delivered, it was initially criticized by various parties. They believed that because he was a civilian officer, Hoshino Naoki could not be responsible for military actions. Modern international humanitarian law takes into consideration commanders' responsibilities and their acts of negligence, largely because of earlier postwar trials such as the Nuremberg and Tokyo Trials. Consequently, the Tokyo Trials verdict made a tangible and important contribution to the development of international humanitarian law.

Researchers also note that the tribunal made a very persuasive ruling on specific findings, such as Japanese wartime atrocities. The historic narrative for the rulings and verdicts became later known as the "Tokyo Trials view of history". Although there were some issues about the charges of conspiracy, it cannot be denied that this narrative profoundly impacted studies of Japan's wartime history. Whether it was known as the "14-year war" (the September 1931 "Mukden Incident" is seen as the beginning of the Pacific War) or the "Asia-Pacific War", Japan's military attacks on China were used as a trigger for the Pacific War. This has become one of the mainstream views in modern history.

4 Summary

As with the trial proceedings, the verdicts for the Tokyo Trials experienced difficulties coming into fruition, and they have left much for future generations to discuss. We do not have to evade criticism, as we know that the Tokyo Trials were pioneering in international law. There are certain legal disputes about the verdict that cannot be avoided, but we can find positives in those discussions. An in-depth examination of the verdict (as well as the individual opinions of judges) can lead to a more accurate and objective assessment of the trials. Furthermore, they can inspire us to think about how humans should face or handle "war and peace" situations. Parties during the trials and serious scholars expected the Tokyo Trials to have an "educational function".

Bibliography

1. Totani, Y. (2008). *The Tokyo War Crimes Trial: The Pursuit of Justice in the Wake of World War II.* Cambridge: Harvard University Asia Center and Harvard University Press.
2. Boister, N., & Cryer, R. (2008). *The Tokyo International Military Tribunal: A Reappraisal.* Oxford: Oxford University Press.
3. Higurashi, Y. (2002). *Tokyo saiban no kokusai kankei--Kokusai seiji ni okeru kenryoku to kihan* [The International Relations of the Tokyo Trials—Power and Norms in International Politics]. Tokyo: Bokutakusha.
4. Nakazato, N. (2005). *Paru hanji--Indo nashonarizumu to Tokyo saiban* [Justice Pal—Indian Nationalism and the Tokyo Trials]. Tokyo: Iwanami Shoten.
5. Röling, B. V. A., & Cassese, A. (1993). *The Tokyo Trial and Beyond: Reflections of a Peacemonger.* London: Polity Press.
6. Mei, X., & Mei, X. (2013). *Mei Ru'ao dongjing shenpan wengao* [The Tokyo Trial Manuscripts of Mei Ru'ao]. Shanghai: Shanghai Jiao Tong University Press.
7. Cohen, D. (2015). *Weibo zhanzhengzui panjue cao'an-dongjing shenpan panjue de ling yi shijiao* [An Alternative Tokyo Judgment: The Draft "President's Judgment" of Sir William Webb at the IMTFE]. Center for the Tokyo Trial Studies: Dongjing shenpan zai taolun [The Restudy on the Tokyo Trial]. Shanghai: Shanghai Jiao Tong University Press.
8. Zhang, X., Xiang, L., & Xu, X. (Trans.). (2015). *Yuandong junshi fating panjueshu* [The Judgment of the International Military Tribunal for the Far East]. Shanghai: Shanghai Jiao Tong University Press.

CHAPTER 5

Other Asian Trials for Japanese War Crimes

The Tokyo tribunal was the only court established by the Allies in Asia after WWII to try Class A war criminals. There were also a "quasi-Class A" court and a number of courts spread over the Asia-Pacific region trying Class B and C war crimes. The trials in these courts lasted much longer than the Tokyo Trials (1945–1952), but they were perhaps more complete than those carried out by the Allies in the Far East. This chapter focuses on those Asian Class B and C trials.

1 The Allies' Trials

1.1 *The Establishment of Courts in Asia for the Trials of Japanese War Criminals*

During the late stages of the Second World War, the Allies began considering how to try German and Japanese war criminals. After discussions and consultations with allied nations, they finally set up two major international military tribunals in Nuremberg and Tokyo, to try German and Japanese state leaders. Many people were also brought to trial at military courts (ran by military committees under the jurisdiction of the Allies) in war-stricken areas. There were a large number of these courts, and the number of trials they carried out was much greater than those of the two major tribunals. In Asia, the Tokyo tribunal was referred to as the "Class A tribunal", while others were known as "Class B" and "Class C" tribunals. So what exactly are Class A, B and C tribunals?

Z. Cheng, *A History of War Crimes Trials in Post 1945 Asia-Pacific*,
https://doi.org/10.1007/978-981-13-6697-0_5

In October 1945, the US government released the "Policy of the United States in Regard to the Apprehension and Punishment of War Criminals in the Far East", and distributed it to its Allies. The proposal recommended that the Allies prosecute war criminals in the whole Pacific region, and that they discuss the basic principles for an international tribunal (the 'Tokyo Tribunal'). It also recommended that several smaller courts should be formed, which would fall under the jurisdiction of each allied nation. The first chapter of the proposal was split into three parts and defined different categories of crime: crimes against peace (Section A), conventional war crimes (Section B), and crimes against humanity (Section C). Crimes against peace would be tried by the Tokyo tribunal. Conventional war crimes and crimes against humanity would be tried by smaller courts. So what was most important in distinguishing the Tokyo tribunal from other Asian courts was that it fell under a different jurisdiction. Since the defendants that were accused of crimes against peace were mostly state leaders, and those accused of conventional war crimes and crimes against humanity were mostly military officers and soldiers, people often assume that Class A, B and C war criminals were divided according to rank. Even in the West, Class B and C trials are often referred to as the "minor war crime trials". However, the US proposal makes clear that a more accurate translation of "Class A war crimes" should be "Category A war crimes". In October 1946, UNWCC Chairman Sir Robert Wright said that "minor war crimes" was a misleading expression. The Tokyo tribunal sentenced people much more severely for Class B and C crimes, than it did for crimes against peace. In this chapter, we still use the terms "Class B" and "Class C" for a clear narrative (Fig. 1).

Crimes against peace were the subject of great controversy in jurisprudence, while Class B and C crimes were grounded in sound and clear legal documents: the 1899 and 1907 Hague Conventions (also known as the Laws and Customs of War on Land and Related Regulations); and the 1929 Geneva Convention on the Treatment of Prisoners of War. This effectively meant that the allied countries/organizations could apply the relevant laws and punishment procedures to their own trials. Britain, Australia and the United States predominantly adopted land laws and regulations as their international treaties, in line with the Anglo-American legal system. However, countries such as Holland, China and Indonesia, which followed civil law, applied both domestic criminal law and international law. The United States also considered exceptional

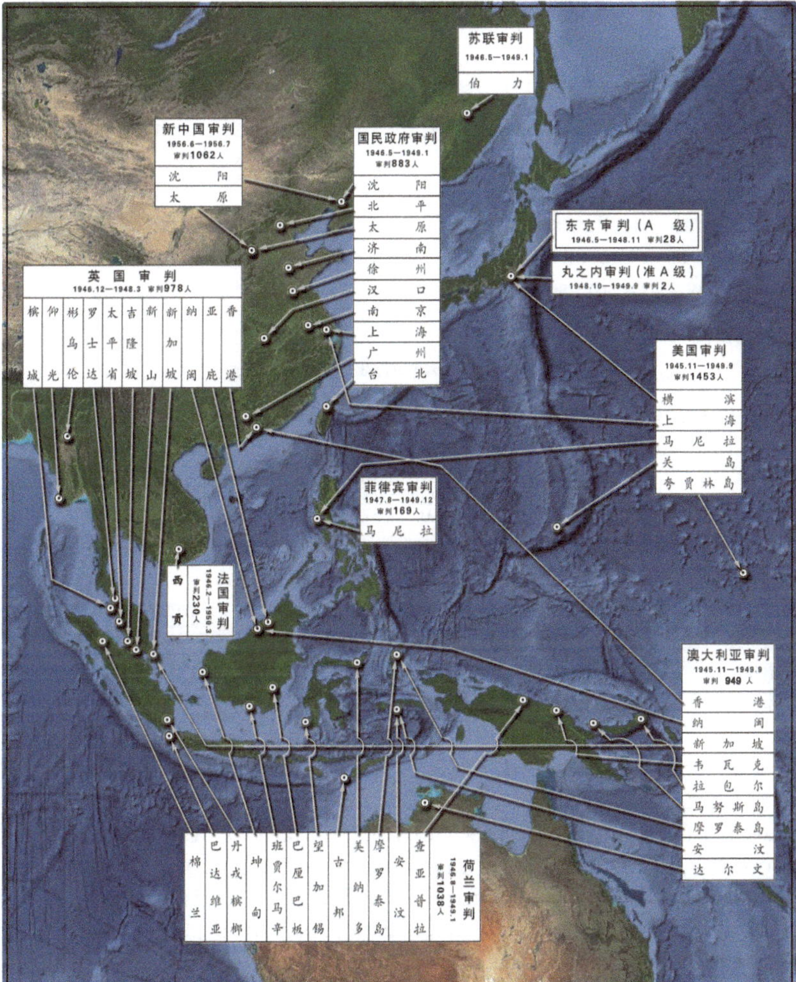

Fig. 1 Distribution of courts (Drawn by Zhao Yuhui)

circumstances regarding where the trials were conducted—for example, with Guam, the trials used local criminal law.

After the Allies reached an agreement on their war criminal policies, they began to set up small courts. In October 1945, the US military tried Tomoyuki Yamashita in Manila. It was the first public trial of Class B and Class C crimes in Asia. However, in February the same year, the US Navy had also tried a Saipan-born police officer in Guam for murder, the details of which were not made public until much later. Between late 1945 and mid-1946, Australia, the United Kingdom, France, China and the Netherlands conducted trials in succession. After the Philippines gained its independence in July 1946, it took over the US military's investigation and began its own independent trials the following month. If we include the People's Republic of China and the Soviet Union, eight nations (with nine governments) set up courts to conduct trials against Japanese war criminals.

1.2 Crimes and Criminals

The Hague Convention and the Laws and Customs of War on Land made provisions for war crimes and crimes against humanity. In May 1944, the UNWCC, the Allies' highest policy-making organ for war crimes, submitted a list of 33 war crime acts. The allied nations either changed or slightly adjusted their own regulations based on this list. The United States, China, the Philippines and Australia stated that they would try "crimes against peace" depending on their own circumstances. But no Class A war criminals appeared in Class B or C courts (Table 1).

In October 1946, the Republic of China issued a law on the trials of war criminals, and it listed 38 criminal acts. It included five new acts: the deliberate bombing of hospitals; the enforcement of collective torture; malicious insults; the plundering of historical, artistic or other cultural treasures; and other acts violating the laws of war, including acts of cruelty or destruction by the military, forcing people to do things beyond their obligation, or acts hampering the exercise of legal rights. It removed the "imposition of collective penalties" act, and split the "abduction of girls and women for the purpose of enforced prostitution" act into two (kidnapping children; and kidnapping women and forcing them to become prostitutes). It also changed some wording in some acts. "Directions to give no quarter" was changed to "ordering wholesale slaughter"; "The use of deleterious and asphyxiating gases" was changed to "the use of poisonous gas or bacteriological warfare"; and "the confiscation of property" was changed to "taking money or property by force or extortion".

Table 1 33 acts identified by the UNWCC as war crimes in May 1944

Murders and massacres; systematic terrorism	*Attempts to denationalize the inhabitants of occupied territory*	*Attack on and destruction of hospital ships*
Putting hostages to death	Pillage	Deliberate bombardment of hospital ships
Torture of civilians	Confiscation of property	Breach of other rules relating to the Red Cross
Deliberate starvation of civilians	Exaction of illegitimate or of exorbitant contributions and requisitions	Use of deleterious and asphyxiating gases
Rape	Debasement of currency, and issue of spurious currency	Use of explosive or expanding bullets, and other inhuman appliances
Abduction of girls and women for the purpose of enforced prostitution	Imposition of collective penalties	Directions to give no quarter
Deportation of civilians	Wanton devastation and destruction of property	Ill-treatment of wounded and prisoners of war
Internment of civilians under inhuman conditions	Deliberate bombardment of undefended places	Employment of prisoners of war on unauthorized works
Forced labor of civilians in connection with the military operations of the enemy	Wanton destruction of religious, charitable, educational and historic buildings and monuments	Misuse of flags of truce
Usurpation of sovereignty during military occupation	Destruction of merchant ships and passenger vessels without warning and without provision for the safety of passengers and crew	Poisoning of wells
Compulsory enlistment of soldiers among the inhabitants of occupied territory	Destruction of fishing boats and of relief ships	Indiscriminate mass arrests

After the war broke out, the Allies began collecting information on Japanese war crimes, including the crimes committed during the Burma-Siam Railway Incident and the Bataan Death March, the murders of overseas Chinese in Singapore and other atrocities against civilians and prisoners of war. As a result, the Potsdam Declaration stated that "stern justice shall be meted out to all war criminals, including those who have visited cruelties upon our prisoners".

After Japan was defeated, the Allies enlisted a number of liaison agencies to act as cooperatives among nations in investigating war crimes. One important agency was the Tokyo-based legal department affiliated with the General Headquarters for the Supreme Commander of the Allied Powers (GHQ, SCAP). It had five branches in Australia, the United Kingdom, Canada, China and the Netherlands. Through these branches, American staff could exchange information on war criminals with investigators in other countries, and carry out arrests and extradition. A similar agency was the War Criminal Coordination Office, which was affiliated with the Allied Land Forces South East Asia (HQ, ALFSEA). The office had headquarters in British Ceylon (now Sri Lanka) and Singapore, as well as 17 branches in Bangkok, Taiwan, Hong Kong, Kuala Lumpur, Labuan, Medan, Penang, Yangon, Saigon, Shanghai and Tokyo.

After Japan was defeated, a large number of rescued prisoners of war leaked intelligence on war crimes, and the investigative agencies made lists of war criminals based on it. By March 1948, there were 440 Japanese suspects on the UNWCC's list of war criminals. In August 1945, the Far Eastern and Pacific Subcommittee in the Chinese municipality Chongqing produced an additional list of 127 Japanese war criminals. Its subcommittee received 26 lists, which detailed 3158 suspects and witnesses. Around September 1945, the Allied Forces in South East Asia also produced 25 lists of war criminals. Meanwhile, the GHQ began arresting those on the lists, and placing military police personnel and other relevant people in prison camps. Statistics from the Legal Investigation Department of Japan's First Demobilization Bureau say that by early October 1946, over 1000 people had been apprehended and arrested.

1.3 *An Outline of the Trials*

Since each nation had its own way of preserving, compiling and disclosing relevant data, it is difficult to give the precise figures of all the trials. There were 51 known war crime courts in the Asia-Pacific region for prosecuting Class B and Class C crimes. According to statistics from Japan's Ministry of Justice, Hirofumi Hayashi found that the smaller courts (excluding those in the Soviet Union and the People's Republic of China) conducted 2244 trials against 5700 defendants. It should be noted that statistics widely differ on how many Class B and Class C trials

Table 2 Outline of the trials against Japan in Asia

	USA	*UK*	*China*	*Australia*	*France*	*The Netherlands*	*The Philippines*	*Total*
Number of cases	456	330	605	294	39	448	72	2244
Number of defendants	1453	978	883	949	2330	1038	169	5700
Death sentence	140	223	149	153	26	226	17	934
Life imprisonment or fixed-term imprisonment	1033	66+	355	493	135	733	114	3419
Not guilty	188	116	350	267	31	55	11	1018
Other	89	83	29	36	1	14	27	279

Source Hirofumi Hayashi: *Trials against Class B and Class C war criminals*, Iwanami Shoten Publishers, 2005

were carried out. This chapter quotes figures from Hirofumi and Chaen Yoshio's research for the purpose of qualitative analysis only.

Most crimes that were indicted involved the abuse, torture, or massacre of civilians and prisoners, as well as acts of forced labor, sexual violence, economic plunder and drug trade. Some countries also had their own concerns, for example, the Philippine court handled cases of cannibalism and the United States had additional cases involving the prisoners' bodies.

Over three-quarters of the defendants were soldiers. Among them, half were low-level noncommissioned officers, and they were mostly given the death penalty. The proportion of gendarmes (and equivalent naval special police) was also quite high. Most of the prison camp victims were civilians and prisoners of war. The courts attached much importance to the killing of civilians and prisoner of war abuse (Table 2).

2 The "Quasi-Class A" Trial

The so-called quasi-Class A trial specifically refers to the trial carried out by the SCAP on October 27, 1948 in Marunouchi, Tokyo. The defendants were Soemu Toyoda and Hiroshi Tamura, Class A war criminals who were accused of Class B and C war crimes.

2.1 *The Concept of the Trial Subsequent to the Tokyo Trials*

This unique "Quasi-Class A" trial was arranged ahead of the Tokyo Trials. In the Autumn of 1945, the GHQ arrested over 100 Japanese Class A war criminals suspects, including politicians and tycoons. Following negotiations, the Allied Nations decided to try 28 of those arrested at the Tokyo Trials, and detain the rest in Sugamo Prison. The Allies had not reached an agreement at the time over whether to conduct subsequent Class A war trials.

The Head of the IPS Joseph B. Keenan supported subsequent trials. On several occasions, he said that he would proceed with prosecuting Japanese tycoons. At first, the US government supported the idea of following up the Nuremberg Trials and cleaning up the roots of Japan's war. However, in early 1946, the United Kingdom expressed doubts about further Class A war criminal trials, while suspects were still in custody. The Commonwealth prosecutors said that the Allies should immediately release these suspects, as they had insufficient evidence. They also suggested that the United States should take over the investigation. However, suspects were released slowly, and by August 1947, 22 were still in custody. The IPS was unhappy with this, and many prosecutors voiced their view that unjustified long-term detention would damage the reputation of the IPS and even the Allies. Douglas MacArthur urged Keenan to make a swift decision. So the IPS carried out investigations, at by late October, they had decided to prosecute 19 suspects. The remaining three were released immediately.

Intriguingly, Keenan had doubts at the time. He told MacArthur that it would be better for this group of people not to receive Class A trials. He felt that the new international trials were both time and energy-consuming, and also costed money. Even though the trial proceedings would be repeated, he felt that they would attract less attention than in the current international context. But he did not approve of releasing the 19 suspects and suggested that the GHQ's legal department should take over the investigation and prosecution of Class B and C crimes. The army agreed with him.

The legal sector chief Alva C. Carpenter took over and began a new round of investigations into the suspects being held in custody. In his first report to MacArthur in April 1948, he proposed the following: (1) Prosecuting the eight members of the Pearl Harbor cabinet on the basis of cabinet responsibility. Owing to a lack of relevant precedents, they could wait for the Tokyo ruling to come out and then make further plans; (2) Prosecuting Soemu Toyoda (Commander of the Yokosuka Naval District and Commander-in-Chief of the Combined Fleet) on the basis of commanding responsibility; and (3) Conducting further investigations into Yoshio Kodama and Ryoichi Sasakawa for potential trials.

In September, Carpenter suggested that Hiroshi Tamura should also be tried. In November, the Tokyo tribunal announced its verdict. It clarified a principle that if a member of a cabinet fails to perform his duty, he should be held criminally responsible for neglect. Carpenter concluded by saying that the Tokyo Trials had failed to set out a compelling precedent to justify the further prosecution of cabinet members, highlighting that only Shigemitsu Mamoru had been convicted according to this principle and was given a lighter sentence (seven years in prison). So the legal sector aborted this plan and released some 20 suspects including members of the Pearl Harbor cabinet. Only two international proceedings followed the Tokyo Trials: the Toyoda Trial and the Tamura Trial.

2.2 *Quasi-Class A Tribunals and Their Results*

Before the trials began, the GHQ's Public Information Office sent invitations to the allied countries, asking them to nominate judges to sit on the tribunal. Therefore, the Quasi-Class A tribunals were not considered US military commissions—even though they may be called "GHQ Military Tribunals"—but international courts within the scope of the Joint Chiefs of Staff (JCS)'s Directive No. 40. Australia, China and the Soviet Union accepted the invitation. The Australian military's John W. O'Brien served as presiding judge over the Toyoda Trial, and James S. L. Yang from the Tokyo Chinese Mission served as head of the tribunal for the Tamura Trial. The judge sent by the Soviet Union was rejected because he could not communicate in English (Figs. 2, 3, 4, and 5).

On October 27, 1948, an order was issued by the GHQ and SCAP to establish two military tribunals in Tokyo, in accordance with the April 24, 1946, JCS Directive. They also sent a letter to the presidents of military tribunals, prescribing the rules and regulations on governing trials. The same day, a press release was issued by their headquarters announcing the commencement of the Toyoda and Tamura trials, with detailed information about them. The new military tribunals set up base inside the No. 11 Mitsubishi Building in Marunouchi, Central Tokyo

Fig. 2 GHQ Trial/Marunouchi Trial

(which was behind the GHQ building). The Toyoda Trial courtroom later moved to the Japan Youth Building in Aoyama Gaien, a major structure overseen by the occupation authorities. Consequently, the Quasi-Class A Trials were also known as the GHQ Trial, Marunouchi Trial or Aoyama Trial.

The defendant Toyoda was born in 1885. He graduated from the Japanese Imperial Navy Academy. He was promoted to Admiral in 1941, and was Commander-in-Chief of the Kure Naval District. Before the Pacific War, he refused to serve as Navy Minister in Tojo's cabinet. Toyoda was appointed Commander-in-Chief of the Combined Fleet in May 1944. In April 1945, Toyoda instructed the Yamato battleship to go on its final one-way mission to Okinawa. In his role as Chief of Navy General Staff and Supreme Commander of the Japanese Imperial Navy, Toyoda argued that the Japanese people should defend their nation until the very end.

Fig. 3 Defendant Tamura was at the trial

The defendant Tamura was born in 1894 and he graduated from the Japanese Imperial Army Academy in 1916. He was appointed Second Lieutenant in the army artillery and took military posts in both Taiwan and Thailand. When the Pacific War broke out, he was appointed Major

Fig. 4 Defendant Toyoda was walking into the courtroom

General. He was later appointed Chief of Staff of the Kwantung Army and Head of the Prisoner of War Information Bureau. In 1945, he became Lieutenant General.

Fig. 5 Manila tribunal

The trials lasted over ten months. On February 23, 1949, the tribunal attached criminal responsibility to Tamura for tolerating his subordinates abusing allied POWs. He was sentenced to eight years of hard labor. Toyoda was charged with atrocities against POWs, but he was acquitted and later released on September 6, 1949.

These trials were much smaller than was originally envisaged due to various factors, such as the lengthiness of the Tokyo Trials and the loss of interest in the Allies' subsequent trials. However, they provided further scope into the legal concept of "commanding responsibility". They also proved important in helping future generations understand and deliberate what war responsibilities the state, organizations and individuals should take.

3 Class B and C Trials Conducted Within the Allied Nations

3.1 The United States

The US Army held its trials against Japanese war criminals in Manila, Yokohama and Shanghai. The US Navy held its trials in Guam and Kwajalein. The Army followed the "Regulations for the Trial of War Criminals", which was drafted by the US Pacific Army Command in late 1945. The Navy followed local criminal law. 1409 defendants were tried, 1229 were found guilty, and 136 were sentenced to death and executed.

The US was the earliest of the Allies to begin its trials. The Army's Manila trials of Yamashita Tomoyuki (October–December 1945) and Honma Masaharu (January–February 1946) were the first public hearings in Asia against Japanese war criminals. The two defendants were commanders in the 14th Area Army. Yamashita was convicted for

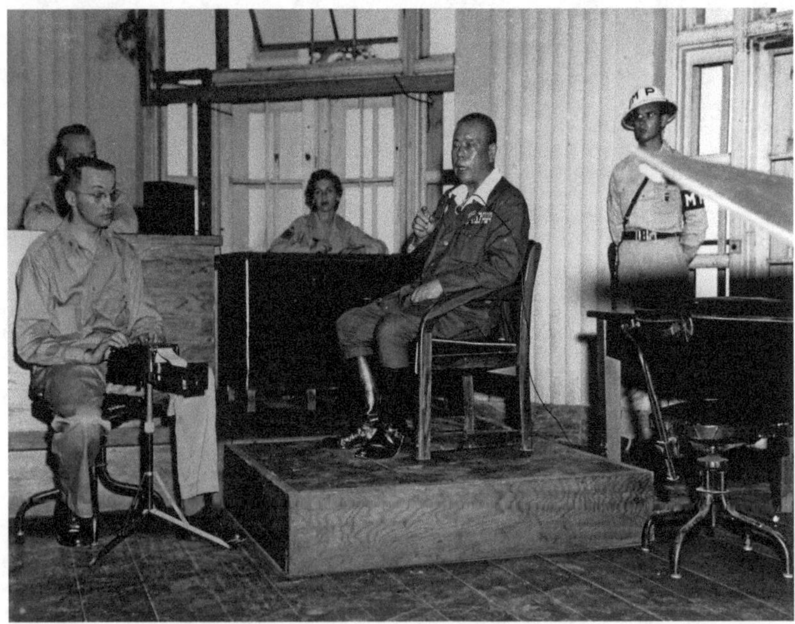

Fig. 6 US Army's Manila trials of Yamashita Tomoyuki

Fig. 7 US Army's Manila trials of Honma Masaharu

allowing troops under his command to commit atrocities against prisoners and civilians in the Philippines and Singapore. Honma was convicted of ordering atrocities during the notorious "Bataan Death March". Both men were hanged. It was the first judicial verdict in human history to be handed under the principle of commanding responsibility—commanders bearing the responsibility of their subordinates during wartime and violating international law.

The Navy's Guam and Kwajalein trials began much earlier. 123 people were prosecuted, 113 were found guilty and 30 were sentenced to death. However, the US Navy issued an order saying that "those who carried out the extermination orders of their superiors should not be sentenced to death". So the number of people sentenced to death was reduced to 10, because most of the accused were charged with killings. Relatively speaking, the penalties for naval trials were lighter than those of other

Fig. 8 US Army's Yokohama trial (The photo was taken on May 7, 1948. Five Japanese defendants were charged with killing 62 US military pilots in 1945)

courts. The Japanese Ministry of Foreign Affairs reported that the Navy's trials were "fair and prudent". Since then, much research on the US military trials has been carried out, especially around the Yamashita trial.

The US military trials attached much importance to the issue of POWs being ill-treated. Out of all of the cases, the proportion of crimes against prisoners was as high as 81.3%. They were mainly for the maltreatment or murder of US captives, but they also included cases of neglect, slander and even cannibalism. During the longest and largest Yokohama trial (December 1945–October 1949), the percentage of crimes against POWs reached 97%. The court held that defendants were accountable for ill-treating prisoners at various prison across Japan.

Fig. 9 US Army's Yokohama trial (The photo was taken on March 11, 1948. Chief Counsel Frank Seidel was speaking)

The Shanghai court (February–September 1946) ruled that the Japanese army had committed crimes against American POWs on the Chinese battlefield, during the "Hankou Incident" and the "Doolittle Raid".

The US military trials also looked at other types of crimes, such as the "Huagang Incident", in which Chinese workers were killed. Some of the defendants were nonmilitary personnel, such as the ordinary Japanese who abused B-29 bomber pilots; and the doctors and nurses who undertook biopsies on captives at the Kyushu Imperial University. In general, the US military tried Japanese war criminals for a wider range of crimes, but the courts were more concerned about the maltreatment of US prisoners of war. This was quite different from the British military trials (Figs. 6, 7, 8, 9, and 10).

Fig. 10 Some defendants and defense counsels at the Yokohama trial

3.2 Britain

L. Louis Mountbatten, the Supreme Commander of ALFSEA, was in charge of overseeing Britain's war crimes trials. His seventeen investigative teams worked across Southeast Asia except in the Philippines. Britain had a common law system with a profound litigation tradition, and so it advocated strict procedures for the trials and verdicts of war crimes. It followed the Regulations for the Trial of War Criminals, and some secondary legislative documents were attached to the British Royal Warrant in 1945. There were also some guiding rules issued by the GHQ and the ALFSEA.

From January 1946, the United Kingdom began setting up military courts in Singapore, North Borneo (now Sabah, Malaysia), Malaya (formerly known as the Peninsular Malaysia), Myanmar and Hong Kong. Scholars have not been able to reach a consensus on the statistics related

Table 3 Outline of British Army's trials

Location	*Number of defendants*	*Types of the victims*				
		Local civilians	*Western civilians*	*POWs*	*Indian POWs*	*POWs/ civilians*
Singapore	464	182	26	160	33	63
Malaya	169	169				
North Borneo	29	25			4	
Myanmar	132	113	1	17	1	
Hong Kong	124	61	5	50		
Total	918	550	32	227	38	71
Percentage (%)	100	60	3	25	4	8

Source As shown in Table 2, there are differences between the two tables due to different statistical methods

to these trials. Hirofumi Hayashi's statistics indicate that there were 918 defendants, and 281 were sentenced to death. Another prominent western scholar Prichard believes that there were 890 defendants, and 237 were sentenced to death. Overall, the Singaporean court handled the largest number of cases, followed by Myanmar, Hong Kong and Malaya.

What was most important about the British trials was that they paid great attention to the Japanese army's crimes against locals, whereas the US military courts only paid attention to their own prisoners of war. If both local prisoners and civilians had been included, about two-thirds of the victims would have been Asian, especially Chinese. During the high-profile Massacre of Overseas Chinese in Singapore case,[1] seven Japanese military officers were found criminally responsible. Two of them were sentenced to death and five were given life imprisonment (Table 3).

[1]After the fall of Singapore, the Japanese military launched a clean-up operation against the local Chinese. A large number of Chinese that were suspected of fighting against Japan were brutally killed. Japanese forces carried out the operation secretly, and so it is hard to confirm the death toll. The figures presented in the British trials ranged from 25,000 to 50,000.

On the one hand, the British trials refuted the view that "the Allied trials only cared about the victims and prisoners of war in their own countries", as they looked at the impact on Asian victims. On the other hand, many scholars argue that Britain did this in the hope of regaining the confidence of its colonial people. Japanese attacks forced British troops stationed in Southeast Asia to make wild retreats, meaning that it lost prestige in the colonies. While the postwar colonial independence movement was surging, the Chinese-dominated communist fighters chose to turn against the British in 1948, while India, Singapore and Malaysia strived for independence. All of these factors cast a political shadow over the British trials.

3.3 Australia

Australia was the first country among the Allies to begin investigating war criminals. Between 1943 and 1945, the government established three investigative commissions. Sir William F. Webb, the future president of the Tokyo Trials, was chairman three times. The commissions carried out extensive and meticulous investigations in the Southwest Pacific region, and provided a wealth of evidence for the Australian trials against Japanese war criminals. The third Webb commission also investigated crimes of aggression, i.e. Class A crimes against peace.

During its war criminal trials, Australia ignored the political pragmatism of the United States and Britain, and instead urged the Allies to prosecute the Japanese Emperor. Even though Webb and Alan Mansfield were appointed judge and prosecutor at the Tokyo tribunal, the commission's final report only detailed Class B and C war crimes. It did not make mention of the emperor because the Tokyo tribunal had decided not to prosecute him (Table 4).

The Australian trials followed the 1945 War Crimes Act (Act No. 48 of 1945) and the Regulations for the Trial of War Criminals (No. 164 of 1945), which contained similar wording to British Royal Warrant. After the November 1945 Weiwak trial, courts were established for trying Japanese war criminals in Labuan, Morotai, Rabaul, Darwin, Hong Kong, Singapore and Manus.

The crimes tried in Australia were mainly against captives, and 81.1% of the accused were charged. The prosecution charged defendants with massacring surrendered troops, maltreating prisoners and cannibalism.

Table 4 Outline of Australia's trials

Location	*Number of defendants*	*Guilty*	*Not guilty*	*Death sentence*	*Imprisonment*
Weiwak	2	1	1		
Labuan	145	128	17	7	121
Morotai	148	81	67	25	56
Rabau	390	266	124	87	179
Darwin	22	10	12	1	9
Hong Kong	42	38	4	5	33
Singapore	62	51	11	18	33
Manus	113	69	44	5	64
Total	924	644	280	148	496
Percentage (%)		69.7	30.3	23	77

Source As shown in Table 2, there are differences between the two tables due to different statistical methods

Of all the cases, the most representative incidents were the "Sandakan Death Marches". In 1945, some 1300 Sandakan prison camp captives were forced to move to the Ranau prison camp in northwest Borneo. A large number of prisoners died of disease, starvation or murder both during the march and after arriving at the camp. By the end of the war, only six Australians had survived. Mortality rate was close to 100%. During the June 1947 Rabaul trial, Lieutenant General Baba Masao, commanding officer of the 37th Japanese Army, was found responsible for the Death March atrocity and was sentenced to death.

The victims in the Australian trials came from various countries. There were many Asian, as well as European and American victims. Of the total 294 atrocities committed by the Japanese, 128 were related to the Chinese, Indonesians, Indians or other South Pacific Islanders. At the Rabaul trial, the Japanese argued that the victims were Japanese soldiers, but the court found them to be captives. This shows another way in which the Allies paid considerable attention to the atrocities imposed on Asian communities.

The Australian trials were known for lasting a long time. Although the Far East Commission recommended that they conclude on September 30, 1949, they continued until mid-1951. They lasted a year and a half longer than those of other allied nations.

3.4 *China*

China was the biggest victim in the Japanese war of aggression. In February 1944, the national government set up an investigative committee in Chongqing to investigate war crimes. The Ministry of Foreign Affairs, the Ministry of Justice and Administration and the Ministry of Military Affairs also participated. In May 1944, the UNWCC established a Chongqing subcommission. These two institutions investigated Japanese war crimes and were involved in China's war criminals trials. Because almost half of China became a battlefield during the war, enemy-occupied areas still existed, and it was difficult to collect evidence. Before the end of the war, mission groups could only gather statistics on the losses and casualties in KMT-run areas. But despite these difficulties, the Chinese government was able to gradually advance with its trials, and started to produce a list of war criminals. In October 1945, the Chinese government issued the Investigation Method of Enemy Crimes, and in February 1946, it formulated the Trial of War Criminals, the Treatment Method of War Criminals and the Implementation Details of War Crimes. Later, the war crimes committee established courts to try Japanese war criminals in Beijing, Nanjing, Shanghai, Hankou, Guangdong, Shenyang, Taiyuan, Xuzhou, Jinan and Taipei (Fig. 11 and Table 5).

The Chinese trials had several key characteristics:

1. Their overall size was relatively small. Despite being the biggest victim in the Japanese war of aggression, China had less courts than the Netherlands (which had 11), and it had fewer total defendants than the United States, Britain, Australia and the Netherlands. This was mainly due to the large mobility of the army during the war, and the frequent displacement of people. Even if there were many plaintiffs accusing the Japanese of atrocities, it was difficult to identify the names of the soldiers, meaning that it became especially difficult to identify and arrest suspects.
2. More than 90% of the cases were atrocities against civilians. This was because many areas in China became battlefields, or were occupied by Japanese troops during the war. The courts predominantly tried Japanese soldiers for murder and abuse, but they also tried them for looting (destroying) residents' property, forcible

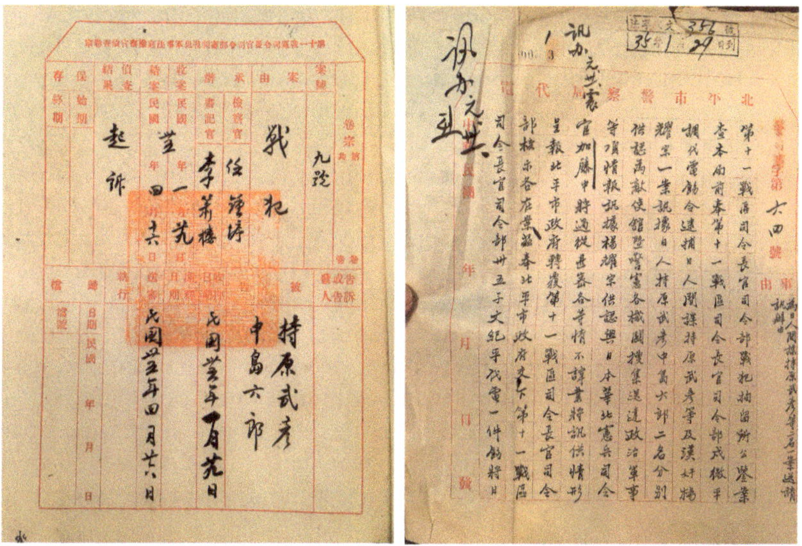

Fig. 11 Photocopy of the defendant Takehiko held by the Peiping court

Table 5 Outline of the trials in China

Location	*Number of defendants*	*Guilty*	*Not guilty*	*Death sentence*	*Imprisonment*
Peiping	112	73	39	28	45
Nanjing	37	26	11	8	18
Shanghai	183	122	61	13	109
Hankou	151	49	102	7	42
Guangdong	171	116	55	48	68
Shenyang	136	56	80	23	33
Taiyuan	11	6	5	2	4
Xuzhou	25	22	3	8	14
Jinan	24	18	6	9	9
Taipei	21	18	3	1	17
Total	871	506	365	147	359
Percentage (%)		58.1	41.9	29.1	70.9

Source Chaen Yoshio: Class B and Class C war criminals—statistics of China and France's trials, 1992

extortion, enslaving education, drug trafficking and even the act of "inciting aggression", i.e. mounting crimes against peace. It was only in the Wuhan court that soldiers were tried for the crime of gas warfare, even though it was committed by the Japanese army in many other places.

3. The number of accused senior military leaders came second only to the United States, and was proportionally highest among the Allies. This showed that China hoped for them to be tried on the basis of commanding responsibility. However, except for a few people such as Hisao Tani (in the Nanjing Court) and Hisakazu Tanaka (in the Guangzhou Court), commanding defendants were not punished severely. Most of the sanctioned soldiers were gendarmerie, of which 40% were found guilty, and only half of that figure were executed. These were the people that had had direct contact with civilians in Japanese occupied areas, and were found to have committed the highest number of bullying or abusive acts.
4. The Chinese had the highest proportion of acquittals during their trials, an approximate 41.9% (which was followed by the Australian trials). It is generally believed that these were influenced by the political factors of the time, namely, the civil war between the KMT and the CCP. With civil war becoming increasingly unfavorable to the Kuomintang, many trials were abruptly ended. The Kuomintang wanted to use the Japanese army to contain the Chinese Communist Party. Take the case of Okamura Yasuji, a Japanese military leader in charge of China's imperial army. He ran the "Three Alls Policy" (Kill all, burn all, loot all) in North China's Communist Party-controlled areas, which led to tremendous damage. However, his crimes were not included in the national government trials and he was ultimately acquitted.

At the end of January 1949, the Shanghai trials came to a close, and all of the national government trials against Japanese war criminals ended. Within a month, all of the war criminals that were serving sentences were sent back to Japan. In October 1949, the People's Republic of China was founded. Seven years later, New China began its independent trials against Japan.

3.5 *The Philippines*

When Japan surrendered, the Philippines was still an American dominion. Therefore, the April 1945 investigation into Japanese war crimes committed in the Philippines was conducted by the US Army Pacific War Criminal Investigation Agency. On July 4, 1946, the Philippines gained independence. The Filipino government followed the example of the United States' investigation in dealing with its war crimes cases. In August 1947, the Philippine trials were conducted in Manila. The crimes tried in the Philippine courts were somewhat similar to those of the Chinese courts: 92.7% were allegations of atrocities against civilians (with China's, the figure was 94.6%). The prosecution also faced similar difficulties as China in testifying against specific suspects, because of the frequent entry and exit of the Japanese army, or the death of military personnel. However, the main difference was that 79 of its 169 accused were sentenced to death, a much higher percentage than China's. That being said, only 17 people were finally executed. In 1953 on the Philippines National Day, an amnesty was granted, and death row inmates who had not yet been executed had their sentences reduced to life imprisonment. They were extradited back to Japan, which some scholars believe was the Philippines showing its good intentions because of Japanese compensation.

3.6 *The Netherlands*

The majority of crimes tried in the Netherlands' Class B and C courts were mainly committed by the Japanese in its Dutch East India colony (now Indonesia). What made the Dutch trials special was that the authorities conducted investigations and trials amidst an unstable political situation. During Japan's surrender, Indonesia declared independence. When officials from the Netherlands reentered Indonesia as a sovereign state, they were resisted by local independents. Consequently, it was not until June 1946 that the Netherlands enacted its relevant trial regulations (Table 6).

About half of the trials carried out in the Dutch courts were related to crimes against local civilians, with a smaller figure being against Europeans (predominantly Dutch residents). The proportion of atrocities committed by military personnel was under 20%. Japan set up detention centers in many areas to prevent wartime spying, but its detainees

Table 6 Outline of the Netherlands' trials

Location	*Number of defendants*	*Death sentence*	*Types of the victims*		
			POWs	*Western civilians*	*Local civilians*
Batavia	357	62	63	306	234
Medan	137	24	38	92	73
Tanjung Pinang	11	1	0	3	6
Pontianak	36	16	1	28	35
Balikpapan	88	18	50	18	85
Makassar	93	32	27	10	56
Kupang	25	6	1	1	23
Ambon	79	14	2	11	75
Manado	59	28	1	7	51
Morotai	65	8	0	0	65
Hollandia[a]	67	9	43	0	17
Total	1047[b]	228	233	499	742
Percentage (%)		23	15.8	33.9	50.3

[a]Now Jayapura, Papua province, Indonesia

[b]Since one defendant may be related to different types of victims, the number of victims has been counted repeatedly

Source As shown in Table 2

in both Java and Sumatra far exceeded that of any other center, reaching over 80,000. Detainees were subjected to various forms of inhuman treatment. They were starved, deprived of medicine, abused and even murdered. Many local civilians were arrested, tortured and massacred by Japanese forces, allegedly for suspected anti-Japanese acts or espionage.

The Dutch trials attached great importance to crimes of sexual violence. The prosecution's evidence found that many Dutch and Asian women were forced to become "comfort women" during the war. Japan's war crimes against the Dutch people greatly affected diplomatic relations between the two countries. After the Tokyo Trials, while most allies began to resume diplomatic relations with Japan, the Dutch government expressed no signs of friendship. Even after the 1951 Treaty of Peace signing in San Francisco, the Dutch government continued to exert pressure on Japan to resolve compensation.

During the rise of Indonesian independence, many remaining Japanese soldiers joined the movement. The Netherlands regarded this as a subsequent war against Java. This made the nature of the Dutch trials unclear—several defendants were accused of violating the Armistice Treaty because they handed their weapons over to the Indonesian Independence Army, rather than the Dutch authorities. There was no such equivalent in other countries' trials. With the Netherlands failing to impose politics, military or diplomacy on the Indonesian people, it completely withdrew from Indonesia in late 1949. The 700 war criminals still in custody were transferred to the Sugamo prison, and the Class B and C war criminal trials ended. The outcome was very similar to that of the KMT-governed trials in China. Compared to the United Kingdom, whose trials were also conducted in its colonies, the Dutch trials saw prominent conflict while "trying war criminals" amidst "ending colonialism". A similar thing also happened with the French trials.

3.7 France

The French court for trying Japanese war criminals was located in Saigon, French Indochina (Ho Chi Minh City, Vietnam). During World War II, the French Indochina authorities surrendered to Japan after France was occupied by Nazi Germany. To prevent the authorities from joining forces with the Allies, Japan disarmed them in March 1945. Japan announced the independence of Vietnam and Cambodia (actually ruled by Japan), and massacred the French Indochina government and military. After the 1945 August revolution, Vietnam declared independence on September 2. Amidst France, Japan and Vietnam's complicated relationship, the French authorities launched an investigation into Japanese crimes. It did this while suppressing Vietnam's national independence movement. The Saigon trials followed French jurisprudence, and the trials followed the same procedures as those trying German war criminals. They applied domestic criminal and military law, namely the August 1944 "War, War Crimes and the Treatment Method of War Crimes" act. From February 1946 to February 1950, 230 people were accused. 63 were sentenced to death, 23 were given life imprisonment, 112 had other prison sentences and 31 were found innocent.

In court, the prosecution accused the Japanese of "massively murdering" French prisoners of war, by "decapitation", "torture", abuse and forcing them to do work which violated international conventions. Japanese troops also killed French prisoners, civilians and members of

Indochina resistance organizations. However, their acts against locals were largely ignored by the courts. Out of the 230 defendants, only 30 were charged with the crimes, and most were linked to crimes against the French. Some scholars have been critical of the French trials for their seeming passivity about these kinds of crimes. Studies show that, with the outbreak of the first Vietnamese War, it was the ambition of recolonizing Indochina that dominated the French trials of Vietnam.

3.8 The People's Republic of China and the Former Soviet Union

Apart from the above seven countries, two other nations in Asia also carried out trials against Japan: the former Soviet Khabarovsk and the People's Republic of China. These two courts were not included in the Allied War Crimes tribunals.

The Soviet Khabarovsk trials commenced on December 25, 1949. This court attracted the attention of future generations because its focus was on Japan's wartime manufacture and use of biological weapons. 12 military officers were accused of this, including Otozo Yamada, commander of the Kwantung Army. According to Hirofumi Hayashi 's research, some 300 Japanese prisoners were tried. Most of them were detained in Manchuria before standing trial. Since Japan did not occupy the Soviet Union during the war, the Khabarovsk court mainly prosecuted defendants for espionage and counter-revolution. The Soviet

Fig. 12 Courtroom of the Special Military Court of Shenyang, People's Republic of China

中華人民共和國最高人民法院 特別軍事法庭送達回證

一九五六 年度特 軍 字第 四 號一案

送達文件：起訴书副本、起訴书译本、指定辩护人通知、指定辩护人通知译本 各乙件

收件人：武部六藏 送達地點：戰犯管理所

審判長 書記員

收到時間：1956 年 6 月 25 日 午 6 時 20 分

收件人簽名蓋章或捺指印 武部六藏

不是本人親收應記明理由

附記：

一九五六年六月廿五日 時

送達人

Fig. 13 Related documents of Rokusashi Takebe at the Fushun War Criminals Management Office (The receipt for the indictment and other documents that was served to the suspected Rokusashi Takebe at the Fushun War Criminals Management Office by the Supreme Court of the People's Republic of China. Rokusashi Takebe was sentenced to 20 years in prison by the New China Shenyang Court in July 1956, but then released and returned to Japan due to encephalopathy)

Fig. 14 Special Military Court of Taiyuan, People's Republic of China (June 12–20, 1956, eight Japanese war criminals were tried at the Taiyuan Special Military Court)

Union abolished the death penalty between 1947 and 1950, so each defendant was given a sentence of hard labor. In 1956, the Soviet Union resumed diplomatic ties with Japan, and it sent these defendants and other Siberian laborers back to Japan.

In July 1950, 969 Japanese war criminals were transferred from the Soviet Union to the Fushun War Criminals Administrative Center, under a joint agreement by Chinese and Soviet officials. At the same time, 140 Japanese soldiers were taken to the Taiyuan War Criminals Administration. These were people who had assisted Yan Xishan and had later become captives of the Communist Party. The New China government had guidelines on ideological education and reformation for its prisons of war. It had different policies on war criminals to other countries, in that it strived to make them reflect and confess, while ensuring they received humane treatment (Figs. 12, 13, and 14).

In April 1956, the National People's Congress Standing Committee decided to grant leniency to war criminals. Between June and July 1956, 45 people were tried in the Shenyang and Taiyuan courts. The remaining 1017 were exempted from prosecution. Prosecutors alleged crimes such as child abuse, murder, economic plunder and cultural aggression. All of the defendants were found guilty, but none of them were sentenced to death. Since their jail time was calculated after 1945, groups of prisoners began to return to Japan upon completion of their sentence, or on getting a commutation. By April 1964, all of them had returned to Japan. Some scholars believe that the "more reform, less punishment" policy adopted during the New China trials was not only consistent with the CPC's policies, but it related closely to China's internationalism at the time.

4 After the Trials

4.1 Serving a Sentence and Releasing POWs

Apart from those that had been executed, most war criminals served their sentences in the place where their trial had been held. But with the rapidly changing situation internationally after the war, many people were transferred to the Sugamo prison in Tokyo. In China, the outbreak of civil war between the Kuomintang and the Communist Party meant that the KMT transferred 260 of its war criminals to Sugamo in February 1949—a month after its local trials. In 1950, the Netherlands, France and the United Kingdom also transferred war criminals. The subsequent wave of national independence meant that it was difficult for Southeast Asian colonies to manage their POW camps. In August

1951, the Australian courts transferred war criminals from their Hong Kong and Singapore bases. In 1953, prisoners of the Rabaul and Manus courts were transferred to Sugamo along with prisoners of the Philippine courts. After the September 1951 Treaty of Peace with Japan was signed in San Francisco, the GHQ handed over jurisdiction of Sugamo to the Japanese government. However, it was still up to the United Nations to decide over who to pardon, commute and parole. China did not participate in the San Francisco Peace Treaty, but shortly after the April 1952 "Treaty of Peace between Japan and the Republic of China" was signed in Taipei, the national government released its remaining 91 war criminals.

At that time, there was building momentum in Japan for war criminals to be released. In May 1952, the "war prisoners' world conference" was established, which promoted the release of war criminals. The following month, the Japanese House of Representatives and the Senate passed several resolutions on the release of war criminals. Public opinion tended toward portraying war criminals as victims of war. The Japanese government lobbied for support in the West during the Cold War, for the full release of war criminals and the reconstruction of military power. With such influence, France (in 1954), Australia (in 1957), the United States, Britain and the Netherlands (in 1958) all released war criminals. By the end of 1958, all remaining war criminals had been released.

It is worth mentioning that after the People's Republic of China's independent trials, over a thousand people exempt from prosecution were immediately sent back to Japan. By 1960, all of its war criminals had returned to Japan. Later on, the "China Returnee Liaison Committee" was established, which proved an important civil organization in promoting Sino-Japanese peace and reconnaissance after the war.

4.2 *Unsettled Problems*

Recent studies have pointed out that there are two problems in some Class B and C trials.

1. Crimes that went unpunished.
   The first was wartime sexual violence. The courts in various countries have prosecuted for "enforced prostitution", but this was not enough, and charges were never brought for "rape" by any independent count. It is also important that neither the Tokyo Tribunal

nor any other Class B/C court brought a ruling on "comfort women". There was not an international consensus until 50 years after the way that wartime sexual violence should be punished as a crime against humanity, when the International Criminal Court and the United Nations Security Council adopted relevant documents.

The second was Japanese biochemical warfare. After the war, investigations in the Pacific uncovered mass evidence of human testing and gas warfare by the Japanese military. Both the Australian and Chinese courts have prosecuted such cases. However, there are a number of similar acts that have gone unprosecuted. The most obvious example is at the Kwantung Army's (Unit 731) Epidemic Prevention and Water Purification Department in Manchuria, where human testing was carried out. It went unprosecuted because the United States was afraid that it would be politically restrained.

The third was crimes against the colonial people, and where there were colonial war criminals. During an era of territorial expansion, Japan educated the colonial people on "imperialization" and war mobilization, forcing many Korean women to become sex slaves of the Japanese army. After the war, the Allied forces filed lawsuits against Taiwan, North Korea and the Saipans who had served the Japanese empire. However, they had paid little attention to colonial victims. The colonial war criminals who were tried were also abandoned by their sovereign states. They neither received legal assistance nor were granted the same treatment as Japanese soldiers.

2. Differences among courts.

The allied nations tried Class B and C war criminals independently. Different national conditions (applicable laws, judicial personnel, etc.) meant that imbalances existed in different courts. Yuma Totani's research on the Anglo-American courts found that the rules on submitting evidence in Australian and Britain courts were not strict because they were afraid that the trials would run on for too long, and violate the 1929 Geneva Treaty. Other studies suggest that there were wrongful convictions and that suspected Japanese war criminals were abused. However, some scholars believe that most of the victims of Japanese atrocities were never entitled to a fair trial. If critics have not based their assessment on a thorough reflection on these crimes, they might be seen to be actually excusing the perpetrators of responsibility.

5 Summary

The overall scale of Class B and C trials conducted by the Allies after WWII (based on the number of courts and defendants) far exceeded that of the Tokyo tribunal, the only Class A war criminal court in Asia. Although the Class B and C courts were under the sole jurisdiction of each allied nation, their investigations and policies were organized, or determined by international agencies, so they still had some international or interallied features. The Tokyo tribunal prosecuted conventional war crimes as well as Class A crimes. During its prewar investigations and during specific trials, the Tokyo tribunal shared vast amounts of intelligence with other Class B/C Asian courts. So these two types of trials presented similar characteristics and were often influenced by the same political factors. There were, however, differences among Class B and C courts in terms of what laws they followed, their trial procedures, and their penalties. Although this chapter is divided into countries, further reading will show that there are still huge differences among Class B and C trials led by the same country. For example, the US military was criticized for its sloppy procedures and rules on evidence during the Tomoyuki Yamashita trial. Meanwhile, the Yokohama trial was seen to be adequately implemented and followed the principle of a fair trial. Did the postwar trials of Japanese war criminals achieve "justice"? To answer this question, researchers still need to conduct more detailed and in-depth research.

Bibliography

1. Hayashi, H. (1998). *Sabakareta senso hanzai: Igirisu no tainichi senpan saiban* [Judged War Crimes: The United Kingdom's War Crimes Trials Against Japan]. Tokyo: Iwanami Shoten.
2. Hayashi, H. (2005). *Bishikyu senpan saiban* [Trials for Class-B and -C War Crimes]. Tokyo: Iwanami Shoten.
3. Chaen, Y. (1987). *Bishikyu senpan Firipin saiban shiryo* [Trial Documents from the Philippines for Class-B and -C War Crimes]. Tokyo: Fuji Shuppan.
4. Chaen, Y. (1992). *Bishikyu senpan Chugoku Fukkoku saiban shiryo* [Trial Documents from China and France for Class-B and -C War Crimes]. Tokyo: Fuji Shuppan.
5. Higurashi, Y. (2002). *Tokyo saiban no kokusai kankei—Kokusai seiji ni okeru kenryoku to kihan* [The International Relations of the Tokyo Trials: Power and Norms in International Politics]. Tokyo: Bokutakusha.

6. Japanese War Criminals Trial Literature Series Committee. (2016). *Wanzhinei shenpan wenxian (gong 18 ce)* [Documents of the Marunouchi Trials (18 vols.)]. Beijing: National Library of China Publishing House.
7. Totani, Y. (2015). *Justice in Asia and the Pacific Region, 1945–1952: Allied War Crimes Prosecutions.* New York: Cambridge University Press.
8. Liu, T. (2015). *Guomin zhengfu dui riben zhongyao zhanfan de shenpan* [Trials Conducted by the Nationalist Government Against Major Japanese War Criminals]. Nanjing: Military History Research.
9. Yan, H. (2016). *Tongxiang zhanhou shenpan zhi lu: mengguo dui erzhan zhanzuicheng niyi lunshu* [The Road Leading to the Post-war Trial: The Proposed Process for Punishment of the War Criminal by the Allies in the World War II]. Nanjing: Nanjing Journal of Social Sciences.
10. The Acting 9. (1974). *Political Adviser in Japan(Sebald) to the Secretary of State*, October 29, 1948 (Vol. VI). United States Department of State: Foreign Relations of the United States, 1948, the Far East and Australia. Washington, DC: U.S. Government Printing Office.
11. Pritchard, J. (1996). British Postwar War Crimes Courts: The Gift of Clemency Following British War Crimes Trials in the Far East, 1946–1948. *Criminal Law Forum*, *7*(1), 15.

Part II

CHAPTER 6

A Reevaluation of the Tokyo Trial Argument

The argument about Tokyo trials is continuous because there are right-wing challenges. Besides, the hasty decision, the wide and complex issues and the difficulty in preparing it are also relevant.

1 Following Discussions on the Issues of the "Ex Post Facto" Law

The issues of the "ex post facto" law were not beyond the expectation of the prosecution. In the opening statement, Keenan emphasized that the war launched by Japan did harm to the whole humankind, that is to say, Tokyo and Nuremberg trials are the beginning of the history of the human trials. Meanwhile, he quoted "dawn" and "progressive" in International law which justice Benjamin Cardozo talked about in the Supreme Court of the United States. The reason why Keenan talked about this point was mainly to suggest "avoiding destruction" is superior to anything when humans face death. Laws, especially international law, develop with the development of human practice.

It is obvious that Tokyo and Nuremberg trials make great break-through in laws. Otherwise, the epoch-making significance of the two trials after the war for the development of international law and international criminal trial cannot be discussed. When Henry Lewis Stimson, an important promoter of the postwar trials and the wartime secretary of the US army, faced the named accusations that the Nuremberg charter

Z. Cheng, *A History of War Crimes Trials in Post 1945 Asia-Pacific*,
https://doi.org/10.1007/978-981-13-6697-0_6

violated "the principle of all crimes being stipulated by law", he pointed out: this understanding was based on the "wrong concept of the overall nature of the laws of various countries", "an authoritative written law cannot cover international law which is the accumulation of the cases and gradually expresses the moral trial of the civilized world". On the other hand, as the prosecution of Tokyo Trials showed in the court that the illegal view of war had not only taken root but also that those who launched the war shall bear corresponding responsibility had become the common sense of international community through treaties and agreements.

The related discussions after the Tokyo trial are focused on the issues of the prosecution and the defense in the court. Because the Tokyo trial didn't try "crimes against humanity" actually, the discussions are mainly concentrated on "crimes against peace". As a whole, deniers' views were basically the platitudinous remarks of the defense. The supporters' views (including the basic supporters) such as prosecution started from the law. From where the supporters stood, firstly, the views of wars against the law was established with the assignment of a series of international treaties and agreements since modern times especially the Pact of Paris in 1928. Secondly, inquiring the war instigators was expressed or implied by the most countries of international community in Tokyo trial. Thirdly, the work of codification of the United Nations was underway. Fourthly, the awareness of law normative after the war was unbreakable.

In retrospect, the established argument of the prosecution from "legal basis" and "the reasons" said by the supporters have the pressure of "ex post facto" law. However, the defense ignored the grounds of law proposed by prosecution and spread the named opinion that the court failed to answer the issue of jurisdiction put forward by the counsel Kiyose Ichiro, which is not the truth.

Except the supporters and deniers, there are different opinions between the two parties. For example, Bernard Victor A. Roling, a justice from Netherland, argued that "crimes against peace" in the Tokyo Chart was actually "ex post facto" law but the new understanding of this serious crime needn't be focused on this point. He said that "crimes against peace" should and could give special interpretation. Roling discussed it many times in the interview by Italian famous jurist Antonio Cassese. To be generalized, there are three aspects of his opinion.

First, war crimes have the attribute of crime in the International law. However, in the terms of domestic laws, it is appropriate to attribute the war crimes to the named "political crimes". That is, it emphasizes the harm to the society compared with the traditional "immortality". These criminals would rather be called enemies than be called criminals. Corresponding to this, compared to the "law revenge", it is a "political revenue".

Second, the justification of law starts from the war and the war grants the winners to maintain the peace which may endanger the new order. Thirdly, the general application of the new law can be realized by the losers. The opinions of Roling are not ex post. Except the opening statement of the court by Keenan, American chief prosecutor Robert H. Jackson admitted that "trials on crimes against peace" were unprecedented in the Nuremberg trial. Jackson emphasized that trying crimes against peace was due to its "malignancy" and "destructiveness" which "civilization" cannot tolerate as the unavoidable and major responsibility.

Therefore, on the one hand, crimes against peace have the root. On the other hand, the pioneering meaning is a breakthrough.

2 The Issue of Conspiracy

Charter of the International Military Tribunal for the Far East 2.5.1: Crimes against Peace: Namely, the planning, preparation, initiation or waging of a declared or undeclared war of aggression, or a war in violation of international law, treaties, agreements or assurances, or participation in a common plan or conspiracy for the accomplishment of any of the foregoing. In this article, "conspiracy" is the most important accusation as the general list of "crimes against peace" in the Tokyo trial. "conspiracy" in the fifty-five counts presented by public prosecutors ranks first and all defendants were accused of guilty of this crime. Except Matsyui Iwane and Shigemitsu Mamoru, other twenty-three defendants were sentenced to be guilty of this accusation.

This prominent crime has been considered as the beyond accusation deviated from the facts by the defendants, the defense counsels and deniers. Until now, the deniers of the Tokyo trial still think of this crime as unacceptable. It is inappropriate to quote the crime of conspiracy in the Nuremberg trial because the political system of Japan is different from the Nazi German.

The main ground of the assertion that the accused was guilty was that the Japanese army was continuous to invade the territory of neighboring countries since 1928. One-third of the judgment which was the longest one in the history of Tokyo Trials described the accomplishment of the "military ambition" of the Tanaka Giichi Cabinet to prove that these conspirators dominated Japan at that time and they determined and carried out their policies.

The "continuous invasion" of Japan proved by Tokyo trials is an undeniable fact. Before the Pacific war, although the military actions of the Japanese army without notice were objected or restricted by the central government, the Japanese army were not prohibited and the central government always had to recede such as "no expansion" required by the Wakatsuki Reijiro Cabinet on September 18 and "no expansion" required by the Konoe Fumimaro Cabinet on July 7. In terms of this aspect, the main political and military leaders of Japan should be responsible for not stopping the wars.

There are major differences whether the responsibility and "conspiracy" are equivalent. In the judgment of the Tokyo court, "conspiracy" can be divided into "initial conspirators and subsequent participants. If the subsequent participants agree with the goal of the common plan or conspiracy, they are the conspirators". The "conspiracy" not only refers to the "plan" and "preparation", but also means the "implementation". If a criminal wages a war, the participants in carrying out this war commit the crimes. The wide recognition does have the deficiency that the responsibility cannot be distinguished easily and the trials do not work and lose meaning. Actually, no matter Tokyo trials or Class B and C trials in different areas, they didn't—actually couldn't—trial in accordance of the standard of "once participation". From the other aspect, Tokyo trials didn't determine the accused according to the wide standard of "once participation", which means that the measure of real implementation is severe not lenient.

Before the "whole country" "attacked" Pearl Harbor, no matter the military actions of Japan are out of premeditation or by accident, they are waged by grassroots. If there are difficulties in determining "conspiracy", this has to be the most important aspect. Japanese scholars have many comments on the "irresponsible" mechanism. For example, one section of the Chapter Two *Staff of the Army* in the book *Proof of Responsibility for the War* edited by Yomiuri Shinbun specially talks that the actions of Japanese Army are controlled by "the staff of the Army". The title of this section is *Chief Commander Arbitrarily Expands the Military Actions.* In the book *The Lessons of Tokyo Trials* written by Hosaka Masayasu, he thinks that only prosecuting the persons liable for military administration but letting go of the persons liable for military operations can avoid that the Emperor would be involved in the issue of leadership right. Because the criminal law of Army stipulates that those who arbitrarily instigate the army shall be sentenced to death or life imprisonment. The famous staffs of army who instigate the army after Showa from Ishihara Kanji and Itagaki Seishiro who instigated the "September 18th Incident" to Masanobu Tsuji and Hattori Takushiro who investigated the "Nomonhan Incident" didn't be sentenced to any or even light criminal penalties. Therefore, the irresponsibility of Japanese wartime system was serious.

Ikuhiko Hata who did the research on Sino-Japanese wars for a long time said:

> A system has the proposal right but shall not responsible, which is an issue. The order of Emperor is drafted by the chief of the General Staff and becomes the sacred decision after the Emperor signs his name. The Emperor who signs his name shall take the responsibility but according to the Meiji Constitution the Emperor shall not be liable. On the other hand, the chief of the General Staff takes no responsibility for the plan and implementation of the failed war. In the Class B and C trials, many officers were prosecuted to be sentenced to hanged but nearly no staff were sentenced.

"As above so bellows" Hata said and the postwar trial are not the same, while "irresponsibility" and "no responsibility" have something in common. (That Tokyo trial prosecuted the crimes of Itagaki Seishiro can trace to Kwantung Army, but mainly because of the acts of the staff of the army, Ishihara Kanji couldn't get away.) In the Chapter Five *Proof of Responsibility for the War*, Shinichi Kitaoka said, "Prime Minister is not the member of the army camp and there is no person responsible from start". In the Chapter Nine, when Kohno Hitoshi was asked the responsibility of "special attack", he said, "the army follows the order and there is no "special attack" and "failure". While the decision mechanism of the Japanese army is ambiguous and irresponsible. No one knows Who and when to give orders. Here "no one knows" does not mean complete confusion but means the ambiguity of person who shall be liable because this book has narrated the reasons that after Battle of the Philippine Sea Fushimi Hiroyasu suggests to oppose US army with "something special" and Onishi Takijiro proposes "special attack" as the "only revenue" to win at the Imperial Japanese Army General Staff Summit (Onishi Takijiro subsequently was appointed as the chief of the 1st Air Fleet).

Although the specified contents of the foregoing "responsibility" are different, "irresponsibility" is common.

From the "responsibility", "irresponsibility" itself is a kind of responsibility. Besides, it is a fact of the increasing expansion after Showa times. So the Japanese hierarchy cannot be separated from the conspirators (It means that the Pacific war is consistent with "conspiracy" before the Pacific war.). The problem here is that the "conspiracy" is the responsibility of the country and there is difficulty in proof of evidence to prove the individual responsibility. From the aspect of trial, it is related with the individual responsibility from three aspects. Firstly, the problem is whether the person participates in the conspiracy. Secondly, the problem is whether the "conspiracy" who participates in determines the actions or affects the policies. Thirdly, the problem is whether there is conspiracy on the premise. On the other hand, the core of "conspiracy" has no relation with the position or wars or the active participation in the wars. Despite the fact of the history is not the same as the articles specified, right or wrong tends to be different in degree. For example, what's the duty? What's the "conspiracy"? Sometimes it is difficult to distinguish. However, from the principle, What the "conspiracy" is and whether to participate in "conspiracy" should have strict lines. That is, only participation in the "conspiracy" concerning with the "plan" about wars can be defined as this crime. Otherwise, even if the chief of the government and army, he shall take different responsibility. The reason why President Webb drafted another judgment is that the judgment of the majority is not adequate enough in the individual responsibility.

As soon as the allied countries entered into Japan, they started to define Class A suspects but they were still confused about whom responsible for the aggressive law. Minister of Intelligence of allied countries felt awkward when he received the name list from Macarthur because he did not know who should be responsible. From the increasing number of name list, class A suspects owned eminent ranks and nearly all wartime political, military, financial leaders, eminent right-wing thinkers, chiefs of right-wing group and main media directors were included. Sato Kenryo, the chief of the Military Affairs Section who was sentenced to life imprisonment, once said, "At the beginning of the war, I am the director. I am honorable to be a Class A criminal with the ministers!" What he said became quite famous later. His remarks mean that the Class A criminals are equivalent to the eminent figures. A majority of the Class A suspects listed by allied countries were not prosecuted later. The special stance of the United States was one of the reasons. Whether to participate in the "conspiracy" may not the core of the judgment. According to the strict standard of "conspiracy", most of these suspects had no relation with the "conspiracy". Those who were related with the "conspiracy" such as the foregoing famous "Staff" Ishihara Kanji and Masanobu Tsuji were not listed. From this point, the crime "conspiracy" itself is a question, so the Whether Class A suspects responsible for this crime judged by Tokyo trials should be sentenced is a question. That is, the list of Class A suspects would be different if it is prosecuted.

There is another difference between "countries' policies" and local conspiracy. The conspirators of local wars also have the whole plot and local wars sometimes become the start or remote cause of the total wars. However, the local wars are different from the wars waged by the countries. From this aspect, "the conspirators" who should be responsible are without doubt that "the Japanese leaders" quoted the words of former minister of intelligence of allied countries in Japan. Therefore, when the allied countries determined the Class A suspects, they also considered this aspect and then focused on "the eminent figures". This consideration was appropriate because "the conspiracy" should be put on the high level as the state-scale aggressive wars. The problem is that there is a subsequent untenable argument. Japan waged wars against the United States, which was correspondent with the standard of "conspiracy", while the wars against China weren't waged by the top officers, which doesn't accord with the standard of "conspiracy". However, the crime of conspiracy itself was the crime of invasion in the crimes against peace. There was a doubt whether Japan's attack against the United States was in the west and the aggressive wars against China were never denied by the majorities in Japan. Many serious public opinion polls of Japan are like that. For example, at the 60th anniversary after the World War II, Yomiuri Shinbun carried out a survey of integrated public opinion polls. 68% believed that Japan lunched aggressive wars against China, which accounted for a majority, while 10% thought the wars were not invasion. Only 34% believed Japan's attack on the United States was aggressive, less than 44% who thought the wars were not aggressive. Therefore, it is hard to copy "the conspiracy" of Nuremburg trial to punish Japan.

However, on the other hand, if the conducts of Nazi German were the standard of the conspiracy, wartime conducts of Japan would be the transformation of "the conspiracy". It is narrow to use the standard to measure the transformation. Besides, if the Emperor Hirohito were not exempted, even if the disagreement about "conspiracy" didn't be eliminated, at least could be reduced. The fourth section in this chapter will continue to discuss the responsibility of Emperors.

3 The Issue of Crimes Against Humanity

The race massacre is not rare in human history. In the civilized society especially the western civilized society, the destructive massacre of a certain race such as Nazi Germany was unprecedented. From history to now, Nazi made the most thoughtful plot, and adopted the most scientific means and the largest scale of crimes. Therefore, the conventional war crimes punishment against Nazi could not match the crimes of genocide and the punishment was not enough. That's special demand why International Military Tribunal Charter (Nuremburg Charter) set crimes against humanity in the London conference. Tokyo Charter evolved from Nuremburg Charter. Compared with the Nuremburg Charter, in Article 5, Paragraph 3 of Tokyo Charter, there are two deletions about crimes against humanity. The one is all civilian population and the other is religions. Deleting the religions, according to the report of the United Nations War Crimes Commission and the Development of the Laws of War, "is meaningless if it was stipulated in the Charter because Class A Japan war criminals have no such crimes". Deleting all civilian population considered the different conditions of Japan and German:

> In the Charter of the International Military Tribunal for the Far East, there was no distinctive stipulation about crimes against humanity as the crimes against peaceful civilian population while the Nuremberg Charter emphasized it with the aim of including the crimes of Nazi against the German civilian population.

It was generally acknowledged that deleting "civilian population" enlarged the scope of crimes against humanity. Italian Jurist Antonio Cassese who recorded the thoughts of Netherland justice Roling about Tokyo trials said:

> The beginning of the Tokyo Charter deletes "civilian population" with the result of enlarging the scope of crimes against humanity (the enlargement

makes it possible for the punishment of killing the enormous soldiers in the illegal wars).

Namely, what "the enlargement" meant could include "killing the enormous soldiers" said by Cassese as well as considered the differences between Japan and German. However, in terms of "crimes against humanity" repeatedly emphasized by the prosecution of Tokyo trials and the court, Japan was not exempted from crimes against humanity because of the differences between Japan and German in the Tokyo trial. Japan's general opinions differed in this point—the Japanese except the minority who insist on reflecting the war crimes held the views that the Tokyo court knew the "inexistence" of "crimes against humanity" but deliberately mixed them. Before the trial of Yokohama Class B and Class C war criminals, the head of the Allies' judicial department interpreted Class ABC as levels. That is, "so-called Class B referred to the heads of the army such as Yamashita and Honma who were responsible for the of acts of killing, abuse and slavery. Class C referred to committing the foregoing crimes. So-called Class A war criminals were the political leaders like Prime Minister Tojo Hideki". Although the way that categorizes Class A and BC was not strict, it was generally appropriate. However, until now some Japanese still thought this categories as the distortion of facts. For example, Chaen Yoshio 茶园义男 dragged this talk into the Regulations Governing the Trial of Conventional War Criminals in Yokohama that published before the talk and claimed that the Classes ABC were absolutely without the meaning of levels.

That Japan had no Class C (crimes against humanity = genocide—original note) was the fact investigated by the American army. Therefore, general headquarters which was lost in dilemma was drafted as a Class C = war criminal. It deliberately made an imagination of genocide.

As the foregoing said, Tokyo trials didn't exempt Japan from crimes against humanity because of the differences between Japan and German. Therefore, so-called intention was distorted by himself. From the other hand, crimes against humanity in the Tokyo trial had no distinctive differences with the common war crimes. Roling said:

The concept of crimes against humanity was applicable in the Tokyo trial but is furnished with "(conventional—original note) war crimes". Killing slaveries and citizens is war crime and should be sentenced to capital punishment. Therefore, the concept of crimes against humanity doesn't work in the Tokyo trial.

The war crimes here are the Japanese translated version of conventional war crimes. Although Tokyo Charter listed "crimes against humanity" clearly, the third category (No. 53–5) in the 55 counts is conventional war crimes and crimes against humanity whose meaning is conventional war crimes. Except the third category and the first category "crimes against peace" (Counts No. 1–36), the second category (No. 37–52) is also conventional war crimes.

On the other hand, Tokyo trial wasn't prosecuted as "crimes against humanity" so that nowadays some Japanese accepted the mistake and think of the documents of Japanese Army's Atrocities presented in the Tokyo trial as the accordance with crimes against humanity. As professor Kitamura Minoru of Ritsumeikan University said, "because there are crimes against humanity in the Tokyo trial, Nanjing Massacre existed just to find the corresponding crimes." Domestic scholars believe the judgment about Nanjing Massacre in the Tokyo trial is in accordance with "crimes against humanity" but they don't distinguish the conventional war crimes from "crimes against humanity", which is opposite to the views of Kitamura Minoru.

Here we can find: firstly, Tokyo Charter listed crimes against humanity which was evolved from Nuremberg Charter. Secondly, the actual hearing of Tokyo trials didn't adopt "crimes against humanity". Thirdly, although "crimes against humanity" were not adopted, it didn't stop people from recognizing "crimes against humanity" as the main accusation in the Tokyo Trial. Fourthly, as for recognizing "crimes against humanity" as the main accusation in the Tokyo Trial, some Japanese believed it was appropriate while some domestic people believed the atrocities Japan committed were equivalent to crimes against humanity. The core didn't rely on whether Japan's Army atrocities and expansion in the war violated "humanity" but relied on whether it deserved "crimes against humanity" of Tokyo Charter. Because the conventional war crimes were also against humanity, besides the conventional war crimes, "crime against humanity" should be a limited specific reference but not be against humanity in the general meaning.

"Crimes against humanity" in the two postwar trials referred to the inhuman conducts of large-scale massacre, annihilation, slavery, forced migration against citizens (deletion after Tokyo Charter) and persecution based on politics and races. In this section, we have mentioned that Tokyo Charter was evolved from Nuremberg Charter and Nuremberg Charter is designed for Nazi German. Therefore, although "crimes against humanity" listed several important crimes and other inhuman conducts, they could include a wider range but generally emphasized these features: first, it was against citizens regardless of enemy states or homeland, wartime or peacetime—it is the whole difference from the conventional war crimes; Second, it especially emphasized the reference to the specific race. It was closely related with Nazi genocide, especially holocaust.

Look back on history, it is easy for us to find that whether Japan promoted "Five Races under One Union" in Manchukuo or advocated "greater east Asia co-prosperity" in a wider range, the premise was that they were "led" by "Yamato". In the prewar publications of Japan, the race superiority that regard themselves "the voters" was visible. In a book entitled *What Will Become of Japan*, Shinohara Yoshimasa shockingly states that the "Japanese race" is the "most excellent race in the world", and he even paints Japan's "mountains, rivers, grass, trees, dogs, horses and fish" as "the best in the world". Nowadays, some Japanese quote the proposals of equality of nationality in the Paris Peace Conference to prove that Japan has no racial discrimination, which contradicts the ethnic memory of such countries as China and Korea and doesn't check through the references. From the other hand, the International Supervision Bureau didn't compare the Japan's Army Atrocities as "crimes against humanity" which took genocide of Nazi German as a prototype to present the differences between the two.

Many years ago, Japan's right-wing magazine *Shokun!* conducted a questionnaire survey on the Nanjing massacre. The 16th question was: "Was the 'Rape of Nanjing' a crime similar to the Fascist holocaust?". It is worth noting the great massacre school (those who believed the existence of large-scale holocaust of Japan's Army) unremittingly disclosing and condemning Japan's war crimes for a long time but not the fabrication school and middle ground school. A prominent figure of the great massacre fraction Fujiwara Akira, who was alive at the time, said:

> It was different from the holocaust (specific reference to Nazi genocide). The so-called holocaust was extermination of a certain race based on national policy. However, the cause of the Japanese army's random killing

> and raping of Chinese civilians was the neglect of commanders and fanaticism of soldiers.

Members of the great massacre school who participated in the questionnaire answered differently but no one believed the Nanjing Massacre was holocaust.

Chinese people will definitely think that the word "neglect" is too gentle, but this is irrelevant to the stance of Fujiwara and the great massacre school. As a matter of fact, it is difficult to prove these issues regarding the Nanking Massacre. In the recent years, by comparing the evidence of the accused who attacked Nanjing and witness in the Tokyo trial with their diaries, the difference between them was not by accident and some of them were perjury. At the same time, studying all records of Japan, we still couldn't find that Japan's army high level had a Nazi holocaust plot. From the existing documents of Japan's Army about attacking Nanjing and diaries of Japan's army high level, there was no clear top-down orders of conducting atrocities except the few diaries of the regimental commander Nakajima Kesago of the 16th Division which recorded the order of killing the captives. Therefore, it has difficulty that the Tokyo trial sentenced the first responsible person of Nanjing massacre Matsyui Iwane to the ultimate penalty but it referred to his passive responsibility (No. 55 cause of action). From this point, the actual hearing of the Tokyo trial didn't adopt "crimes against humanity". It was illustrated that Japan's atrocities in the East-Asian regions were different from "crimes against humanity" according to the standard at that time.

4 The Reevaluation of the War Responsibility of the Showa Emperor

The war responsibility of Emperor Hirohito is an issue that has been discussed at home and abroad. In the Chinese world, there is no objection to the war responsibility of Emperor Hirohito and the pertinent discussion mainly puts emphasis on the two aspects, which will not be repeated again. One is that Emperor Hirohito shall bear but fail to bear the war responsibility; the other is that the situation is incurred by the American's selfish decision. In this section, we intend to discuss other two issues: first, it is a misjudgment that the United States holds that

Emperor Hirohito bears no war responsibility; second, failure to ascertain the responsibility of Emperor Hirohito results in a defect in the identification of the Japan's overall war responsibility.

4.1 The Judgment Made by the United States That the Emperor Bore No Responsibility Due to His Negative Response

There were two aspects of the war responsibility of Emperor Hirohito. First, why the responsibility of Emperor Hirohito was not ascertained? Second, did Emperor Hirohito himself bear the war responsibility? The confirmation of the latter served as the premise of the former, because there was no question of exemption if Emperor Hirohito was not accountable. We used to pay more attention to the former aspect and considered that lack of the investigation of Emperor Hirohito was mainly due to the expediency of the Commander-in-Chief of the Allied Powers in Japan, MacArthur. In fact, the dominant idea of the United States that there was no investigation of Emperor Hirohito has already been formed in the early stage of the war. The idea covered both strategic factors and the judgment of no war responsibility of Emperor Hirohito. When Elmer Davis, the director of the United States Office of War Information (OWI), was confronted with the question why the radio concerning Japan did not "attack" or "embarrass" Emperor Hirohito on December 9, 1942, he answered that:

> The basic principle of this issue is that the Emperor has permanently not had a voice about what happened in Japan. Any attack on him must be stimulating and not be accepted properly, for the Emperor is regarded as a god. There is a quantity of evidence that the Emperor has nothing to do with the Japanese politics. The problem lies in the power of the Military Department.

Since then, there was no lack of the request of the punishment on Emperor Hirohito from the Allies and the United States, especially that Australia repeatedly requested Britain, the United States and the United Nations War Criminals Commission to regard Emperor Hirohito as a war criminal. However, as the war progressed, especially with the US occupation of Japan, the fear that the trial of Emperor Hirohito might provoke a revolt in Japan became a growing weight. On January 25,

1946, MacArthur's letter to Dwight Eisenhower, the US Army Chief and the former Commander of the European Allied Powers, was a typical example:

> In the past decade, there hasn't been any clear evidence that the behavior of Emperor Hirohito in different situations is related to the various political decisions of the Empire of Japan. The results of our exhaustive investigation demonstrated that the involvement of Emperor Hirohito in the national affairs was largely passive with only a mechanical response to the words of ministers who assist him. It was believed that even if Emperor Hirohito had his own mind, as long as it was against the popular opinion manipulated by the ruling warlords, his efforts may render him dangerous.
>
> If we impose a trial on Emperor Hirohito, then the plan of occupation must undergo major changes. Consequently, preparations should be completed before the actual actions are taken. If the Emperor is reported, it is inevitable to cause great riots among the people of Japan and its influence will never be overestimated. The Emperor is the symbol of the Japan's national integration and this state will fall apart without the Emperor.

This letter was quite long and later stressed that the trial of Emperor Hirohito was difficult to control the situation and complete the transition of Japan to democracy, etc. The letter of MacArthur was from the inferior to the superior, but the immunity of Emperor Hirohito was firmly in the hands of the United States. (Countries involved in the Tokyo trial had the power to select the suspects in war criminals, but the disposal of the Emperor was controlled by the State-War-Navy Coordinating Committee.)

The exemption from prosecution of Emperor Hirohito was an arbitrary decision by the United States. In terms of the foregoing content, the decision was based on two considerations, but its main purpose aimed at avoiding intensifying the revolt in Japan and stabilizing its occupation. Without such a consideration, it was not necessary for the United States to stand in opposition to other allies. Emperor Hirohito could have at least been treated as a suspect in war criminals like the Royal Nashimoto Morimasa, which was absolutely obvious. However, if there was no judgment that the Emperor had no real power, the United States would confront much more pressure from the allies when exempting the Emperor from war responsibility. Therefore, whether the Emperor had no voice or had nothing to do with the various political decisions of the Empire of Japan, that is, whether the imperial power of the prewar Japan was as symbolic as the United States thought was indeed the key to the exemption of Emperor Hirohito.

4.2 *The Narration of the Decision-Making in National Affairs by Emperor Hirohito Himself*

If we turned to the prewar Japan, we could not keep silence about the improper judgment that Emperor Hirohito had no real power. Article 1 of Chapter 1 of the postwar new constitution stipulated that the Emperor was only the symbol of the Empire of Japan and the symbol of the union of Japanese nationals. Article 4 explicitly provided that the Emperor had no power to intervene national affairs. However, the situation was completely different before Japan's surrender. First, the Meiji Constitution stipulated that the Emperor served as the head of state and commanded the sovereignty (Chapter 1, Article 4). The sovereignty included parliament, law, officials, the army, declaration of war, negotiation of peace, enforcement of internal martial law, amnesty and commutation, etc. (from Article 5 to Article 17 of Chapter 1), which were all the most important powers of a state. Second, the sovereignty owned by Emperor Hirohito was not only signing and making his marks as the foregoing Japanese scholars expressed. The Emperor exactly had a supreme voice, even though he did not express his opinion all the time. Third, Emperor Hirohito was in fact highly concerned and engaged in the war rather than being indifferent to the national affairs (Fig. 1).

There was no difficulty in proving from the perspective of system and history that the role of the Emperor before the war or during the war was not only a symbol. However, it was indeed difficult to prove that the actions of the Emperor were active behavior rather than a mechanical response to the ministers who assisted him from the perspective of system and public or private literature. Yet we happened to have the most evidence to prove the role of the Emperor, which was his monologue to his subordinates and relatives soon after the war. This conversation later published and named *The Showa Emperor's Monologue* was documented by Terasaki Hidenari who served as a general official of the Imperial Household Ministry (a job title). After decades, these documents were revealed and delivered to experts by his daughter Mariko Terasaki Miller (who was of mixed Japanese-American descent and ignorant of Japanese) and other families. They were known as the rare historic documents after Emperor Hirohito died. Through such a

Fig. 1 MacArthur and Emperor Hirohito

conversation, we could see that Emperor Hirohito in imperial politics was far from a passive involvement.

The Monologue was of special value to the understanding of the role of Emperor Hirohito in Japanese wartime politics, not only because it was the self-bearing of Emperor Hirohito, but also because the conversation was before the Tokyo trial that called for the investigation of Emperor Hirohito at home and abroad, which was the same time as the foregoing MacArthur's letter. Therefore, even if Emperor Hirohito did not intentionally cover up, he at least would not incur the suspicion on himself. In this particular point, the time of this conversation was actually due to the tacit understanding between Emperor Hirohito and the United States, especially MacArthur. The conversation mentioned several times that Emperor Hirohito depended on the words of who assisted him except the *226 Event* (a coup launched by some Japanese Tōseiha faction young officers) and the end of the war because of the rumor that the Emperor sympathized with Tanaka incurred by compelling the Tanaka Yoshikazu Cabinet to resign. He also did not make the opposite decisions to the words of his ministers, which were almost the copy of a mechanical response to the words of who assisted him as MacArthur said. In the end of *The Monologue*, if the war decision was overruled, then "my confidants will be killed and my life will not be guaranteed". This was exactly what MacArthur said that the Emperor's opposition to the popular opinion would render him dangerous. Thus, in the context of such a conversation, Emperor Hirohito only needed to narrow his role and had no reason to exaggerate it; so, the role of Emperor Hirohito we could see from *The Monologue* was only the lowest limit of the actual situation, not magnified, even in the so-called "private" conversation.

According to *The Monologue*, Emperor Hirohito was nearly passive except in the effect of Tanaka's resignation, the *226 Event* and the end of the war, even *The Monologue* in this case was totally unmatched. There were a number of the relevant examples in *The Monologue* and here were only a few examples of proof. In the section of "Shanghai Incident" (the first battle of Song Hu), concerning the armistice, Emperor Hirohito said:

> In Shanghai, controlling combat zone in such a way as to prevent the expansion of the incident was the contribution of General Shirakawa Yoshinori (Yoshinori --- the original note, similarly hereinafter). The March armistice was not because of his obedience to imperial orders, but because I ordered him not to expand the incident.

Not the obedience to imperial orders meant that Shirakawa's action was not based on the drafting and signature of the Military Department. Thus, Emperor Hirohito not only did not have to wait for the words of who assisted him and obey the law, but also had the power to violate the system (violation of the system originally referred to describing the officials, but after Meiji Restoration, Japan was known as a constitution state, so borrowing the term was proper). In fact, he also surpassed the system. The section of China Incident and Triple Alliance mentioned to increasing troops to Shanghai in the second battle of Song Hu. At that time, the first minister of General Staff, Ishihara Kanji, thought that the urgent task for Japan was the defeat of the Soviet Union and the safety of Manchukuo. He was against to the expansion of the war in Shanghai, which was opposed by Japanese militants. Eventually, Ishihara Kanji resigned and left, so the Japanese army continued to increase its troops and the war was continuously expanded. From this section, it could be seen that the increase of troops was promoted by Emperor Hirohito. In the section of Nomonhan Incident, Emperor Hirohito said:

> Both parties can say that the other side is illegally invading, for the Soviet-Manchurian frontier (it should have been the Manchuriann- Mongolian frontier) near Nomonhan is not clear. At that time, I once ordered the commander of the Kwantung Army, Yamada Otozo (the mistake of Kenkichi Ueda, Yamada was the commander of the Kwantung Army at the end of the war), to strictly abide by the territory of Manchukuo. So, there was a reason for the war between the Guandong army and the invading Soviet army. At the same time, the Manchurian army was justified in the fight from the standpoint of the full defense agreement.

This was also the order of Emperor Hirohito. In the section of the event of cabinet Umezu, Emperor Hirohito said that he appointed Umezu Yoshijiro or the Equerry Hata Shunroku the Prime Minister because the rumored candidate for the Minister of the Military Department (military and naval minister, here was the Military Minister) was not appropriate. In the section of cabinet Yonai and the Military Department, Emperor Hirohito said that he appointed Yonai the Prime Minister in order to restrain the German–Japanese Alliance. When granting the authorization, Hata was required to be present and support Yonai. In the section of dispatching envoys to the Vatican, Emperor Hirohito said that it was his idea to firstly dispatch envoys to the Vatican since the war.

Although Emperor Hirohito did not take positive measures in some events, he was not powerless. In the section of Triple Alliance, he said,

> In terms of the result, I agreed with the German-Japanese Alliance, but it was by no means satisfactory. Matsuoka believed that the United States would not join the war. I was not convinced by his opinion that the German Americans would stand on the side of the German-Italian Alliance. But I also did not believe Matsuoka lied to me, so I was

> skeptical. Meanwhile, I asked Fumimaro to pay more attention to the Soviet-German relationship.

The situation of forming the cabinet before the war between Japan and United States was similar. In the section of Fumimaro's resignation and Tojo's formation of his cabinet, Emperor Hirohito said,

> In Fumimaro's handwriting, we saw that he flattered Naruhiko Higashikuni into the Prime Minister. This was recommended by the army. I did not think it appropriate that the royal family served as the political leaders. In this way, if the royal person was the Prime Minister, the royal family must bear the war responsibility as long as the war broke out. I thought it was inappropriate and Naruhiko Higashikuni also did not possess such an intention, so I did not accept the army's request and let Tojo form his cabinet.

It was not difficult to see that Emperor Hirohito was not powerless but unwilling to bear the war responsibility. His negative attitude in various situations was actually based on the calculations of such gains and losses. In the section of the decision to war after the previous section, Emperor Hirohito's doubts about the war were mainly whether Japan could win.

Tojo was regarded as the most powerful Japanese Prime Minister in the war and people were also used to listing him, Hitler and Mussolini as the equal "dictators". Even so, he was just a "minister" inferior to the Emperor. Emperor Hirohito said in the section of the domestic affairs of the Tojo cabinet that he wanted to talk about why the Tojo cabinet fell from power and why the person who let the Tojo cabinet fell from power was not Emperor Hirohito himself. Although the following words only discussed the reasons for the downfall and did not involve his foregoing questions, Emperor Hirohito had the power to "let him fall from power". In this section, the Emperor expressed that his mood could not be conveyed to all the officials through Tojo, nor could it be conveyed to the nationals. However, the reason was not that Tojo overrode the Emperor but that Tojo was busy with his multiple posts. In the section of Tojo himself, Emperor Hirohito talked about an unprecedented report requesting the cancelation of what the Emperor had approved. It was as follows: in 1944, because of the internal dissent, Tojo no longer served as the chief of the staff and he had consulted with Fushimi that

Ushiroku Jun might take this position. But Fushimi thought it improper. When Tojo reported to the Emperor, Emperor Hirohito said,

> The Marshal's advice was reasonable. I asked him if he had some more valuable suggestions. After Tojo withdrew, he wrongly sent the report that suggested Ushiroku to be the chief of the staff, but I still approved it. Tojo seemed to sense what I meant, so regardless of my approval, he requested to cancel the report again and recommended Umezu Yoshijiro. Tojo's request of the cancellation of report was the only one example.

What this example demonstrated most was that not only the explicit order of Emperor Hirohito but also his meaning had a deep influence. (The comment of Emperor Hirohito on Tojo in this section was fairly positive, such as his insight, diligence, thoughtfulness, competence, observation of public opinions, etc. Emperor Hirohito also tried to defend Tojo. For example, in the spring and summer of 1943, Tojo's visit to the East Asia criticized by the Japanese top as the "self-publicity", but Emperor Hirohito said that this was his permission.)

Since the Koiso cabinet came into power, Japanese army continued to fail. The contradictions between the army and the navy were increasingly sharp, so Koiso was forced to resign. K. Suzuki, one of the candidates, did not be willing to assume the role of the Prime Minister. He did not accept it until Emperor Hirohito persuaded him. Therefore, at that time, regardless of Tojo, no one could or could try to disobey the Emperor. The threat of the mutiny felt by Emperor Hirohito was all in the disguise of ridding the Emperor of evil ministers to support the Emperor. Although Emperor Hirohito ordered to suppress the *226 Event*, the executed perpetrators all shouted, "Long live the Emperor" before execution. Thus, in the outsider's view, there was no power to pose a threat to the imperial power in Japan during the war.

Since Koiso cabinet came into power, Japanese army continued to fail. The contradictions between the army and the navy were increasingly sharp, so Koiso was forced to resign. Kantaro Suzuki, one of the candidates, did not be willing to assume the role of the Prime Minister. He did not accept it until Emperor Hirohito persuaded him. Therefore, at that time, regardless of Tojo, no one could or could try to disobey the Emperor. The threat of the mutiny felt by Emperor Hirohito was all in the disguise of ridding the Emperor of evil ministers to support the Emperor. Although Emperor Hirohito ordered to suppress the *226*

Event, the executed perpetrators all shouted "Long live the Emperor" before execution. Thus, in the outsider's view, there was no power to pose a threat to the imperial power in Japan during the war.

For a long time, we have always put emphasis on that the acceptance of the Potsdam Proclamation by Emperor Hirohito was the key to the end of the war, which had a dominant influence in Japan. Many Japanese intended to describe such an announcement as a holy decision. For example, Harako Shozo flattered the so-called Emperor of all ages into the supreme culture in the world. He also stated in the book A View of the Emperor of Japan From the World History that the best manifestation of the quintessence of this state was the holy decision and that Emperor Hirohito was a supporter of peace. In fact, the reason why the war would not be ended timely was Emperor Hirohito's fluke mind. For example, before the battle of Leyte Gulf, Emperor Hirohito inclined to hit the United States in order to create a room for compromise. Such an idea was not only before the battle of Leyte Gulf, but also with the US army's counterattack. Even though Japan's chances of victory were increasingly fading, Emperor Hirohito still held such an idea. As he said,

> I thought that the victory was hopeless after the breakthrough of the Stanley Mountains in New Guinea (September, the 18th year of Showa Emperor's times). So, I was thinking where we could strike the enemy to obtain a chance to make peace.

In the Japan's war fever at that time, it was indeed difficult to give up the war without a complete failure. However, at least it could be said that Emperor Hirohito did not make a meaningful attempt at peace before the end of the war.

By means of Emperor Hirohito's monologue, I assume that there is no doubt whether the role of Emperor Hirohito during the war s in conformity with the words of MacArthur. As a result, we can say that the reasons for Emperor Hirohito's exemption do not hold water, or if Tojo and other people should be responsible for the war, then Emperor Hirohito must be the first person who bears the war responsibility. As for the various questions of the Tokyo trial itself, they are the other matters. Conversely, it can be said that if Emperor Hirohito can be exempted, then as the French judge Henri Bernard in the Tokyo trial said, it is at least unfair to the other A class war criminals condemned guilty in the Tokyo trial.

4.3 The Exemption of Emperor Hirohito Dismissed the Core of the Crime of Conspiracy

There was no need to avoiding pointing out that no investigation of the war responsibility of Emperor Hirohito had a deep influence on avoiding the resistance of Japanese troops at the end of war, reducing the cost of maintaining Japan's stability by the allies and incurring the Japan's turbulence during the transition period. However, Emperor Hirohito's improper exemption also caused irreparable consequences. Among them, the most significant negative influence on Tokyo trial was whether the crime of conspiracy was appropriate.

The Charter of the International Military Tribunal for the Far East 2.5.1 stipulated that crimes against Peace: namely, the planning, preparation, initiation or waging of a declared or undeclared war of aggression, or a war in violation of international law, treaties, agreements or assurances, or participation in a common plan or conspiracy for the accomplishment of any of the foregoing.

As the general outline of the crime of anti-peace, the joint consultation in this provision was the most important charge of the Tokyo trial. Not only the crime of joint consultation ranked first in the 55 offenses proposed by the prosecution, but also all the defendants in this case were accused of guilt. In addition to Matsui Iwane and Shigemitsu Mamoru, the other 23 defendants were also convicted of this accusation.

This prominent accusation was also the falsest accusation deviated from the fact which was agreed by the defendants, the defense attorney and the ex curia opponents. Even to this day, opponents of the Tokyo trial still considered this crime most unacceptable, for Japan's politics was completely different from that of the Nazi Germany. In their view, Japan adopted the modern parliamentary democracy after the Meiji Restoration and there was no qualitative change when the war broke out; not only the policies of the parties and the policies of the frequently changed cabinets were different, but also the policies of the cabinet and the military were different. Even in the government, there were contradictions between the Ministry of Foreign Affairs and the Greater East Asia Province established after the outbreak of the Pacific War and between the Planning Institute and the Military Service Province. The disagreement between the navy and the army sometimes came to a very high degree, so there was no joint consultation and there was impossibly joint consultation. Those who held the view believed that although

Germany also had contradictions between the S.S. and the national defense forces, the situation in Japan was fundamentally different. Because Japan did not have a German style leader (a dictator as Hitler), a political party (the dictatorial National Socialist Party) and the one doctrine (the state socialism), quoting "the crime of conspiracy" of the Nuremberg trial was completely unsuitable.

Prosecutor's prosecution and court decisions were mainly about Japan's grand history of aggression since 1928. From the perspective of a fait accompli, this conclusion was still powerful; the problem was that there was a gap between its relevance to the defendant's liability. It was a pity that the argument of the Court President Webb from the defendant's personal point of view was not open at that time, but the key was that the emperor of Hirohito who strung the conspiracy line was not investigated. It was precisely because of the spirit of this series that the defendants seemed to be scattered and unrelated in joint consultation. It could be said that if the emperor was not exempted, the defendant's so-called mutual disagreement and the original opposition and so on would be disqualified. Then the defense would not have excuses for the argument of the crime of conspiracy.

5 Summary

The Tokyo trial, just as the different opinions of the judges that year, deserves the discussion. But it is not to say that it is meaningful that the deniers of Japan totally repudiated. Prime Minister Shinzo Abe stood for the deniers and declared that the Tokyo trial is the trial by the winners in the official occasion like the House of Representatives Budget Committee. As for this point, we want to quote a true story to tell Abe and the deniers of Japan what "the victors' trial" is.

The Case of Zhou Jitang.

On January 28, 1938, Japanese Central China Area Army council of military court trialed a case of the so-called "violation of military laws". This case has a vague record in the *Journals of Japanese Central China Area Army Council of Military Court*.[1]

[1] Military law conference is often translated into "Council of Military Court". However, Japan set up the military disciplines conference to trial the soldiers and people in the occupied areas. The court established by the occupation army during US occupation of Japan was presented as Chinese characters "军事法庭". The military court was equivalent

The journals of judicial department of the Japanese army and council of military court could reflect the conditions of military disciplines originally. However, as the Japan's army began to destroy the related documents in a large-scale before the end of the wars, the journals of judicial department and council of military court we can find today are *the Journals of the 10th Judicial Department* of the 10th Division who landed Jin Shanwei and *Journals of Japanese Central China Area Army Council of Military Court* of latterly established to coordinate the 10th Division and military command agency of Shanghai expeditionary forces Central China Army. The two journals were fluke to be reserved because of the chief of the judicial department of 10th Division Okawa-Sekiziro.

In the *Journals of Japanese Central China Area Army Council of Military Court* January 27, 1938, which named "send to director of the Legal Section", there was "a report on the request of a trial" and the words of such six members as Zhou. Because the records had no "brief facts of the crimes" and judgments and there were no related records of "the announcement of the handling events" in the end of the journal. *The Journals of 10th Judicial Department* also had no clues, which suspended this case. Later, *Okawa-Sekiziro's Diaries* was published and solved the puzzle.

Okawa-Sekiziro's Diaries records the situation of the trial and sentence of six persons such as Zhou on January 28th:

> The six persons such as Zhou were trialed due to their violations of military disciplines at 9a.m. The head Zhou Jitang as the chief of the second district, used to be a hooligan, that is, rascal, swordsman and he managed 500 people so we could find that he was steadier than others. The trial ended at about 1p.m and prepared to be executed at once. At 5p.m, it was executed. I present at the trial as the prosecutor and ordered the gendarmes as the executing commander. The criminals absolutely denied the disadvantages of themselves but had no bad attitude when execution. When they entered into the execution ground, they were steady, fearless and silent. It ended without any barriers. The names of criminals (original note—the number means the age.): Zhou Jitang(34), Fang Jiaquan(28), Yang Guangyuan(21), Xu Xiangqing(17), Zhang Mangun(23), Gu Chuanyun(30) and Chen Kunlin(29).

to military disciplines conference, and to avoid confusion, council of military court was adopted here.

The diaries didn't record such criminals as Zhou Jitang. From January 24th and 26th diaries, Zhou Jitang and other people were sentenced for guerrilla. January 24th recorded:

> Investigate the violation of military disciplines of Zhou Jitang and other people all days. The undesirable youth collected as einsatz gruppen and actively acted in the Shanghai battles based on the so-called guerrilla and with the purpose of troubling the Japanese rear. After Nanjing was occupied by the enemy, they came to Guangdong and only few still acted underground activities. Most people were rascal (original note—hooligan) and participated because of the force of life.

January 26th recorded:

> Complete the summary of the violation of military disciplines of Zhou Jitang and other five persons. The summary is "the accused colluded as a party. It was a group that would jeopardize the imperial army. Their acts not only did harm to the imperial army but also stopped the Japan's peace which the imperial expected. Therefore, there was no doubt that these ferocious people should be annihilated and given strict sanction and the most severe punishment."

The details of this case are unknown today. For example, what crimes the accused committed? How they defend themselves? What laws the punishment is pursuant to? The military disciplines conference[2] was determined to give "the most severe punishment" before the trial. The trial was a form. From the opening to the sentence and from the sentence to the execution, it took only one day and the form was too easy. Some Japanese often claimed that Japanese army trialed the Chinese army and citizens by the military discipline conference and the underlying meaning was that it was "lawful". The case of Zhou Jitang told us that such trials were meaningless. Besides, if we study the cases that some Japanese emphasized to trial Japanese army crimes by the council of military court, we can find that the trials are unfair.

In the cases of Japanese army's raping trialed by the 10th division and council of military court of central China army, the most severe punishment was 4-year-prisonment and offense of intentional homicide and

[2]The people in military disciplines conference were the same as those of council of military court.

raping were exempted from prosecution. For example, the homicide case of such people as Tsuji (considering so-called reputation, when the journals and diaries were published, the names of the parties only left a word) in the first artillery of Backing mountains:

> The accused killed three Chinese people because they were drunk and driven by the strong hatred towards the enemy at 5p.m in November 29th, the 12th year of Showa (1937) in the Jia Xing camp.

In the "summary of the criminal facts", the so-called "drunk" and "hatred towards the enemy" actually were to seek leniency and leave a hint for the council of the military court of the Japanese army. Nowadays, some Japanese still think of "drunk" as "a reason". However, firstly, according to the criminal laws of Japanese army, murder shall be determined to death penalty, life imprisonment and long sentence. Secondly, killing three people was more serious than killing one. Thirdly, although it was understandable, it had the bottom lines and the heavy sentence couldn't be reduced to the light sentence and exempted from the sentence. However, Tsuji killed three people without reason and was exempted from prosecution due to the so-called "Article 301 Notice" in the council of military court.

Another example was the raping case of the 6th division army and the 6th Division infantry the 45th wing the 7th squadron private first class.

> When the accused went to Feng Ting town to collect grains and fodders in the daytime of November 27th, the 12th year of Showa, he saw a Chinese girl (15-year-old) trying to run away, then he caught her and raped her.

The accused undertook the official business and raped in the daytime, which was arrogant. However, he was also exempted from prosecution due to the "Article 301 Notice" of the council of the military court.

Not only was the sentence inappropriate, but also the investigation of the suspects was unfair. For example, there was enough evidence about one of the reserve private first class killing someone. However, he was still psychiatrically evaluated by the lieutenant Hayao Torao(professor of Kanazawa Medical University)of the military medical department. As many as seven categories and nearly thirty subjects were identified, such as the so-called "ability of guidance", "ability of acceptance", "ability of memory" (especially the ability to remember something new), "memory", "knowledge", "criticism", "delusion and illusion", "conceptual connection", "coercion concept", "feeling", "will" and so on. The conclusion of his identification was also complex. It was mainly that Zhi was drunk so that before the first consciousness awakened, he was dominated by the second consciousness (original note—extremely primitive). As a result, he misread the facts and took inappropriate actions. No one can get a "normal" result by such complex check. So it was more justification for the suspect than an identification. Such investigation and the sentence against such Chinese people as Zhou were as different as night and day.

The details of the case of Zhou Jitang and other people were unknown but it was sure not to cost the property of that Japanese army. The records and diaries had the record of the case of Li Xinmin, Lu Danshu and other people throwing the native grenades and the Japanese army free from damages. If it caused serious damage to the Japanese army, it must have records. Therefore, the severe punishment against Zhou Jitang and other people and the light punishment against Tsuji and other people illustrated that although the military disciplines conference had the name of trial, the repression was the facts. The trial has no relation with justice regardless of the "law" itself.

Compared Zhou Jitang case and the Tokyo trial which gives the defendant full right of defense thus long-delayed, it is clear that what the winners' trial is and what the civilized trial is.

Bibliography

1. Kyokuto Kokusai Gunji Saiban Kohan Kankokai (Eds.). (1948). *Kyokuto kokusai gunji saiban kohan kiroku* [Trial Records of the International Military Tribunal for the Far East]. Tokyo: Fuzanbo.
2. Nitta, M. (Ed.). (1968). *Kyokuto kokusai gunji saiban sokkiroku* [Stenographic Records of the International Military Tribunal for the Far East] (Vol. 1). Tokyo: Yushodo Shoten.
3. Tokyo Saiban Shiryo Kankokai (Ed.). (1995). *Tokyo saiban kyakka miteishutsu bengogawa shiryo* [Rejected and Unsubmitted Documents of the Defense Side in the Tokyo Trials] (Vol. 8). Tokyo: Kokusho Kankokai.
4. Asahi Shinbun Hotei Kishadan (Ed.). (1946). *Tokyo saiban* [The Tokyo Trials] (Vol. 1). Japan: Nyususha.
5. Kyokuto Kokusai Gunji Saiban Kenkyukai (Ed.). (1947). *Kyokuto kokusai gunji saiban kenkyu* [Research on the Trials of the International Military Tribunal for the Far East] (Vol. 1). Tokyo: Heiwa Shobo.

6. Kyokuto Kokusai Gunji Saiban Kenkyukai (Ed.). (1948). *Kyokuto kokusai gunji saiban kenkyu* [Research on the Trials of the International Military Tribunal for the Far East] (Vol. 2). Tokyo: Heiwa Shobo.
7. Takayanagi, K. (1948). *Kyokuto saiban to kokusaiho* [The Far East Trials and International Law].
8. Stimson, H. L. (1947, January). The Nuremberg Trial: Landmark in Law Foreign Affair. *Foreign Affairs.*
9. Tanaka, M. (1952). *Paru hakasejutsu, shinri no sabaki, nihon muzairon* [Justice Dr. Pal's Statement, Judging Truth, and the Theory That Japan Was Not Guilty]. Japan: Taiheiyo Shuppansha.
10. Takikawa, M. (1952–1953). *Tokyo saiban o sabaku* [Judging the Tokyo Trials] (Vols. 1 and 2). Tokyo: Towasha.
11. Hayashi, I. (1962). *Kyokuto kokusai gunji saiban* [Trials of the International Military Tribunal for the Far East]. Tokyo: Jinbutsu Oraisha.
12. Kiyose, I. (1967). *Hiroku Tokyo saiban* [Confidential Documents and the Tokyo Trials]. Tokyo: Yomiuri Shinbunsha.
13. Kitaoka, T. (2006). *Tokyo saiban wa dechiage datta* [The Tokyo Trials Were a Fabrication]. Tokyo: Sogo Horei Shuppan Kabushiki Kaisha.
14. Hosoya, C., Ando, N., & Onuma, Y. (Eds.). (1984). *Tokyo saiban o tou: Kokusai shinpojiumu* [Questioning the Tokyo Trials: International Symposium]. Tokyo: Kodansha.
15. Tokyo Saiban Kenkyukai (Ed.). (1984). *Kyodo kenkyu Pal hanketsusho* [Joint Research: Pal's Judgment Document] (Vols. 1 and 2). Tokyo: Kodansha.
16. Minear, R. H. (1985). *Tokyo saiban: shosha no sabaki* [Victors' Justice: The Tokyo War Crimes Trial] (N. Ando, Trans.). Tokyo: Fukumura Shuppan Kabushiki Kaisha.
17. Shioda, M. (1988). *Tenno to Tojo Hideki no kuno--A-kyu senpan no isho to shusen hiroku* [The Suffering of the Emperor and Hideki Tojo—Testaments of Class-A War Crimes and Confidential Documents at the End of the War]. Tokyo: Nihon Bungeisha.
18. Awaya, K. (Ed.). (1989). *Tokyo Saibanron* [Theory of the Tokyo Trials]. Tokyo: Otsuko Shoten.
19. Yamagiwa, A. (Ed.). (1990). *Shiryo Nihon senryo 1 tennosei* [Documents on Japanese Occupation 1, the Emperor System] (M. Nakamura, Trans.). Tokyo: Otsuko Shoten.
20. Terasaki, H. (Ed.). (1991). *Showa tenno dokuhakuroku: Terasaki Hidenari goyoka nikki* [Records of the Showa Emperor's Monologues: The Journal of Hidenari Terasaki]. Tokyo: Bungei Shunjusha.
21. Fuji, N. (1995). *"Nankin daigyakusatsu" wa kou shite tsukurareta--Tokyo saiban teki giman* [This Is How the Rape of Nanking Was Created—Deception in the Tokyo Trials]. Tokyo: Tendensha.

22. Röling, B. V. A., Cassese, A., & Kurihara, K. (Commentary). (1996). *Rerinku hanji no Tokyo saiban* [Justice Röling's Tokyo Trials] (N. Kosuge, Trans.). Tokyo: Shinchosha.
23. Ogawa, S. (2000). *Aru gun homukan no nikki: Furoku* [Journal of a Military Law Officer: Supplement]. Tokyo: Misuzu Shobo.
24. *Shokun!* (2001). *Maboroshiha, chukanha, daigyakusatsuha goudou daian-keeto* [The Fiction Faction, the Middle Ground Faction, and the Massacre Faction: Major Joint Study of Three Factions]. Tokyo: Bungei Shunjusha.
25. Higurashi, Y. (2002). *Tokyo saiban no kokusai kankei* [International Relations of the Tokyo Trials]. Tokyo: Bokutakusha.
26. Chaen, Y. (2003). Senpan saiban no hoteki datosei o tou [Questioning the Legal Validity of War Crime Trials]. In Taiheiyo Senso Kenkyukai (Ed.), *Tokyo saiban* [Tokyo Trials]. Tokyo: Shinjinbutsu Oraisha.
27. Ushimura, K. (2005). *Bunmei no sabaki o koeru—Tainichi senpan saiban dokkai no yomi* [Beyond the Judgment of Civilization: The Intellectual Legacy of the Japanese War Crimes Trials]. Tokyo: Chuo Koron Shinsha.
28. Yang, X. (2005). *Nanjing datusha shiliao ji: 7 dongjing shenpan* [A Collection of Historical Materials Relating to Nanjing Massacre: 7 Tokyo Trial]. Nanjing: Jiangsu People's Publishing and Phoenix Publishing House.
29. Awaya, K. (2006). *Tokyo saiban e no michi* [Road to the Tokyo Trials]. Tokyo: Kodansha.
30. Yomiuri Shinbun Senso Sekinin Kensho Iinkai (Ed.). (2006). *Kensho senso sekinin* [Verifying Responsibility for War] (Vol. I). Tokyo: Chuo Koron Shinsha.
31. Cheng, Z. (2007). *Cong dongjing shenpan dao dongjing shenpan* [From "Tokyo Trial" to Tokyo Trial]. Shanghai: Historical Review.
32. Onuma, Y. (2007). *Tokyo saiban, senso sekinin, sengo sekinin* [The Tokyo Trials, Responsibility for the War, and Responsibility After the War]. Tokyo: Toshindo.
33. Higurashi, Y. (2008). *Tokyo saiban* [The Tokyo Trials]. Tokyo: Kodansha.
34. Hosaka, M. (2008). *Tokyo saiban no kyokun* [Lessons of the Tokyo Trials]. Tokyo: Asahi Shinbun Shuppan.
35. Totani, Y. (2008). *Tokyo saiban: Dainiji sekai taisengo no ho to seigi no tsuikyu* [The Tokyo War Crimes Trial: The Pursuit of Justice in the Wake of World War II]. Tokyo: Misuzu Shobo.
36. Boister, N., & Cryer, R. (2012). *Tokyo saiban o saihyoka suru* [Tokyo International Military Tribunal: A Reappraisal] (K. Awaya, H. Fujita, Y. Takatori, & R. Okada, Trans.) Tokyo: Nippon Hyoron Sha.
37. Totani, Y. (2015). *Futashika na seigi–Bishikyu senpan saiban no kiseki* [Uncertain Justice—The Trajectory of Class-B and -C War Crimes Trials]. Tokyo: Iwanami Shoten.
38. Center for the Tokyo Trial Studies. (2015). *Dongjing shenpan zai taolun* [The Restudy on the Tokyo Trial]. Shanghai: Shanghai Jiao Tong University Press.

CHAPTER 7

Evidence-Take Nanjing Massacre as Example

For a long time, the Japan's right wing has alleged that the Tokyo trial is dominated by winners which is unfair. Yamada Fuji, who served in the second demobilization department and claimed that participated in most of the trials, wrote the Tokyo trial is "extremely unfair" when examine the evidence given by the prosecution and the defense in his book,"The Nanjing Massacre was Created in this way -- the Deception of Tokyo trials".

> The judgment of the court is based on the evidence and the final statement of the prosecution ... I am not saying that the evidence presented by the prosecution is all wrong, but that the evidence presented by the defense is all right. I just mean that as a Japanese with common sense, when examining the evidence of both prosecution and defense, I truly think that the evidence presented by the prosecution contained a great deal of distortion, exaggeration and fiction, and at the same time I felt that the evidence presented by the defense was more reasonable.

In the 1980s, Masaaki Tanaka, the representative figure of fiction school in Japan, made up a "fact" in the "Fiction of the Nanjing massacre" in order to deny the Nanjing massacre from its root. That is, before the Tokyo trial, the world didn't know that there were "Nanjing massacre" which were completely fabricated by the Tokyo trial.

Z. Cheng, *A History of War Crimes Trials in Post 1945 Asia-Pacific*,
https://doi.org/10.1007/978-981-13-6697-0_7

Tanaka's "fiction" theory is widely quoted in Japanese right-wing works. In "the real Nanjing massacre", Sakura Um said, "It is the far east international military trial that describe Nanjing massacre as a problem at first. Actually, there is no saying of "Nanjing massacre" at that moment." Matsumura Toshio said in "the big question about the Nanjing massacre" that through "careful review of contemporary information, the documents from Far East International Military trial and Nanjing military court, as well as the newly prepared information of China and witness's testimony after the problem arose again, to see the growth process of this matter as a rumor is pretty clear". In the 1980s, Aroken-ichi (Hatakenaka Hideo), who interviewed more than 40 "parties", said in "Documentary: Nanjing massacre":

> I think most of the exhibits and testimony claiming to prove the Nanjing massacre contain false contents. Starting from the materials put forward before the court of Tokyo trials, there are a large number of reports posted on the first-class newspapers and other media, so it is more difficult to see the truth of Nanjing massacre. We get lost when deciding what kind of exhibits and testimony is trust worthy.

The fiction school unanimously think that the Tokyo trial to determine the case of the Nanjing massacre was entirely favoring the prosecution, ignoring the "true" and "reasonable evidence" of the defense. Is that true? In this chapter, we examine the defense's "reasonable evidence" with firsthand materials.

1 The Reevaluation of the Testimony of Matsui Iwane

There are 11 statements in Matsui Iwane's affidavit, the first responsible person of the Nanjing massacre, and we will select the most important to refute as follows.

1.1 Is It an "Accident" to Attack Nanjing?

The first statement of the affidavit said that the reason for Japanese troops stationed in the south of the Yangtze River after the "813 incident" were that "the soldiers and civilians who staying in Shanghai were threatened", and the Shanghai garrison was formed to "protect the life and property safety of residents in the vicinity of that place". The second statement says, "I am specially transferred to Shanghai's dispatched troops as their commander from the reserve service" in order to "quickly solve the incident on the spot, so as not to aggravate the military tension between two parties". In his fourth statement, "the composition of China's army and the decision to attack Nanjing", he said,

> Selecting the Nanjing as the base area, the China army was gradually developing to the north to get prepared for a large-scale war, and ready for attacking Jiangsu and Zhejiang. If we could not seize Nanjing, it was impossible to maintain the security of the central china, and thus the rights and interests of our side could not be maintained. Therefore, in order to restore the overall peace of the south of the Yangtze River, Japan decided to seize Nanjing.

How did the "8.13 incident" break out? Is the attack on Nanjing a plan or an accident? These question about Nanjing atrocities was not the same thing. There are two reasons for me to clarify that difference: one is that the above statement made by Matsui Iwane in Tokyo trials covered up his performance, and the other is that this cover-up affected the identification of his liability.

From the existing Japanese literature, it can be seen that the initial dispatch order of Japanese senior officials did limit their aim to "wipe out the enemy near Shanghai and occupy the important boundary of northern Shanghai". Even with the increasing investment of both sides and the overall escalation of the war, the Japanese joint staff issued two orders which order the troops could not cross the Wufu boundary and Xicheng boundary. Constantly violating orders of the Japanese central command and expanding the war, especially the attack on Nanjing, is completely the result of the Japanese "ambition", among which Matsui Iwane will undoubtedly play the greatest role. Looking at the diary of Matsui himself and his family, he covered up his performance when engaging in the trial in Tokyo.

Matsui Iwane lied that his diary had been burned down when he was questioned by the court. When the Nanjing massacre caused fierce controversy in Japan in the 1980s, Masaaki Tanaka found a batch of documents of wartime and postwar period, including Matsui Iwane's diary in the relics storeroom of the 34th company of self-defense forces (which his wife stayed). Diary from November 1, 1937 (Suzhou river battle) to February 28, 1938 (the year also called "triumph") is complete, but the part before October is missing. When this existing volume was published by hibiscus study in Japan under the title "the Diary of Matsui Iwane during wartime", Japanese scholars pointed out that the collector Tanaka had tampered with the original diary in more than 900 places. Therefore, the Japanese veteran accompany club revised the punctuation and select the abridged parts to add into the "Nanjing war history data collection". In 1992, the researchers of the Department of war history of the Japan Defense Research Institute returned to the same library and found the Matsui Iwane's diary from August 15 to October 30. This part and the supplement has been collected and published in "the Nanjing war history data collection II" (perhaps to avoid misunderstanding, reprinting version omitted punctuation). Now let's take a look at what Matsui Iwane himself wrote in his diary.

The next day after the "813 incident" broke out, Japan decided to set up "Shanghai dispatch troops", and appointed Matsui Iwane as commander. In the afternoon, receiving the order given by the vice minister of army ministry to via express telegram which command him to go to Beijing, Matsui quickly arrived at the official residence of Sugiyama Hajime, the Japanese army minister from the hotel in that night. He recorded the feeling of meeting this time in the diary:

> The army has not yet determined whether to take the China as the main battlefield. Instead, they only want to send their troop to shanghai in order to back up the Navy. At this time, the government withdrew the previous orders which require to limit the scale of war and solve it by local battles because the central China was sending troops. It urged the Nanjing government to behave and restore the comprehensive relations between China and Japan. The naval authorities took a tough stance, but the army, especially the staff headquarters, has not yet had an explicit attitude. The army still targeted to contain the army of northern China, and the government's attitude is still unanimous. The foreign affairs authorities also vainly hope to solve it through diplomatic negotiations, and the intention to avoid military conflicts has not faded. The attitude of our government and the Ministry of military affairs is quite worrying for the future development of the current situation.

Okada and other defense witnesses once said Matsui felt "regretful" for the Sino-Japanese war, so did Matsui Iwane "worry" about it? There is a definite answer in Matsui's diary of the first day. In his diary on August 15, he said, "we should raise the hammer to awaken the Chinese authorities and let them feel the pain of war". The next day when he meets with Sugiyama:

> The current situation today has entered to the stage that the so-called non-expansion policy cannot work. Considering the comprehensive policy towards China and the war with the china national army, it is advisable to devote all efforts to oppress Central China, especially the Nanjing government, through force and economy to tackle this problem totally. If our army looks forward to avoiding fighting, or cares too much about Russian or other foreign relations, it can only make our future national policies in danger ... For the above reasons, our army should send the necessary troops (five divisions) to China for the purpose of annihilate the Nanjing government at one stroke. Besides the military force, economic and financial coercion shall be more effective.

Matsui Iwane said that Sugiyama responded to his suggestion: "Personally I have no objection" to his proposal, but he "didn't agree" after he considered the opinions of this department. Matsui showed "great regret" for "lack of determination" of army departments. That afternoon, Matsui met with Yonai Mitsumasa, the minister of the navy, and "the minister's opinion on the current situation is coincident with me", so Matsui was "very glad". Later, in the days before departure, Matsui visited military and political leaders repeatedly and promoted his proposition—"wiped out the Nanjing government at one stroke". Because the Japanese high-level officials at that time still insisted that the purpose of stationing troops in Shanghai is to fight a local war, Matsui felt disappointed because of the attitude of key figures, though he got some echo among military and political officials who held no real power. For example, on the 17th, he visited Fumimaro Konoe, the prime minister, and Fumimaro "did not make his own attitude clear", which made Matsui feel "regretful". On the 18th, Matsui met with Hayao Tada, who has just taken over as the deputy chief of staff headquarters; Nakajima Tetsuhide, minister of general affairs; Kanji Ishiwara, minister of operations; and Masaharu Homma, minister of intelligence, etc. Matsui felt "deeply regretful" because of the "negative" attitude of them, especially Ishihara. The specific content of this meeting is not contained in Matsui's diary, but it is recorded in detail in the diary of the chief of staff of Shanghai's dispatch army. Matsui believed that "the local solutions and no-expansion policy should be abandoned", and "necessary forces should be resolutely used to make quick decisions in the traditional spirit". It is more necessary to use it in Nanjing than to use the main force in the north China, and "Nanjing should be captured in a short time".

This aim of occupying Nanjing and overthrowing the Nanjing national government was constantly put forward by Matsui and never changed before the Japanese high-level officials finally decided to attack Nanjing. For example, on September 17 when the battle of Songhu was fought inextricably in Baoshan, he attached his "personal opinion" which set "invading Nanjing" as the third stage of war in his "opinions of the army" to the deputy chief of staff. At that time, it was completely unexpected that Chinese troops would collapse and retreat at the end of October, so he expected the third stage to start in March next year. It can also be seen that Matsui's determination to attack Nanjing is unshakable. In late October, when the war in Shanghai came to an end, Matsui wrote in his diary on the 20th, "I entrusted Colonel Suzuki to pass my opinion to the deputy chief staff officer". With the end of the campaign in western Shanghai, there should be at least two front armies, and the operational goal of the army should be Nanjing. After three days, he wrote, "on this day, Major Nakayama returned to capital, and I entrusted letters to minister Sugiyama. The main message is: ...Thirdly, the goal of fighting in Southern of Yangtze River should be Nanjing anyway...; Fourthly, Japan's policy should focus on overthrowing the Nanjing government at present". On November 15 when Eisa Aki, the head of the strategy department of staff and Shibashiyama Kaneshiro the head of the military affair department on a business trip to Shanghai dispatch army, Matsui urged "the necessity of capturing Nanjing". On November 22, in its "statement of opinions on future operations" he said once again the front army of central China should "take advantage of the enemy's current decline to conquer Nanjing" (Matsui clearly recorded in his diary that this opinion was "personal opinion"). On November 25, Hayao Tada, the deputy chief of staff called and said that the Japanese military action could be extended to Wuxi and Huzhou, but it should not go west anymore. Matsui dismissed it as "following the principle of appeasement, which is incredible absurd" in his diary.

From Matsui's diary, it can be seen that his statement about the explanation of the troop rally and attack on Nanjing before the court of Tokyo trials obviously covered up the truth. This cover-up directly affected the court's determination of his liability.

1.2 *Did Matsui Iwane Constantly Emphasize the Bearing and Discipline of the Army?*

In the Article 2 of Matsui's affidavit, he mentioned the twelve years of his career in China. In addition to his devotion to the Sino-Japanese goodwill, Matsui mainly explained that he particularly ordered the subordinates to carry out this spirit thoroughly and then made the following instructions on the occasion of the troops so that this dispatch would not result in the long-term mutual resentment of the two countries and lay the foundation of the future goodwill. Firstly, the battle in the vicinity of Shanghai was specially designed to the enemies who challenged the Japanese army and the army should endeavor to conciliate and care for the Chinese officers and people. Secondly, the army should pay attention to the noninvolvement of the residents and troops of all countries and maintain a close communication with the officers and troops of all countries in order to avoid misunderstandings. In the Article 3 "the war situation in the vicinity of Shanghai", Matsui said that he repeatedly ordered his subordinates to protect and conciliate Chinese law-abiding people and respect the rights and interests of foreign countries. For example, based on his order, the battle near the south area of Shanghai was ended without destroying the city. In the Article 5 "the disposal on the occasion of the Nanjing occupation and the so-called Nanjing plunder and atrocities", he said that he endeavored to confine the war to a general battle in accordance with the consistent policy of their government. Also, on the basis of his belief that Japan's nurturance could produce the coprosperity of Japan and China, Matsui tried his best not to make this battle into an overall national struggle. Therefore, he proposed the careful attention of the army. Due to the foregoing purpose, he specially ordered to attach importance to the bearing and discipline of the army.

The related statement by Matsui Iwane was consistently proved by the defense. For example, Iinuma Mamoru said that General Matsui repeatedly instructed the army to completely eradicate the unlawful practices; Ogawa Sekijiro, the chief of judicial department said that Commander Matsui demanded the strict bearing and discipline of the army and the strict application of law in order to protect the rights and interests of Chinese law-abiding people and foreign countries. Due to the special situation of Iinuma Mamoru and Ogawa Sekijiro, Iinuma Mamoru said that some instructions were personally conveyed by him (as on December 4) and Ogawa Sekijiro' was in charge of the bearing and discipline of the army. Therefore, it was difficult to make a substantial refutation without powerful internal evidence. The prosecutor of the Tokyo trial did not argue because of the lack of such evidence.

Today, it is surprising that the record of these incidents happens to be the disproof of their testimony in the Tokyo trial through opening up the diaries of the parties concerned. By checking Matsui Iwane's diary, there was no record of ordering the strict bearing and discipline of the army, no matter in the battle of Songhu or in the whole process of the attack on Nanjing. Not only did Matsui's diary lack such record, but also there was no record of Matsui's demand for the bearing and discipline of the army in *The Diary of Iinuma Mamoru* from August 15 to December 17. Generally speaking, whether there was record could not simply equal to whether it was a fact—if a diary was a rough note and something was not important, the possibility of not recording might not be excluded. The difference between Matsui Iwane's diary and Iinuma Mamoru's diary was that both of them were fairly detailed. The key was that not only Matsui and Iinuma but also other defense witnesses said that these instructions were specially emphasized by Matsui. Consequently, the related record could not be completely missed. Its absence in the diary could only prove that their testimony in the Tokyo trial was not true. The first mention of the bearing and discipline of the army in Iinuma's diary and Matsui's diary was on December 8 when the Japanese army was blamed for their performance after entering Nanjing. Because their performance made the Japanese supreme military and political authorities feel pressure by the protests from Western media and western people in China, especially in Nanjing. The coincidence of them could also prove from the other side that Matsui Iwane never gave instructions of the so-called strict bearing and discipline of the army until December 17.

If Matsui Iwane and Iinuma Mamoru deliberately confused the facts, then Ogawa Sekijiro's testimony was completely fabricated (later in detail).

1.3 Did Matsui Iwane Have the Intention of a Comprehensive Cooperation and Negotiation with the Chinese Government?

Matsui Iwane stated in the Article 6 "Action After the Occupation of Nanjing" of his affidavit that it was necessary to fully cooperate and negotiate with the administration of Chiang Kai Shek. He specially sent people to Fujian and Guangdong to get in touch with Chen Yi and

Song Ziwen when promoting Chinese around Shanghai to make efforts together.

Was it possible to make a judgment by Matsui Iwane's self-narration based on the foregoing Matsui's continuous appeal for the conquest of Nanjing and the overthrow of the Chinese government? Although the so-called cooperation and negotiation in Matsui's affidavit was after the occupation of Nanjing, it was unreal in terms of his aforementioned persistent proposal. Here, we might as well check Matsui's diary after the Japan's occupation of Nanjing again so that we could discover whether Matsui had different considerations at that time. He wrote on December 30 and 31:

> Today, I met Li Zeyi, Chen Zhongfu and Xuan Ye et al., instructing the future strategy and adopted their suggestions. It was said that the peace movement in Shanghai has gradually matured and gathered force. Recently, Li has been to Hong Kong to get in touch with Song Ziwen et al. in the purpose of the future trend of the National Government. I told him that he might exploit Song Ziwen, but she could never participate in the new regime. According to Chen's words, Juzheng's wife in Hankou came to Shanghai to find out our intentions. I generally told her that there was no special requirement currently except for anticommunism and the proposal of Asia. In addition, Juzheng and some people in the National Government hoped to peacefully negotiate with Japan under the premise of Chiang Kai Shek's resignation. I told them that the prerequisite of the new regime was to dismiss the current National Government after Chiang's resignation.

Matsui also wrote in the margin of this day's diary:

> As the representative of Tang Shaoyi, Wen Zongyao came to visit and expressed that Chiang must resign and go travelling in any case (referring to going abroad – the quotation) and the independence of Guangdong and Guangxi must be based on severing ties with the United Kingdom. I agreed with his opinion. Wen Laichun went to Guangdong with Tang's intention. We also sent Colonel Takaji to assist him. We had to deal with Guangdong and Guangxi because our army intended to attack Guangdong. Therefore, this matter was worth studying.

He wrote the report of Tsukada Osamu who was the chief of the front army of central China and returned from Tokyo and Matsui Iwane's opinion on January 2:

> Chief Tsukada returned from Tokyo. According to his report: firstly, in terms of the operations of the army (referring to the foregoing army – the quotation), the General Staff was extremely passive and unwilling to extend the future range of operations; secondly, the government had not made any decisions on the future aftermath. It was surprising that there was still no draft of the compromise with the National Government or the establishment of a new regime; thirdly, the General Staff had no passion for the army's strategy and certainly disagreed with my suggestion to dispatching staffs. It especially did not reply to the letter I directly wrote to the minister, but ask major general Tsukada to negotiate with the undersecretary again. Its indecision surprised me. In a word, our government's realization of the current National Government was the prerequisite for the future operations and strategies.

On January 4, he wrote that Matsui Iwane discussed the aftermath of the situation with the Japanese ambassador to China Kawagoe Shigeru and the minister of foreign affairs Kawai Tatsuo. Article 1 was that the government must deny the National Government in some form. The next day, Matsui summoned the staffs of the navy and Funatsu Tatsuichiro to convey the content of the discussion of the day before. Funatsu Tatsuichiro came to China for a private negotiation after the war broke out. His public identity was the chairman of the Textile Industry Association in China and then the consultant of Dadao Government. Matsui wrote on January 6:

> Wen Zongyao visited to consult the independence movement of Guangdong and Guangxi. He would set out from Shanghai to Hong Kong on January 8 in order to reach an agreement with local people. In accordance with our agreement, we would send Colonel Takaji to Hong Kong. If possible, we would send Lieutenant Nakai to Hong Kong for assistance.

He wrote on January 7:

> Recently, I contacted the embassy and the navy and learned that our government had decided to deny the National Government. We unanimously agreed that the declaration of statements in some form was crucial to the future operations and strategies. I submitted this suggestion to the minister and the general secretary. Meanwhile, I let the navy and the embassy respectively submit their proposals. I also asked the director of personnel to submit a private letter to the Prime Minister Fumimaro, the Foreign

Minister Hirota and the General Sugiyama. The letter referred to several problems and put forward the related solutions. For example, with respect to the future operations and tasks associated with the foregoing general policy, a special organ for implementation would be established under my jurisdiction in Shanghai. It aimed at recruiting staffs for the ministry of finance of overseas naval affairs and the ministry of commerce and studying the future problems of military affairs, politics and economy, etc.

He also wrote in the margin of this day's diary:

I got in contact with the tenth division for the sake of such affairs as the occupation of the Longhai Railway near Xuzhou, the cut of salt transportation and the expansion of the regime in Zhejiang.

He wrote on January 10:

According to the mainland's news report, the cabinet meeting was held in Tokyo yesterday. The cabinet negotiated with the supreme headquarters and discussed with the participants. It seemed that they had made more specific decisions on the future China-oriented policies. Although the content was unclear, our government's policy became gradually clearer. It not only made the army's operations and strategies clearer, but also aroused the attention of Chinese people. I appreciated that a clear result led to a more positive action.

He wrote on January 15:

Envoy Ito came to visit and inform us of the government's attitude. The government still hesitated to move forward because the mediation of Germany had not yet ended. (Ito said that) the government should be impelled to make decisions, which was astonishing. Therefore, I summoned the major general Harada and asked for his opinion on the front army for now. Meanwhile, I also ordered him to return to Beijing and castigated the authorities.

He wrote on January 16:

Today, the government issued a statement that from now on the National Government no longer served as an object of the negotiation (that is, the denial of the National Government – the quotation). Although the true meaning was not yet clear, but there was no doubt that this action took a

> step closer to our proposal. The government's decision was still disturbing, so I thought that all aspects should offer advice to the government at this moment to consolidate the future understanding and the future corresponding strategy, definitely, not to say that the battle must be further. After having a deliberate discussion with Envoy Ito, major general Tsukada and major general Harada, I ordered to make the local policies promptly in accordance with our decision.

On January 15, the Japanese government decided to no longer recognize the Chinese government after the cabinet liaison meeting of the Japanese supreme headquarters, so the aforementioned content quoted stopped when Matsui knew that the Japanese government no longer recognized the Chinese government. Although Matsui Iwane's activities to actively overthrow the Chinese government in the future were far beyond the limits of orders, let us put this responsibility on the account of Japan's supreme authorities.

The reason why this section introduces Matsui Iwane's diary during this period in detail is mainly that it is crucial to determine what kind of responsibility Matsui Iwane should bear.

1.4 Was Matsui Iwane Particularly Concerned About the Protection of Western Interests?

Article 2 of Matsui's affidavit stated that attention should be paid to the noninvolvement of residents and armies of all countries. Article 3 stated that he repeatedly ordered his subordinates to respect the rights and interests of foreign countries. Article 6 stated that he was keen to contact with the commanders of the British and American navy and the civil and military officers of all countries in order to appropriately deal with the events in the fighting.

Did Matsui Iwane particularly respect the rights and interests of foreign countries? We still had to check his diary. On August 26, 1937, the British ambassador to China S. M. Knatchbull-Hugessen took the car from Nanjing to Shanghai, being strafed by the Japanese military aircraft near Wuxi and got seriously injured, which made British and other western countries strongly unsatisfied. Japan immediately apologized. Matsui wrote this event on August 30. His mood could also be seen through his record of this event after a few days. He said that he thought it was their naval aircraft. Yesterday, there was the Chinese aircraft painted Japanese

National Flag. Therefore, it could not be asserted that it was the behavior of our army:

> Even if our army strafed, it was inevitable that internal and external people who passed the battlefield without warning might be implicated. Therefore, it was not necessary for our government to express its regret in a hurry. Because it made people feel that the attitude of our government and Shanghai's ministry of foreign affairs and the navy was overly flurried.

In the diary of the same day, Matsui also expressed his dissatisfaction with that the trade activities of British merchant ships were still in progress after the war. He keenly felt that the navy should impose a severe blockade on the Chinese coast. Matsui had a hostile attitude not only to British warships, but also to those warships of all western countries. These warships only normally cruised in the Huangpu River and the Wusong estuary. On September 1, when the third division attacked Wusong Town, a French warship happened to pass by, which was called a prank by Matsui in his diary of the day. Matsui asked the third fleet and the Japanese embassy to make a serious protest to France and demonstrated that the army could not guarantee the safety of the French warships if it happened again in the future. On September 20, he wrote that British merchant ships at the lower reaches of the Huangpu River should leave and said:

> If these ships did not comply with this warning and were still moored at the present location, our army would not bear the responsibilities for their future casualties due to the war.

Matsui wrote in the diary of the next day:

> Today, we sent several shells to the waters near the British ships for threat purposes. These British ships had recently been moored at the lower reaches of the Huangpu River. Two of them suddenly and rapidly set sail, which facilitated us to achieve our goal. One was still stubbornly stopping in the place…

This was Matsui Iwane's real attitude. If Matsui did not completely have no realization of the rights and interests of foreign countries, it could at least be said that it was negligible compared with the needs of the Japanese army. In the diary on October 1, Matsui wrote down that he asked the Japanese embassy to influence western journalists. It was evident that Matsui did not completely ignore the foreign public opinion, but Matsui did not aim at requiring the positive performance of his own army, but aim at the obedience of others and the opposition to the negative reports of foreign media to the Japanese army. When Matsui asked to influence western journalists, he used the word "manipulate" in Chinese characters. He said the reason why he keenly felt it necessary to use the word "manipulate" was that the League of Nations adopted the illegal resolution condemning Japan's bombing of Chinese cities on September 28. There was a note under the word "illegal" in *The Collection of Nanjing War History* including the diary, which referred to the resolution of reproach. Then it also recorded the following paragraph:

> It was surprising that the embassy in Shanghai had never used any methods to bribe the foreign journalists. It was feared that if the military officers of the army and the navy did not make effort and did not take emergency measures, they would bring extremely unfavorable results to the propaganda war in the future.

Matsui Iwane had a special preference for Chinese culture. He continuously wrote poems (most of them were seven-character poems) even during the fierce war. So, his true meaning was to let the Chinese people get the understanding at a glance by the Chinese characters of "manipulate" and "illegal".

After the breakthrough of the Chinese army's defense line in the suburbs of Shanghai, such as Dachang, the Japanese army's shellfire spread to the city and had a direct conflict with the interests of some western countries. On October 29, the third division of the Japanese army bombarded many places in Shanghai. Its bombardment in the Jessfield Park (now the Zhongshan Park) caused the casualties of several British soldiers, so Britain made a protest against the Japanese army. Although Matsui expressed his regret in his diary, but he thought the reason was that the British army did not withdraw to the Zhongshan Bridge in accordance with our request. On the same day, the Japanese army bombarded the Avenue Joffre in the French Concession (now the Huaihai Road). Matsui thought it was the prank and strategy of the Chinese army. On October 31, Matsui said in his diary that the spread of bombardment into the British jurisdiction was due to the British army adjacent to the area protected by the Chinese army. There was a following sentence that could highly reflect Matsui's displeasure: "the British and French armies took the sympathy and support of the Chinese army from the beginning". Therefore, he believed that the Japanese army should take a tough position.

With the collapse of the Chinese army, the attitude of the Western embassies and the army in Shanghai army began to soften. Therefore, Matsui was more relaxed than before. On November 2, he wrote in the diary that Britain, America, France, Italy and other countries had a general understanding of our policy. So, Matsui did not add proviso when requiring divisions to protect the property of foreigners in southwestern Shanghai. However, this was not to say that Matsui's position had been fundamentally changed. There was no change in his position of the Western countries' obedience to the Japanese army. There was a record in the diary of November 10 that could reflect the opinion of Matsui:

> The First Meeting with the Captain of the British Fleet
>
> Today, I meet the captain of the British fleet and the commander of the army in the school of Jiangwan. The British captain changed his rough manners in the past and repeatedly expressed that the British army did not intend to obstruct the Japanese army's fighting. I'd rather say that he tickled me by pretending to be poor. After I greeted him with the general international etiquette, I announced that our army would use the Suzhou River, the Huangpu River and the railway for recharge, and take the necessary means of self-defense against the obstructers no matter they were Chinese or foreigners. The British chief said he would consult with the consul general and other people about measures, which I thought it necessary to make them act completely in accordance with the will of the Japanese army…
>
> After the meeting, I also met with the British, American, French and Italian military officers of their embassies in China. I mentioned the foregoing words of the British captain and hoped that the governments and the armies of all countries could properly handle them. The attitude of these military officers was modest and courteous. It seemed that they expressed their respect for the Japanese army and me. In fact, they were afraid of the power of the Japanese army.

It could be seen from this record that the premise of Matsui Iwane's international etiquette was that the western countries did not intend to obstruct the Japanese army. On November 17, Matsui went to the British navy flagship to pay the captain of the British fleet a return visit. The British captain was extremely courtesy. Matsui not only expressed a gentle attitude like the day before, but also said no harm to the rights of all countries and the peace of Japan, etc. However, when Matsui summoned Envoy Ito Nobufumi who was on his side on the same day, his true thoughts were another different tone:

> Today, I summoned Envoy Ito to come to the headquarters and talked about my opinions on the disposal of the Shanghai concessions in the future. He completely agreed with me and agreed to make effort to urge the foreign authorities in the future. In addition, in terms of the general international situation, there was no need to worry about the British and American navies. Speech and action should take advantage of the war situation that was in my favor. In the future, the common concession as well as the French concession should strive for prohibiting the Chinese government and Chinese people from the anti-Japanese behavior. Therefore, the Chinese government would be clearly aware of giving up the so-called will of the dependence on Europe and America and the sustained Anti-Japanese War.

On November 21, Matsui Iwane ordered the Japanese military officer in China, Harada Kumakichi, to transfer to the authorities of French concession to prohibit the anti-Japanese activities, and threatened if they could not meet our requirements, our army would take measures in accordance with the needs of the war. On November 24, when the French commander of the army visited Matsui for the first time, his attitude was extremely courtesy as the British captain. However, the French embassy and its authorities were reluctant to the requirements of the Japanese army, so Matsui directly said some tough words. For example, if the French authorities could not understand his sincerity (referring to be obedient to the Japanese army—the quotation) but blindly advocate the privilege of the French concession, he would take resolute measures against the French army near the south city. On November 26, the captain of the French navy in Shanghai and Consul General of Shanghai paid a visit to Matsui. Matsui wrote in his diary:

> In addition to their ceremonial visits, their intention was to hope that our army would take a firm attitude towards the actions of the French concession. I said the French army must cooperate with the Japanese army in the

> French concession, especially in the south city. To this end, for the sake of our army's supply liaison in south city, our army needed to use part of the river bank of the French concession for transportation. They had no objection to the cooperation with our army, but they were hard to recognize from the treaty and the rights of France that the armed soldiers would pass through the French concession. I said, in this way, we would have to consider taking measures against the French army in the south city. I hoped that they could block the national bank of China in the concession while intimidating them...

On December 3, the 101st division of the Japanese army demonstrated in the public concession in Shanghai. When it went to Nanjing Road, the division was thrown with hand grenades by passers-by, which caused three Japanese soldiers and one embassy inspector injured (young men who cast bombs were shot on the spot). The concession authorities were forced to agree that if the Japanese army thought it necessary to carry out the self-defense, they could take their own action to clean up the enemies in the concession. Matsui said it was contributed to the explosion after recording this event.

From the aforementioned content, if Matsui Iwane did not completely ignore the rights and interests of foreign countries, his behavior at most reflected that who complied with him would thrive and differed from the model for the protection of foreign rights and interests as he tried to disguise himself in the Tokyo trial.

1.5 Did Matsui Iwane Apologize for the Event of HMS Ladybird?

Eventually, let's take a look at the actual performance of Matsui in the event of HMS Ladybird. Article 11 "HMS Ladybird, USS Panay and other foreign affairs" of the affidavit stated that Colonel Hashimoto found several ships on the morning of December 12 in the thick fog. These ships carried Chinese soldiers and sailed in the Yangtze River. Colonel Hashimoto ordered to bombard them and the HMS Ladybird was occasionally hit. Matsui immediately ordered the commander of the tenth division to apologize to the captain of the British navy. He also immediately visited and apologized to the commander of the British navy Little after he returned from Nanjing to Shanghai.

On December 12, the day before the fall of Nanjing, four British warships and merchant ships, including the HMS Ladybird, were bombarded near Wuhu by the 13th wing of the field heavy artillery of the Japanese tenth division and got injured. In the afternoon of the same day, the US warship USS Panay and three ships of Exxon Mobil Corporation were bombarded by the planes of the 12th air force of the Japanese navy in the upper reaches of Nanjing and then sunk. This event caused a strong protest of the United Kingdom and the United States. At that time, Japan was not ready to complete a showdown with the United Kingdom and the United States. So, the Japanese government expressed their "Chen Xie" (apology) on December 13. On the next day, Japanese Foreign Minister Hirota Koki wrote to the British and American ambassadors to Japan. In addition to his apology, he also said he would compensate for the loss. The actual pressure on Japan at that time exceeded the Nanjing atrocities themselves. Not only the Japanese government responded quickly, but also people from all walks of life expressed their apology to the United Kingdom and the United States, especially the apology to the United States. For example, the undersecretary of the Ministry of Navy, Yamamoto Isoroku, apologized to the American ambassador; the famous publisher, Iwanami Shigeo, proposed to donate one thousand yen in response to the fund-raising and ship-building compensation initiative of the *Tokyo Daily Newspaper*, etc. The army and the navy sent the commissioners to the present investigation and took some measures because the military was under pressure at that time. For example, Hashimoto Kingoro who later became a famous war criminal was forced to leave the army from the position of the captain of the 13th wing of the field heavy artillery.

The naval air force was who bombard the USS Panay, which was not under Matsui Iwane's jurisdiction. Here, we only checked Matui's attitude toward the HMS Ladybird. The first time Matsui wrote this event in his diary was on the next day. At that time, he had a foreboding that it would cause a quantity of problems in the future. But he also said at the same time: "It was inevitable that the nationals and ships of the third country in this dangerous area suffered from unexpected calamities. Moreover, we had already given notice to the danger of the battlefield in this area". This day's diary ended with this sentence. Obviously, Matsui did not think it was the fault of the Japanese army. The second mention of the event of the HMS Ladybird in his diary was on December 16, three days after the event. At this time, he had been informed of the Japanese government's apology, so the beginning of this day's diary was the following event:

> The Event of the British Warships in Wuhu with regard to the sinking of British warships and merchant ships on December 12, the Japanese government immediately apologized for the protest of the United Kingdom in complete ignorance of the truth, which was overly flurried. But at this point, I could only investigate the truth and sent a telegram to Tokyo of the unnecessary result of the punishment of those responsible.

There was no longer any record of this event in Matsui's diary afterwards. According to Matsui's habit of recording the daily events in detail, if it was true as he said in the Tokyo trial that he immediately ordered the commander of the tenth division to apologize to the captain of the British navy and immediately visited and apologized to the commander of the British navy Little after he returned from Nanjing to Shanghai, his diary could not be left without a single word. There was indeed a mutual visit between Matsui and Little in Matsui's diary. But it did not happen after the event of HMS Ladybird or after Matsui returned from Nanjing to Shanghai, not to say the expression of apology. The meetings of Matsui and Little in the diary were only the foregoing visit of the captain of the British fleet to Matsui on November tenth and Matsui's return visit on November 17. Matsui noted the captain of the British fleet here as "リットル" in the diary of November 17 and he stated in his affidavit that "リットル" referred to "little". Thus it could be seen that Matsui's testimony in the Tokyo trial of the event of the HMS Ladybird was a highly false double perjury. Not only the immediate visit was not true, but also the truth of the apology was definitely the opposite of his actual performance.

Some aspects of the review in this section were too trivial to have an influence on the sentencing even if they were stated in fact, such as the performance of Matsui Iwane in the event of the HMS Ladybird. It was explained in detail in order to show that the false words provided by Matsui in the Tokyo trial were not occasional misstatements but a clear preparation for the purpose of the trial.

As the prosecutor and the court of the Tokyo trial did not have substantial doubts about Matsui's testimony, the tribunal exempted 37 out of 38 crimes prosecuted by the prosecutor, especially the 27th "crime against the implementation of the aggression against China", which should have been inevitable. As a result, there was left an issue whether taking the negative crime of omission as the standard of hanging (the highest sentence) was appropriate and even a problem whether Matsui could be judged as an A class war criminal.

2 A Review of the Testimony of Ogawa Sekijiro

Ogawa Sekijiro was the chief of the judicial department of the tenth army who was most senior among the Japanese full-time legal officers at that time. The tenth army was one of the main forces of the Japanese army attacking Nanjing.

Ogawa landed in November 1937 with the tenth army in Jin Shan Wei. After that, the tenth army headed west to Nanjing along Jiaxing, Pingwang and Huzhou. At the end of December after the conquest of Nanjing, the tenth army moved to Hangzhou and Ogawa never left the army. On January 7 of the next year, Ogawa went to Shanghai to form the council of military court of the front army of central China (the front army was an institution of operation command to coordinate the tenth army with the Shanghai expeditionary army without the judicial department). On February 14, the systems of the front army of central China, the tenth army under its jurisdiction and the Shanghai expeditionary army were revoked. A week later, Ogawa, Commander Matsui Iwane, Chief Tsukada Osamu returned to Japan. As one defense witness in the Tokyo trial on the Nanjing atrocities case, Ogawa was a fairly special one. His special identity was not that he was a person who had experienced the event. Most of the witnesses at that time had personally experienced the Nanjing atrocities. His special identity was also not due to his higher rank. At that time, in addition to some junior military officers, there were also some witnesses who were the high-rank military officers, such as the chief of the Shanghai expeditionary army, Iinuma Mamoru. The special identity of Ogawa was that he was in charge of the two branches of the judicial department of the tenth army and the front army of central China. The bearing and discipline of the army was his profession. Therefore, his testimony was more likely to be regarded as the authoritative testimony by the third outsiders, or at least the professional testimony. Moreover, unlike many witnesses denying that the Japanese army implemented any atrocities, he acknowledged that the Japanese army had limited atrocities. To some extent, it increased the degree of credibility. Although we could not judge what role Ogawa's testimony had played on the determination of the responsibility of the Japanese army in the court at that day, it was of special significance that Ogawa's testimony had not been interrogated by the court and the prosecutor.

2.1 *The Affidavit of Ogawa Sekijiro*

The Affidavit of Ogawa Sekijiro (Defense Document No. 2708, Exhibit No. 3400):

a. I was appointed as the chief of judicial department of the tenth army (Its Commander was lieutenant general Yanagawa) in the end of September 1937. I landed on the North Bank of the Hangzhou Bay and participated in the battle of Nanjing. On January 4 of the following year, I was attached to the front army of central China and directly subordinated to Commander Matsui.
b. After the tenth army landed in the Hangzhou Bay, the army was commanded by the front army of central China. Commander Matsui ordered to strictly abide by the bearing and discipline of the army, including the strict protection of the Chinese law-abiding people and the rights and interests of foreign countries in conformity with law definitely.
c. So far, I had punished 20 offenders concerning the bearing and discipline of the army. Among them, the difficulty of dealing with the offenders concerning the bearing of the army was the charge of rape or adultery.
   The reason was that it was common that Chinese women themselves flirted with the Japanese soldiers. However, once the sex was found by the law-biding people or others, the women immediately changed their attitude and overstated that it was rape. But no matter whether it was rape or not, I would prosecute and deal with the offenders one by one based on severity, such as the severe punishment of them by means of coercion.
d. I entered Nanjing at noon on December 14. When I patrolled part of the military garrison area of the tenth army (southern Nanjing) in the afternoon, I only saw six or seven corpses of Chinese soldiers and no others. The tenth army evacuated Nanjing on December 19 and moved to Hangzhou. When I stayed in Nanjing, I had never heard of the wrongful acts of Japanese soldiers or any wrongful cases that were prosecuted. The Japanese army was in the battle and the military discipline was fairly strict. Neither the order that Commander Matsui handed down to allow any wrongful acts nor the order to tolerate any wrongful acts was possible.
e. The soldiers of the gendarmerie strictly adhered to the order of Commander Matsui. Lieutenant Kamisago (the gendarmerie) protested against the judgment that I was not prosecuted in trial due to my petty misdemeanor and he thought the judgment was too tolerant.

Therefore, the wrongful acts of the Japanese soldiers were severely prohibited.

f. In January 1938, when I met General Matsui in Shanghai's headquarters, General Matsui ordered to severely deal with the crimes with a particularly stressed tone. I implemented my task strictly in accordance with this order.

The written statement in Tokyo on October 6, the 22rd year of Showa (1947)

Ogawa Sekijiro

Ogawa's testimony was read out in the morning of November 7, 1947. Different from the repeated interrogation by the prosecutor of the former Iinuma Mamoru and the latter Sakakibara Kazue, the prosecutor and the court did not interrogate Ogawa's testimony.

The length of Ogawa Sekijiro's testimony was not long in the testimony of the defense, but all contents concerning Matsui did not conform to the fact, such as Matsui's order to strictly abide by the bearing and discipline of the army, a small amount of atrocities, the uncertainty of rape or adultery, only six or seven corpses in Nanjing, no information of wrongful acts, the strict prohibition against wrongful acts and Matsui's special emphasis on the bearing and discipline of the army, etc. Now, we will make a comparison between the journals of the two branches of the judicial department of the tenth army and the front army of central China and Ogawa's records at the time of the incidents.

2.2 Did Commander Matsui Order to Strictly Abide by the Bearing and Discipline of the Army?

The accused and Matsui Iwane had a tacit understanding in the Tokyo trial. They claimed with one voice that Matsui had repeatedly emphasized the bearing and discipline of the army when the Japanese army came to China. This was proved to be untrue by Matsui's testimony. In order to completely check Ogawa's testimony, we would not omit to make a review of Ogawa's diary. Ogawa mentioned twice in his affidavit that Matsui talked about the bearing and discipline of the army. One was the strict compliance with the bearing and discipline of the army and law. The other was the special emphasis. The tone was so prudent that the content was not routine or occasional cliché. According to Ogawa's habit of recording daily experience in detail, these oral instructions could not be omitted. Therefore, when we read all the texts of Ogawa's diary without finding any similar speech of Matsui, we could definitely conclude that the testimony was untrue. However, it was not only because there was no record in the diary, but also because the diary directly exposed Ogawa's self-defeating. Article 6 of his testimony stated that he met General Matsui in Shanghai's headquarters on January 4, 1938, etc. The time, place and characters were all quite accurate, so we could image that the prosecutor had no reason to interrogate Ogawa at that time. However, thanks to the accuracy, we could make a comparison with the diary. Ogawa's diary of January 4 recorded his two visits to lieutenant general Yanagawa Heisuke who was the commander of the tenth army. He talked about the case of the involved major (the names of all the people involved were hidden when the diary was published) with Yanagawa Heisuke and participated in the farewell party held by ministries of weapons, military doctors, veterinarians and justice. He did not leave the headquarters of the tenth army in Hangzhou. Ogawa left Hangzhou to Shanghai to report to the front army of central China on January 7. He did not meet Matsui until January 15 (Figs. 1 and 2).

Ogawa's diary of January 15 recorded his meeting with Matsui in detail and Matsui excitedly talked about the political strategy, such as how to overthrow the regime of Chiang Kai Shek, how to establish a pro-Japanese regime and how to achieve a hundred-year plan of the Japanese mass migration from Japan to China, etc. However, not only there was not a single word mentioning the bearing and discipline of the army, but also there were some curious feelings:

> Did the Commander (the original note: General Matsui Iwane) maintain dignity or he was born arrogant? He was indeed strange compared with the generals who I had contacted with so far. The chief did not stand on his dignity and made it easier for subordinates to understand his policies. I thought it was great because there was no need to stand on his dignity. It was inevitable that too much dignity might hinder the understanding of the listeners. Therefore, it would be difficult for the superiors to understand the various considerations. The relationship between the chief and the subordinates were especially particular. It would never be useless that the subordinates fully understood the chief's opinion and the chief fully considered the subordinates' opinions and listened to the advisors' advice… (The ellipsis was quoted from the original text – the quotation) So, why did the Commander need to stand on his dignity?

In terms of Matsui Iwane, there were various descriptions, but no one had ever said that he was arrogant or stood on his dignity. The reason why Matsui's impression on Ogawa was different was due to the bearing and discipline of the army which made Matsui fall into an awkward position.

After the Japanese army entered Nanjing, since the former reporter of *New York Times* Durdin (F. Tilman Durdin) who was expelled from Nanjing issued the first report on December 17, the Western Journals began to report a large quantity of Japanese military atrocities; the western people of the Nanjing International Committee of the Security Zone began to submit complaints and protests to the Japanese embassy in Nanjing every day since the third day that the Japanese army entered Nanjing. These complaints and protests were immediately transmitted to the Japanese supreme political and military authorities. Under this pressure, the central authorities of the Japanese army had to order and send officers to urge the front army of central China to restrain the bearing and discipline of the army. The pressure made Matsui utterly embarrassed and his joy of conquering the capital of the enemy state was completely swept away. The council of military court was temporarily pieced together under this background, which was not of Matsui's free will. So, confronted with Ogawa whose age and experience were similar to his and who he did not resent, Matsui conveyed his resistance to the pressure of the bearing and discipline of the army by being arrogant and standing on his dignity, whether it was true or not.

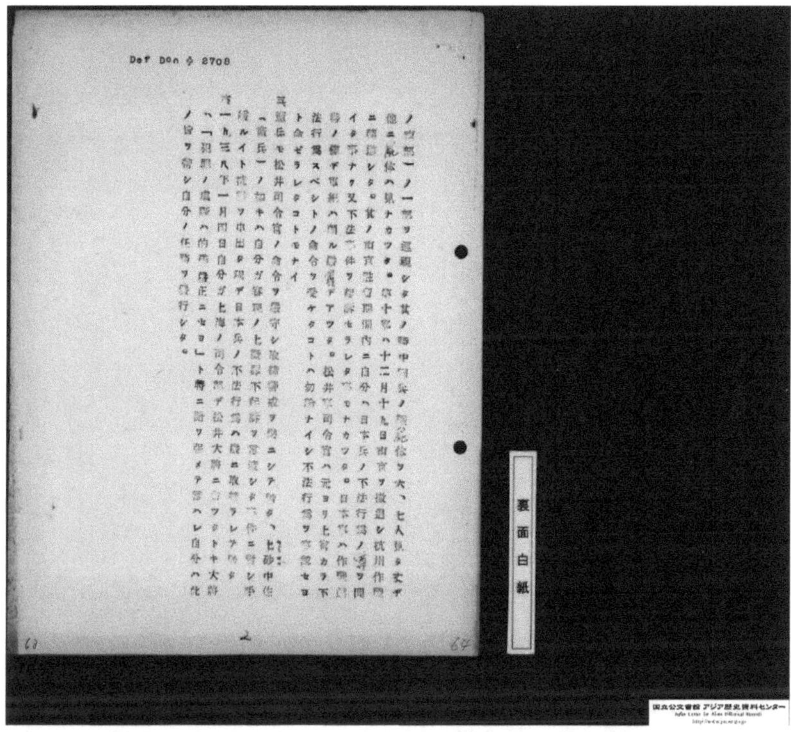

Fig. 1 The affidavit of Ogawa Sekijiro (Ogawa Sekijiro stated in his affidavit that he was asked to strictly deal with the crimes when meeting general Matsui in Shanghai on January 4, 1938)

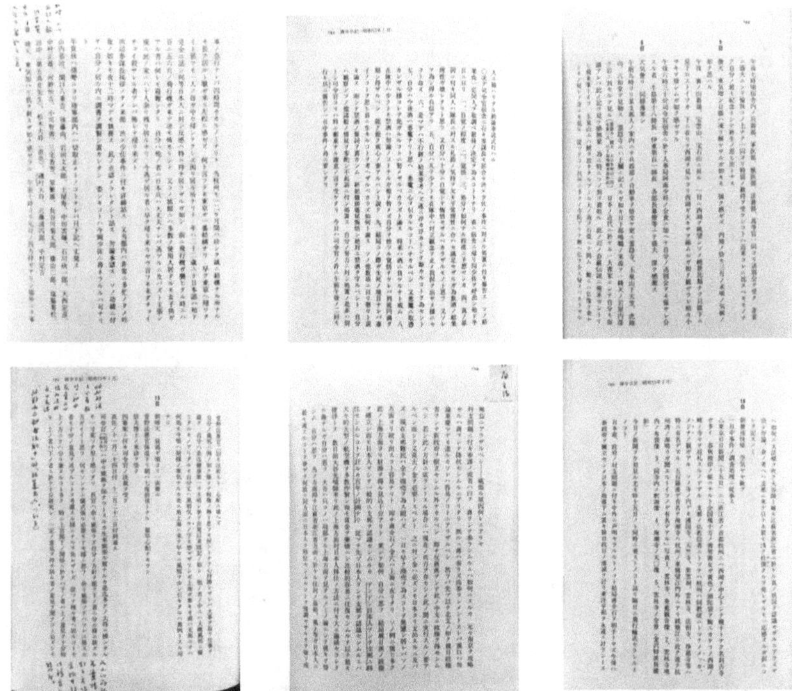

Fig. 2 The diary of Ogawa Sekijiro (The diary of January 4, 1938 recorded Ogawa's activities in detail that he did not leave the headquarters of the tenth army in Hangzhou. It also recorded in detail that when Ogawa met Matsui on the January 15, 1938, Matsui's long speech did not mention a single word about the crimes and the bearing and discipline of the army)

2.3 *Was There the Uncertainty of Rape or Adultery?*

The atrocities of rape of the Japanese army have been deeply rooted in Chinese national memory through various records, especially in literary and artistic works. However, the situation in Japan is different. In addition to the group of massacre which has few members and the group of fiction which it is difficult to argue with, the mainstream society has always avoided mentioning it. This can be reflected by the general account of the Nanjing incident that only recorded the massacre without the atrocities of rape. The denial of the rape of the group of fiction began to be strengthened after the 1990s. They not only called the record of the incident as a rumor and resolutely denied it, but also further thought that the truth of rape was the voluntary prostitution, or the behavior of the Chinese soldiers in the disguise of the Japanese soldiers, or the anti-Japanese task of the Chinese soldiers. Although the denial of rape has become more and more prominent in the recent years, it can be found the source in the Tokyo trial as the denial of other atrocities. The so-called uncertainty of rape or adultery by Ogawa was the beginning of the current denial of rape.

The denial of rape was closely related to that victims themselves rarely initiated the prosecution. Except the weak position of facing the occupying forces, it was also related to Chinese view on virtues and chastity. The Chinese people always put emphasis on the righteousness from ancient times. When moral integrity, they had no alternative but to sacrifice their life for righteousness. A woman's duty of righteousness was her supreme chastity (when Guo Qi discussed the atrocities of rape of the Japanese army in *A Record of the Blood and Tear of the Fall of Nanjing*, he said that a woman's chastity was above everything). Therefore, if a Chinese woman was raped, especially by a brutish soldier, her whole life was completely destroyed. Even if she did not commit suicide, she could only swallow the insult and humiliation silently rather than stand out to initiate a prosecution. As a result, a report to the Japanese occupying forces was a doomed request, so few people intended to find justice with their real names after the war. However, with a rough reading of the journal and diary, there were not only a large number of cases of rape in Shanghai, Hangzhou and Huzhou, but also the detailed records of the pleadings, the verdict, the accusations and the statements of the two parties. The latter was quite surprising. Therefore, the so-called uncertainty of rape or adultery and the words that the rape was only hearsay would be self-destructive. We could quote some related materials for proof.

The tenth army began to land in Jin Shan Wei on November 5, 1937. On November 8, Ogawa went ashore with its headquarters. On the same day, the judicial department received the report that the bearing and discipline of the army was nonbinding due to the atrocities near Jin Shan Wei submitted by the captain of the gendarmerie, Kamisago Shoshichi. Then there usually came the news of fire and robbery. The journal of the judicial department of the tenth army of November 15 firstly mentioned the compulsory obscene event reported by the gendarmerie. It clearly recorded that the rape happened after one day:

> At 8:30 in the morning, Lieutenant Kamisago who was the captain of the gendarmerie came to discuss about the prosecution of the frequent occurrence of the events of plunder and rape with Ogawa.

Here, the phrase of frequent occurrence was noteworthy. In the past, when we talked about the cause of the Japanese army's atrocities, in addition to emphasizing the barbarous character of the so-called militarism of the Japanese army, we mostly regarded the fierce fighting and the revenge as objective causes. It could be seen from the journal of the judicial department that the events of rape were accompanied by the Japanese army from the beginning. The external cause was not of importance. The first case of rape was recorded in the journal on November 25:

> At 3:30 in the morning, Lieutenant Matsuoka who was the captain of the gendarmerie of the Jin Shan Wei military station came to contact Minister Ogawa and accepted search and command because five corporal soldiers of the army under the jurisdiction of the sixth division became rapists and murderers or criminals who attempted to rape and murder.

In the journal of the same day, Ogawa ordered Tajima Riuichi, a member of the judicial department, to search the crime scene at Ding Jia Lou in the morning. The case was tried on December 22. People involved in the case were the secret service soldier Shima□□□ of the small luggage department[1] of the headquarters of the third group of the 13th wing of the sixth division's infantry (In consideration of the so-called reputation of the parties, only the first word in the publication was kept and the rest was hidden by the boxes.), the private first-class Tana□□□ of the 12th lochus of the same group, Leader Uchi□□□ and Tsuru□□□ of the ninth lochus of the same group. There was the detailed record in the judgment left in the journal of the council of military court of the front army of central China. Therefore, this case was so typical that I excerpted the main case as follows:

[1] The small (or big) luggage department of the Japanese army referred to the troops carrying goods of the troops ranking above the group. The small luggage department was responsible for the goods directly related to the war, such as the ammunition. The big luggage department was responsible for the goods indirectly related to the war, such as the food and others.

Firstly, at about 10 o'clock in the morning on November 24 of the same year, defendant Uchi□□□ was near the foregoing empty room. Defendants Shima□□□, Tana□□□, Tsuru□□□ and the aforementioned deceased Fuji□□□ (he was a private first class of the 12th lochus who met the other defendants on his way from Jinshan to Fengjing. According to Ogawa's diary, he committed suicide later – the quotation) went to the nearby villages and sought for Chinese coolies in order to transport their luggage. Tsuru□□□ went back to Uchi□□□ on the way. Other defendants jointly planed to seek for and kidnap Chinese women for rape.

a. At about 11 o'clock in the morning of the same day, the defendant Shima□□□ was near the house of Pan △△ (18 years old) on the Din Jia Road in the same county (referring to the Ding Jia Lou recorded in the journal of the judicial department of the tenth army). He found the woman who escaped because she saw the defendants. So he chased after her, aiming at her with the rifle carried and threatened her. Then he brought her by force when she gave up running away because of fear. At 4 o'clock in the afternoon of the same day, he entered the house of Li △△ (18 years old) in the same village. He also brought this resistant woman by force.
b. At noon of the same day, when the defendant Tana□□□ sought for Chinese women in the foregoing village, he saw Zhang △△ (20 years old). So he chased after her and threatened her with the bayonet carried. Then he brought her by force when she gave up running away because of fear.
c. At 4 o'clock in the afternoon of the same day, the deceased Fuji□□□ found that Zuo △△ (23 years old) and Zuo ◎◎ (22 years old) were working in a boat moored in a small river near the foregoing village. He approached them and threatened them with the gun carried. Then he brought them by force when they gave up running away because of fear. Then he entered the house of Lu △△ (16 years old) at the same time. He said to the woman: "Come! Come!" The woman disobeyed, so he kicked her several times and brought her by force when she was afraid of him.

   The aforementioned six Chinese women were hijacked to the empty house that was the foregoing camp over one mile from the same village by boat, which made the defendants achieve their goal of plunder.

   Secondly, at about 8 o'clock in the afternoon of the same day, the defendants Uchi□□□ and Tsuru□□□ went back to the foregoing dormitory and saw several Chinese women in the room. They knew that these women were plundered by the aforementioned defendants for lust. The deceased Fuji□□□ said that everyone raped one woman. The defendant

Uchi□□□ obtained Pan △△ for the purpose of rape and the defendant Tsuru□□□ obtained Zuo ◎◎ for the purpose of rape.
Thirdly, the defendants Shima□□□, Tana□□□, Uchi□□□, Tsuru□□□ and the deceased Fuji□□□ jointly planned to rape the foregoing Chinese women at about 9:30 in the afternoon of the same day in the foregoing empty house when these women were too afraid of the defendants' threaten to resist them. The defendant Shima□□□ raped Li △△. The defendant Tana□□□ raped Zhang △△. The defendant Uchi□□□ raped Pan △△. The defendant Tsuru□□□ raped Zuo ◎◎. The deceased Fuji□□□ raped Zuo △△.

Fourthly, the defendant Shima□□□

a. At about 11 o'clock in the morning of the same day, he was near the foregoing house of Pan △△. He saw Tan Youlin (53 years old), so he beckoned to her and asked her to come over. The woman did not agree and the defendant attempted to kill her. He shot the woman with the rifle carried and hit her heart in the left breast. The woman died immediately because of the perforating gunshot wounds.
b. At about 2 o'clock in the afternoon of the same day, he saw He-chen Shi (26 years old) in the vestibule of her house and said: "Come! Come!" The woman fled to the house because of fear, so the defendant attempted to kill her. He shot at the back of the woman with the rifle carried. The woman's right thigh was not wounded by the perforating gunshot wounds. Therefore, the defendant did not achieve his goal of killing.
c. At about 5 o'clock in the afternoon of the same day, when monitoring the Chinese women plundered in the foregoing boat, he saw that one unnamed Chinese showed up near the boat and led the way for soldiers who intended to arrest him. So he concluded that they came to retake the foregoing women and attempted to kill them. Then he shot them twice with the rifle carried, but he missed twice and did not achieve his goal of killing
...On November 24, there was the report of the plunder and killing of Chinese women by the Japanese soldiers in the Shajiabang, Jinshan County, Jiangsu province. The result of the search was the arrest of the aforementioned defendants and Fuji□□□ who raped those Chinese women at about 11:40 in the afternoon of the same day in the house of Lu Longqing near Ding Jia Road.

The characteristics of the case were not only the collective rape, but also no sign of resistance of Tan and He. As long as Shima□□□ was not satisfied, he would wantonly shoot other people by gun. The characteristic of compulsion was especially remarkable. The records in the journal of the tenth army and the front army of central China concerning this case proved that the uncertainty of rape and adultery Ogawa said in the Tokyo trial; according to the journal of the tenth army, Ogawa was clear that the captain of the gendarmerie accepted his instructions and he sent people to do the research.

Then, was it possible that the records in the journal were not accurate? Maybe Ogawa did not know the truth. This should not have been a problem. Because no matter whether the journal was personally recorded by Ogawa, its custody by Ogawa should rule out that he did not know the truth. However, in accordance with the consistent performance of the so-called circumstantial evidence of the Japanese group of fiction, they must think that it could not be concluded whether Ogawa knows the truth. Fortunately, we can still see the diary of Ogawa which is the most direct evidence today. Compared with the brief record of the judicial department of the tenth army on November 25, Ogawa's diary recorded not only more detailed information of the same day, but also retained his psychological feelings at that time:

> Last night at 3:30, Lieutenant Matsuoka of the gendarmerie reported a major event late at night that five soldiers of the sixth division (including one leader) hijacked several women ranging from teenage girls to 26-year-old women in a village about three miles away and wantonly raped them in an empty house. Meanwhile, a 55-year-old woman who escaped was shot and killed and another woman's right thigh was shot and injured. The extent of their violation of the bearing and discipline of the army was too appalling to be described in words.
>
> △ (the original symbol in the diary – the quotation) The Japanese government declared that even if it was against the Chinese government, it would not be hostile to the nationals in the future. However, what the Japanese soldiers did to the people who had no guilt was extremely appalling. How did they think about the further anti-Japanese ideology of the Chinese people after such behavior? The consideration of the future of the Japanese Empire chilled people to the bone.

Not only did they wantonly rape Chinese women but also the extent was too appalling to be described in words. The similar expression of pain and sorrow was not rare in the diary of Ogawa. Here were other two examples before the foregoing day and after the foregoing day for proof. Ogawa recorded in the aforementioned diary of November 23:

> It was unspeakable humiliation that the Japanese soldiers wantonly raped Chinese women wherever they went and did not regard predatory or arson as the wrongful acts. As Japanese, especially the young men who would be the support of Japan, what effect would be on the future ideology of the whole Japan if they made a triumphant return with such an unscrupulous psychological habit? The consideration chilled people to the bone. I thought that the Japanese government should make a research and implement a comprehensive reform in ideological issues. This was a slightly extreme statement. However, as someone said, Japanese soldiers were more brutal than China soldiers, which made us sob. I heard that the Chinese people called Japanese the beasts and called Japanese soldiers the beast soldiers. From the perspective of Chinese people, it was indeed the truth. As Japanese, the regrettable examples of the actual behavior of the Japanese soldiers were too countless to enumerate.

He wrote on November 26:

> From all aspects of observation, not only the frontline troops but also the cunning soldiers of the rear troops were deliberately left behind to enter the houses of civilians and do evil things. The aforementioned defendants of murder, robbery and rape were this kind of people. As a result, the honest and serious soldiers who fought bravely in the front line died because of a little negligence. It was not too much to call the cunning fellows who act wantonly and never participate in any battle traitors, opponents or black sheep, which made people increasingly feel regret.
>
> (Omission of the middle part) As soon as they saw the Japanese soldiers, they fled at once. Women and children seemed to be extremely afraid of the Japanese soldiers, which was resulted from the evil things did by the Japanese soldiers. If they never did any evil things, Chinese people would not escape. It was indeed a pity.
>
> What was the dignity of the Imperial Army? Japanese themselves could not judge the beginning of the so-called war. However, in terms of the foregoing Chinese feelings of Japanese, the impact of the quality of Japanese soldiers on young men in the future would only be disappointing.

In the light of Ogawa's chill, regret and disappointment to the atrocities, such as the wanton rape, Ogawa's testimony of the uncertainty of rape or adultery in the Tokyo court was definitely perjury.

2.4 *Did Ogawa See Only Six or Seven Corpses of Chinese Soldiers in Nanjing?*

The heated debate on the Nanjing incident in Japan was basically different from our attention to the Nanjing massacre. For example, were the dead soldiers or civilians? Were the soldiers killed by the combatants in the battle or the captives who had laid down their weapons? Did the executed captives abide by the obligations of the captives stipulated in international law? Was there a legal trial? Did the killed civilians resist? Could they be regarded as neutral civilians? etc. These problems were not only under no consideration, but also were hardly accepted by our emotions. But no matter how to interpret these problems, the group of fiction always attempted to decrease the number of the dead as much as possible. This attempt also started from the defense of the Tokyo trial. The so-called testimony of Ogawa that he only saw six or seven corpses of the Chinese soldiers in Nanjing was also a typical example.

At the end of the war, Japan handed down orders to destroy official document files, especially those of the army, so the relevant information hardly remained. However, only few Japanese documents could still prove that there were a large number of corpses when the Japanese army conquered Nanjing. Therefore, it might contribute to our understanding of this event by quoting the diary of Colonel Yasuyama Koudou who served as the surgeon of the navy and the surgeon of the headquarters of the fleet in China.

Yasuyama Koudou arrived in Nanjing on December 16 by seaplane. At two o'clock in the afternoon, he visited the battlefield with the chief executive and the chief controller of the fleet. He wrote in the diary of this day:

> From the Xiaguan wharf, we drove along the broad road built into a straight line. Rifle bullets were scattered on the road as the sand covered with brass and the corpses of the Chinese soldiers were scattered on the grass and were left exposed.
>
> Before long we drove from Xiaguan to the Yijiangmen where led to Nanjing. An arched road was under the towering stone gate and its one-third height was buried with soil. After we went into the gate, the road became a ramp from the perspective of Xiaguan. The car slowly moved forward and I felt it was moving slowly on the rubber bag full of air. In fact, the car was moving on the corpses of countless enemies buried. It was probably moving on where the layer of soil was thin and suddenly the meat came out of the soil. The miserable scene was truly beyond words.

> Finally, we left the stone gate and drove into Nanjing. The countless corpses of the enemies became black coke. The iron pockets and the bayonets were also smoked into black. Metal wires used for wire netting overlapped with remnant wood of burned door posts. The accumulated soil was also burnt into black. The chaos and misery were unspeakable.
>
> There was a sentence on the hillock on the right side of the door that China was always at daggers drawn with Japan, which showed that Chiang Kai Shek made propaganda for the anti-Japanese war. When we approached to the city, the plain blue cotton-padded jacket abandoned by the enemies made the road like shabby clothes. The corpses of the enemy officers lying on the back with stiff hands and feet who wore yellow army uniforms and leather leggings could also be seen everywhere.

The above content was only one fragment that Yasuyama Koudou saw in Nanjing on the first day. He encountered a quantity of corpses everywhere in the three days when he stayed in Nanjing. For example, on the morning of the second day (December 17), he saw countless corpses in other two places in Xiaguan. He also personally saw that a Chinese soldier with full of blood begged for mercy and was shot at close range by a reserve soldier from behind (the old soldiers who were re-recruited when the standing military service had been full). He saw countless corpses along the Zhongshan North Road in the morning. When he inspected Jiang ting in the lower reaches of Xiaguan in the afternoon with Okochi Denshichi who served as the commander of the special marine corps of the navy in Shanghai, he saw countless corpses of the enemies became black coke. He also saw in the river bank sixty or seventy corpses of the enemies who had tasted the fierceness of Japanese swords. On December 18, he firstly saw the abandoned corpses of the enemies here and there in the Lion Grove. Then he saw the scattered corpses outside the foothills of the barracks and the scattered corpses of the enemies in the Zhongshan Park.

Yasuyama Koudou's testimony and other similar testimony could completely prove that Ogawa's testimony of six or seven corpses of Chinese soldiers was not true. There was no doubt about this. The question remained to be solved in this section was whether Ogawa intended to commit perjury for himself or whether Ogawa only saw six or seven corpses of Chinese soldiers. We continued to check the diary of Ogawa. His testimony stated that the date of entering Nanjing was December 14. Let's check the diary of Ogawa of the same day. The diary of this day was fairly detailed. When he entered Nanjing, the situation was as follows:

> The soldiers of the Chinese regular army (The word of corpses was mentioned in the foregoing same sentence and was omitted in this sentence – the quotation) on the side of the road were overlapped and burnt by fire. It seemed that the Japanese soldier were used to the corpses under their feet. We could see that soldiers who passed through the burning corpses due to heavy traffic became totally used to human corpses. We gradually arrived at the south gate. The walls completely constructed by the stones were about three feet high and the battle of yesterday had destroyed part of the walls. However, the wall was as thick as the car road, so the ordinary artillery was hard to collapse them. As soon as I entered the door, I saw the corpses of the Chinese soldiers on the both sides.

In fact, although Ogawa claimed that he only saw six or seven corpses of the Chinese soldiers, what he truly saw was countless corpses. No matter what motivated him to testify, his testimony could only be considered as perjury compared with his diary. Actually, since he landed in Jin Shan Wei, Ogawa encountered the corpses of the Chinese people almost everywhere.

For example, when Ogawa was on the way to Zhang Yan town on the morning of November 14, there are all countless in the rivers, pools and fields. When he arrived at Jin Shan in the afternoon, there were even some naked corpses. On November 17, there were still corpses of the Chinese people. On November 28, when he was on the way to Huzhou, he saw countless corpses and quite a few of them wore civilian clothes. On December 10, he recorded that there were countless corpses of the Chinese people here and there. Such a large number of corpses made him feel numb, as he said in his diary of December 11:

> When I first set out from the house of Li to Jinshan and saw the corpses of the China people on the way, I always had a strange feeling. However, when I gradually saw a large number of corpses, I became accustomed to them. The feeling at this time was like seeing the remains of dogs in the mainland.

Ogawa's feeling for the body was from feeling strange to being accustomed, but he would not ignore them or eliminate them from the memory. Particularly, he would not maintain the opposite memory.

As the chief of judicial department, Ogawa was not in the frontline of the battle, so there was no fierce competition in his diary. However, in his diary there was no lack of the record that he personally saw the

Japanese soldiers abused the Chinese people. The aforementioned diary of November 25, he recorded this passage:

> I saw the Japanese soldiers enslaving the Chinese people and pointing to them with rifles, which exactly treated them like cats and dogs.

He wrote on November 29:

> Some soldiers let the Chinese people carry their luggage. As long as the Chinese people showed a little disobedience or disobedience, they would be immediately punished, which made people speechless. I saw on the way that two soldiers pulled out the swords and stabbed a Chinese person lying on the back. to stab a rising Chinese man. Another Chinese person was filled with blood and pain. Confronted with this scene, I extremely felt pity for the nationals of the defeated country.

It was very common that the Chinese people were forced into slave labor with the army at that time. He wrote on December 11:

> These Chinese people tried their best to carry the luggage and a considerable number of them were old people. There was no one more fortunate than those who lost their country. On such an occasion, they would be punished immediately by our soldiers as long as they showed a little disobedience. If they had escaped, they would have been executed immediately. Therefore, the Chinese people were in a dilemma and had to obey any order.

Although Ogawa used the subjunctive mood, his conclusion from his own personal experience was not baseless. The tenth army was not strongly resisted after landing, so a considerable number of the corpses left behind by the tenth army were the victims of such a random execution. Ogawa also recorded in the diary of the second day:

> According to the report of Lieutenant Kamisago who was the captain of the gendarmerie in the afternoon, the situation near Jin Shan Wei was that the plunder of the city was serious and the useless killing was extremely miserable. If this was the case, it would be a great and disturbing problem.

The sentence that the useless killing was extremely miserable was associated with Ogawa's every strong regret and disappointment of the Japanese army in his diary. Although he did not resolutely say that he had not seen any corpses in the Tokyo court, he had deliberately tried to commit perjury.

2.5 *The So-Called Severe Prohibition of the Wrongful Acts of the Japanese Soldiers*

The basic position of the defense in the Tokyo trial was the denial of a large scale of atrocities of the Japanese army in Nanjing and the severe punishment of the limited wrongful acts of the Japanese army. Wakisaka Jiro who was the captain of the 36th wing said that there was a most typical example that his subordinate was punished by the military discipline because he picked up a shoe. Due to the limitation of the evidence, although the prosecutor put forward quite a number of opposite evidence, the words of the prosecutor were almost against those of the defense. The prosecutor had not accordingly interrogated the other similar testimony of the defendant, so today in Japan there were still people who think that the treatment of the evidence of two parties in the Tokyo trial was extremely unfair.

Ogawa entered Nanjing on December 14 and went to Huzhou on the morning of December 19. In Nanjing, he participated in "entering the city", "soothing style" and other activities. He also met with the officers from the bureau of justice of the ministry of the army and the minister of justice of the Shanghai expeditionary army. Ogawa's diary when he was in Nanjing did not record the wrongful acts of the Japanese army except the fire. Therefore, that the wrongful acts of the Japanese army were severely prohibited and the severe punishment in his testimony referred to not Nanjing but other places. The Tokyo trial did not investigate the atrocities of the two armies under the jurisdiction of the front army of central China outside Nanjing. Ogawa's testimony aimed at proving the internal evidence by the external evidence. He intended to prove that there were no atrocities in Nanjing because there was no wrongful act outside Nanjing. It was meaningless at all. The reason was very simple because no wrongful act outside Nanjing was not equivalent to no atrocities in Nanjing. However, Ogawa's testimony could not prove the atrocities of Nanjing, but it provided an important basis for us to verify the authenticity of Ogawa's testimony.

The foregoing content mentioned that when Ogawa still stayed in Jinshan on November 25, he sent a member of judicial department Tajima Riuichi to investigate the rape case of Ding Jia Lou. In his diary of the next day, Ogawa wrote that the situation of the field investigation was much worse than his imagination. There were a quantity of records in Ogawa's diary about the wrongful acts of the Japanese army and his regret and disappointment as mentioned before. So were all of these wrongful acts punished severely?

There were 118 people involved in the cases recorded in the journal of the judicial department of the tenth army. 60 people of them were not prosecuted, accounting for over half of the people. Besides, 16 people were not dealt with promptly when the construction of the tenth army was revoked, so the actual treatment rate was less than 36%. The people involved in the cases who were immune from prosecution included 24 murders, one person who abetted the murder, five people who assisted the murder, one person who injured and caused death of others, one person who raped and intentionally injured others, one person who plundered and raped others, three rapists, seven plunderers, one person who committed the atrocity, one person who intentionally injured others, two arsonists, one person who committed compulsory indecent crimes, three people who acted indecently toward others, two thieves, one person who threatened and plundered the chief due to the atrocities of the chief, one person who insulted and coerced the chief into preparing the murder and caused negligence injury, two people who violated the rules of convening the army, and three people who violated of the rules of the enforcement of military service. We could see that felonies such as murder, rape, plunder and arson accounted for most of the crimes, except a few conflicts between the Japanese officers and soldiers.

Let's look at three specific cases of the immunity from prosecution.

a. The Massacre by Second Lieutenant Youshi □□□ from the Fourth Lochus of the Fourth Group of the Reserve Infantry of the Tenth Army and Other People

(1) When Second Lieutenant Oka □□ worked in the Jinshan branch of the field clothing and grain factory, he was driven by the uneasiness and complained to Second Lieutenant Youshi □□□ who was also the police chief because many Chinese who inhabited near his dormitory seemed to have the unsafe words and deeds or steal articles.

(2) Therefore, Youshi □□□ ordered 26 subordinates to arrest the aforementioned 26 Chinese people on December 15, the 12th year of Showa. On the way back to the same gendarmerie, the attempt to escape of the

arrested Chinese people raised him to kill them. (The list of murderers and people who assisted the murder would be listed in detail later – the quotation)

All 26 people were killed in the case. Jinshan was the stable rear of the Japanese army at that time, so no one would dare to beard the lion in his den (My mother lived in Zhapu, which was not far away from Jinshan. She said that the general public was avoiding the Japanese army rather than irritating them.).[2] Even if the doubt of Oka □□ was true, the Chinese residents were just stealing articles, which was still doubtful. There was no reason to kill people due to the so-called doubt; since the crime was not enough to be punished, the so-called attempt to escape also could not be a crime; when 26 soldiers escorted the same number of civilians (During the Nanking Massacre, the number of people under escort was often a dozen times as many as the number of Japanese and they were all soldiers.), any people with a little reason would not attempt to escape. If there was an attempt, it would not be implemented. Even if someone truly escaped, it was impossible for the rest to continue to run away regardless of their lives as long as the Japanese soldiers fired their guns or shot any person. Therefore, although it was obvious that the statement of the complaint tried to plead for the Japanese army, it was still impossible to cover up the facts of deliberate massacre.

b. The Killing by the Private First Class Tsuzi□□ from the First Lochus of the Reserve Artillery and Other People

At about 5 o'clock on the afternoon of November 29, the 12th year of Showa (1937), the defendant was completely drunk because of the Chinese wine in the camp of Jiaxing. Driven by the strong hatred, he produced evil thought and killed three passing Chinese people with the bayonet carried.

It was difficult to imagine that a person who was completely drunk could kill three people by a bayonet unless the victims had been caught.

[2]There was no lack of records of obedience of the people in Ogawa's diary. For example, the records of Ogawa in Jinshan stated that the local residents were submissive and respectful to them like Bodhisattvas after they came t Jinshan. Especially the children gave the highest respectful salute in the immovable posture, so people could not help having compassion for them. (*A Diary of an Officer of Justice*, page 59.)

Moreover, if a person was completely drunk, he would not recognize or care about any people. The statement of the defendant that he was driven by the strong hatred only aimed at the immunity from the crime. The record of the judgment was entirely based on the facts. Even if it is not partial to or tolerate the defendant, the defendant would not be able to get rid of the fact that he assisted the murder or was not conscientious enough.

c. The Compulsory Indecent Crimes by the First Private Class Taka□□□□ from the First Lochus of the 114th Wing of the Engineers of the 114th Division and Other People

> The defendant was in the camp of Huzhou at about 2:30 on the afternoon of December 31, the 12th year of Showa. When he was near the Tai Liang Bridge in the Huzhou city, he saw a passing Chinese girl (8 years old) and brought her to the nearby empty house to rape her by his blandishments (rape was the crime of this case – the quotation). Then he was arrested by the gendarmerie.

During the Japanese occupation of Nanjing, the age of the victims of the sexual violence ranged from grandmothers to granddaughters. For example, Miner Searle Bates demonstrated in his literature that women aged between 11 and 53 years old were raped. A lot of such records were recorded in Western literature at that time. For example, James McCallum wrote in the letter that girls aged 11 or 12 and women aged 50 also did not escape (the sexual violence). It was appalling that girls aged 11 or 12 were raped. However, the case of Taka□□□□ recorded in the journal showed that it was not the lowest limit of age. Even if the defendant used blandishments to induce and deceive an innocent girl without violence, it was still rape.

Through the above three cases of serious crimes that were immune from prosecution, it was self-evident whether the wrongful acts of the Japanese army had been severely punished. In fact, even without the most convincing cases immune from prosecution, we could also prove that the severe punishment was not true by only three cases that had been punished.

a. The Rape and Killing by Private First Class Chi□□□□ from the Tenth Lochus of the Sixth Wing of the Engineering of the Sixth Division

Chi□□□□ committed the gang rape of a woman whose surname was Cai with his colleague on December 14. Then they went back again:

> At about 3 o'clock on the afternoon of December 17, Chi□□□□ felt obsessed with the foregoing woman whose surname was Cai, so he left the dormitory to commit the rape again. He met the aforementioned Fuji□□□ (one of the former Gang Raptor) and asked him to go to the house of Cai △△ together. They called the woman out of the house. Her husband Cai ○○ happened to be at the door. He walked towards the defendants as he screamed out something. (The defendants) promptly judged that he was trying to stop them, so they attempted to kill her husband. The defendants continuously fired three shots to the man and two shots hit the back of his head and his left chest. As a result, the man died immediately because of the non-perforating gunshot wounds.

They were too rampant to open the rape and call the woman on a public occasion. Besides, when they saw the husband of the victim, they not only had no sense of shame but also shot him at once. Such an abominable crime was only sentenced to four years in prison.

b. The Rape and Intentional Injury by the Private First Class Huru□□□ from the Thirteenth Infantry Regiment of the Sixth Division and the Rape by Kawa□□□

> The two defendants were in the camp of Jinshan in Jinshan County.
>
> (1) On December 25, the 12th year of Showa, when the defendant Huru□□□ was in an unknown village which was three kilometers north of Jinshan in order to confiscate the vegetables, he intimidated an unknown woman (18 or 19 years old) in a Chinese farmhouse of the same village. Then he raped the woman when she could not resist him because of fear.
> (2) On December 27 of the same year, the defendant Huru□□□ also came to Cao Jia Bang in Jinshan County to confiscate the vegetables. He captured a Chinese boat because he worried that the assembled over 40 people might detained him. When he withdrew, he shot the assembled people with the gun carried in order to prevent them, which caused the waist of a Chinese man was shot but the bullet did not come out of his body. In the same night, when the defendant slept in a farmhouse in the Shi Jia Lou in Jinshan County, he invaded the neighborhood in

> the middle night and raped a Chinese woman (32 years old) who was sleeping with violence. The foregoing defendant Kawa□□□ had once slept in the house of a Chinese woman. After he knew that Huru□□□ raped a Chinese woman in the neighborhood, he came to the same house immediately. Then he threatened the same woman by the bayonet carried, frightening her and raped her.

In this case, Huru□□□ was a recidivist because he raped the Chinese woman twice. He even captured a boat and intentionally injured other people in the second time. However, he was only sentenced to two years in prison and Kawa□□□ was only sentenced to one year in prison.

c. Case of Murder Committed by Private First Class Asa□□□ from the 4th Company, 124th Infantry Regiment, 18th Division

> The defendant was in the Huzhou quarter. On 29 November, Year 12 of Sowa period, he went to collect vegetables with his colleagues. They picked about 5kanmes (1 kanme is about 3,75 kilograms- quote) of vegetables grown in a nearby field. The defendant went to the nearby farmhouse and demanded three Chinese women to wash the vegetables. One of the Chinese women (named Liu A'sheng according to the log of the Area Army-quote) said something quickly, as if she was reluctant. (The defendant) considered this as scorn towards the Japanese soldiers, so he shot her dead with his rifle.

Apparently, the defendant did not understand what the victim was saying, but he shot her dead in any case. This voluntary manslaughter was only sentenced to one and a half years in prison.

According to the Japanese Criminal Law in wartime, murder and rape were felonies. "Robbery and rape", for instance, should be sentenced to "life imprisonment or punishment of over seven years" (Article 86 of the Army Criminal Law). Therefore, the case prosecuted by the Judicial Department of the Tenth Army received lenient judgments which were not in line with the crimes. The soldiers were not severely punished at all.

2.6 Confusion as Chief of the Judicial Department

The issue of how to handle the crimes committed by the Japanese forces had been a conundrum troubling Sekijiro Ogawa as Chief of the

Judicial Department. As Ogawa's diary kept many relevant records, I want to make a summary so as to reveal the incompetence of the Judicial Department in face of unruly Japanese soldiers and the contradiction between the function of the Judicial Department and the mechanism of the Japanese forces.

The Japanese court-martial was composed of members of the Judicial Department (professional military law officers) and the so-called "judges with sword" (military personnel). Nominally speaking, there was no difference between the powers of military judges and those of "judges with swards". However, as the editor of *Modern History of Japan...Military Police* said, the legal officers could only serve as the weak commissioners when the military officers equaled to the judges with sword. Besides, the Japanese council of military court provided that only the commanders or the chiefs of the divisions could serve as its chief, which demonstrated the consistency between the jurisdiction and the command of the army. This institutional provision restricted the professional legal officers from the rule of law.

In addition to the institutional provision, it was fairly serious that the headquarters did not attach the importance to the judicial department. There was a quantity of records in Ogawa's diary that the ministry of adjutants intentionally did not allow the judicial department to go along with the commander and the judicial department was discriminated in terms of the treatment, etc. The final jurisdiction of the Japanese council of military court was in the hands of the commanders at all levels who served as its chief. Therefore, as the ministry that was responsible for the daily affairs, it was necessary for the judicial department to maintain close contact with the commander at any time. It aimed at not only the high-efficient function but also the normal operation. Ministries of staff, adjutants, management, weapons, managers, military doctors, veterinarians and justice should have gone along with the commander. So the judicial department should have been next to the commander unless it was deliberately arranged. However, based on the diary of Ogawa, the ministry of adjutants repeatedly tried to separate the judicial department from the army and Ogawa was very dissatisfied with this. For example, he wrote on November 24:

> We should proceed to Jiaxing tomorrow, but it was postponed suddenly to the day after tomorrow because of the unknown reason. We protested against it for the following reasons.

> … Secondly, all affairs of the council of military court depended on the jurisdiction of the command, so our affairs could not be carried out without the commander. If the commander was separated from us, then we would not be informed of the decision of the commander and the most important procedures of the council of military court would be delayed. Now, we detained three suspects of arson. Although the investigation of the prosecutor had ended, it could not be prosecuted without the order of the commander, so the disposal of the incident could only be delayed.

He also wrote in this section:

> Our position was not exclusive. However, it was a pity if people thought we were useless.

The so-called uselessness was not the unwarranted suspicion of Ogawa, because it could be seen from many things that the judicial department was so ignored that it was unpopular. The following trivial matter was taken as an example of the treatment of the ministry of justice. The headquarters of the tenth army went from Huzhou to Lishui on December 10. Many ministers and adjutants flew by the plane, but Ogawa was arranged to take a bus. So, he thought it was discrimination and wrote down his indignation in his diary that day. This situation was indeed related to the general low status of the civil service. The following account of Ogawa's diary on December 12 was a true portrayal of this:

> Our civil officers had no alternative but to accept this kind of discrimination. (In particular, the power of the army was increasingly fierce and extremely arbitrary. The original note: the original text in brackets was removed.) If we only depended on the bestowal, we might be the object of jealousy. However, we were actually regarded as encumbrance on any occasion.

However, the discrimination against the judicial department was not only because the military officials often disdained the civil officials, but also because the function of the judicial department was in conflict with the bearing and discipline of the Japanese army. So the military officials might deliberately disdain the civil officials.

The diary of Ogawa recorded on December 8 that Minister Tsukamoto negatively treated everything and did not implement anything. Tsukamoto referred to the aforementioned Tsukamoto Hirotsugu who was the chief of the judicial department of the Shanghai expeditionary army. According to Ogawa's diary, the reason for the non-implementation and negative treatment was the lack of internal harmony. But at that time, it was hard to imagine that the non-implementation of everything was only because of the interpersonal relationships. The reason for the non-implementation should be associated with that the operation of the judicial department was obstructed. Not a few Japanese soldiers mentioned the protests made by various troops to the judicial department in the Tokyo trial, including Tsukamoto Hirotsugu. The reason was that the punishment of the judicial department was too severe. He said: "all the troops blamed the judicial department of the Shanghai expeditionary army for its severe punishment and its correction of misdemeanors". Iinuma Mamoru who was the chief of the Shanghai expeditionary army also said that the 16th division protested against the judicial department because the military discipline was extremely strict (It meant that the military discipline was overly strict in accordance with the original text—the quotation.). The so-called strictness was completely nonsense based on a large number of cases of minor punishment or impunity recorded in the journal. However, even if the judicial department was very tolerable, its nature still determined that it could not be accepted by the Japanese military officials and soldiers.

The blame said by Minister Tsukamoto could be proved through the experience of Ogawa. When Ogawa visited the front army in January 1938, he felt that the difference between the front army and the army was that there was no force directly under the jurisdiction, so it was not necessary to consider the interpersonal relationships:

> (When I was in the army,) it was necessary to take into account that the army should bear the direct responsibility of the crimes committed by the subordinates and the chief had certain opinions on the subordinates in terms of the interpersonal relationships. Therefore, we had to think deeply and cautiously about the opinions of the chief.

The so-called certain opinions referred to the blame of various troops said by Tsukamoto Hirotsugu.

The professional legal officers were in a weak position at that time. When the daughter of Ogawa was young, she had a symbolic experience. Mitsuyo (Ogawa) Nagamori said that when she was in primary school, the color of her father's official collar and the hat were special (white; red symbolized the army; black symbolized the navy; green symbolized the cavalry; blue symbolized the air force) and their number was rare, so people were always curious. Her classmates even asked: "Is your father a Chinese soldier?" For this reason, the teenager Nagamori was very upset. She thought: "I would be so proud if my father was an ordinary soldier, but I feel sorry for myself".

Tsukamoto Hirotsugu had no alternative but to negatively treat everything and not to implement anything and the reason was explained above. The situation of the tenth army was better than that of the Shanghai expeditionary army, but the judicial department was still in a dilemma. So many cases could only be ignored by the judicial department, which caused the dissatisfaction of the gendarmerie of law enforcement. Ogawa wrote on December 25:

> Lieutenant Kamisago came to consult some affairs. He said that most of the recent rape cases were not prosecuted and the laborious accusation of the gendarmerie was wasted in the end. I answered that it might be true. However, I thought that we could not ignore the situation of the war, the mentality of the prisoners, the view on chastity of the Chinese women, the number of crimes so far (the original note: the actual number was quite large), the comparison between the number of the people who were not accused and the number of the people who were occasionally accused, etc. In addition, theoretically, we could not assert that all the victims of the rape at that time were the so-called people who were unable to resist in conformity with Article 1, 7 and 8 of the criminal law. We should take into account that some people were easy to accept the requirements. Thus, it was hasty to define rape immediately when people were raped. The circumstances of the crimes should be further considered and then the disposal could be decided. Therefore, I did not immediately agree with the requirements of the lieutenant.
>
> Besides, I was as worried as the lieutenant about that the number of the rape cases would increase after the truce in the future, which would affect the conciliation. I might think so. On the other hand, the establishment of the comfort facilities might be able to prevent the increase. Moreover, it was unnecessary for people to give their lives away in war. The contact with women was like facing the last test of impulse. So it was unnecessary to worry about the increase of the rape cases after the truce.

The captain of the gendarmerie, Kamisago Shoshichi, had said in *Thirty-one Years of the Gendarmerie* that some Japanese veterans were disinterested about the corruption of the bearing and discipline of the tenth army and thought it was a lie. For example, Major Yoshinaga Sunao who was the staff officer of the tenth army said: "The statement of Kamisago was a pity". The foregoing record of Kamisago himself could prove that the denial of the memory of Kamisago was a slander.

At that time, it was often the case that the gendarmerie was dissatisfied with the non-prosecution. For example, on the next day (26th) that Kamisago came to the judicial department, Lieutenant Matsuoka expressed his dissatisfaction with the non-prosecution of a major:

> It was unfair that the cadres were not investigated. If the captain did not properly deal with it, I would not report any incidents of his soldiers in the future.

There were a lot of repeated records in the diary of Ogawa that he was not reconciled to be ignored by the judicial department. We quoted the diary of Ogawa in the third section to prove that he knew the rape. However, when he was confronted with the dissatisfaction of the gendarmerie, he pretended to be a considerate man. At that time, this was the only way Ogawa could take whether he truly thought that some rape might be adultery. We could saw that he was in a dilemma in his diary of December 3:

> If I did not have many works and was leisure, other people would consider that the judicial department was useless and despise it. However, if I had a lot of works and was busy, it would at least upset the relevant parties. I would rather say that it was inevitable to be criticized if we were too serious.

Two days before Kamisago expressed his dissatisfaction with the non-prosecution of the rape cases, the diary also left an important guideline which was not found in the journal (23rd):

> In terms of the rape cases, we adopted the policy that we only prosecuted the most vicious cases so far in order to deal with the negative standpoint. If the similar events continued to occur frequently, we had no alternative but to consider the related disposal.

It was not important that this policy was the decision of the chief or the self-determination of Ogawa or the judicial department. It was of importance that it told us that the military law system of the Japanese army indeed had a clear policy of indulging the atrocities.

3 Summary

To sum up, we can conclude that the inaccurate testimony of Matsui Iwane, Ogawa Sekijiro in the Tokyo trial—as well as Iinuma Mamoru who was the chief of the Shanghai expeditionary army and many other witnesses—was not due to the occasional memory error but the purposeful perjury. The group of denial of the Japanese Tokyo trial demonstrated that the testimony of the defense was the reasonable testimony in conformity with the facts, which completely failed to be tested by the facts.

Bibliography

1. Kamisago, S. (1955). *Kenpei sanjuichinen* [Year 31 of the Military Police]. Tokyo: Raifusha.
2. Usui, K. (Commentary). (1964). Gendaishi Shiryo (Vol. 9). *Nicchu senso* [The Second Sino-Japanese War] (Vol. 2). Tokyo: Misuzu Shobo.
3. Nitta, M. (Ed.). (1968). *Kyokuto kokusai gunji saiban sokkiroku* [Stenographic Records of the International Military Tribunal for the Far East] (Vols. 5 and 7). Tokyo: Yushodo Shoten.
4. Hora, T. (Ed.). (1973). *Nicchu sensoshi shiryo* [Historical Documents on the Second Sino-Japanese War] (Vol. 8). *Nankin jiken* [The Nanking Incident] (Vol. I). Tokyo: Kawade Shobo.
5. Boekicho Boei Kenshujo Senshishitsu. (Ed.). (1974). Senshi Sosho. *Chugoku homen kaigun sakusen 1: Showa jusannen sangatsu made* [Naval Strategy in the China Region 1: Up to March 1938]. Tokyo: Asagumo Shinbunsha.
6. Takahashi, M. (Ed. and Commentary). (1982). Zoku Gendaishi Shiryo (Vol. 6). *Daijugun (Yanagawa heidan) homubu jinchu nikki* [Field Journals of Legal Staff in the Tenth Army (Yanagawa Army Corps), *Gunji keisatsu* Military Police]. Tokyo: Misuzu Shobo.
7. Onuma, Y. (1985). *Tokyo saiban kara sengo sekinin no shiso e* [Thoughts on Post-war Responsibility Since the Tokyo Trials]. Tokyo: Yushindo Kobunsha.
8. Tanaka, M. (1984). *"Nankin gyakusatsu" no kyoko: Matsui Taisho no nikki o megutte* [The Fiction of the "Rape of Nanking": Reviewing the Journal of General Matsui]. Tokyo: Nihon Kyobunsha.
9. Tanaka, M. (Ed.). (1985). *Matsui Iwane taisho no jinchu nikki* [General Iwane Matsui's Field Journal]. Tokyo: Fuyo Shobo.
10. Chinese Cultural and Historical Press. (1985). *Zhang Zhizhong huiyilu* [Memoirs of Zhang Zhi Zhong's]. Beijing: Chinese Cultural and Historical Press.
11. Nankin Senshi Henshu Iinkai. (Ed.). (1989). *Nankin senshi* [Nanking War History]. Tokyo: Kaikosha.

12. Nankin Senshi Henshu Iinkai. (Ed.). (1993). *Nankin senshi shiryoshu* [Collection of Nanking War Historical Documents] (Vol. II). Tokyo: Kaikosha.
13. Shimizu, M. (1991). *Kokusai gunji saibansho kensho dai 6 jo c ko, "Jindo ni taisuru tsumi" ni kan suru kakusho* [Memorandum Regarding "Crimes Against Humanity", Article 6 Item C of the Nuremburg Charter]. *Tokyo Jogakkan Tanki Daigaku kiyo* [Tokyo Jogakkan Junior College Bulletin] (No. 14).
14. Nankin Jiken Chosa Kenkyukai. (Ed. and Trans.). (1992). *Nankin jiken shiryoshu* [Collection of Documents on the Nanking Incident] (Vol. 1). *Amerika kankei shiryohen* [Document Edition Related to the United States]. Tokyo: Aoki Shoten.
15. Fuji, N. (1995). *"Nankin daigyakusatsu" wa kou shite tsukurareta--Tokyo saiban teki giman* [This Is How the Rape of Nanking Was Created—Deception in the Tokyo Trials]. Tokyo: Tendensha.
16. Tokyo Saiban Kenkyukai. (Ed.). (1996). *Kyodo kenkyu Pal hanketsusho* [Joint Research: Pal's Judgment Document] (Vol. 2). Tokyo: Kodansha.
17. Fujioka, N., & Jiyushugi Shikan Kenkyukai. (Eds.). (1996). *Kyokasho ga oshienai rekishi* [History That History Books Don't Teach] (Vol. 2). Tokyo: Sankei Shinbunsha.
18. The Second Historical Archives of China and Nanjing Archives. (1997). *Qinhua rijun Nanjing datusha dangan* [Archives of Nanjing Massacre by Japanese Invaders]. Nanjing: Phoenix Publishing House.
19. Matsumura, T. (1998). *"Nankin daigyakusatsu" he no daigimon* [Major Doubts About the "Rape of Nanking"]. Tokyo: Tendensha.
20. The Editorial Board of the Collection of Historical Materials Relating to Nanjing Massacre by Japanese Invaders and Nanjing Library. (1998). *Qinhua rijun Nanjing datusha shiliao* [A Collection of Historical Materials Relating to Nanjing Massacre]. Nanjing: Phoenix Publishing House.
21. Fujioka, N., & Higashinakano, O. (1999). *"Za reipu obu Nankin" no kenkyu: Chugoku ni okeru "johosen" no teguchi to senryaku* [Research on the "Rape of Nanking": Methods and Strategies in China's "Information War"]. Tokyo: Shodensha.
22. Itakura, Y. (2000). *Honto wa ko datta Nankin jiken* [How the Nanking Incident Really Was]. Tokyo: Nihon Tosho Kankokai.
23. Ogawa, S. (2000). *Aru gun homukan no nikki* [Journal of a Military Law Officer]. Tokyo: Misuzu Shobo.
24. Higashinakano, O. (2000). "*Daigyakusatsu" no tettei kensho* [Thorough Verification of the "Massacre"]. Tokyo: Tendensha.
25. Nihon Kaigi Kokusai Koho Iinkai. (Ed.). (2000). *Saishin "Nankin daigyakusatsu": Sekai ni uttaeru Nihon no enzai* [Reinvestigating the "Rape of Nanking"—The World's False Charges Against Japan]. Tokyo: Meiseisha.

26. Yu, Z., & Yun, Z. (2000). *Ba yi san songhu kangzhan* [August 13 Battle of Song-hu]. Shanghai: Shanghai People's Publishing house.
27. Kitamura, M. (2001). *"Nankin jiken" no tankyu--Sono jitsuzo o motomete* [Investigating the "Nanking Incident": Seeking the Actual Image]. Tokyo: Bungei Shunjusha.
28. Ara, K. (Ed.). (2002). *"Nankin jiken" nihonjin yonjuhachinin no shogen* [Testimony of 48 Japanese Regarding the "Nanking Incident"]. Tokyo: Shogakukan.
29. Cheng, Z. (2002). *Nanjing datusha shi dongjing shenpan de bianzao me?* [Was the Nanjing Massacre Fabricated by the Tokyo Tribunal?] Beijing: Modern Chinese History Studies.
30. Cheng, Z. (2002). *Rijun tushaling yanjiu* [Study on Massacre Order of Japanese Army]. Beijing: Historical Research.
31. Yang, X. (2005). *Dongjing shenpan* [Tokyo Trial]. *Nanjing datusha shiliao ji di 7 juan* [A Collection of Historical Materials Relating to Nanjing Massacre] (Vol. 7). Nanjing: Jiangsu People's Publishing Ltd and Phoenix Publishing House.
32. Yang, X. (2005). *Guoji jianchaju wenshu* [Records of the International Prosecution Section]. *Nanjing datusha shiliao ji di 29 juan* [A Collection of Historical Materials Relating to Nanjing Massacre] (Vol. 29). Nanjing: Jiangsu People's Publishing Ltd and Phoenix Publishing House.
33. Hata, I. (2007). *Nankin jiken--gyakusatsu no kozo* [The Nanking Incident—The Structure of the Massacre] (Augmented Ed., Chapter 9). *Nankin jiken ronsenshi* [History of the Controversy About the Nanking Incident] (Vol. 1). Tokyo: Chuo Koron Shinsha.
34. Cheng, Z. (2008). *Songjingshigen zhanzheng zeren de zai jiantao* [Re-evaluation of Iwane Matsui' s War Guilt]. Beijing: Modern Chinese History Studies.
35. Cheng, Z. (2010). *Xiaochuanguanzhilang zhengci de zai jiantao* [Reexamination of Ogawa Sekijirō's Testimony]. Nanjing: Jianghai Academic Journal.

CHAPTER 8

Tokyo Trials and International Rules of Law

After the World War II, it is the first time for human beings to establish the International Military Tribunal above the national sovereign, to trial the countries' leaders who waged the aggressive wars and solemnly declare the aggressive wars and the illegal acts in the wars as international crimes. The Tokyo trial resorts to the international criminal justice for the pursuit of the permanent peace of human beings, which reflects the ration, civilization and progress of human society. As the President Webb declared at the beginning of the trial, there is no more important criminal trial in the whole history. There is no doubt that both Tokyo trials and Nuremburg trials promote the development of international criminal laws and humanitarian law, starts the modern international criminal justice practice and reshapes the new order of international community through the rule of law. The Tokyo trial is of great importance for the human civilization of rule of law, which tells us that waging the aggressive wars is international crimes and the crimes should be punished and forbidden to take place for the peace of the generations.

1 The Origin and Formation of the Views of Illegal War

For a long time, war stands for honor, hero and reputation. The military theorist Karl Philip Gottfried von Clausewitz once said, war is another continuation of politics. The two world wars overruled the war tradition

Z. Cheng, *A History of War Crimes Trials in Post 1945 Asia-Pacific*,
https://doi.org/10.1007/978-981-13-6697-0_8

of human. International community changes the consensus toward war. War and peace become the important theme of international laws.

The Nuremburg and Tokyo trials after the World War II demonstrated the efforts of the international community to contain war and fight for permanent peace through international criminal justice trial. Tokyo trials, together with Nuremburg trials, defined the war as international crime and punished the individual who waged the aggressive war. In the terms of law, it was the milestone of international rule of law that established new views of war rules. Just like the saying of UNESCO, even if war starts from the thoughts of human, we can build peace from the thoughts of human.

1.1 Restriction on the Resort to the Jus Ad Bellum and Wartime Rules

Human thoughts about war and war rules exist for a long time. To clarify it is helpful for us to understand the topic and historical meaning of the two postwar trials.

Jus ad bellum of the countries is restricted from 1899 and 1907 Hague Peace Conferences in the terms of International law. This two conferences prudently discussed the issue of the state's right to engage in wars without restriction. In 1899, Hague peace conference concluded *Convention for the Pacific Settlement of International Disputes* which stipulated that with a view to obviating, as far as possible, recourse to force in the relations between States, the Signatory Powers agree to use their best efforts to insure the pacific settlement of international differences. In case of serious disagreement or conflict, before an appeal to arms, the Signatory Powers agree to have recourse, as far as circumstances allow, to the good offices or mediation of one or more friendly Powers. In 1907, Hague Peace Conference revised *Convention for the Pacific Settlement of International Disputes* and concluded *Convention Respecting the Limitation of the Employment of Force for the Recovery of Contract Debts* which stipulated that the Contracting Powers agree not to have recourse to armed force for the recovery of contract debts claimed from the Government of one country by the Government of another country as being due to its nationals. This undertaking is, however, not applicable when the debtor State refuses or neglects to reply to an offer of arbitration, or, after accepting the offer, prevents any compromise from being agreed on, or, after the arbitration, fails to submit to the award.

Convention for the Pacific Settlement of International Disputes is the earliest to stipulate the settlement of international disputes and its function and value are not limited with the ways of settlement of international disputes. This is the first time to limit countries' jus ad bellum.

International community is also devoted into limiting the acts of war and making jus in bello to reduce the damage and cruelty of wars. The earliest jus in bello can be traced to 1621 Military Legal Provisions Observed in the War promulgated by Sweden which stipulated that neither the colonel nor the lieutenant shall order the soldiers to do anything illegal, and the offenders shall be punished in accordance with the judgment of the judge.

In 1863 during US civil war, *Lieber Code* was widely regarded as the best summary of the first customary laws and customs of war, which was a binding document approved by president Lincoln and became the origin of 1874 *Brussels Declaration* and *Hague Convention.*

The *Saint Petersburg Declaration of 1868* is the first formal agreement prohibiting the use of certain weapons in war. The article of the appendix of Hague Convention IV of 1907 *Convention Respecting the Laws and Customs of War on Land* stipulated that family honor and rights, the lives of persons, and private property, as well as religious convictions and practice, must be respected. The other articles of this agreement also provided protection against culture and private property. The prelude of *Hague Convention* acknowledged itself imperfect but promised that until the complete code of laws of war was issued, populations and belligerents remained under the protection and empire of the principles of international law, as they resulted from the usages established between civilized nations, from the laws of humanity.

The series rules of means and methods of warfare were called Hague Law. In 1913, a commission of inquiry sent by the Carnegie Foundation to investigate the atrocities committed during the Balkan Wars used the provisions of Hague Convention IV as a basis for its description of crimes. Immediately, following World War I, the Commission on the Responsibility of the Authors of the War and on the Enforcement of Penalties, established to examine allegations of war crimes committed by the central powers, did the same. It was not until Nuremburg and Tokyo trials that the behaviors against Hague Convention were prosecuted.

Meanwhile, thanks to the International Committee of the Red Cross, an international conference with 16 countries was held in Geneva in 1864 and adopted the first *Geneva Convention* for the amelioration of the condition of the wounded in armies in the field with the aim of protecting the sick, wounded soldiers and such war victims as non-combatants, slaves and civilians. On this basis, the humanitarian norms of "the law of Geneva" was developed. The principle of the humanitarian norms of the law of Geneva was realized by restricting and regulating the means and methods of warfare. Besides, the treaties of the law of the Hague were signed in the spirit of humanitarian. Therefore, the law of Geneva and the law of the Hague were coherent in restricting wars, implementing humanitarian protection.

1.2 The Formation of the Views of Unlawful Wars

Although there have been many destructive wars in European history, in many cases, most participating countries seemed not to get any lessons and engaged in a new war. Nineteenth century European militarist asserted that regardless of the strategic goal of the wars, the wars themselves were a beneficial activity. They think wars can make people cheer up. The World War I not only presented the end of imperialism in the field of western mainstream thoughts but also denied that the war is a kind of need or an unavoidable opinion. Human generally acknowledged that waging the wars deliberately wasn't considered as justice. The heads of all countries started to organize international union to prevent new wars.

In 1919, the *Covenant of the League of Nations* (hereinafter referred to Covenant) referred in the prelude, "in order to promote international co-operation and to achieve international peace and security, by the acceptance of obligations not to resort to war". The Article 13 of the covenant required that they will not resort to war against a member of the league which complies with the award or decision. Meanwhile, pursuant to the Article 16, should any member of the league resort to war in disregard of its covenants, it shall ipso facto be deemed to have committed an act of war against all other members of the league, which hereby undertake immediately to subject it to the severance of all trade or financial relations, the prohibition of all intercourse between their nationals and the nationals of the covenant-breaking States, and the prevention of all financial, commercial or personal intercourse between the nationals of the covenant-breaking States and the nationals of any other State. It shall be the duty of the Council in such case to recommend to the several Governments concerned what effective military, naval or air force the Members of the League shall severally contribute to the armed forces to be used to protect the covenants of the League. The league of nations tried to limit the countries' right of resorting to the wars through the collective security system based on international organizations.

The concept that aggressive war is illegal even a crime is reflected in the latter documents of league of nations. Article 1 of *Draft Treaty of Mutual Assistance* drafted by league of nations in 1923 but finally ineffective declared aggressive war is an international crime and contracting parties undertake that none of them will be guilty of its commission against another. In 1924, league of nations adopted *the Geneva Protocol for the Pacific Settlement of International Disputes* which acknowledged the joint relations among the members of international community and that aggressive war destroyed the relationship was an international crime. On September 24, 1927, league of nations adopted *Declaration on Aggression* according to the proposal of Poland delegation. It pointed that all peaceful ways should be used to solve the disputes which may happen in the countries and aggressive wars cannot be the way of solving international disputes. Aggressive war, therefore, is an international crime. All aggressive wars shall be prevented forever. On February 18, 1928, one of the resolutions adopted by the 6th Pan-American Conference pointed that aggressive war constituted a crime against human…all aggression was illegal and therefore declared prohibited.

There is no doubt that 1928 *Kellogg-Briand Pact* (*Pact of Paris*) is the epitome of these efforts. The pact was pioneering in renunciation of war as an instrument of national policy and made great contributions to establishing the two principles of international laws of settling international disputes by peaceful means, refraining from the threat or use of force.

2 Aggressive War Is an International Crime

2.1 War: From Illegal to Crime

Pact of Paris is decisive in the development of international law which prohibits wars and constitutes base of positive law which confirms aggressive war as an international crime. The preamble of *Pact of Paris* pointed that *the time has come when a frank renunciation of war as an instrument of national policy… Convinced that all changes in their relations with one another should be sought only by pacific means and be the result of a peaceful and orderly process, and that any signatory Power which shall hereafter seek to promote its national interests by resort to war a should be denied the benefits furnished by this Treaty.*

Oppenheim's International Law comments on it: The Pact constitutes a radical change in International Law. War cannot now legally, as it could be prior to the conclusion of the Pact, be resorted to either as a legal remedy or as an instrument for changing the law. "Resort to war is no longer a discretionary prerogative right of States signatories of the Pact; it is a matter of legitimate concern for other signatories whose legal rights are violated by recourse to war in breach of the Pact".

By 1939, among the 67 countries, 63 approved *Pact of Paris* including China and Japan. This convention then became applicable worldwide and is still effective until now. This convention is often accepted by national practice and is the basis of other bilateral and multi-lateral treaties of renunciation of war.

Pact of Paris failed to prevent the World War II because aggressive political party deliberately ignored their obligations under international law and lunched a war. Also, this convention has come weaknesses. It and prohibitive provisions of war means are based on a narrow formal war concept. Moreover, as part of the collective measures of the league of nations, the use of belligerent force is still allowed because war is a renunciative instrument of national policies but not the international policies. Besides, through the declaration submitted when signing the convention, all parties clearly stated that this convention didn't restrict their right to self-defense. However, since there is no definition of the legal measures of self-defense in the convention itself, it leaves the danger of abusing the right to self-defense.

There is no doubt that in the late 1930s, the standpoint of international law toward war dramatically changed. Aggressive war was no longer considered as a rational policy but limited largely to lose its legal position. Aggressive war has become a crime under the customary international law. However, the range of crime must be determined on the basis of the only precedent so far. Those are Nuremburg and Tokyo trials.

People often ask whether all crimes prosecuted by the international military tribunals in Nuremberg and Tokyo—crimes against peace, war crimes and crimes against humanity—become crimes under international law when implemented. Based on the different standpoints, there are indeed different opinions on this question. In order to understand and respond to this question correctly, we should go back to Nuremberg and Tokyo trials which were examined as an international criminal judicial trial.

The Far East International Military Court has convincingly proved the criminality of the aggressive war from the international law. The prosecution pointed that aggressive war was an international crime and it was enough to depend on the legal documents as direct evidence when the tribunals were set up. However, when the argumentation, the prosecution referred to more evidence to prove that aggression or the acts which violated international treaties was against international law. Chief president of The Tokyo tribunal Keenan provided three definitions about "aggression". Firstly, aggression is "a first and unprovoked attack, or act of hostility; the first act of injury or first act leading to a war or a controversy; an assault; also the practice of attack or encroachment; as, a war of aggression". Secondly, aggression is an act that "a nation that refuses to arbitrate or to accept an arbitration award, or any other peaceful method, in the settlement of a dispute but threatens to use force or to resort to war". Thirdly, aggression is that "the aggressor being that state which goes to war in violation of its pledge to submit the matter of dispute to peaceful settlement, having already agreed to do so". These three definitions described the illegality of aggression. The Tribunal for Tokyo trials concluded the existence of aggressive plan, preparation, launching the wars and implementation as the premise of the individual duty. Tribunal carefully evaluated the military situation when the Manchurian Incident broke out in 1931, which confirmed that "Manchurian Incident" was not a simple "individual incident" but a first step of Japanese aggressive war with relation to the latter military actions against China, Southeast Asia and Pacific areas. The tribunal pointed no matter how difficult the overall definition of "aggressive war" gives, such attack can only be defined as aggressive war. *The Judgement of International Military Tribunal for Far East* defined the nature of aggression: the aim of aggressive war is to rule another country or to gain territory of another country. This is consistent with the judgment of Nuremberg trial. So-called self-defensive war has also become defense reason for the defendant and defense lawyer in the Tokyo trial. For example, the defense argued that the two military conflicts between Soviet Union and Mongolia (Zhang Gufeng incident and Nomonhan incident) in the so-called border line of Manchukuo was the "self-defensive war" of Japanese Manchukuo. The tribunal checked and decided Japan made the plan and preparation of the war in the "border line" before the event and rejected the claim of defense. That meant The Tokyo tribunal considered aggressive war as a major international crime. Except following the international law accepted by all civilized countries, the tribunal was responsible for the prosecution of the war. To show acquiescence in condoning criminal acts was to trample on the common interest of humankind.

2.2 *The Nature of War Crime: Dimension of International Law*

The two world wars completely destroy the basic values of the international community—peace, safety and welfare, which provides an international dimension for war crime and turns it into a crime under the international law. As this kind of crime influences the so-called international community as a whole, to punish the international crime becomes the task of international community and the norm of international criminal law can penetrate "the armor of state sovereignty". Thus, the relations between criminal law and the interests of international community provide its special rationality.

All the international crime has the background in which violence is widely used. As a rule, it is a group that takes the responsibility for violence, typically it is a country. For crimes against humanity, the organized violence is made up of a kind of wide or systematic attack toward civilians. For the war crimes, the organized violence is made up of a series of armed conflicts and the armed conflict between countries must destroy the world peace, so the crime must have happened. As a result, the criminalization which is against the war laws is aimed to reduce the effect of the armed conflicts to the minimum in case of intensifying the conflicts. For crimes against peace, the organized crime itself is criminalized. Therefore, aggression is crimes against peace in the direct meaning.

The basic values of the international community—peace, safety and welfare are protected in the international law. The punishment of the international criminal sanction toward war is aimed to prevent the war from breaking out again and punish war criminals. The prosecution and punishment by the Tokyo tribunal on the aggressors is to realize the greater common goal of "ensuring international peace". In this sense, the legal principle of crimes against peace insisted by The Tokyo tribunal should be given a positive evaluation. What is more meaningful is that the process of prosecution toward the war criminal suspects and the prosecution itself through legal means can help a lot to form the world public opinion and can gain a relationship with the long-time war prevention so as to contribute to the world peace. In another word, people can realize that pursuing international justice corresponds to the joint benefits of the humankind through the education of Nuremberg and Tokyo trials.

2.3 Legality: Principle of Justice

The main dissenting opinions toward the Nuremberg-Tokyo trial mode are about its political rationality and legal basis. From the law, the criticism of Tokyo trials is mainly that the trial of crimes against peace is the violation of the principle of a legally prescribed punishment for a specified crime and non-retroactivity of law.

Legality requires that written or unwritten norms must exist and the description of criminal acts must be clearly stipulated in the definition of the crimes as far as possible, so that the crimes can be established under the international law. Legality is part of customary international law and the legal basis accepted by the Tokyo and Nuremberg tribunals. Legality plays a major role in the Tokyo trial.

Actually, the proverb "nullum crimen sine lege" is not a limitation for sovereignty and is a principle of justice. The principle of non-retroactivity of law cannot be aimed at protecting the abuse of rights in violation of international law from punishment.AS Japan's politician Kushima Kaneburo said before the judgment of Tokyo trials was released, "our life is not for the life, instead, law exists for our life". Thus, "only those people who don't understand law allow the atrocities that leads the world to collapse for without no precedent."

The highest aim of law is to realize justice, and it is necessary to accuse the aggressors. Critics only stick to the incompleteness of the positive law and ignore the important fact of whether the object of the trial is actually criminal. It is important to grasp the essence of the criminal acts. If it owns the nature of crime substantively, there will be corresponding reasons to punish it instead of ignoring the fact of crimes based on the practical standpoint of law and the incomplete form.

The principle of a legally prescribed punishment for a specified crime, the predecessor of principle of legality, is the important product of Enlightenment Movement. Its core aim is to limit the national power through limiting judicial abuse. Its fundamental aim is to protect the happiness of mankind. It is originally the product of western tradition of civil disobedience. Evaluating the principle of legality should be in light of the history tradition of the people's own country. If it is not regarded as a civic tradition but a symbolic interpretation mechanism, it is easy to draw a dangerous and wrong conclusion. Besides, forbidding ex post laws is applicable to the aims of protecting individual freedom from infringement by state power, while the exercise of this principle to protect those who abuse state power contradicts the original concept. Therefore, one of the famous jurists and a member of the Tokyo trial defense team, Kainō Michitaka, believed that to make the principle of a legally prescribed punishment for a specified crime come true must be to protect the freedom of political activities and thoughts. Therefore, to follow the principle of a legally prescribed punishment for a specified crime legitimately must protect the freedom of political activities and thoughts correctly. In Japan, it is absurd that those who exercised state power to suppress the political and ideological freedom before or during the war tried to support Class A war criminals to avoid punishment on the basis of the principle of a legally prescribed punishment for a specified crime when facing the Tokyo trial after war. The Tokyo trial correctly rejected the claim of the defense and believed that the proverb of nulla poena sine lege didn't refer to the limitation on the sovereign but a general justice principle.

The Tokyo trial's view on the wars—wars are not recognized by the international community. Aggressive wars, international illegal acts, become international crimes. The individual criminal responsibility of the leaders of the countries who waged the aggressive war can be investigated—have become the consensus of the international community today. Tokyo trials made specific contributions to the establishment of the law and the realization of justice and correctly foresaw the future trend of international law. The Nuremberg-Tokyo law principle established by the Nuremberg and Tokyo trials established as customary international law, which becomes part of the international legal system and is important in the contemporary international rule of law.

3 The Establishment of Individual Criminal Responsibility

3.1 From Versailles to Tokyo

The idea of establishing universal criminal justice can find its root in the early stage of human history. The actual first international trial took place in 1474. Peter von Hagenbach was put on trial for the atrocities committed during the occupation of Breisach. He was guilty of war crimes, and beheaded. However, the enlightening experiment of international trial in the middle ages was soon replaced by the principle that the state sovereign was sacred and inviolable established by *the Peace Treaty of Westphalia* in 1648. 1899 and 1907 Hague Convention affirmed responsibilities and duties for each contracting country but didn't affirm individual criminal responsibilities.

In the international law, the efforts to establish individual criminal responsibilities can be seen in the *Treaty of Versailles* On June 28, 1919. Article 227 of *Treaty of Versailles* stipulated that a special military tribunal will be constituted to try German Emperor William II of Hohenzollern for waging the wars. So, Commission on the Responsibility of the Authors of the War and on the Enforcement of Penalties was established as the first commission on the international investigation of war crimes. The commission consisted of the representatives of the USA, the British Empire, France, Italy, Japan and China for investigate individuals responsible for the World War I and whether there was a fact and legal reason for trying those responsible for the war and acts in the war. In other words, the commission was on responsibility for the Violation of the Laws and Customs of War, charged with deciding whom to indict for crimes committed during the war.

In the investigation report of the commission, Japanese and US delegations expressed their reservations for establishing the international military tribunal and trying the state leaders. They started the argument about the major law issues of the individual criminal responsibility and command responsibility of the war initiators. These disagreements and opinions about the legal issues of the war responsibility cannot be ignored, which deeply reflected the caution and concern of mankind as a community about the prompt punishment of war criminals by legal means. The concern partly came from meticulous legal supremacism not complacent victors or cunning arguments of losers, which proved that war crimes trials were not "shows" by major powers. The arguments continued to the Nuremberg-Tokyo trial, developed until now and affects legal thoughts of mankind about wars and peace.

German Emperor William II gent to exile in the Netherlands. German Supreme Court in Leipzing tried the 12 defendants and most defendants acquitted and released in the audience's cheers. The allied countries lost the opportunity to punish war criminals and rebuild peace order through the establishment of international justice system.

Although the international court envisaged in the *Treaty of Versailles* didn't establish and it didn't trial the German Emperor, the groundbreaking significance of the *Treaty of Versailles* shouldn't be underestimated. This is the first time that prosecuting the individual criminal responsibility of the war initiator and those who committed crimes in the war has been clearly stipulated in an international treaty. This concept is unprecedented—the leaders of the countries can be held accountable for the decision to launch the war. There has been a clear start to punish the perpetrators and leaders of the war in the international community.

After the World War II, Nuremberg and Tokyo trials provided revolutionary standpoints. *Charter of the International Military Tribunal* and *Charter of the International Military Tribunal for Far East* suggested that in the International law, crimes against peace, war crimes and crimes against humanity shall produce individual responsibility. This means that the individual may be considered to shoulder the criminal responsibility of war crimes in the international criminal trial. It is also for this reason that the defendant and the defense lawyers raised their defense against the court's jurisdiction over these crimes. Waging an aggressive war is an act of the country, while international law is dominated by the countries and it lacks the sanction means against individuals. It is impossible for individuals who involved in the war to satisfy the "intentional" condition necessary for the establishment of crimes. Therefore, individuals shouldn't bear criminal responsibility for crimes against peace.

Nuremberg tribunal cited "Ex Parte Quirin" to prove that international law prescribes rights and duties for individuals and there are numerous precedents of punishing individuals under international law. Meanwhile, each person not only has the duty to know and follow laws and Ignorantia ju-ris non excusat but also it is impossible that the defendants "have no intention to commit crimes" when destroying the treaty and occupying other countries. The crimes in violation of international law are committed by humankind not by an abstract entity. Only by punishing the individuals who committed these crimes can these provisions of international law be implemented. Based on this, the tribunal determined the theoretical basis of the principle of individual responsibility in the aggressive war. This also becomes the precedent followed by Tokyo tribunal.

3.2 Conspiracy and Individual Criminal Responsibility

The Article 5 of the International Military Tribunal for the Far East stipulated that *The Tribunal shall have the power to try and punish Far Eastern war criminals who as individuals or as members of organizations are charged with offences which include Crimes against Peace. The following acts, or any of them, are crimes coming within the jurisdiction of the Tribunal for which there shall be individual responsibility:*

a. Crimes against Peace: Namely, the planning, preparation, initiation or waging of a declared or undeclared war of aggression, or a war in violation of international law, treaties, agreements or assurances, or participation in a common plan or conspiracy for the accomplishment of any of the foregoing;

c. Crimes against Humanity: Namely, murder, extermination, enslavement, deportation, and other inhumane acts committed against any civilian population, before or during the war, or persecutions on political or racial grounds in execution of or in connection with any crime within the jurisdiction of the Tribunal, whether or not in violation of the domestic law of the country where perpetrated. Leaders, organizers, instigators and accomplices participating in the formulation or execution of a common plan or conspiracy to commit any of the foregoing crimes are responsible for all acts performed by any person in execution of such plan.

In this article, the last sentence which differs from Nuremberg charter becomes the main basis of the prosecution in the Tokyo trial. The prosecution thinks that conspiracy is an international crime. According to the common law, this crime is known to all and recognized by most civilized countries. The international community takes objective ethical order as its cornerstone, and conspiracy is the flexible form of self-protection model. The so-called conspiracy means two or more people as a whole to take coordinated actions and realize a crime or an illegal aim through crimes or illegal measures. The aim of the conspiracy may be consistent, that is, conspiracy may plan many illegal acts or activities. To start with this, the first cause of the indictment, that is, Tojo Hideki and other all defendants, as the leaders, organizers, instigators or accomplice, were involved in making or implementing the conspiracy and took responsibility for the acts of the individuals or the executors from January 1, 1928 to September 2, 1945. The prosecution also proposed that conspiracy can be confirmed by indirect evidence and it was not a necessary condition that the defendants knew that other people had completed the conspiracy. This means that non-resistance to the current situation is the tolerance for conspiracy.

The prosecution's theoretical basis is that war crime is a special form of crime which is not committed by an individual but occurs in the form of collective resolution, issuing or order execution, group activities, etc. in the process of preparing to wage a war or in a state of war. However, the intentional behavior of individuals is prerequisite for the crimes. The acts stipulated in the crimes against peace actually are guided by different stages of the crimes from planning, preparing, waging to implementing aggressive wars. The fact that you participated in the aggressive war only after it began is sufficient for this crime. This manifested that part of the crime involved implementing aggressive wars. This is why the defendants of the crimes against peace in the Tokyo trial are former political or military leaders. But it must be clear that the key is the possibility of effective control or leadership not the legal position. The perpetrators needn't make a decision about war and peace, but they must participate in such activities as planning, preparing, waging or implementation. Because the defendants are part of the entire aggressive war plan, their "negligence" or lack of resistance would make the mistake worse.

The defense proposes that criterion of liability expands conspiracy and is too strict for the defendants. It should be replaced by a more restrictive definition and conspiracy should be limited in the process of core decision. However, based on the investigation, the tribunal supported the prosecution's view. President Webb believes that although the conspirators may never meet, know or talk directly or indirectly, it doesn't prevent war criminals from jointly committing crimes against peace under the premise of lack of conspiracy communication. Therefore, the tribunal's opinion is that the crime of conspiring to wage an aggressive war or an illegal war is established when two or more people agree to commit the crime. The stage of war planning and preparation will be entered upon the conclusion of conspiracy. The criminals who participated in this stage may be the initial conspirators or the followers. If the latter accept the aim of the conspiracy and plan and prepare for the wars, they will become conspirators. In this sense, all the defendants will face the accusation of conspiracy. We may find that the perpetrators of the conspiracy are also involved in planning and preparation, so there is no need to distinguish the two. The defense's argument about the military department and government in opposition to each other is only one side of the whole truth. Judging from the short-sighted historical evaluation, it may not be wrong. But if we re-examine it from an all-round perspective, it seems that the former distorts the facts.

People in the civil service against hawk don't always hold opposing opinions and once voluntarily participated in and directed the planning and implementation of aggressive wars. Once these related facts are clearly presented in court, the logic basis for the defense to argue that civil officers shouldn't be held accountable no longer exists.

The court judgment reviewed the historical facts of Japan's long-term aggressive wars against China and the Pacific and concluded that Japan made its military expansion policy after seizing the power since 1920s. Through re-dividing its ultimate expansion goal of "the greater East Asia co-prosperity sphere", Japan, on the one hand, controlled all territories between India and Myanmar. On the other hand, Japan controlled Australia and New Zealand. The judgment analyzed Japan's military expansion policy, which revealed the process of implementation to explain the villainy committed by the defendants for the rise of militarism and thus to confirm the individual criminal responsibility of these people.

The extensive planning for waging the aggressive wars and the long-term complicated preparation for the wars cannot be completed by one person but many leaders are involved to accomplish the common plan. Although they may not know each other well and don't "plot" in one room even have different opinions and oppositions, their common goal is to ensure the dominant position of the great Japanese empire, so they instigate, implement and join in the war. The common goal is the basis for their common actions. Even if there is no specific contract, it doesn't prevent all defendants from making "contributions" to war crimes.

Indeed, there is no more serious crime than waging an aggressive war or conspiring to wage an aggressive war. The implementation of the common plan is bound to be accompanied by massive death and pain.

The legal principle of determining criminal responsibility for crimes against peace based on conspiracy reveals that a collective with less strict organization even with opposing opinions also can produce common war crimes. This criterion of liability runs through the trial of the International Military Tribunal for Far East, and even such justices who hold skeptical attitude toward this criterion as Roling are also willing to admit that the court's judgment on crimes against peace has a certain basis and makes it clear that civil officers may be responsible for war crimes. This is a major contribution made by the International Military Tribunal for Far East.

3.3 *The Legal Meaning of Determining Individual Criminal Responsibility*

The establishment of individual criminal responsibility faces two main legal barriers. The one is that the country is the only subject in the jurisprudence of classic international law. Thus, in order to establish individual criminal norms in the international law, individuals should be recognized as subject of the international law. The other is to overcome the defensive attitude of the countries toward external interference based on the notion of sovereignty and interest orientation.

The massive atrocities in the World War II "shock the human conscience" and the foundation of human civilization was shaken. This inspired international community to deeply reflect on traditional theory of international law. People realized that "culture of impunity" was an important reason why atrocities recur. The country becomes a shelter for individuals to commit serious crimes behind the theory of sovereign immunity. This legal problem must be solved through legal self-renovation.

Based on the existing legal theory and principle and the particularity of the war crimes, the International Military Tribunal for Far East proposed that determining war crimes must break through the traditional legal principles of governing inter-country affairs and penetrate into the domestic field of the involved countries to pierce through "the armor of sovereignty". The crimes in violation of international law are implemented by people instead of an abstract subject like countries. Only by punishing individuals who commit these crimes can international law be truly implemented. Those leaders who directly participate in decision making must be tried in international court. The court illustrated the principle of such legal issues as conspiracy, the responsibility of commanders and negative crime. Besides, it provided many creative legal interpretations about individual criminal responsibility principle and finally determined the individual criminal responsibility of the defendants through the evidence-centered trial.

The Tokyo and Nuremberg trials made it clear that those who commit crimes that constitute crimes against peace, war crimes and crimes against humanity should bear individual criminal responsibility and be subject to criminal punishment. The "individual responsibility" means: first, leaders, organizers, instigators, and accomplices who participated in the decision or execution of the conspiracy shall be responsible for the acts committed by anyone who implemented the plan. Second, the official offices of the criminals cannot be the basis for exempting them from criminal responsibility. That is, anyone including heads of the countries and the responsible officials of various government apartments shall not make the excuse that he was on behalf of the country or the government when he was committing the crimes and emphasized that their acts are the country's acts rather than individual acts so as to abdicate individual responsibility. Third, people who specifically committed war crimes couldn't be exempted from individual responsibility for "following the orders". That is, people who specifically committed war crimes couldn't be exempted from individual responsibility even if they acted according to the order of the government or a superior or chief commander. Fourth, the acts of the defendants didn't violate the domestic law where the defendant was located, which couldn't be the reason for being exempted from individual responsibility. In this case, the penalty can be reduced considering the actual situation when committing the crime. This also promotes the development of international criminal law.

Japanese social democracy hasn't developed during the war, and the state power is in the hand of leaders. If International Military Tribunal in Tokyo lacked the knowledge of establishing individual criminal responsibility and took a conservative stance of state responsibility and collective responsibility, war responsibility would be shifted to the people who were not allowed to make any political statements and suffer from the war, and the real responsibility would be covered. Thankfully, all abstract theories of state legal person were firmly rejected by the Tokyo trial.

In this way, not only have the two legal barriers been successfully overcome, Tokyo court has also been the pioneer of establishing individual criminal responsibility for international war crimes and promoted the development of international criminal law.

4 Strengthening the Concept of Humanity and Human Rights

4.1 Humanitarian Is the Foundation of the Trial of War Crimes

War is bound to cause death and injury. Naturally, it is immortal. Only under the strict conditions where the war prevents more death can the war be justified. The punishment for war crimes stems from caring for the fate of individuals in the war. The more attention is paid to the basic rights of individuals, the more urgent is the desire to punish war crimes.

The Enlightenment Movement in the eighteenth century triggered a "humanitarian revolution" in the west. The revolution gradually placed humanity, human rights, the sympathy and concern for the weak and tolerance for others at the core of people's moral consciousness. The Geneva law system and Hague law system, which were formed and continuously developed in the nineteenth century, were devoted to improving the conditions of individuals affected by wars and protecting the basic individual rights in the armed conflict. The two systems jointly formed today's international humanitarian law. International humanitarian law and law of war shared origin and existence and it was the main content of the law of war. Serious violation of international humanitarian law may constitute international crimes.

On May 24, 1915, France, Great Britain and Russia stated in their declaration condemning Turkey's massacre of the Armenian that all members of the Ottoman government and those of their agents who are implicated in such massacres will hold personally responsible for crimes against humanity and civilization. In 1919, the report of Commission on the Responsibility of the Authors of the War and on the Enforcement of Penalties of Versailles conference stated that the acts of murders and genocide, systematic terrorism, putting hostages to death, torture of civilians, deliberate starvation of civilians, rape, abduction of girls and women for the purpose of enforced prostitution, deportation of civilians, internment of civilians under inhuman conditions, forced labor of civilians in connection with military operations of the enemy, imposition of collective penalties, deliberate bombardment of undefended places and hospitals were crimes against humanity. Although the US and Japanese delegations believed the concept of "humanitarian law" was too vague, the report of commission still insisted that "humanitarian law" did exist and someone who violated the law should bear criminal responsibility.

For a long period of time, although the concept of humanity has become increasingly popular, effective sanction mechanism and judicial practice for the violations of international humanitarian law lacks. After the World War II, this situation changed in the two trials. *Charter of International Military Tribunal* and *Charter of International Military Tribunal for Far East* included crimes against humanity into the jurisdiction of the court.

The two international military tribunals believed that crimes against humanity are extremely serious international crimes under the international law and violated the common interest of international community and the common values shared by all mankind. Crimes against humanity are not only directed against certain groups and individuals, but also against the crime acts of all mankind. If these acts of crimes are not punished or stopped, the basic values on which the international community depends will be damaged.

The provisions of the Tokyo charter on crimes against humanity have the following characteristics: first, crimes against humanity don't distinguish between "pre-war or wartime"; Second, the specific implementation forms of crimes against humanity are various, including killing, genocide, enslavement, forced migration, etc. Third, crimes against humanity was recommended as a crime in the international law. Even if the certain acts are lawful pursuant to the domestic law, if such acts conform to the requirement of crimes against humanity, they will also be punished by international law. Finally, different from Nuremberg charter, the crime of persecution under crimes against humanity doesn't need religious reasons.

This means that "humanity" has transcendence. First of all, it is beyond the state and political power, returns to the human rights themselves and protects all mankind as a community with a shared future. It also puts the value of "human" prior to "civilization". It is believed that civilization should not be superior to human. Any act of destroying and enslaving citizens or ethnic groups in the name of reviving civilization and consolidating political power or with the excuse of the historical will and the direction of progress is a crime.

The indictment of Tokyo trials didn't make a clear distinction between war crimes and crimes against humanity but combined them as the third cause of action—war crimes and crimes against humanity. Tokyo court also didn't judge crimes against humanity but took all documented cases of atrocities as war crimes. However, it not only didn't weaken the humane stance of Tokyo trials but also highlighted the speculation and understanding of crimes against humanity by the international military tribunal in Tokyo. In the Tokyo tribunal's view, crimes against humanity lies in the special crime motive that is based on the race, nationality, culture community and beliefs of the victims. With this motive, systematic acts of violating human life, physical health and freedom can constitute crimes against humanity.

The statute of the international criminal court further improved the definition of crimes against humanity and clearly stipulated that the criminal responsibility of defendants who committed crimes against humanity should be investigated not only against one party of the conflicts but also against the acts in violation of humanity. To a large extent, this developed the trial of the two international military tribunals after the World War II and demonstrated the universal appeal of humanity.

Some rules which formed in the two major postwar trials of punishing the crimes against peace, war crimes, crimes against humanity gradually developed as war Jus Cogens and established the responsibility of a state for the whole international community, i.e. “obligatio erga omnes”. For the interest of the all human, no matter whether a state has a treaty, it must undertake duty of cracking down on and punishing international crimes for the whole international community.

The emergence of modern international criminal law is actually the result of the continuous attention of mankind to humanitarian, or the creation and development of the international criminal law is to defend humanitarian. Humanitarian is the foundation on which war crimes are proved. Tokyo trials of the war crimes also promote the spirit of humanitarian. Although international criminal law and international criminal rules have gradually developed, safeguarding humanitarian is always the unswerving pursuit in a whole.

4.2 Trial Makes the Concept of Human Rights Awaken

The establishment of individual criminal responsibility in the Tokyo trial is different from the traditional state-centered mode of international law. Tokyo trials have confirmed the subject status of individuals in the international law. Individuals can have rights in the international law and must perform their obligations required by international law. As a result, as the milestone of international criminal justice events, Tokyo trials improved the legal status of human to an unprecedented level. National citizens transformed into world citizens, especially leaders of the countries, must assume individual legal obligations for world peace. This is far from a revolution of international law, which led to fundamental changes of international law system.

The laws and principles applied and developed in the Tokyo trial became the important source of international criminal law. As a new branch of law, the international criminal law took the individual’s act as its object of regulation and the liability as individual responsibility. The result of the trial was not only a victory of justice, but also awakened the concept of individual rights and declared the end of dark age of totalitarianism and coming of the times of individual rights. International criminal law and human rights law achieved their own breakthrough by the epoch-making international criminal justice events.

The Tokyo trial clarified the criminal nature of the aggressive war. Punishing war criminals means that the ultimate value of the rule of law is the individual. This open trial of the century conveyed to the world an idea that the life and rights of each individual can be protected and respected by law, and the fate of human is linked and nobody is an isolated island. We must work together to make peace.

The protection of basic rights of human pursued by the Tokyo trial is all-round. The trial established the individual criminal responsibility of the defendants and fully guaranteed the individual rights of defendants.

At that time, Japanese citizens felt that the shameful people like war criminals needn't defend themselves. However, not only Japanese people but also the American lawyers who once were lawyers of "enemy's country" defended the defendants. They wholeheartedly defended the defendants, which deeply shocked and moved many nationals and jurists.

Acknowledging that the defendants has the same right to debate in court as the prosecution gave the deepest impression on the Japanese who were accustomed to the authoritative prosecution and weak defendants. A large number of Japanese jurists like Dleto Shigehikaru gave a positive comment on Tokyo trials and believed that it can be considered as the greatest contributions to the Japanese criminal trial and had profound meaning for the history of Japanese criminal law. It also proved once again that the Tokyo trial was not a revenge drama but a vivid picture of the international community's efforts to seek for law and justice.

5 The Demonstration of Judicial Justice

People have made various comments on Tokyo trials, evaluating it as the "winners' trial", "the trial beyond winners", "the moral trial" and "civilized trial". As an epoch-making international criminal justice trial in human history, we must consider the requirements of the independent and fair trial in accordance with the principle of the rule of law to judge whether the trial is qualified and successful. Since the international community selected legal method to punish the criminals, the form and spirit of law must be respected. The justice of Tokyo court Henry Bernard pointed, “the moral nature of the law applied in Tokyo trials must be subject to respect for procedure justice. The legitimacy of the Tokyo court depends on whether the allied countries can give the defendant a fair trial”. Through an analysis of the proceedings and litigation process, we can find that the Tokyo trial is a just trial which was based on a solid principle pf rule of law and followed due process.

5.1 The Nature and Procedural Standards of Tokyo Court

The consensus of the legal community is that International Military Tribunal for Far East is international military tribunal in nature.

In November 1948, after the end of Tokyo trials, because of one-tier trial system, the American defense lawyers of the two defendants Dohihara Kenji and Hirota Koki appealed to the US Supreme Court that McArthur has no right to establish military court to trial Japanese war criminals, and Tokyo court is only an American military court and requests to release defendants. According to the international agreements participated by the US government and its international obligations to the allied countries, US supreme court should have rejected immediately. However, the US supreme court unexpectedly decided to accept the appeal, which caused a stir in the international community. The allied countries blamed US supreme court for “the amazing mistake”. If the final judgment made by the international military court is subject to a separate review by a state court, the future decisions and actions of the inter-countries will face a separate review and revocation, and the cooperation and mutual trust will no longer exist. US Department of Justice pointed out to the US supreme court that it had no right to review the agreement with its allies on the punishment of war criminals during the war. Its improper interference will damage international justice and the authority of international law. What’s more, it will destroy the efforts aimed at cooperation, especially United Nations work.

After careful consideration and evaluation, the US supreme court corrected its decision and decided not to hear the appeal of Dohihara Kenji. Also, it clarified that pursuant to the US constitution, the US supreme court has no right to review the acts of General McArthur by the supreme commander of the Japanese forces. McArthur established the court in accordance with the *Potsdam Proclamation* and the policies of Far Eastern Commissions organized by *Moscow Declaration*. Although the basic principles of establishing the Tokyo court was not recorded in the Article 10 of *Potsdam Proclamation*, Japanese emperor and the government both promised to follow and obeyed the orders and decisions by the supreme commander of the allied forces or other representatives appointed by the allied forces in the *Japanese Instrument of Surrender*, which made McArthur beyond his right to execute the provisions of *Potsdam Proclamation*. The Judgment of Tokyo trials also clarified that McArthur was not as an American citizen but as an agent of the allied countries to establish the court. According to *Potsdam Proclamation*, *Japanese Instrument of Surrender* and basic principles of international law, Tokyo court can be considered as international military court.

The State-War-Navy Coordinating Committee (SWNCC) was responsible for the establishment of international court for far east. SWNCC made US policy on arrest and punishment of war criminals for far east as a document of litigation against the far east war criminals and hoped to rapidly promote the preparation of the trial. Justice Robert H. Jackson also believed that compared with Nuremberg mode, the establishment of a unified procuratorial system based on multi-country consultation was more conducive to the trial preparation and proof of evidence, which was more efficient. Therefore, McArthur was responsible for a series of trial preparation such as investigation of war criminals, the special agencies of litigation, the appointment of justices, the formulation of applicable laws and trial procedures by Nuremberg precedent. However, the facts proved that most of McArthur's power was superficial and was not what people thought to be the monopoly of power. Considering the independence of the judiciary, McArthur did not have the right to interpret the charter and the law applicable to the court. His speech before the hearing was refused and the principle of speedy trial based on the charter after the trial didn't promote the process of the trial. No original documents proved that McArthur manipulated the Emperor Hirohito's immunity from prosecution. In fact, McArthur had no official or unofficial power to decide issues of Emperor Hirohito. It can be said that McArthur had little individual influence on the Toyo trial.

In late January 1946, eight Allied Powers nominated the judges. On this basis, pursuant to the orders of the US government, McArthur announced the establishment of International Military Tribunal for Far East and promulgated the Charter of the International Military Tribunal for Far East on January 19 of the same year, and he appointed nine judges including the representative of United States a month later. After the successful establishment of the court, the US government sought approval from the Far East Commission. The Far East Commission acknowledged. It suggested that Tokyo court was established based on the consensus among countries.

The procedure model of the Tokyo court is a summary procedure based on US military commission and set up for trialing the foreigners. It was applied in the case of Ex parte Quirin and was adopted in Nuremberg Charter. It stipulated that the court can adopted and use efficient and non-technical procedures to the greatest extent.

This procedure model adopted the international common standard applied to stand trial for foreigners in the local country from 1946 to 1948. According to Harvard Research Group Draft Convention, if "no fair and humane treatment is given to a foreigner who has accepted prosecution or punishment, and no fair judgment is made in an independent court but excessively cruel, unusual punishment and unfair discrimination are imposed on him", it will lead to an unjust result. The postwar trial must guarantee foreigners' rights of due process, including free access to the court, the acceptance of formal charges, public trial, the right to hire lawyers, the right to cross-examine, etc. Other domestic trial requirements such as the right to appeal, the right to ask for the ratio decidendi and the right to request a jury trial are not necessary in the international law.

This procedural mode and litigation standard are fully reflected in the charter of Tokyo court. Five chapters seventeen articles in the charter of Tokyo court made specific provisions about "the mechanism of the court", "jurisdiction and general regulations", "fair trial of the defendants", "the power of the court and the operation of the trial" and "judgment and penalty". Besides, it also clarified the important procedures of court organization, the trial procedures and the rules of evidence.

5.2 *The Judicial Independence of Tokyo Trials*

5.2.1 The Independence of the Prosecution

Tokyo trials followed the doctrine of commencement of action by law, doctrine of prosecuting discretion and the doctrine of separating prosecution from trial. As the foregoing said, based on the doctrine of prosecuting discretion, Tokyo court adopted more unified hierarchical prosecution system. The IPS was responsible for the prosecution function.

On November 30, 1945, President Truman appointed Keenan as the chief prosecutor to prosecute Japan's top war criminals. According to the Article 8 of the charter regarding the Chief of Counsel, the Chief of Counsel is responsible for the investigation and prosecution of charges against the war criminals within the jurisdiction of the tribunal, and will render such legal assistance to the supreme commander as is appropriate. Eleven countries participating in the International Military Tribunal for Far East respectively may appoint an Associate Counsel with rich experience of prosecution and abundant knowledge of law to assist the Chief of Counsel. Chief of Counsel and Associate Counsel are different in their functions and respectively responsible for the different stages of the proceedings. The former is mainly responsible for the opening and closing statements. The Latter is responsible for preparing materials of evidence and combining the contents of the cases. They often have a long discussion on the case with each other.

On April 29, 1946, International Prosecution Section submitted indictment to the International Military Tribunal for Far East and sent the suspects who are in the Sugamo prison.

On May 3, 1946, the International Military Tribunal for Far East held hearings, and the bailiff read the indictment. The indictment explains the basic reason for this prosecution, that is, Japan which is controlled by militarism and ethnic groups, together with Germany and Italy, is trying to dominate the world. The indictment consists of 55 causes of action in three categories, charging 28 defendants with crimes against peace, murder and other war crimes and crimes against humanity. Taking Nuremberg as an example, it clearly stated the actions of each defendant in waging or deepening this aggressive war and charged them separately. However, unlike Nuremberg's comprehensive detailed allegations in the appendix to the indictment, this indictment explains the contents of each defendant's criminal activities item by item, thus there are many duplicate contents. In addition, five appendices are listed after the indictment to explain each cause of action in detail.

On the whole, the indictment is long and complicated. Each charge contains many accumulative accusations, which leads to excessive individual charges. For example, the one charge of crimes against peace includes over 750 individual accusations. The prosecution's intention is to leave the indictment to the court to decide the important parts to the law and facts. Actually, the court did the same, and the final judgment reduced 55 causes of action to 10.

The prosecution exercised its discretion in accordance with the charter and procedural rules, which met the legal requirement, strictly followed the principle of cause of action and achieved the separation of prosecution and trial.

5.2.2 The Independence of Judges and Court

It is often criticized that Tokyo court is "the winners' court". In fact, this opinion stems from only seeing the external form of the tribunal but ignoring or misunderstanding the essence of the Tokyo tribunal.

The judges of The Tokyo tribunal have profound professional knowledge of law and rich experience of legal practice. More importantly, they hold a fair and impartial judicial position. This has a significant positive impact on the fair trial. 6 of the 11 judges all have a professional background in common law and have profound legal literacy. Most of them are the well-known criminal lawyers in China. President Sir William Flood Webb was a President of the Queensland Court of Arbitration and judge of the High Court of Australia. All judges signed a joint confirmation, promising to duly administer justice according to law, without fear, favor or affection, according to our conscience, and the best of our understanding. As the foregoing said, President Webb and all judges are staunch judicial independents and actively resist McArthur's efforts to manage the court, which eventually led to McArthur's negligible influence on the court and trial.

In terms of the court components, there are no Japanese judges among the members of the judges although Japan is a surrender country and a country concerned. However, as the defense lawyer Shimanouchi Tatsuoki of the defendant Oshima Hiroshi in the trial said, it is impossible both in theory and fact that the accused who unconditionally surrendered and the judges all stand on the bench. It is hard to imagine integrating the courts of all countries with supreme power. Even entrusting neutral countries to try and punish war criminals is only the utopian fantasy.

In terms of the trial organization, the Tokyo and Nuremberg tribunals are for the first time to establish supranational organization which transcend national power in human history. It can be said that it is the disastrous aftermath of the World War II that promotes human to reconsider the basic issues of countries and state sovereignty. The conclusion is that there is humankind above the countries and the state sovereignty should be restricted by the international law in the international community and by the legitimacy in the domestic country. Based on the limited sovereignty theory, The Tokyo tribunal and Nuremberg tribunals officially started human punishment on the international crime actions about state sovereignty. The independence of The Tokyo tribunal lies in that it doesn't represent the victorious country or a victorious group of the countries but the entity with the state sovereignty and the trustee of the supranational international community. The Tokyo tribunal was established on the principle of the equal sovereignty of the countries, which is an important part of the new order reconstruction of the international community after the World War II. Its jurisdiction has a sufficient basis in international law and it shouldn't ignore the judicial independence due to the external form of its "special court of ocupation troops".

5.2.3 The Rights Protection of the Defendants

The Chapter 3 of *Charter of the International Military Tribunal for Far East* is named *Fair Trial for Accused* to clarify the due process protection of the accused and provide the accused adequate protection of their rights so as to ensure a fair trial. Article 9(A) of the Charter stipulates that the indictment should give clear, accurate and adequate statement of the crimes prosecuted and prepare a Japanese copy to be delivered to each defendant as soon as possible so as to guarantee the rights to know of the accused, as well as provide the accused enough time to prepare the defense before the trial. Article 9(B) requires that the trial should be conducted in English and in the language of the accused. Translations of documents and other papers shall be provide as needed and requested.

Different from the Nuremberg precedent, the accused of the Tokyo trial are provided adequate right of defense. Article 9(C) stipulates that each accused shall have the right to be represented by counsel of his own selection, subject to the disapproval of such counsel at any time by the Tribunal. If an accused is not represented by counsel and in open court requests the appointment of counsel, the Tribunal shall designate counsel for him. Article 9(D) establishes the right of the accused to conduct their defense through themselves, including the right to examine any witness, subject to the witness summoned by the prosecution. Article 9(E) guarantees that an accused may apply in writing to the Tribunal for the production of witness or of documents.

The defendants of the Tokyo trial were given a luxurious legal team. The Japanese defense team includes two outstanding Japanese lawyers Kenzo Takayanagi and Kiyose Ichiro and famous jurists Kainō Michitaka, etc. US legal team has high professional spirit, which is of great significance to Japanese defense lawyers who lack defense experience and are not accustomed to the common law system. Thanks to the efforts of the huge legal team, the accused had the opportunity to challenge the legality of the tribunal and the crimes in the indictment. In the tribunal, the defense had 187 days to respond to the prosecution. Under the adversarial lawsuit mode, it can be said that the prosecution and the defense are equal.

Compared with the historical situation at that time, this right is even more precious. Cordell Hull, a 1945 Nobel Peace Prize winner and former secretary of state, once argued that the existing laws and conventions on war crimes were no longer sufficient to deal with such crimes as the Nanjing massacre. So abandoning the trivia of the laws and shooting the most heinous criminals is more helpful for the pursuit of law. The reason is that their crimes are too serious and beyond the judicial procedures. Churchill also held the same view to line them up and shoot them. At the strong atmosphere that tends to execute these war criminals immediately, it is amazing that the accused have the opportunity of the right to defense.

The tedious criminal proceedings of Tokyo trials have silenced the so-called winners' revenge. The protection of the accused's right to defense is a strong proof against the victors' court.

5.3 The Judicial Fairness of Tokyo Trials

Tokyo trials adopted a mixed mode of lawsuit which is dominated by adversarial mode of lawsuit of common law and has some features of inquisitorial mode of lawsuit. The whole proceeding followed the procedural rules and evidence rules in the *Charter of the International Military Tribunal*.

The tribunal didn't adopt a jury to trial. Pursuant to Article 11(B) of the Charter, the tribunal shall have the power to interrogate each accused and to permit comment on his refusal to answer any question. This is consistent with the judicial characteristic that judges in the civil law system can interrogate the accused to seek truth.

The official languages of the tribunal are English and Japanese. However, to guarantee the right to know, French and Russian are also used in different stages of the trial. Due to the difficulty in the translation of different language, the tribunal especially set up a Language Arbitration Commission and provided simultaneous interpretation. At the same time, the trial is conducted in combination with written evidence.

The tribunal, subject to Article 15(B), allowed the prosecution, the accused or the counsel to make an opening statement in each stage of the trial. The prosecution and the defense may offer evidence and the admissibility of the same shall be determined by the tribunal. The prosecution and each accused may examine each witness and each accused who gives testimony. In the end, the prosecution and defense may address the tribunal. The tribunal will deliver judgment.

The evidence rules of the International Military Tribunal are complicated with combination of the evidence rules of the military commission and British royal to certify and trial war criminals, and the tribunal shall not be bound by technical rules of evidence and the statement of the accused can be accepted as the evidence. Although the Charter stipulates that the tribunal has the power to make supplementary rules of evidence, The Tokyo tribunal didn't do so.

In fact, the Tokyo trial faces greater difficulties than Nuremberg trial such as more countries' struggle, the differences of legal systems, cultural differences and Japan's destruction of important documents. However, The Tokyo tribunal would rather abandon the basic requirements of "promptness" in the Charter but adopted procedural justice to ensure the fairness of the trial.

A total of 817 court sessions were held in Tokyo and lasted 416 days. The prosecution and defense spent half of the time in sending evidence. Among the 1194 witnesses, 419 appeared in court and accounted for 35%. In the trial, the accused fully exercised the right to defense, right to remain silent and right to cross-examination, and filed an application for challenge and objection to jurisdiction. The defense counsel of the accused played a full role. The prosecution and defense had a lengthy debate on the enormous unrelated documents.

Tokyo trials met the requirements of due process, which reflected the efforts to establish comprehensive international criminal procedures. The valuable experience and lessons of the Tokyo trial were absorbed by the rules and statues of the international military tribunal and international military court. The protection of the defendants' right was confirmed by the Article 14 of the International Covenant on Civil and Political Rights.

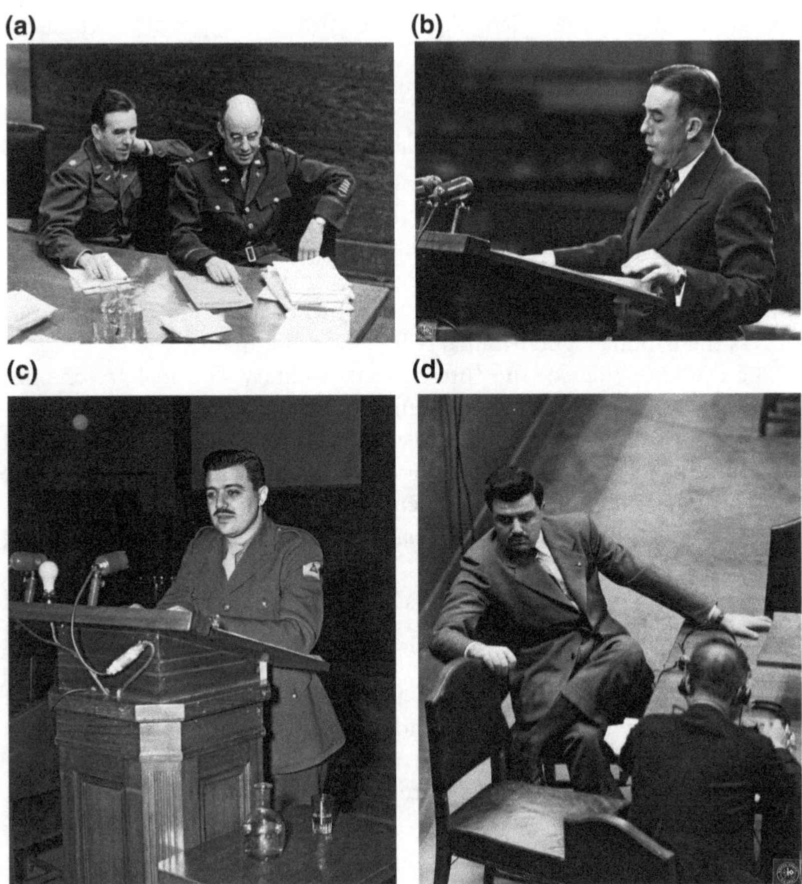

Fig. 1 The defense councils (The US defense councils in the Tokyo trial mostly were soldiers and wore military uniforms at the beginning of the trial. After presentation of the prosecution case, they all wore suits) (**a**) UMEZU Yoshijiro's defense council Major Blakeney in military uniform and MUTO Akira's defense council senior captain Furness (Later he was promoted as major) (**b**) Blakeney in suits (**c**) the defendant HATA Shunroku's US defense council in military uniforms (**d**) Lazarus in suits

In March, Erima Harvey Northcroft from New Zealand wrote in a memorandum to the Prime Minister, "the decision of the tribunal is based on the available evidence and made after giving the opportunity to express dissenting opinions. Besides, I believe it is impartial" (Fig. 1).

6 Summary

If the development of the law is the result of the darkness in human history, Tokyo and Nuremberg war crimes trials after the World War II are no doubt the most gratifying dawn after dark.

Ethnic, religious, racial, cultural and national conflicts often occur due to the different interests and values. The hundreds of years of wars make people realize that some common interests of human can be beyond the interests of a single country.

At the beginning of the twentieth century, the law of war, which was considered as an unenforceable moral norm, has required a rigid status in the international law and made the countries and their leaders more consciously abide by the international law than ever before. Morality, humane care and the concept of rights largely promote the transformation of war views from illegality to criminalization. In turn, through the two postwar international criminal trials, the human society's appeal for peace and justice, and its aversion to violence and war reached the peak. Then, war becomes an international crime recognized by the international community. The countries' leaders who waged wars must take responsibility for breaking the world peace.

Law serves as justice. "If you want peace, please work for justice". Tokyo trials and Nuremberg trials reflect the legal consensus of that era. The members of international community selected supranational international criminal justice mode for the first time and finished a great legal practice.

The Tokyo trial followed the requirements of procedural justice. Some even commented that the whole process was extremely boring. According to the criminal procedures, "everything has to be done step by step". Evidence is the center of the tribunal. The judge ruled out the interference inside and outside, and the independence, fairness and openness of the justice are guaranteed. In an era when the accused's right to defense was still fresh to Japan, this long trial is undoubtedly an open legal course and a textbook on the rule of law. It has left us a large number of legal achievements which runs through our understanding and development of modern international law in a profound way.

The Tokyo trial is different from the Nuremberg trial in that not only more countries has participated in the tribunal, but also it is more difficult to identify crimes due to the destruction of evidence. The process of the national aggressive policy formed by the conspiracy of the accused is more complicated. What's more, it is a trial beyond race and Eastern and

Western civilizations. The censures faced by the Tokyo trial are not from legal criticism but are mixed with many unspeakable positions and emotions. Only these barriers break can the warning, forgiveness and reconciliation pursued by the trial come.

Brazil professor Mahmoud Cherif Bassiouni, the famous international criminal law expert, once said that law is part of history. History is like a river, sometimes stagnant, sometimes slow, sometimes it rushes to the unpredictable destination with deep strength. The law has its own life. The evolution and innovation of law is based on human thoughts about their own destiny and the pursuit of common values, People believe that the world is established on the three pillars—peace, security and welfare. Tokyo trials break the barrier of law strongly and opens up a new road of history so as to open a new way of international law and rule of law.

Bibliography

1. Cheng, Z., Gong, Z., & Zhao, Y. (2013). *Dongjian shenpan yanjiu shouce* [Handbook of the Tokyo Trial Studies]. Shanghai: Shanghai Jiao Tong University Press.
2. Zhu, W., Leng, X., & Zhang, B. (2010). *Zhanzhengzui* [War Crimes]. Beijing: Law Press.
3. Lu, Y. (2007). *Zhanzhengzui xingshi zeren yanjiu* [Study on Criminal Responsibility of War Crimes]. Beijing: Law Press.
4. Werle, G. (2009). *Guojixingfa yuanli* [Principles of International Criminal Law] (S. Wang, Trans.). Beijing: The Commercial Press.
5. Bassiouni, M. C. (2010). *Guojixingfa daolun* [Introduction to International Criminal Law] (X. Wang, Trans.). Beijing: Law Press.
6. Nishihara, H. (1997). *Riben Xingshifa de xingcheng yu tese-riben faxuejia lun riben xingshifa* [The Making and Features of Japanese Criminal Law] (H. Li, et al., Trans.). Beijing: Law Press.
7. Ryuichi, H. (2016). *Xingfa de jichu* [Foundations of Criminal Law] (H. Li, Trans.). Beijing: China University of Political Science and Law.
8. Iriye, A. (2016). *Di er ci shijie dazhan zai yazhou ji taipingyang de qiyuan* [The Origins of the Second World War in Asia and the Pacific] (X. Li, Trans.). Beijing: Social Sciences Academic Press.
9. Buruma, I. (2015). *Zuinie de baoying: deguo he riben de zhanzheng jiyi* [The Wages of Guilt: Memories of War in Germany and Japan] (T. Ni, Trans.). Guilin: Guangxi Normal University.
10. Tuck, R. (2009). *Zhanzheng yu heping de quanli: cong gelaoxiusi dao kangde de zhengzhi sixiang yu guoji zhixu* [The Rights of War and Peace: Political

Thought and the International Order from Grotius to Kant] (J. Luo, etc., Trans.). Beijing: Social Sciences Academic Press.
11. Whitman, J. Q. (2015). *Zhanzheng zhi yu: shenglifa yu xiandai zhanzheng xingtai de xingcheng* [The Verdict of Battle: The Law of Victory and the Making of Modern War] (J. Lai, Trans.). Beijing: China University of Political Science and Law.
12. Pinker, S. (2015). *Renxing zhong de shanliang tianshi: baoli weishenme hui jianshao* [The Better Angels of Our Nature: Why Violence Has Declined] (W. An, Trans.). Beijing: CITIC Press Group.
13. Zhaoqi Cheng. (2007). *Cong dongjing shenpan dao dongjing shenpan* [From <Tokyo trial> to Tokyo Trial]. Shanghai: Historical Review.
14. Neil, B., & Cryer, R. (Ed.). (2008). *Documents on the Tokyo International Military Tribunal: Charter, Indictment, Judgments.* Oxford: Oxford University.
15. Neil, B., & Cryer, R. (2008). *The Tokyo International Military Tribunal: A Reappraisal.* Oxford: Oxford University.
16. Yuma, T. (2008). *Tokyo War Crimes Trial: The Pursuit of Justice in the Wake of World War II.* Cambridge, MA and London: Harvard University Asia Center.
17. Casses, A. (2013). *Casses's International Criminal Law* (3rd ed.). Oxford: Oxford University.
18. Ambos, K. (2013). *Treatise on International Criminal Law.* Oxford: Oxford University.

CHAPTER 9

Tokyo Trials and World Peace

The pursuit of peace is an eternal theme of mankind. More than 70 years since the end of the world war II, the international conflict often occurs, but they are local. Looking back on the history and reviewing the origins, we can find that the postwar trials of the two international military tribunals played an important role in world peace after war. It is no exaggeration that Nuremberg trials and Tokyo trials are the important milestone of the international peace order after the trial.

Chief prosecutor of Tokyo trials Keenan made it clear that "safeguarding peace" is the "order" of Tokyo trials. In his opening speech, he reiterated, "the trial today is not an ordinary trial but save human civilization". The prosecutor pointed out the meaning of Tokyo trials: safeguard world peace.

1 Deny Japan's National Aggressive Policy, Reject Militarism

The Tokyo tribunal tried Japan for its aggression against other countries since modern times, which revealed the aggressive nature of Japan's militarism and laid a foundation for Japanese to abandon militarism so as to promote the peace and democracy of Japanese society. Japanese scholar Kainō Michitaka believed that the Tokyo trial has revolutionary nature that breaks the Japanese militarism and strengthen the tendency of democracy.

Z. Cheng, *A History of War Crimes Trials in Post 1945 Asia-Pacific*,
https://doi.org/10.1007/978-981-13-6697-0_9

1.1 Deny the Theory Basis of the Thoughts of Japanese Expansion

Kodo and Hakko Ichiu, the theory basis of Japanese militarism, runs through the course of Japan's invasion and expansion. The beginning of Part B of Tokyo trial Judgment makes definitions and explanations about how Kodo and Hakko Ichiu are used by militarists.

The so-called "Hakko Ichiu" means the bringing together of the corners of the world under one roof, or the making of the world one family. This was the alleged ideal of the foundation of the Empire; and in its traditional context meant no more than a universal principle of humanity, which was destined ultimately to pervade the whole universe. Kodo is a concept of virtue and a maxim of conduct. Hakko Ichiu is the moral goal, and loyalty to the Emperor is the road which led to it. Kodo and Hakko Ichiu were originally the idea of the emperor in the pre-modern society for the funding of the country. Limited by the social development at that time, the so-called Hakko Ichiu is to establish a feudal empire in the limited space and advocates the establishment of an empire through the benevolent rule of the emperor, which is Kodo.

In the nineteenth century, with the development of capitalism and the establishment of the colonial system, the concept of the "world" was largely expanded. It is undoubtedly inappropriate for Japanese militarism to transplant the traditional political concept into the politics of the twentieth century. In December 1940, Hashimoto Kingoro reiterated his view which was expressed in August 1936. The armed forces of the whole country should unite in the spirit of Kodo. The spirit of Kodo made it possible to realize the target of Hakko Ichiu or dominating the world. The Tokyo tribunal believed that the imperial rescripts issued by Emperor Meiji expressed the concept of Kodo and Hakko Ichiu. However, at that time, these concepts represented the core of reorganization of the country and the appeal to Japanese patriotism. But in the decade before 1930, the two concepts were adopted by Japanese scholars or politicians who advocated expansion and became the reason why Japanese expanded its territory. *The Judgment of the International Military Tribunal for Far East* pointed out that Again and again throughout the years that followed measures of military aggression were advocated in the names of Hakko Ichiu and Kodo which eventually became symbols for the world domination through military force.

1.2 *Reveal the Aggressive Nature of Japan's Modern Policy*

Tokyo trials revealed the aggressive nature of Japan's so-called liberating Asia and coexistence national policy of Greater East Asia Co-prosperity Sphere.

On August 7, 1936, Hirota Koki hosted a Five Minister Conference to determine the basic principles of *National Policy* which was a long-term national policy of the Japanese government. The principles were to consolidate Japan from both domestic and abroad and make Japanese empire "nominally and actually a stabilized force in East Asia, ensure the peace of East Asia and make contributions to the peace and welfare of the world". Furthermore, it was to make diplomacy and national defense complement each other, consolidate the empire's position in East Asia and develop southern ocean that the nature of the national policy was aggression.

The first paragraph of article one of the national policy stipulated that "it is the concrete reflection of the spirit of Kodo to rule out the hegemonic policy of the great powers in East Asia according to the propositions of real coexistence and common prosperity and happiness sharing. It is also the directive spirit that our country should implement on the foreign policy". Through the trial of Japan's "14-year-trial", Tokyo trials revealed, "first, this policy would inevitably lead to the conflict between the countries with rights and interests in the East. Japan must rule out the hegemonic policy of the great powers and follow Japan's 'coexistence and co-prosperity'. The Japanese government was clear that its expansion must destroy the interests of the powers in Asia. It tried to reduce its resistance to expansion in Asia, and even hoped that Asian countries can become Japan's cooperative forces against western countries under the excuse of 'coexistence and co-prosperity'".

After the "July 7 Incident of 1937", the Konoe government held the attitude to insist the policy of not expanding the conflicts and to solve the issues in the local area quickly. However, Japanese Army's aggressive activities in China expanded rapidly. With the continuous victory of the Japanese Army in China, the Japanese government began to compromise with the army. In November 1938, the Konoe government issued a statement on the decisive relationship between China and Japan, "after occupying Nanjing, the imperial government remained patient to give the government of Nationalist China the last opportunity to reflect themselves. But the Nationalist government didn't understand our country's intention, rushed to launch the war of resistance and ignored the sufferings of the country and the peace of East Asia. Therefore, the imperial government no longer cared about the Nationalist government and expected the establishment and development of the new regime that was really worth cooperating with the empire". The Japanese government owed its responsibility of waging aggressive wars and destroying the peace of East Asia to the war of resistance of the Chinese government and put forward the proposition of establishing "new order of East Asia" on the grounds of "the increasing responsibility of empire for the peace of East Asia". The Tokyo tribunal revealed that Japan "closed the door of negotiation and built a platform to continue its aggression and support the local regime with the ultimate goal of establishing Chinese 'new regime' that could cooperate with Japan".

In July 1940, Konoe Fumimaro formed a cabinet for the second time and confirmed the outline of the basic national policy. It stipulated that the imperial state was established based on the spirit of 'Hakko Ichiu' and took the establishment of world peace as fundamental. The first was to establish a new order of greater East Asia centered with the empire and based on the combination of Japan, Manchukuo and China. After establishing goal of the Asia-Pacific policy of the "great East Asia Asia-Pacific new order" that is "Greater East Asia Co-prosperity Sphere", the Japanese government started to implement Southward Policy substantively. Under the cover of liberating the Asian from the oppression of the white and in the principle of "friendly neighbors", "common defense against communists" and "economic support", it made Japan's actions in China legalized and laid a "just" foundation for Japan's expansion in Asia. The Tokyo tribunal denied this one by one: the basic premise of "friendly neighbors" was the superior status, privileges and responsibility of Japan in East Asia; due to the need of "common defense against communists", Japan must reserve the military right and supervision right over all traffic and communication facilities, and Japan must station troops in north China and Mongolia; economic support meant Japan, Manchukuo and China were mutually beneficial to complement the natural resources with each other, and it was emphasized to obtain the resources buried in north China which Japan and Manchukuo lacked, especially mining resources. The natural resources actually were controlled by north China and Mongolia.

In April 1938, Japan set up two companies related to national policies, that is, North China Development Company and Central China

Promotion Company. Except for the daily affairs, these two companies must obey the order of Japanese government, accept the dominance of Japanese government and managed the public business, transportation and natural resources in north China and Central China. In January 1939, Japanese Planning Bureau passed "the plan of China's economic development" but didn't inform Manchukuo and China, and the plan was decided and implemented unilaterally by Japanese. Part of the iron ore excavated and the remaining pig iron produced by the subsidiary company of North China Development Company Lung Yen Iron Mining Company was transported to Japan. Of the total output of 4.3 million tons, 700,000 tons were used in the production of pig iron, 1.4 million tons were transported to Manchukuo, and millions of tons were transported to Japan. When developing coal resources... to ensure the continuous supply to Japan, the measures to control the supply to China were taken. Japan's so-called "economic support" actually was a mad plunder of resources in the occupied areas.

In order to disrupt China's resistance, the Japanese government did whatever it could. Before the Sino-Japanese war broke out, the government of Nationalist Chinese was determined to eliminate opium. In June 1936, the Nationalist government issued provisions to suppress drug addicts and the provisions took effective. To attack the morale of Chinese nationals and prepare funds for all levels of Japanese government and wars, Japan developed a number of drug trade in China. The prosecution collected numerous evidence which proved that "since 1937, the opium trade of China had been associated with Japanese Army, Japan's foreign affairs agencies and Asia Development Board. The special service agencies of Japanese Expeditionary Army were set up in many cities and were entrusted with the sale of opium".

Since 1935, the Japanese government had started to implement the strict news inspection system and inspected all public opinions extensively. Newspaper and radio became the tool of the government. When Tokyo trials inspected and revealed the Japanese atrocities in detail, Japanese nationals were deeply shocked. Japanese society started to doubt the basic national policy which was regarded as the cornerstone and model.

1.3 Attribute "14-Year-War" as Wars of Aggression

The International Military Tribunal for Far East took 1928 as the starting point of prosecuting Japanese aggressive war crimes and tried the

14-year-war from 1931 "September 18th incident" to 1945 when Japan surrendered.

After the "September 18th incident" which was the first step to invade China (the Tokyo tribunal called it Mukden Incident or Shengyang incident), Japanese military ministry owed the responsibility of the incident to China to avoid possible condemnation and punishment by the international community. Besides, it took advantage of media to fabricate and distort the facts and made propaganda in the domestic and international community. Furthermore, it disguised the armed aggression deliberately created by Kwantung Army as the self-defense due to the attack of Chinese Army and tried to legalize its aggression. After the "September 18th incident", at the request of the Nationalist government, League of Nations once sent Commission of Enquiry to north China to investigate the truth. Due to the various reasons, the Commission of Enquiry failed to fully reveal the truth. After the war, the prosecution of the International Military Tribunal for Far East submitted a large amount of evidence to the tribunal which proved that the "Shengyang incident" was plotted in advance by the staffs of the Japanese military headquarters, the staffs of the Kwantung Army, members of the Sakurakai and others. Based on a large amount of convincing evidence, the tribunal adopted the charges of the prosecution. Hashimoto Kingoro and Itagaki Seishiro was found guilty of creating and assisting "September 18th incident".

To gain the support of Japanese nationals, two factions formed in Japan. One faction advocated the use of force to achieve the goal; the other faction was some politicians and bureaucrats who advocated peaceful means or at least more cautious choice to use force to expand Japan. When the faction who advocated force believed they overwhelmed all opposition forces, they gradually carried out the attacks for the ultimate goal of ruling the far east.

"In 1931, they waged aggressive wars against China and occupied Manchuria and Jehol. By 1934, Japan started to invade north China, stationed troops in north China and established various puppet governments to serve its purpose. Since 1937, Japan continued large-scale aggressive wars against China, invaded and occupied Chinese territory and set up various puppet governments following the above-mentioned pattern. Besides, Japan also exploited China's economic and natural resources for Japanese military and general needs". "At the same time, they made plans and preparations for waging the aggressive wars against

Soviet Union for a long period of time". "On December 7, 1941, the conspirators waged aggressive wars against the United States and Britain".

The Tokyo tribunal decided that since 1931, a series of wars waged by Japan were wars of aggression and "there was no greater crime than plotting and executing a war of aggression. The security of the world and its people was threatened by this plot and destroyed by this war. The only possible outcome, which, was the great sufferings the world would face". The Tokyo tribunal not only attributed the expansion of Japan since modern times as aggressive wars, but also deeply revealed the harm Japan's conduct brought to the world and recorded it in the Judgment of International Military Tribunal for Far East which was reserved forever and warned the future generations.

After the trial in the tribunal, the Tokyo tribunal not only combed through Japan's erroneous national policies since modern times and revealed the aggressive nature of the Japan's war route, but also tried, convicted, sentenced and punished the government leaders who were responsible for Japan's erroneous national policies and war route. Thus, the general liquidation of Japan's erroneous national policies and war route laid the foundation for the emergence of a peaceful and democratic new Japan.

2 Open Up International Judicial Precedent, Prosecute War Criminal Responsibility

The two world wars in the twentieth century brought unprecedented disasters to mankind. However, disaster promoted human reflection. The two international organizations formed after the two world wars—League of Nations and United Nations, which was important practice of political idealism that mankind reflected on the catastrophe of war and sought permanent peace. The two organizations tried to establish a mechanism to prevent wars and maintain permanent peace for mankind. However, League of Nations failed. The cost of the failure was the world war II which was even more bitter, widespread and destructive. The establishment and operation of United Nations was successful, which maintain overall peace for over 70 years. The peaceful environment of the world is the result of many actors of the development of social politics and culture and technology. Also, the role of United Nations shouldn't be overlooked. The precedent set by the trial of Fascist and militarism of Axis countries in the two international military tribunals—the Nuremberg tribunal and the Tokyo tribunal after the world war II, which is confirmed, maintained and developed through United Nations, is the important milestone of the postwar world peace.

2.1 Open Up the Precedent of "Prosecuting Individual Criminal Responsibility"

As the forgoing said, in the traditional international law, individual is not the subject of international law. War responsibility generally is borne by the state which is the subject of the international law, and individual cannot take criminal responsibility due to the violation of international law. Even a war of aggression, the leaders of the defeated countries wouldn't be punished for the identity of individual. The defeated countries were often punished for ceding territory and paying indemnities to the victorious countries. On June 28, 1919, *Treaty of Versailles* prepared to prosecute the war responsibility of the initiator of world war I German Emperor William II, but due to Holland's refusal to extradite the Emperor, the allied powers missed opening up the precedent of prosecuting the leaders individual war responsibility in human history. The two international military tribunals after war undertook this important mission. Nuremberg trial established the international law principle of prosecuting the individual criminal responsibility and tried and sentenced Nazi leaders with this principle. Tokyo trials further practiced his principle. Nuremberg trial and Tokyo trials jointly opened up the international judicial practice of investigating and punishing individual criminal responsibility of aggressive wars.

The establishment of United Nations effectively reduced the local wars, avoided world wars and made great contributions to maintaining world peace. As the United Nations Form Panel pointed in its report, "without the United Nations the post-1945 world would very probably have been a bloodier place. There were fewer inter-State wars in the last half of the twentieth century than in the first half. The United Nations contributed a lot". The purposes of the United Nations are:

> To maintain international peace and security, and to that end: to take effective measures for the prevention and removal of threats to the peace, and for the suppression of acts of aggression or other breaches of the

> peace, and to bring about by peaceful means, and in conformity with the principles of justice and international law, adjustment or settlement of international disputes or situations which might lead to a breach of the peace.

And it stipulated that…

> All members shall settle their international disputes by peaceful means in such a manner that international peace and security, and justice, are not endangered… All members shall refrain in their international relations from the threat or use of force against the territorial integrity or political independence of any state, or in any other manner inconsistent with the Purposes of the United Nations.

Avoiding the use of force, peaceful settlement of disputes and maintaining world peace is one of the main purposes of United Nations.

However, although similar provisions existed as early as Hague Convention of 1899 and 1907 and 1928 *Pact of Paris*, the two world wars inevitably broke out. Why can the similar provisions under the framework of the United Nations prevent large-scale armed conflicts?

It must be said that this is due to the two international military tribunals established after the world war II to try war crimes. According to the traditional international law, the defeated countries were often punished for ceding the territory and paying indemnities to the victorious countries. These punishments finally were passed on to the people, returnees, war orphans and widows who were not allowed to make any political statements and suffered from the scourge of war, while the leaders of the defeated countries sheltered in the country and were difficult to be punished. Nuremberg trial and Tokyo trials initiated the international practice of investigating the individual criminal responsibility of the leaders, and the individuals couldn't shelter in the "umbrella" of the country. For leaders who want to seek war means to achieve their national goals, the punishment of the individuals would give warnings to urge them to give up wars and to seek national interests by the peaceful means. This doctrine was recognized by the whole international community through the resolution of the United Nations Assembly. The peaceful means of developing economy, strengthening the influence of culture, shaping the image of a responsible country becomes the mainstream ways for all countries to seek national interests.

2.2 Open Up "Prosecuting the Command Responsibility for Failure to Stop Atrocities"

Commanders must take responsibility for the crimes committed by their subordinates. This concept had similar provisions in the documents of the seventeenth and eighteenth centuries in the West. However, the international judicial practice through establishing international military tribunal to try and punish the aggressive war initiators for "not preventing the atrocities" was established in the trial of military tribunal after the world war II. The groundbreaking case is "Yamashita Tomoyuki Case".

In September 1944, Yamashita Tomoyuki who was called Tiger of Malaya was appointed as the commander-in-chief of the 14th Army of Philippines and was responsible for the defense of the Philippines and to fight against US Army. On October 2, 1945, a month after Japan surrendered, Manila Special Military Tribunal prosecuted Yamashita Tomoyuki. From October 19 to December 7, after the two-month-trial, the tribunal sentenced Yamashita Tomoyuki to be hanged. Different from the general indictment, Yamashita Tomoyuki was prosecuted for his "command responsibility" but not for his individual acts. From 1945, Japanese Army carried out indiscriminate massacre and other atrocities such as raping, torturing and arson at the same time. According to the statistics, in Manila, three-quarters of the buildings were destroyed and 125,000 Philippines were killed. In addition to the Philippines, foreigners living in the area also suffered atrocities. During the whole slaughter, Yamashita Tomoyuki didn't take measures to prevent or control the conducts of the Army. As the commander of Japanese Army fighting with the US and its allied countries… allowed his subordinates to carry out atrocities and other major crimes. The commander ignored the obligations to control the conducts of the subordinates. Thus, Yamashita Tomoyuki violated the laws and regulations of law and was sentenced to be hanged.

The consequent Nuremberg and Tokyo trials further practiced the theory of "command criminal responsibility". Both the Nuremberg tribunal and Tokyo tribunal didn't clearly stipulate "command criminal responsibility" in the charter of the tribunals. However, the trial involving the command criminal responsibility was made. There were verdicts against Koiso Kuniaki and Shigemitsu Mamoru in the Tokyo trial. They were convicted on the following charges:

> they deliberately and recklessly disregarded their legal duty to take adequate steps to secure the observance and prevent breaches thereof, and thereby violated the laws of war.

Tokyo trials are different from Nuremberg trials in that Nuremberg trials were limited to prosecute the military command criminal responsibility, while Tokyo trials extended the scope to prosecute the non-military personnel, that is the officers. Former Japanese Prime Minister Hirota Koki was a non-military commander who was convicted according to this doctrine and sentenced to death (Fig. 1).

At the beginning of Japan's all-round aggression against China, Hirota Koki served as the foreign minister of Konoye Cabinet who was not a military commander in the general meaning and neither responsible nor commanded Japanese Army against China.

However, subject to the count 55 of the Tokyo tribunal indictment, the Defendants deliberately and recklessly disregarded their legal duty to take adequate steps to secure the observance and prevent breaches thereof, and thereby violated the laws of war, and the following Defendants were responsible for the same. In accordance with the evidence presented in the trial, the Tribunal found,

> As Foreign Minister, he received reports of these atrocities immediately after the entry of the Japanese forces into Nanking. according to the Defense, evidence credence was given to these reports and the matter was taken up with the War Ministry. Assurances were accepted from the War Ministry that the atrocities would be stopped. After these assurances had been given, reports of atrocities continued to come in for at least a month. The Tribunal is of opinion that Hirota was derelict in his duty in not insisting before the Cabinet that immediate action be taken to put an end to the atrocities, failing any other action open to him to bring about the same result. He was content to rely on assurances which he knew were not being implemented while hundreds of murders, violations of women, and other atrocities were being committed daily. His inaction amounted to criminal negligence. The Tribunal finds Hirota hanged under Counts 1, 27.

Although it is still controversial about Hirota to be sentenced to death, Tokyo trials undoubtedly made groundbreaking contributions to the establishment of the doctrine of "command responsibility" in international law.

Fig. 1 Yamashita Tomoyuki

On May 25, 1993, the United Nations Security Council adopted Resolution 827 to establish the International Criminal Tribunal for the former Yugoslavia. The article 7 paragraph 3 of the statute of the tribunal clearly stipulated (Fig. 2).

Fig. 2 Hirota Koki

The fact that any of the acts referred to in articles 2 to 5 of the present Statute was committed by a subordinate does not relieve his superior of criminal responsibility if he knew or had reason to know that the

> subordinate was about to commit such acts or had done so and the superior failed to take the necessary and reasonable measures to prevent such acts or to punish the perpetrators thereof.

On November 8, 1994, the Security Council adopted resolution 955 to establish the International Criminal Tribunal for Rwanda. As for the command responsibility, it was the same as the statute of the International Criminal Tribunal for the former Yugoslavia.

The article 28 of the Rome statute of the permanent International Criminal Court established in 2002 stipulated:

> (a) A military commander or person effectively acting as a military commander shall be criminally responsible for crimes within the jurisdiction of the Court committed by forces under his or her effective command and control, or effective authority and control as the case may be, as a result of his or her failure to exercise control properly over such forces, where:
>
> …
>
> (b) With respect to superior and subordinate relationships not described in paragraph (a), a superior shall be criminally responsible for crimes within the jurisdiction of the Court committed by subordinates under his or her effective authority and control, as a result of his or her failure to exercise control properly over such subordinates, where:
>
> …

Obviously, the command criminal responsibility in the current international law includes military commanders and other superiors (non-military commanders), which was directly originated from the case of Tokyo trials. Although there are some legal disputes and confusions in the theory of command responsibility, The Nuremberg trial, Tokyo trial and the consequent war criminals trial provided a significant legal basis for the development of the command criminal responsibility in today's international criminal law. The establishment and prosecution of "command responsibility for the failure to stop atrocities" would urge the commanders to control the acts of the army in the war to prevent and reduce the atrocities in the war.

2.3 *Opening Up International Humanitarian Judicial Protection*

Abandoning war completely is a beautiful idea of human society, but there is still a long way to go. Although no global-scale world war broke out after the world war II, local wars or armed conflicts frequently occurred. Compared with prohibiting the wars, international humanitarian law developed a lot.

International Military Tribunal for Far East Charter stipulated that conventional war crimes mean violations of the laws or customs of war. The laws or customs of war can be divided into two parts. One part is about the start and termination of wars or armed conflicts, and principle, rules and regulations on belligerents, belligerents and neutral powers or non-belligerents during this period. Another part is about jus in bello, that is, weapon, other means of war and the principles of protecting civilians, combatants and victims of war. The second part is usually called International Humanitarian Law in the international practice and western works of international law. Conventional war crimes didn't include the acts against humanity before the war. It can be said that crimes against humanity was especially established for this gap.

Based on the groundbreaking international judicial practice of Nuremberg trial and Tokyo trials and the development of post-war international law, on July 1, 2002, the Rome Statute of the International Criminal Court officially took effect. Under the framework of United Nations, the first permanent International Criminal Court was established. The ICC has the jurisdiction to prosecute individuals for the international crimes of genocide, crimes against humanity, and war crimes. It is intended to punish the crimes that seriously endanger the common interests of the international community and to maintain peace and justice of the world. International Humanitarian Law is designed to balance humanitarian concerns and military necessity, and subjects warfare to the rule of law by limiting its destructive effect. It is aimed at protecting persons who are not participating in hostilities and restricting and regulating the means and methods of warfare available to combatants. The core of International Humanitarian Law is "protection". It protects civilians, places, goods and environment. There are several basic principles of International Humanitarian Law. Principle of humane treatment is applicable in all wars and armed conflicts. It protects the victims of the war. Non-combatants must receive respect, protection and humane treatment. The principle of distinction means that the combatants and non-combatants must be distinguished in the war. The principle of necessity means attacks on the military personnel and objects in the war are lawful but must limit the harm and loss as possible. The principle of proportionality means when protection is not absolute, humanitarian and military need are restricted with each other in a good will. The principle of reprisals prohibition means prohibiting the reprisals to the objectives protected by International Humanitarian Law. This principle is absolute. Even if the other party has already committed a violation of international humanitarian law, any reprisal can't be adopted.

1864 *Geneva Convention* has started to establish the principles of the sick and wounded, which is the first step of codification of laws and rules of war on land. 1899 *Martens Clause*, 1907 *Hague Convention IV* (laws and rules of law on land), 1929 *Geneva Convention* (Convention relative to the Treatment of Prisoners of War) and other conventions gradually improved the treatment and protection of prisoners of war. However, in the two world wars, there were still abuses of prisoners of war and atrocities against civilians, and the conventions and regulations were not followed. Most prisoners and civilians were treated properly in the military conflicts after the world war and this has much relations with the two postwar international military tribunals.

Although the prominent crime is crimes against peace in the two postwar international military tribunals, only the defendants who committed atrocities and were responsible for the atrocities in the war were sentenced to death. Even the severity of the sentence was proportional to the degree of atrocities. Therefore, the two major international military tribunals are also of landmark significance in punishing war atrocities and maintaining humanitarian. Half a century later, the International Criminal Tribunal for the former Yugoslavia and the International Criminal Tribunal for Rwanda were established one after another, which were the judicial practice of international humanitarian in the new era and the continuation and development of the two major trials after the war.

3 Promote Popularization of Democracy and Establish a Peaceful Order

The process of Tokyo trials, also the process of denying the feudal thoughts of keeping absolute loyal to the Emperor, frees Japanese nationals from the militarism and promotes Japanese society from tyranny to democracy.

3.1 The Disillusionment of "Historic View of Imperialism"

The Meiji government, when implementing the policy of centralization of authority, attached more importance to the authority of the emperor and stipulated that the rule of the emperor was Japan's national system, and created a theoretical system to demonstrate the rationality of the imperial system of Japan in order to establish and guarantee the power and status of emperor. This theoretical system was called "historic view of imperialism". The core of "historic view of imperialism" is to describe Japan as the "god's country" which is centered with the Emperor and regards the worship of emperor as its belief. The emperor bears the sacred responsibility of connecting the heaven and common people. He is not only responsible for educating the Japanese people, but also has the qualification to lead other uncivilized or semi-civilized Asian countries, namely China, north Korea and other countries. The imperial Japanese headed by the Emperor has the sacred duty to promote the Japanese spirit of Hakko Ichiu to the whole world. If resistance is encountered, Japanese nationals should sacrifice everything and devote themselves to the sacred war and the glorious cause led by the emperor.

In order to make the "historic view of imperialism" truly influence the consciousness and belief of Japanese nationals, Japanese government issued the emperor's instruction on education in the form of "imperial edict" in 1890 which became the basic guideline to guide Japanese modern education and write the textbooks. This is "educational rescript" ruling Japanese social and ideological education for half a century. The core of the "educational rescript" is that "once something happened, we must protect the infinite imperial fortune of heaven in the spirit of righteousness". "When there is a war, we must be dedicated to the emperor and defend the national system". In the guideline of "educational rescript", Japanese began to cultivate their loyalty to the emperor and their dedication to the emperor from an early age. Based on Japan's big family system, Japan established the ideology system of "views of family and country" and trained Japanese the national moral norms to comply unconditionally with the emperor and to dedicate themselves to the emperor.

In 1935, the Japanese government started a strict news inspection system. Newspaper, radio, etc. could only broadcast information approved by the government. In addition to receiving education on "historic views of imperialism" from an early age, Japanese nationals regarded those who died in the war of aggression as "heroes who sacrificed their lives for their country" and regarded the Japan's war of aggression against Asia as "a just war" of "self-defense" and "liberation of Asia" and "a holy war" for the accomplishment of historical missions.

Therefore, the response of Japanese society was "empty" when Japan declared "ending the war". The writer of Japanese Shirakaba school Nagayo Yoshirō once recorded that on August 13, the friend working in the library of House of Representative said to broadcast important news. At that time, people who realized the war situation was not good for Japan had believed emperor would review himself and encourage nationals to fight the war. If the emperor did so, the whole Japanese nationals would be very grateful and actively participated in the war. However, after hearing the emperor's voice on the 15th, people were "suddenly frustrated" and didn't know what to do. Left-wing social democrats Arahata Kanson wrote in his autobiography, "the response of the Japanese was strange after hearing the emperor's voice. Did the war really end? Many people couldn't stand the emptiness and had no feeling of excitement".

It can be seen that Japanese nationals who received the education of "historic views of imperialism" and were under the control of the news from an early age prepared "a last chance" and regarded sacrifice themselves as a supreme glory. Therefore, they were at a loss when hearing the declaration of ending the war by the emperor.

Before the Tokyo trial, Japan implemented a constitutional system of centralization of monarchy in politics and pursued "historic views of imperialism" in thoughts. The whole society was under the control of militarism. This social system was easy to lead to war of aggression and instability in the regions and world. Tokyo trials ideologically removed the imprisonment of "historic views of imperialism" from the Japanese, politically rejected the centralization of power by the emperor and eliminated militarist control of Japanese society through the trial and punishment of war criminals, and provided conditions for Japanese society to move forwards democracy and peace。

3.2 Promote the Democratic Process of Japanese Society

One of the significance of the Tokyo trial is to promote the democratic process of Japanese society.

The *Potsdam Proclamation* has a provision about the democratization of Japan:

> The Japanese government shall remove all obstacles to the revival and strengthening of democratic tendencies among the Japanese people.

> Freedom of speech, of religion and of thought as well as respect for the fundamental human rights shall be established.

The democratization of Japanese society is also an important goal of occupation of Japan by allied forces. The Allied powers headed by the United States carried out democratic reforms in the fields of Japanese politics, economy and society, which received positive comments from Japanese society.

Generally speaking, political and social changes dominated by foreign countries were unacceptable to any nation. However, in Japan, the democratic reforms led by external forces developed smoothly and was stabilized quickly. This special situation was partly due to the Tokyo trial.

Tokyo trials proved that the so-called "the great Asia sacred war" of Japanese militarism to liberate Asia actually was aggressive war against other countries in Asia. Its aim was not to "liberate Asia" but to replace Western Powers and incorporate Asian countries into Japan's colonial system. After the truth was revealed, Japanese people's support of militarism turned to contempt and disgust. The American Japan hand Edwin O. Reischauer analyzed the minds of Japanese people in his book *The Japanese*:

> Leaders had expected to win through the superiority of Japanese will-power, and the people had responded with every ounce of will they possessed, until they were spiritually drained. Not only was the city burnt out but also the heart of the people was burnt out.
>
> Instead of feeling guilt, the people [the Japanese] felt that they had been betrayed. To their surprise, they discovered that their armies, far from being welcomed in Asia as liberators, were universally hated. The great respect for the military as selfless patriots and servants of the emperor turned to anger and contempt.

The denial of "historic views of imperialism" and militarism ideologically recreated Japanese nationals and created a social development for democratic development so as to lay foundation for the implementation of *Constitution of Japan* and the development of Japan's democratic society.

The Japanese government established the constitutional system of centralization of monarchy and implemented *Constitution of Japan* (that is *Meiji Constitution*). Besides, it followed 1871 *Verfassung des Deutschen Reiches* (that is Bismarcksche Reichsverfassung) where the emperor has absolute sovereignty over the country by integrating sovereignty, legislative power, commander-in-chief power, parliamentary power and diplomatic power. It was through Meiji restoration that Japan was able to get rid of being bullied by the powers and embark on the road of making country rich with military power, and became the only modern country in Asia and joined the ranks of world powers. In addition, the Japanese government educated nationals on "historic views of imperialism" from an early age. Therefore, even if the country was devastated, Japanese nationals held a positive attitude toward the emperor and the Meiji constitution. This was typically reflected in the draft of constitutional amendment submitted by the Shidehara government.

On October 11, 1945, McArthur had a talk with Shidehara Kijuro, requesting Shidehara Kijuro to carry out "liberal reform" to the Meiji constitution. On February 8, 1946, the constitution amendment draft submitted by the Shidehara government made minor adjustment to the Meiji constitution. The "Army and Navy" in the Article 11 was changed to "armed force", and "the emperor commanders Army and Navy" was change to "the emperor commanders the armed force". "the emperor determines the establishment of Army and Navy" in the Article 12 changed to "the law determines the establishment of Army and Navy". This result was clearly not what the United States expected and was unacceptable to the department of civil affairs of allied powers who was responsible for Japan's democratization. On February 13, 1946, General Headquarters submitted a relatively progressive draft of Japan's constitution, that is McArthur's draft, to Japan and requested the Japanese to accept it. This is the draft of the Japanese current constitution *Constitution of Japan* which the Shidehara government made minor adjustment and was passed by the parliament.

Although this constitution reserved the imperial system, the emperor turned from "sacred and inviolable" into "the symbol of Japan" who didn't master any actual power to govern the country. What's more, Article 9 of the constitution stipulated that Japanese people forever renounce war as a sovereign right of the nation and land, sea, and air forces, as well as other war potential, will never be maintained, which was called "peaceful constitution" and also called "McArthur constitution". On November 3, 1946, the constitution amendment draft was officially issued. Consequently, the draft was distributed to all regions of Japan for discussion. On May 3, 1947, *Constitution of Japan* took effect. The draft was officially published and discussed nationwide. Proof of evidence by the prosecution basically ended in the Tokyo tribunal (the testification phase began on June 4 and ended on December 24.), in which the tribunal revealed the atrocities of Japanese Army and aggressive nature of the expansion of Japanese Army. In the early days of the court session, all seats were occupied in the Tokyo tribunal and the corridors were filled with spectators. Japanese media reported the situations and daily process of the tribunal of Tokyo trials. It can be said that the Tokyo trial played an important role in the successful adoption of "peaceful constitution". Generally speaking, the interference of external forces in a country's political process could be confronted with strong resistance. However, Japanese society showed high approval of the "peaceful constitution", which had much to do with the Tokyo trial. The promulgation and implementation of this constitution has also accelerated the democratization process in Japanese society and advanced Japan to move toward peace.

3.3 Laying the Foundation of East Asia Peace Order

First of all, as the major crimes of Tokyo trials, crimes against peace reflected the international community's demand for sever punishment for breaking the peace. Crimes against peace referred to the planning, preparation, initiation or waging of a declared or undeclared war of aggression, or a war in violation of international law, treaties, agreements or assurances, or participation in a common plan or conspiracy for the accomplishment of any of the foregoing. The Tokyo tribunal not only believed that waging or implementing a war of aggression constitutes crimes, but also believed that the preparation for the war also constitutes crimes. Preparation was a step of implementing various plans before the crimes were actually committed. The Tokyo tribunal traced how Japanese militarists gradually controlled the whole Japanese government, how they mobilized the whole society to prepare for the war through national policies and concluded a tripartite agreement with German and Italy to prepare the aggressive wars. Except for Matsyui Iwane, Oka Takasumi, OSHIMA Hiroshi, Shigemitsu Mamoru, Shimada Shigetaro and Togo Shigenori, 19 of the 25 Class A war criminals were judged to have participated in the preparation for the war of aggression.

The crimes against peace extended the scope of the war of aggression to "undeclared war of aggression" and "undeclared war of aggression" or "declared war of aggression" didn't affect the determination of the war of aggression. Some people thought that the aggressive war should start from attack on Pearl Harbor because the Chinese government had never declared war on Japan before that. If the tribunal adopted thus view, the main and major crimes committed by Japan in China would have escaped trial, and the atrocities like Nanjing massacre may slip through the history and become unreliable rumors in the war. If the tribunal didn't trial the crimes committed by Japanese Army in China before Pacific war, more war criminals may have escaped the punishment, which is not conducive for Japanese society and international community to understand the cruel nature of militarism and to eliminate militarism fundamentally.

Extending the scope of aggressive war to "undeclared war of aggression" can prevent aggressive war initiators from "undeclared war of aggression". To a certain extent, it can prevent small incidents developing into uncontrolled wars and thus reduce the occurrence of war.

Secondly, the military trial on the defeated countries through the establishment of international military tribunal reflects the appeal to peace. 1945 *Potsdam Proclamation* declares that "stern justice" shall be meted out to all war criminals, but sanction is not to revenge. And it suggests that "we do not intend that the Japanese shall be enslaved as a race or destroyed as a nation". The traditional international law usually punishes the defeated countries by killing the defeated generals, ceding territories and paying the indemnities. This kind of punishment is immediate and simple, but it is also cruel and brutal, and it is easy to bury hatred. Once the country which is punished recovered its national strength, it will seek opportunity to revenge so as to be in a vicious circle of revenge and bring endless war and turmoil to the world.

The proposal of conducting international trial on the defeated countries faced the issues of coordination between countries, delay of time and huge human and financial cost. As to the punishment of Axis Powers, there are two arguments of "immediate execution" and "international trial" in the Axis countries. "immediate execution" may be more efficient. However, finally the Axis countries selected a tough road to establish international military tribunal to conduct "a civilized trial" against defeated countries. On the one hand, it is to "show justice".

On the other hand, it is to establish a good example for the peaceful settlement of international affairs.

The Tokyo tribunal gave adequate defense right to the accused and rebuilt postwar international order through the peaceful trial on the defeated countries. This process itself revealed that war should be abandoned as the way to seek national interests and the international order can be shaped through peaceful means. Dleto Shigehikaru in Tokyo Imperial University thinks that "the formation of public opinion in the world plays an important role. I believe that this contributes a lot to world peace indirectly". The idea of the pursuit of peaceful settlement of international disputes conveyed in the Tokyo and Nuremberg trials can prevent the wars for a long time through the formation of world public opinion.

Thirdly, the international military tribunal records history and warns the future. It can be said that the establishment of international military tribunal to punish defeated countries through international trials is realized due to the firm support of US secretary of the army Stimson. When trying to persuade president Roosevelt to select international trial, Stimson provides the necessity of international trial "that we should pursue preventive punishment, in other words, educational punishment, not revenge". The whole process of prosecuting war criminal suspects through legal procedure, on the one hand, records history, keeps the crimes committed by Japanese militarism in history through court hearing and warns the world. On the other hand, it educates the people. When the Tokyo trial began, about 1000 people were in the tribunal, including judges, the accused, lawyers, legal staff, Japanese and foreign reporters and common spectators. On November 3, 1948, Asahi Shimbun had a social comment that the judgment of Tokyo trials was important for Japanese and world history in that it reflected the peace determination of the world. Tokyo trials require to bury the old Japan characterized with militarism which cultivated by the former accused. The trial also clearly stipulated that the country that our nation should build in the future is a peaceful country. Tokyo trials provided an opportunity for Japan's reconciliation with the world. In 1951, Japan returned to the international community *through Treaty of Peace with Japan* and its premise is to recognize the trial of Japan by the International Military Tribunal for Far East (Fig. 3).

Fig. 3 The whole scene of the Tokyo trial court

4 Summary

After the world war II, international community established two international military tribunal, opened international criminal practice of punishing war crimes and laid the foundation for postwar international peace order. The Allied Powers gave up simple and quick trial but selected time-consuming and arduous "international trial". Its significance lies in preventing wars and maintaining peace in a better way. The trial of international military tribunal is not only the record of the struggle to suppress evil, but also a huge step to guide the world to a just and fair standard.

Tokyo and Nuremberg trials open up the precedent of prosecuting individual international criminal responsibility so "country" cannot be the "umbrella" of the individual. That can serve as a better warning to the leaders of the countries that wants to wage a war and thus better prevent war. The international trial is not only to punish those who are responsible war, but also to record history, reveal truth, educate the people and establish preventive mechanism for long term. Japanese people can understand the historical truth through the trial of International Military Tribunal for Far East, thus Japan gives up the right of war and cannot retain armed forces, nor can it declare war to make Japan move on the road of democracy and peace. At the same time, the history which might be covered is revealed and recorded through the trial of tribunal. During the period of the world war II, Japan waged war of aggression and committed brutal acts of aggression, which became the undoubtable history though the trial and judgment of the tribunal. Postwar East Asia peace order is established on the judgment of history by the Tokyo trial and the peaceful road selected by Japan. It is recognized that the Tokyo trial is the premise for Japan to return to international community. Peace is not easy to come. It is of great significance to safeguard the outcome of Tokyo trials for peace in East Asia and even the world.

Bibliography

1. Totani, Y. (2016). *Dongjing shenpan: er ci dazhan hou dui fa yu zhengyi de zhuiqiu* [Tokyo War Crimes Trial: The Pursuit of Justice in the Wake of World War II] (Y. Zhao, Trans.). Shanghai: Shanghai Jiao Tong University Press.
2. Tokyo Trial Literature Series Committee. (2013). *Yuandong guoji junshi fating tingshen jilu di yi ce* [Transcripts of the Proceedings of the International Military Tribunal for the Far East]. Shanghai: Shanghai Jiao Tong University Press, Beijing: National Library of China Publishing House.
3. Boister, N., & Cryer, R. (2008). *The Tokyo International Military Tribunal: A Reappraisal.* Oxford: Oxford University Press.
4. Higurashi Y. (2016). *Dongjing shenpan de guoji guanxi-guoji zhengzhi zhong de quanli he guifan* [The Tokyo War Crimes Trial and International Relations: Power and Norm] (X. Zhai, Trans.). Shanghai: Shanghai Jiao Tong University Press.
5. Tanaka, T., McCormack, T. L. H., & Simpson, G. (2014). *Chaoyue shengzhe zhi Zhengyi-dongjing zhanzui shenpan zai jiantao* [Beyond Victor's Justice? The Tokyo War Crimes Trial Revisited] (X. Mei, Trans.). Shanghai: Shanghai Jiao Tong University Press.
6. Cheng, Z., Gong, Z., & Zhao, Y. (2013). *Dongjian shenpan yanjiu shouce* [Handbook of the Tokyo Trial Studies]. Shanghai: Shanghai Jiao Tong University Press.

7. Center for the Tokyo Trial Studies. (2015). *Dongjing shenpan zai taolun* [The Restudy on the Tokyo Trial]. Shanghai: Shanghai Jiao Tong University Press.
8. Center for the Tokyo Trial Studies. (2013). *Dongjing shenpan wenji* [Collected Works of the Tokyo Trial]. Shanghai: Shanghai Jiao Tong University Press.
9. Mei, X., & Mei, X. (2013). *Mei Ru'ao dongjing shenpan wengao* [The Tokyo Trial Manuscripts of Mei Ru'ao]. Shanghai: Shanghai Jiao Tong University Press.
10. Bu, P. (2015). *Zhongri lishi wenti yu zhongri guanxi* [Sino-Japan Historical Problems and Relations]. Beijing: Unity Press.
11. Zhang, X., Xiang, L., & Xu, X. (Trans.). (2015). *Yuandong junshi fating panjueshu* [The Judgment of the International Military Tribunal for the Far East]. Shanghai: Shanghai Jiao Tong University Press.
12. Research Department of Party School of the Central Committee of C.P.C. (1996). *Kangzhan Waijiao* [Anti-Japanese Diplomacy (vol. 2)] (X. Juan, Trans.). Beijing: CPC History Publishing House.
13. Qi, H. (2010). *Zhanzheng yu zhixu: zhongguo kangzhan yu dongya guoji zhixu de yanbian yanjiu* [War and Order: Study on China's Resistance War Against Japanese Aggression and the Evolution of the East Asia International Order]. Shanghai: Fudan University Press.
14. Bu, P. (2011). *Kuayue zhanhou: riben de zhanzheng zeren renshi* [Post-war: Japanese Perception of Their War Responsibility]. Beijing: Social Sciences Academic Press.
15. Nishihara, H. (2012). *Riben de qiantu yu yazhou de weilai* [The Future of Japan and Asia] (Jianjun Song, Trans.). Beijing: China Renmin University Press.
16. Lael, R. L. (2016). *Shenpan shanxia fengwen: zhanzhengzui yu zhihuiguan zeren* [The Yamashita Precedent: War Crimes and Command Responsibility] (H. Han, Trans.). Shanghai: Shanghai Jiao Tong University Press.
17. Zang, Y. (2009). *Jindai riben yatai zhengce de yanbian* [The Evolution of Japanese Asia-Pacific Policy in Modern Times]. Beijing: Peking University Press.
18. Men, H. (2015). *Dongya zhixu lun: diqu biandong, liliang boyi yu zhongguo zhanlue* [East Asian Order: Region Changes, Strength Gambling and Chinese Strategy]. Shanghai: Shanghai People's Publishing House.
19. Zhu, W. (2015). *Dongjing shenpan yu zhuijiu qinlue zhi zuize* [Tokyo Trial and the Crimes of Aggression]. Beijing: China Legal Science.
20. Yu, Z. (2009). *Guoji rendaofa de jieding ji qi yu zhanzhengfa, wuzhuangzhongtufa de dengtong wenti* [International Humanitarian Law Definition and Conflicts with War Law and Armed Conflict Law]. Xi'an: Journal of Xi'an Politics Institute.

21. Wang, Z. (2014). *"shanxia Fengwen Shenpan" faguan yijian yanjiu* [Study on the Opinions of Judges in Yamashita's Trial—Reexamination of the First Case of the Trial of the Axis War Criminals After World War II]. Shanghai: Exploration and Free Views.
22. Ru, X. (2016). *Lun dongjing shenpan zhong de pohuai hepingzui* [On the Crimes Against Peace in the Tokyo Trial]. Beijing: Chinese Review of International Law.
23. Lu, Y. (2006). *Zhihuiguan xingshi zeren jiben lilun* [Doctrine of Command Criminal Responsibility]. Chongqing: Southwest University of Political Science and Law.
24. Liu, J. (2005). *Lianheguo zai guojiguanxi zhong diwei yu zuoyong de yanbian* [The Evolution of the Position and Role of the United Nations in International Relations]. Beijing: International Studies.

Appendix

People

Judges

1. William Flood Webb
Justice Member from Australia; President of the IMTFE. He was a judge and President of the Queensland Court of Arbitration, as well as the President of the Supreme Court of Queensland. He was made a Knight in 1942. Since 1943, Webb was appointed three times by the Australian government to head investigations into Japanese war crimes. In January, 1946, Webb was appointed President of the IMTFE.

2. Edward Stuart McDougall
Justice Member from Canada. He served in the Princess Patricia Regiment of the Canadian Army in his early years. Later, McDougall was appointed as a judge in the Court of King's Bench of Quebec, the highest appellate court in Quebec. In 1946, McDougall represented Canada as a judge on the IMTFE.

3. Mei Ju-Ao
Justice Member from China. After obtaining his Juris Doctorate from the University of Chicago, he was appointed consultant of the Interior

Z. Cheng, *A History of War Crimes Trials in Post 1945 Asia-Pacific*,
https://doi.org/10.1007/978-981-13-6697-0

Ministry, Legislator of Legislative Yuan, and special member of the Supreme Council for National Defense. On December 12, Mei Ju-Ao was appointed Chief of the Ministry of Justice, Republic of China. After the founding of the People's Republic of China, he was the consultant of the Ministry of Foreign Affairs. He was also a member of the first National People's Congress and a member of the Standing Committee of the National People's Congress.

4. Henri Bernard
Justice Member from France. He was a colonial magistrate who sided with the Free French during WWII when the French authorities joined De Gaulle's fight. He served as the Attorney General of various military courts in Xavier, Greece. After the war, he worked in the first military court in Paris, and later worked for the French occupation forces in Austria. In 1946, he participated in the Tokyo Trials as a French representative.

5. Bernard Victor A. Röling
Justice Member from the Netherlands. He obtained his Ph.D. in law from Utrecht University and was later appointed professor of law at Utrecht University. He was the judge of Utrecht Court. He acted as the Dutch representative for the IMTFE. After the Tokyo Trials, he continued to teach criminology and international law in several universities.

6. Maj.-Gen. Ivan Michyevich Zaryanov
Justice Member from the Soviet Union. Major General of Justice. Member of the Military Collegium of the USSR Supreme Court. In 1935 and 1938, he participated as a judge in the trials of the Trotsky and Bukharin factions.

7. William Donald Patrick
Justice Member from the UK. Former chairman of the British Law Society, judge of the Supreme Court of Scotland. From 1946 to 1948 he represented the United Kingdom at the IMTFE. He became a Privy Councillor in 1949. In 1950 he was elected a Fellow of the Royal Society of Edinburgh.

8. John P. Higgins
Justice Member from the US. Chief Justice of the Massachusetts Superior Court since 1937. Appointed in January 1946 by President Truman to be the United States judge on the IMTFE. Higgins resigned in June, 1946, and was replaced by Major General Cramer.

9. Myron C. Cramer
Justice Member from the US. He served as a judge advocate of the Washington department, the Philippine Department, and the US Army. On July 10, 1946, he was called to serve as a judge of the IMTFE and served as acting director during the return of President Webb.

10. Radhabinod Pal
Justice Member from India. Obtained his Ph.D. in law from the University of Calcutta. Judge of Calcutta Supreme Court since 1940. Of the 11 judges at the Tokyo Trials, he was the only one to exonerate all defendants.

11. Erima Harvey Northcroft
Justice Member from New Zealand. He was formerly a deputy judge advocate general in the New Zealand Army, before becoming a judge of the Supreme Court of New Zealand. Between 1946 and 1948, he was appointed as the New Zealand judge in the IMTFE. His services in the tribunal were recognized by the conferment of knighthood in 1949.

12. Delfin Jaranilla
Justice Member from the Philippines. He served as Attorney General to the Philippines, Secretary of Justice, and Justice of the Supreme Court of the Philippines. He was a Bataan Death March survivor.

Prosecutors

1. Joseph Berry Keenan
Chief prosecutor from the United States of America. He served as a Special Assistant at the U.S. Department of Justice, and Assistant Attorney General of the Criminal Division. In November, 1945, President Truman appointed Keenan as head of a legal advisory team to investigate war crimes committed by Japanese criminals. In 1946, he was appointed as Chief Prosecutor for the IMTFE.

2. Hsiang Che-Chun (Xiang Zhejun)
Prosecutor from China. After obtaining his bachelor's degree in law from George Washington University, Hsiang returned to China and taught law at Peking University, Beijing Jiaotong University, Hebei University

and the China University of Political Science and Law. Since 1927, he became the minister of Justice and Foreign Affairs, Chief Justice of Wu County Court in Jiangsu, Chief Prosecutor of the First District Court of Shanghai, Secretary of the Supreme People's Defense Committee, Chief Prosecutor of the Supreme Court Xiangyue Chamber, and Chief Prosecutor of the Shanghai High Court. On April 1, 1949, he was appointed as the judge of the court. After returning from the IMTFE, he chose to teach at several universities in China. His translated works included *The Discovery of India*.

3. Arthur. S. Comyns Carr
Prosecutor from the United Kingdom of Great Britain and Northern Ireland. In 1908, Comyns Carr was called to the Bar at Grays Inn. He became a King's Counsel in 1924; a Bencher of the Inn in 1938. He became one of the British prosecutors at the Tokyo Trials. He was knighted for this work in 1949.

4. Sergei Alexandrovich Golunsky
Prosecutor from Union of Soviet Socialist Republics. He served as the Attorney General of Moscow. From 1943 to 1952, he worked in the USSR Legal and Treaty Department of the Ministry of Foreign Affairs. He also participated in the Dumbarton Oaks Conference in 1944 and the San Francisco Conference in 1945. He acted as a translator and legal expert for the Soviet delegation at the Potsdam Conference. He was appointed as the USSR prosecutor at the IMTFE.

5. Alan James Mansfield
Prosecutor from Australia. He served as Chief Justice of the Supreme Court of Queensland. He then represented Australia on the International Military Tribunal for the Far East on behalf of the United Nations War Crimes Commission. Between 1946 and 1947, he was the chief Australian prosecutor at the IMTFE. After the trials, he was appointed Governor of Queensland. He was made Knight Commander of the Royal Victorian Order in 1970.

6. Henry Grattan Nolan
Prosecutor from the Dominion of Canada. During the Second World War, he acted as deputy to the Canadian Army Judge Advocate

General. In 1946, he was chosen to be the Canadian prosecutor before the International Military Tribunal trying war criminals in the Far East. In 1956, he was appointed to the Supreme Court of Canada.

7. Robert L. Oneto
Prosecutor from the Republic of France. Chief Prosecutor of the Republic on the Court of Assizes, of the Seine and Marne Department. Assistant to the Director of Personnel at the Ministry of Justice. In 1944, he was a member of the organization against German aggression. After the liberation of France, he served as the chief prosecutor at the Versailles Special Court and tried the Nazis, Vichy war criminals, and their accomplices.

8. W. G. Frederick Borgerhoff Mulder
Prosecutor from the Kingdom of the Netherlands. He practiced as a lawyer in Jakarta before the war. Before being appointed as the Dutch Prosecutor of the IMTFE, he served as a judge in the Special War Crimes Tribunal in The Hague. He arrived on March 4, 1946, but he still managed to add a number of evidence documents to the Dutch-related cases in the indictment.

9. Ronald Henry Quilliam
Prosecutor from New Zealand. Born in 1891. Deputy Adjutant-General of the New Zealand Army and Brigadier between 1939 and 1945. New Zealand Associate Prosecutor at the IMTFE between 1946 and 1948. In the later stages of the trials, he also assumed the work of the Australian prosecutor who returned to Australia.

10. P. P. Govinda Menon
Prosecutor from India. In 1946, he served as an Indian prosecutor in the IMTFE and later resigned. His work was carried out by British prosecutor Comyns Carr. He was appointed as a judge of the High Court of Madras in 1947.

11. Pedro Lopez
Prosecutor from the Philippines. Member of the Philippine Congress.

Members of the Prosecution

The staff of the IPS came from eleven countries, with the largest number from the United States. Among the prosecutors who appeared on behalf of the prosecution, the US prosecutor Keenan was the Chief of Counsel, and the prosecutors sent by each of the ten countries (such as the Chinese prosecutor Hsiang Che-Chun) were Associate Counsels. All the other prosecutors at the court were Assistant Counsels.

Ao, Daniel S.	Lambert, Helen G.
Borgerhoff-Mulder, W. G. F.	Laverge, A. T.
Brabner-Smith, John W.	Liu, James T. C.
Brock, James H.	Llewellyn, Grace Kanode
Brown, W. Glannville	Mahoney, Willis E.
Chiu, Henry	McKenzie, Walter I.
Cole, Charles T.	McKinney, Worth E.
Crowe, Smith N.	Menon, K. Krisna
Cunningham, Floyd W.	Mignone, F. A.
Delaney, T. R.	Morgan, Roy
Damste, J. S. Sinninghe	Morname, Thomas F.
Darsey, John	Morrow, Thomas H.
Davies, Reginald Spencer	Nikolaevich, Lev
Depo, Roger	Nyi, Judson T. Y.
Donihi, Robert M.	O'Neill, Edward E.
Dorsey, Harryman	Parkingson, Kenneth N.
Dunigan, Lester C.	Pashkovsky, Alex A.
Edwards, William E.	Pignatelli, Guido
English, Joseph F.	Prout, William C.
Fihelly, John W.	Robinson, James J.
Fixel, Rowland W.	Rosenblit, S. J.
Gouelou, Jacques	Sackett, Henry A.
Hammack, Valentine C.	Sandusky, Arthur A.
Hardin, Grover C.	Shea, John D.
Hauxhurst, Henry A.	Smirnov, A. T.
Helm, Hugh B.	Steiner, Kurt
Higgins, Carlisle W.	Strooker, Mrs. C. R.
Horwitz, Solis	Sutton, David N.
Hummel, John F.	Tadevosyan, V.
Humphreys, Christmas	Tavenner, Frank S.
Hyde, G. Osmond	Vasiliev, A. N.
Hyder, Elton M., Jr.	Vote, Robert M.
Ivanov, A. T.	Wiley, Robert L.
Kaplan, V.	Williams, Albert
Kunin, A. V.	Williams, Eugene D.
Kwei, Yu	Woolworth, Gillbert S.

The Defense Team

1. Chief defense counsels
American defense team: Beverly M. Coleman (Captain, USNR, resigned on June 18, 1946)
Japanese defense team: Somei Uzawa, the head of the team, and Ichiro Kiyose, the deputy head

2. Defense counsels for the individual defendants

Defendant	*Japanese defense counsel*	*American defense counsel*	*Associate defense counsel*
Araki Sadao	Sugawara Yutaka	Lawrence McManus (June 1, 1946–)	Hasuoka Takaaki Tokuoka Jiro
Dohihara Kenji	Tsukazwki Naoyoshi (–June 4, 1946) Ohta Kinjiro (June 13, 1946–)	Franklin E. Warren (June 1, 1946–)	Kato Takahisa
Hashimoto Kingoro	Hayashi Itsuro	E. R. Harris (September 9, 1946–)	Kanase Kunji Iwama Kohei Sugai Toshiko
Hata Shunroku	Kanzaki Masayoshi	Aristides G. Lazarus (June 3, 1946–) James N. Freeman (July 12, 1948–)	Kokubu Tomoharu Iwanari Taitaro
Hiranuma Kiichiro	Usami Rokuro	Samuel J. Kleiman (May 11, 1946) Franklin E. Warren	Sawa Kunio Mori Yoichi
Hoshino Naoki	Fujii Goichiro	David F. Smith (March 5, 1948–) (June 1, 1946–September 5, 1947, was excluded from proceedings between March 5, 1947 and September 5, 1947) George Yamaoka	Ando Yoshiro Morishima Goro
Hirota Koki	Hanai Tadashi	George C. Williams Joseph C. Howard (September 10, 1946–)	Migita Masao Ryosuke Kanauchi
Itagaki Seishiro	Yamada Hanzo	Floyd J. Mattice (June 28, 1946–)	Sasagawa Tomoji Banno Junkichi

Defendant	*Japanese defense counsel*	*American defense counsel*	*Associate defense counsel*
Kaya Okinori	Takano Tsuruo	Roger S. Rutchick Michael Levin (June 13, 1946–) E. Richard Harris (August 16, 1948)	Tanaka Yasumichi Fujiwara Kenji Yamagiwa Masamichi
Kido Koichi	Hozumi Shigetaka	William Logan (June 1, 1946–)	Kido Takahiko (Kido Koichi's son)
Kimura Heitaro	Shiohara Tokisaburo	Joseph C. Howard (June 1, 1946–)	Tatsumi Koretsune Abe Akira
Koiso Kuniaki	Sammonji Shohei	Alfred W. Brooks (June 1, 1946–June 1947) Joseph C. Howard (June 1947–)	Takagi Kazuya Mimachi Tsunehisa Kobayashi Kyoichi Matsuoaka Tokihiko
Matsui Iwane	Somei Uzawa (–June 4, 1946) Ito Kiyoshi (June 13, 1946)	Floyd J. Mattice (June 28, 1946–)	Jodai Takayoshi Omuro Ryoichi
Matsuoka Yosuke	Kobayashi Shunzo	Franklin E. Warren	
Minami Jiro	Takeuchi Kintaro (–June 4, 1946) Okamoto Toshio (June 13, 1946–)	William J. McCormack (June 13, 1946–October 15) Alfred W. Brooks (October 16, 1946–) Joseph C. Howard (June, 1947–)	Matsuzawa Kondo Giichi
Muto Akira	Okamoto Shoichi	George A. Furness (May 12–July 13, 1946) Roger F. Cole (June 13, 1946)	Chihiro Saeki Hara Kiyoharu
Nagano Osami	Okuyama Hachiro	John G. Brannon (June 13, 1946)	Yasuda Shigeo
Oka Takazumi	Somiya Shunzi	Franklin E. Warren (July 1, 1946–February 19, 1947) Samuel Allen Roberts (February 19, 1947–)	Ono Seiichiro Inada Hitoshi
Okawa Shumei	Ohara Shinichi	Alfred W. Brooks (May 21, 1946–)	Kanauchi Ryosuke Fumiko Fukuoka

Defendant	*Japanese defense counsel*	*American defense counsel*	*Associate defense counsel*
Oshima Hiroshi	Tsukazwki Naoyoshi (–June 4, 1946) Shimanouchi Ryuki (June 13, 1946)	Owen Cunningham (May 3, 1946–)	Uchida Fujio Ushiba Nobuhiko
Sato Kenryo	kiyose Ichiro (–June 4, 1946) Kusano Hyoichiro (June 13, 1946)	James N. Freeman (June 3, 1946–January 1947) John G. Brannon (January 1947–)	Kawamura Saburo Fujsawa Chikao
Shigemitsu Mamoru	Takayanagi Kenzo (–July 26, 1946) Yanai Tsuneo(July 29, 1946–)	Captain George A. Furness (promoted to Major) (May 5, 1946–)	Kanaya Shizuo Miura Kazuichi
Shimada Shigetaro	Takahashi Yoshitsugu	Edward P. McDermott (June 3, 1946) E. Richard Harris John G. Brannon (January 1947–)	Masajiro Takikawa Suzuki Isamu
Shiratori Toshio	Somei Uzawa (–June 4, 1946) Naritomi Nobuo (June 13, 1946–)	Charles B. Caudle (June 3, 1946–)	Sakuma Makoto Hirota Y.
Suzuki Teiichi	Motokichi Hasegawa (–July 29, 1946) Takayanagi Kenzo(September 23, 1946–)	Michael Levin (June 13, 1946–)	Kaino Michitaka Katou Itsupei
Togo Shigenori	Hozumi Shigetaka (–September 20, 1946) Nishi Haruhiko (September 23, 1946–)	Charles T. Young (–July 15, 1946) George Yamaoka (May 5, 1946–July 1946) Maj. Benjamin Bruce Blakeney (July 22, 1946–)	Kato Denjiro Shinobu Seizaburo
Tojo Hideki	kiyose Ichiro	Captain Beverly M. Coleman (–June 19, 1946) George F. Blewett (August 29, 1946–)	Matsushita Masatoshi

Defendant	*Japanese defense counsel*	*American defense counsel*	*Associate defense counsel*
Umezu Yoshijiro	Miyake Shotaro (–July 29, 1946) Mitsuo Miyata (July 30, 1946–)	Maj. Benjamin Bruce Blakeney (May 13, 1946–)	Odajima Sukekichi Ikeda Sumihisa Umezu Yoshikazu (Umezu Yoshijiro's son)

3. A brief introduction to part of the defense counsels

Somei Uzawa

Head of the Japanese defense team. He was born in 1872 in Chiba prefecture, Japan. He graduated from the Law School of Tokyo Imperial University in 1899 and became a Judicial Doctor in 1906. He was appointed the President of Meiji University. He was a member of the Japanese Aristocratic Court from 1930 to 1937. Uzawa represented the accused in a number of famous trials including the May 15 Incident. He was the defense counsel for Matsui Iwane and Shiratori Toshio during the Tokyo Trials.

Ichiro Kiyose

Kiyose was born in 1884 in Hyogo prefecture, Japan. He graduated from the Law School of Kyoto University. He studied in England, Germany, and France, and obtained a doctoral degree. He was elected as a member of the House of Representatives 15 times since 1920, and was the famous criminal defense attorney at the time. He originally favored the "liberal left", but then changed to nationalism. Since 1932, he served as the head of the National League, the secretary-general of the Imperial Rule Assistance Association. After the defeat of Japan, he served as deputy head of the Japanese defense team and defense counsel for Tojo. He had a strong national defense tendency and denied Japan's war aggression. After the trial, Kiyose returned to politics and served as the secretary of the party and the minister of the Ministry of Culture. He served as the Speaker of the House of Representatives and forcibly passed controversial clauses, such as the appointment of the Education Commission and the Security Treaty. He died in 1967.

Itsuro Hayashi

He was the defense counsel for Hashimoto Kingoro during the Tokyo Trials. Hayashi was born in 1891 in Okayama prefecture, Japan. After graduating from the University of Tokyo in 1920, he became a criminal lawyer. He was the president of the Tokyo Bar Association, the general manager of the Japan Lawyers Association, and a professor at the Hosei University in Japan. He was responsible for cases such as the 515 Incident and the Blood League Incident.

Ben Bruce Blakeney
Born in Oklahoma, USA in 1908, he graduated from Oklahoma and Harvard University. In his early years, he worked as a legal counsel at an oil company in Oklahoma. In 1942, he was recruited into the army and was in charge of the wartime prisoner interrogation. He was familiar with Japanese affairs. At the beginning of the Tokyo Trials, Blakeney served as a defense lawyer for Togo Shigenori and Umezu Yoshijiro. He used American materials that were familiar to the Japanese to defend his defendants, and questioned the court on the grounds that the United States also placed the atomic bomb in violation of the Marine Convention; therefore he became a very important member of the defense team. He opened a law firm in Tokyo after the trial. In 1963, he died in an airplane accident.

George A. Furness
Born in New Jersey, USA in 1896, he graduated from Harvard University and became a practicing lawyer in Boston. After the outbreak of the Pacific War, he was recruited into the army. After the war, he first served as a defense lawyer for Lieutenant General Honma Masaharu and Moritake Tanabe on the military court in Manila, and then served as a defense lawyer for defendant Shigemitsu Mamoru in the Tokyo Trials. During the trial he encouraged Kiyose to propose a motion to evade the President, and he also collected a lot of favorable evidence for Shigemitsu. After the Tokyo Trials, he and Blakeney served as defense lawyers for Soemu Toyoda, and eventually Toyota was acquitted. He then settled in Japan and established a law firm in 1950. He died in 1985.

David F. Smith
Born in Washington, USA, he graduated from Georgetown University and received his JD degree in 1925. He acted as a defense lawyer for Hoshino Naoki in the Tokyo Trials. Japan's economic oppression was the focus of his defense. He also questioned the Tribunal about its

operation. On March 5, 1947, because of improper remarks, he was regarded as insulting the court, and he was expelled from the court for refusing to take back his improper remarks and give an apology. He returned to the United States in February, 1948. After the Tokyo Trials ended, he filed an appeal to the US Supreme Court with another defense counsel Logan and asked them to release the accused of the Tokyo Trials; their appeal was dismissed.

A Brief Introduction to the Chinese Delegation

1. Name list

Justice:	Mei Ju-Ao
Secretaries of the Justice:	FANG W.F.S, YANG Shoulin, LUO Jiyi
Prosecutor:	Hsiang Che-Chun
Secretaries of the Prosecutor:	Henry CHIU, Liu, James T. C., ZHU Qingru, Wen-Pin Kao
Legal advisers:	NYI, Judson T. Y. (Chief Legal Counsel), AO Daniel S., Kwei Yu, WU Hsueh-Yi
Translators:	ZHOU Xiqing, ZHANG Peiji, ZHENG Luda, LIU Jisheng, Wen-Pin Kao

2. A brief introduction to part of the members

AO Daniel S.

AO Daniel S. was born in Jiangsu, Yangzhou in 1902. He received his LL.B degree at Lincoln University, graduated from the School of Law in Soochow University in 1928, and then received his J.D. degree at Stanford University. After returning to China, he became a practicing lawyer in Shanghai and doubled as a professor at the School of Law in Soochow University. He became the director of the Shanghai Social Bureau's first department in 1945. In 1946, he was selected to be one of the additional advisers of the Chinese delegation in the Tokyo Trials. He went to Beijing to seek the evidence required by the tribunal and to look for witnesses, including Nanjing massacre survivors Shang Deyi and Wu Changde, US doctor Robert O. Wilson and priest John G. Magee, together with NYI, Judson T. Y. He became a staff member of the administration institute of the Nanjing National Government. Five months later, he resigned and went back to Shanghai to be a professor. After 1949, he became both the dean and councilor of the School of

Law in Soochow University and doubled as a secretary of the director in the Shanghai Flour Industry Association. After 1956, he became a clerk at the Shanghai Federation of Industry and Commerce and a staff member at the Shanghai Research Institute of Culture and History. He passed away in 1970.

FANG W. F. S.

Born in 1914, FANG W. F. S. graduated from the High School Affiliated to Beijing Normal University and entered Soochow University to study law. After graduation, he became the representative lawyer in the Shanghai Municipal Council department of law. During the Tokyo Trials, he became the secretary of Chinese justice Mei Ju-Ao. Then he worked in the Shanghai Matheson. Later, he went to Hong Kong and was employed by Jebsen Group as an administration manager in charge of textiles and machinery business. He passed away in 1976.

Wen-Pin Kao

Born in 1920, he graduated from the School of Law in Soochow University. In 1946, he was employed to participate in the Japanese Class A war criminals trial in the Tokyo Japan International Military Tribunal for Far East. He became the translator in the International Prosecution Section before becoming the secretary in the Chinese Procurators Office. He was responsible for collecting evidence for the Japanese Army war of aggression and translated the testimony into English. Due to his law profession, he became the secretary of Hsiang Chen-Chun. There was a report about the "decapitation contests" in the *Mainichi Shimbun* which was in the documents of Japanese Army archived by the Allied Powers. He was arrested while working in the foreign affairs office of the Institution of Shanghai Military Control Commission. He was reformed through labor in Jiangxi for 27 years and was righted back to Shanghai in 1979. He became a professor of the Shanghai Maritime Academy. He now lives in Shanghai.

KWEI Yu

Born in Zhejiang, Ningbo in 1902, he graduated from the School of Law in Soochow University in 1927. He successively served as a translator in the Shanghai Commercial Press, a judge in the Shanghai First Special District Court, a judge in Shanghai High Court, the secretary of the Supreme National Defense Council, and a staff member of the Judicial Court. In 1946, he was selected as one of the four additional legal advisers and was sent to the International Military Tribunal for Far East to participate in trying Japanese Class A war criminals. After the Tokyo Trials, he served successively as a full-time professor or a visiting professor in Taiwan University, the Law School of Justice, Soochow University, Fu Jen Catholic University and the College of Chinese Culture. He wrote many books including *New Theory of Maritime Law*, *The Maritime Law*, *Insurance Law*, and so forth. He participated in the First United Nations Conference on the Law of the Sea in 1958. Most judges in Taiwan are KWEI Yu's students. He passed away in 2002.

Liu, James T. C.

Born in 1919, LIUT.C. grew up in Shanghai; his ancestral home was Guiyang province. He studied in Tsinghua University. After Japan's occupation of Peiping, Tsinghua moved south and LIUT.C. studied in Yenching University. After Japan was defeated, he went to Japan as a member of the Chinese prosecution in the International Military Tribunal for Far East. His good knowledge of the Japanese language was convenient for the research of evidence in the Japanese documents. In 1946, he studied in the United States. In 1950, he received his doctor's degree at the University of Pittsburgh and taught in the aforementioned school and another school. In 1959, he published *Wang An-shi and His Reform*, which established his position in the study field of the history of the Song Dynasty. In 1960, he became an instructor at Stanford University and entered into Princeton University as a history professor of Princeton University and director of the Institute of East Asia in 1965. In 1993, he passed away at his residence in New Jersey, USA.

LUO Jiyi

Luo Jiyi was born in Fufeng county, Shanxi, in 1896. He graduated from the School of Economics in Tsinghua University in 1921; he then went to Japan to study economics and international law. He was able to speak the languages Japanese, German, English and French. He was appointed as a Chinese ambassador to Korea and Japan and a diplomatic attaché of the Foreign Ministry of the Nanjing National government after he returned to China. After the Sino-Japan War broke out, he went to Hong Kong as secretary of the governor of Hong Kong. He escorted a group of prominent people from Hong Kong to Chong Qing to avoid persecution by the Japanese aggressors. He served as the secretary to judges of the Chinese prosecution in the International Military Tribunal for Far East and participated in the trial of Japanese war criminals. After returning to Hong Kong, he was appointed as a professor of Hong Kong University. He passed away in 1976.

NYI, Judson T. Y.

NYI, Judson T. Y. was born in Jiangsu, Suzhou in 1906. He received his LL.B degree at Soochow University in Shanghai in 1928. He received his J.D. degree at Stanford University in 1929. He served as an honor researcher of the Institute of Law at Hopkins University in the United States from 1930 to 1931. He simultaneously served in Shanghai Soochow University, The Great China University and Chi Chi University to teach international law, international private law, comparison of civil law and Nomology. From 1946 to 1948, as the chief legal counsel of the Chinese prosecution, he participated in the Tokyo Trials and gave an excellent rebuttal in the defense of Doihara Kenji, Itagaki Seishiro and Matsui Iwane. In 1948, he served as the professor of Shanghai Soochow University and doubled as the director of the School of Law. He served as a special committee member in the Foreign Ministry's department of treaty and law and as a legal counsel of the department of treaty and law. He was selected to be a committee member of the international law committee in the 36th General Assembly in 1981. In 1982, he served as a legal counsel of the Foreign Ministry and a judge of the United Nations' international court in 1984. He was selected as acting academician of the Institut de Droit International in 1987 and was transferred to a full membership in 1981. He passed away in 2003.

Henry CHIU

Henry CHIU was born in Jiangsu, Wuxi in 1913. He graduated from both the school of arts and sciences and the school of law in Soochow University in 1933 and 1935. From 1934, he worked in a legal firm. He served as a lawyer in the Shanghai Bing'gong law firm. During this period he had a part-time job, teaching commercial law and laws of the United Kingdom in Soochow University. Moreover, he worked in the banking industry, private industry and commerce. From February 1946 to December 1946, he served as a secretary of the Chinese prosecutors in the International Military Tribunal for Far East. During this period, he found the secret letter which the Japanese ambassador to Tianjin sent to the Japanese Ministry of Foreign Affairs concerning the transfer of Pu-Yi from Tianjin to Shenyang to establish "Manchukuo".

In 1946, he returned to the Shanghai Bing'gong law firm as a lawyer. In 1949, he stopped working as a lawyer and was transferred to the Shanghai Maofeng company. He worked in the Shanghai International Trade Company's department of management. In 1957, he taught in the Shanghai Foreign Trade Cadre School. In 1961, he taught in Shanghai Foreign Trade University. During this period, from 1962 to 1964 and from 1972 to 1981, he taught in Shanghai International Studies University. From December 1985 to January 1984, he served as vice president of Shanghai Foreign Trade University and then became the honor president of Shanghai Foreign Trade University. From April 1985 to April 1990, he was appointed as a member of the Committee for Drafting the Basic Law of the Hong Kong Special Administration Region. He passed away in 2009.

YANG Shoulin

He was born in Wu county, Jiangsu, in 1912. He graduated from the School of Law in Soochow University. In September 1946, he was appointed as the secretary of the Chinese judges in the International Military Tribunal for Far East. After the trial, he was appointed as a Chinese judge in the Allied Powers' Quasi Class Trial (the Toyoda Soemu and Tamura Hiroshi trial). Later, he served as a professor of Soochow University and Fudan University. In 1956, he was transferred to the Shanghai International Studies University. He simultaneously served as a director of the teaching and research section in the School of English, editor of the Journal of Foreign Languages, and deputy editor of the Shanghai Foreign Language Education Press. He engaged in translation, teaching, textbook writing and journal editing. He wrote Course of Translation and other books, and translated The Discovery of India and others. He passed away in 1991.

WU Hsueh-Yi

He was born in Jiangxi, Fuzhou in 1902. He studied in the Kyoto Imperial University School of Law in Japan after graduating from middle school. After returning to China with a master's degree, he successively held the posts of law professor in Nanjing University and Wuhan University. He once served as the assistant of Premier Soong and Foreign Minister Wang. He went to Tokyo as one of the additional four legal advisers of China to participate in the trial preparation at the beginning of the Tokyo Trials. He was responsible for finding evidence in a large number of Japanese documents. After the trial, he served as a law professor of Nanjing University. He passed away in Nanjing in 1966.

ZHANG Peiji

He was born in Fujian, Fuzhou in 1921. He graduated from the English Literature Department of St. John's University in 1945. In the same year, he served as a journalist of The Shanghai Herald and was a contributing writer of The China Critic; he was concurrently a deputy editor of China Yearbook. In 1946, he went to Tokyo as an English translator and interpreter in the International Military Tribunal for Far East. Later, he studied English Literature in the United States at Indiana University. In 1949, he returned to China. He successively held the posts of editor in the Foreign Languages Press, professor at the People's Liberation Army Foreign Language Institute in Luoyang, and professor of the University of International Business and Economics. He translated Rou Shi's *A Slave Mother*, Cao Yu's *Bright Skies*, Yang Zhilin's *Iron Bars But Not a Cage—Wang Ruofei's Days in Prison*, Wang Shijing's *Lu Xun: A Biography*, Liao Jingwen's *Xu Beihong: Life of a Master Painter*, *Selected Modern Chinese Essays* and other works. *Selected Modern Chinese Essays* won first place in the Translators Association of China. He is a famous modern Chinese translator. He currently lives in Beijing.

ZHOU Xiqing

He was born in Hunan, Ningxiang in 1915. He graduated from the Shanghai Jiaotong University School of Management. He received a master degree in Economics at the University of Pennsylvania in 1938. The same year, he returned to China and successively became the vice team leader of the design group at Hunan United Front Work Department, secretary of the Changsha administration, attaché of the Hunan government and concurrently served as the chief editor of Hunan People's Daily. He engaged in the work of the Allied Powers reception, funds and grain raising and organizing personnel to support the front until the win of the Anti-Japanese War. In May 1946, he served in the International Military Tribunal for Far East to participate in the interpreting and translation work of the witness as well as the evidence required by the prosecution of Japanese Class A war criminals.

From July 1947 to March 1952, he served as a technical specialist of the Kuomingtang government's "committee on indemnification and the return of goods and materials to Japan". In 1954, after he returned to China, he joined the Revolutionary Committee of the Chinese Kuomingtang and became a liaison member of All-China Federation of Returned Overseas as well as a member of the Western Returned Scholars Association. In 1964, he taught in the School of English at the Beijing Foreign Studies College. In 1973, he was transferred to the department of English at the Beijing International Studies University. He passed away in Beijing in 2004.

A Brief Introduction to Class A War Criminals

1. ARAKI Sadao
Baron ARAKI Sadao was born to a samurai family in 1877 in Komae, Tokyo. He graduated from the Imperial Japanese Army Academy. He served as a military attaché stationed in Russia, a Provost Marshal General, a principal of the Japanese Army University, a commander of the Imperial Japanese Army (IJA) 6th Division and the Minister of Education. Araki was appointed Minister of War in the cabinet of Prime Minister Tsuyoshi Inuka and Saito after the "May incident" and the "October incident". Kodoha-affiliated officers launched another rebellion in the 1936 "February 26 Incident". Afterwards, he continued to serve as an advisor to the government and as a State Councilor. It was the first time that the minister of the Konoe cabinet and Hiranuma cabinet together were the leaders of "Kodoha" with Jinzaburo Mazaki and Hayashi Senjuro. He was convicted and sentenced to life imprisonment because of a conspiracy to wage an aggressive war but was released 8 years later. Araki died in 1966.

2. DOHIHARA Kenji
DOHIHARA Kenji was born in Okayama City, Okayama Prefecture in 1883. He graduated from the Imperial Japanese Army Academy and Army Staff College. He is fluent in Chinese and gained fame through his nickname "Lawrence of Manchuria". He served as head of the Mukden (Shenyang) and Harbin Special Agency, the mayor of Mukden, the chief adviser of northern China's "autonomous governance", Inspector-General of Army Aviation, commander in chief of the Eastern District Army, commander in chief of the Japanese Seventh

Area Army in Singapore and minister of education. The most important role in his career was working as a spy in China. He actively promoted "the autonomous governance" in northern China and was forced to sign so-called Chin-Doihara Agreement. To isolate northern China from the rest of China, he promoted the establishment of the East Hebei Autonomous Council and plotted to establish in northern China another "small Manchukuo" adjacent to "Manchukuo". He was hanged in the Tokyo Trials.

3. HASHIMOTO Kingoro
Hashimoto was born in Okayama City in 1890, and graduated from Army Staff College. He headed a Russian studies department. He served as head of the Hailar and Manzhouli Special Agency, and he was reassigned as a military attaché to Turkey in 1927. After he returned to Japan, he and some other youth soldiers secretly formed the Sakurakai (Cherry Blossom Society). He advocated connecting Kamal's revolution with his proposed nationalist one-party dictatorship. Kodoha-affiliated officers launched another rebellion in the February 26, 1936 Incident. Due to the bombing of the British warship HMS Ladybird, he retired in order to organize the Great Japanese Youth Party (later changed to the Great Japan Red Council). He was also the minister of the Imperial Rule Assistance Association in 1942. He was sentenced to life imprisonment in the Tokyo Trials. After his release, he was not chosen in the House of Representatives selection. He died of lung cancer in 1957.

4. HATA Shunroku
Born in 1879, Hata was a native of the Fukushima prefecture, and graduated from Army Staff College with highest rankings. He was sent as a military attaché to Germany before the first world war broke out. On his return to Japan, Hata was given command of the IJA. After the "February 26 incident", he became commander of the Taiwan Army of Japan in replacement of Kodoha Yanagawa Heisuke. He served as minister of education; he was also appointed as commanding general of the Central China Expeditionary Army in 1938. He served as minister of war in the Abe cabinet and later the Yonai cabinet. Hata had a pivotal role in bringing down the Yonai cabinet by resigning his post as Minister of War. Hata served as commander-in-chief of the China Expeditionary Army from 1941 to 1944. He was sentenced to life imprisonment; he was paroled in 1954 and died in 1962.

5. HIRANUMA Kiichiro

Baron Hiranuma was born in Tsuyama City, Okayama Prefecture in 1867. He graduated with a degree in English law from Tokyo Imperial University. He was the prosecutor for the 1910 High Treason Incident and was promoted; he became Minister of Justice under the second Yamamoto administration in 1923. He created the Kokuhonsha group and became the chairman. He was appointed Prime Minister in 1939, approving with the Japanese ambassador to Germany and Oshima and the Italian ambassador Bai Yumin to establish a three-nation military alliance. He accepted the post of Home Minister in the second Konoe Fumimaro administration. Before the night Japan was defeated, at the ministerial meeting on whether to accept the Potsdam Declaration, he was clearly opposed to the unconditional surrender of Japan and argued for the continuation of the war. He was given a life sentence in the Tokyo Trials and died in 1952.

6. HIROTA Koki

Hirota was born in Fukuoka Prefecture in 1878. He studied at Tokyo Imperial University and graduated with a law degree. In 1933, Hirota became Foreign Minister in the cabinet of Prime Minister Saitō Makoto and retained the position in the subsequent cabinet of Admiral Okada Keisuke. He also promulgated the Hirota Sangensoku (the "Three Principles" by Hirota) which the Nationalist government rejected. After the "February 26 incident", he was selected as Prime Minister. Under the compromise with the Japanese army, the Hirota cabinet restored the Military Ministers System to be active-duty officers. Hirota returned to government service as a foreign minister in the Konoe cabinet and signed the Anti-Comintern Pact with Nazi Germany and Fascist Italy to further intervene. Before Japan was defeated, he sought a peaceful plan with the Allied Powers through the Soviet Union, delegated by Foreign Minister Togo Shigenori. However, soon after the Soviet Union declared war on Japan and the mediation failed. He was sentenced to death in the Tokyo Trials as the only civilian executed among the 7 defendants sentenced to death.

7. HOSHINO Naoki

Hoshino was born in Yokohama in 1892. He graduated from the school of law in Tokyo Imperial University. Due to his talent in finance, he was sent to Manchukuo. He served as Manchukuo's Vice Minister of Financial Affairs and Minister of Financial Affairs. He served as the chief of general affairs of the Manchukuo in 1937. He was selected to serve as chief of the "Project Department" in the second Konoe Cabinet and chief of the Cabinet Planning board. He implemented the Fascists' new economic system: separation of capital and operation. He was appointed Chief Cabinet Secretary in the Tōjō administration in October 1941, and he doubled as the head of the Total War Research Institute and was a committee member of the National Mobilization Council. He was sentenced to life imprisonment in the Tokyo Trials. He was active in the Japanese financial field after he was released from jail in 1958. He died in 1978.

8. ITAGAKI Seishiro
Itagaki was born in the Iwate prefecture in 1885. He graduated from the Imperial Japanese Army Academy and Army Staff College. He served as a chief staff in the Kwantung Army. He instigated the "September 18 incident" with Ishihara Kanji. He was subsequently a political advisor to Manchukuo, head of the Mukden Special Agency, the highest military advisor to Manchukuo and Chief of Staff of the Kwantung Army. In 1938, Itagaki served as War Minister in the first Konoe cabinet and proposed to conclude a military alliance between Germany, Japan and Italy; he also dealt with the Wang Ching-wei government and Chiang Kai-shek government. He served as chief of the staff of the China Expeditionary Army in 1939. He was reassigned to command the Chosen Army in Korea and 7th division in 1941. He was sent from Singapore to be tried in Tokyo on May 3, 1946. He was condemned to death by the tribunal and was hanged.

9. KAYA Okinori
Kaya was born in the Hiroshima Prefecture in 1889 and graduated from Tokyo Imperial University. He once served as chairman of the Policy Research Council, Minister of Finance, and the Finance Secretary. He was Minister of Finance in the first Konoe cabinet and the Tojo cabinet to manage the budget for the Sino-Japanese War and Japanese-US War. He issued a huge amount of bonds and increased tax to support the huge military expense of the Tojo cabinet, and thus was considered as a Class-A war criminal. He was sentenced to life imprisonment in the Tokyo Trials and was released in 1958. He was elected as a member of the House of Representatives, and was appointed Minister of Justice in the second and third Ikeda cabinet. Among the Class A criminals, he was active for the longest period in post-war Japanese politics.

10. Kido Koichi

Kido Koichi was born in 1889 in Tokyo. He inherited the title in 1917. He graduated from the school of law in Kyoto University in 1915 and held numerous minor bureaucratic posts in the Ministry of Agriculture and Commerce. He continuously served as Minister of Commerce and Industry, minister of Finance and minister of the Industries Control Bureau. Kido became the chief secretary of the Home Ministry under the recommendation of his friend Konoe Fumimaro in 1930. He served as Minister of Education and Minister of Health and Welfare in the first Konoe cabinet in 1937. In 1939, he was appointed Home Minister in the Hiranuma Cabinet. He was recommended to be the minister of Home Ministry by Saionji Kinmochi until Japan surrendered. He influenced the Tojo cabinet, Koiso cabinet and Suzuki cabinet. He submitted his diaries as evidence to protect the emperor and to emphasize that the emperor was not militant. Lastly, he was sentenced to life imprisonment and was paroled in 1955.

11. Kimura Heitaro

Kimura was born in the Saitama prefecture in 1888 and graduated from the Imperial Japanese Army Academy and the Army War College. He served as a military attaché to Germany, an instructor of the Army Service Bureau and commander of The Imperial General Headquarters. He was selected as a member of the Japanese delegation to the London Disarmament Conference in 1929 and actively advocated for Japan's independent development of arms. He was appointed Head of the Ordnance Bureau in 1936. He served as Chief of Staff of the Kwangtung Army in 1939. He served as Vice Minister of War, assisting War Minister Hideki Tojo. In August 1944, he served as commander in chief of the Burma Area Army. The next year, the British army occupied Rangoon and Kimura escaped. After Japan surrendered, he was arrested by the British army in Singapore and was considered as a Class A criminal. He was sent to Tokyo on the day of his trial and was sentenced to be hanged.

12. Koiso Kuniaki

Koiso was born in Tochigi Prefecture in 1880 and graduated from the Imperial Japanese Army Academy and the Army Staff College. He served as a minister of the Army Service Bureau and a minister of military affairs in 1926. In February 1932, Koiso became Vice-Minister of War and in August 1932 he concurrently became the Chief of Staff in the Kwantung

Army. He advocated for establishing a national defense economic system which would be applicable for the total war system; furthermore he planned to establish a subsea tunnel through the Korea Strait in order to achieve the transportation of resources and personnel within the premise of obtaining resources from China. He then assumed command of the Chosen Army in Korea starting from December 1935. He served in the cabinet of Prime Minister Hiranuma Kiichiro as Minister of Colonial Affairs in 1939. Koiso was appointed Governor-General of Korea in 1942. In September 1944, Koiso organized the cabinet of Japan, and during his tenure he attempted to seek peace with the Chongqing Nationalist Government but failed. He resigned in April the next year. He was sentenced to life imprisonment in the Tokyo Trials and died of esophageal cancer, in prison, in 1950.

13. Matsui Iwane
Matsui Iwane was born in Nagoya in 1878 and graduated from the Imperial Japanese Army Academy and the Army Staff College. He served as the head of Harbin Special Agency and the head of intelligence in 1922. After the 1928 Huanggutun Incident, he demanded that the instigator Kawamoto Oku should be severely punished, in order to avoid the adverse comments on the Kwangtung Army. In August 1933, Matsui was dispatched to Taiwan to command the Taiwan Army. He was appointed as commander of the Central China Area Army and the Shanghai Expeditionary Army in October 1937, and during this period a large amount of Japanese atrocities against China, including the Nanjing Massacre, took place. He was recognized as the "China expert" in the Japanese Army. In his early years, he was influenced by Pan-Asianism and supported the revolution of 1911. He was charged with supreme command of responsibility for the Nanjing Massacre and was sentenced to be hanged.

14. Matsuoka Yosuke
Matsuoka was born in the Yamaguchi Prefecture in 1880 and graduated from the University of Oregon school of law. Two years after graduation, in 1902, he returned to Japan and became a diplomat. In 1919 he participated in the Versailles Conference. In 1933, he delivered a speech at the League of Nations, ending Japan's participation in the organization to protest the findings of Lytton report since the "September 18 incident". He served as a director of the South Manchurian Railway Company and assumed the Minister of Foreign Affairs in the second

Konoe cabinet. Matsuoka was a major advocate of Japanese alliance with Nazi Germany and Fascist Italy. Matsuoka also signed the Soviet–Japanese Neutrality Pact with Stalin in Moscow after his visit to Hitler in 1941. However, two months later, Nazi Germany invaded the Soviet Union; his strong attitude to Null Note then became a barrier to Japan-US negotiation. Because of this, Konoe resigned and his cabinet ministers resigned with him in order to get rid of Matsuoka. The frustrated Matsuoka was still considered as a Class A criminal and he died before his trial.

15. Minami Jiro
Born in the Oita Prefecture in 1874, Minami graduated from the Imperial Japanese Army Academy and the Army Staff College. He previously served as commander of the Kwangtung Army, commandant of the Cavalry School, and commandant of the Imperial Japanese Army Academy. He commanded the IJA 16th Division and served as Vice Chief of Staff in the Imperial Japanese Army. He advocated for a national defense strategy that was hardline towards Mongolia and prioritized military affairs. Before the "September 18 incident", he was appointed Minister of War in the second Wakatsuki Cabinet. He knew of the plot and secretly informed the Kwangtung Army to act in advance. Without the approval of the Emperor and cabinet, he arbitrarily commanded the commander of Japanese Korean Army, Hayashi Senjuro, to send an army to support the Kwangtung Army in Shenyang. He received a posting as Commander of the Kwangtung Army in 1934. After the February 26 Incident, Minami was appointed 8th Governor-General of Korea. He was sentenced to life imprisonment and was paroled in 1954.

16. Muto Akira
Muto was a native of the Kumamoto Prefecture and was born in 1892. He graduated from the Imperial Japanese Army Academy and Army Staff College. He was chief of the military intelligence section in 1937. After the Marco Polo Bridge incident, he strongly opposed the non-expansion policy of Ishihara Kanji and advocated for the hardline policy towards China. In the same year, he was promoted to Vice Chief of Staff of the Japanese Central China Area Army. In 1939, he severed as major general in the Military Affairs Bureau of the Ministry of War. He continuously severed in the Abe, Yonai, Konoe and Tojo cabinets. During his tenure, Japan's military power rapidly developed, and Japanese invasion

expanded further. Common political activities and parliamentary politics had stagnated. He served as commander of the Konoe division and the Konoe second division. He was appointed chief of staff of the Japanese Fourteenth Area Army in the Philippines in 1944. He was sentenced to be hanged in the Tokyo Trials. His title was the lowest among the seven defendants sentenced to death.

17. Nagano Osami
Nagano was born in the Kōchi Prefecture in 1880 and graduated from the Imperial Japanese Naval Academy and the Japanese Naval War College. He served as the vice military attaché of Japan's embassy to the United States. Nagano was chief of the Imperial Japanese Navy General Staff and commanded the 3rd Battleship Division. He served as the commandant of the Imperial Japanese Naval Academy and vice chief of the Navy General Staff. He actively advocated for expanding the Navy. In 1933, he was commander in chief of the Yokosuka Naval District. Nagano was the chief naval delegate to the London Naval Conference of 1935; Japan later withdrew in protest. In 1936, Nagano was appointed as Navy Minister under Prime Minister Koki Hirota. In 1937, he was appointed commander-in-chief of the Combined Fleet. From April 9, 1941, Nagano was chief of the Imperial Japanese Naval General Staff until February 1944, when Prime Minister Hideki Tojo removed him from his post; he then he served as the advisor of the Imperial Japanese Navy. In 1943, he was promoted to marshal admiral. As the representative of the Navy supporting the wars, he was deemed responsible for Japan's attack on Pearl Harbor and the Pacific War. In 1947, he died in the course of the Tokyo Trials.

18. Okawa Shumei
Okawa was born in the Yamagata Prefecture in 1886. He was a right-wing writer and a typical Japanese Fascist scholar. He graduated from Tokyo Imperial University in 1911, where he had studied Vedic literature and classical Indian philosophy. Okawa worked as the director of the South Manchurian Railway Company and East Asian Research Bureau. He founded the nationalist discussion group and political club Yūzonsha. He was promoted to chief staff and director general. In 1929, the South Manchurian Railway Company was separated from East Asian Research Bureau and Okawa served as president. In 1931, he formed the Sakurakai with youth soldiers, and he participated in and directed the "March

incident" and "June incident". In 1932, Gyo Chi Sha was reorganized as Jinmu Sha and they continued to advocate for Japanese spirit and Pan-Asianism. He was sentenced to prison due to his involvement in the "March 15 incident" and was released in 1937. He became the political 'think tank' of Konoe Fumimaro. In the Tokyo Trials, the presiding judge concluded that he was mentally ill and dropped the case against him. He died in 1957.

19. Oshima Hiroshi
Oshima was born in the Gifu Prefecture in 1886. He graduated from Imperial Japanese Army Academy and Army War College. He was an assistant military attaché in the Japanese embassy to the Weimar Republic, Budapest and Vienna. He actively promoted the Anti Comintern Pact with Germany and with both Germany and Italy. He was appointed as ambassador to Berlin and attempted to encourage diplomacy between the Axis countries of Japan, Germany and Italy. After the Japan-Germany-Italy military alliance was formed, he returned to Berlin as the Japanese Ambassador in December 1940. After Germany surrendered, he was arrested by the United States. He was informed of being charged as a Class A criminal upon his return to Japan which caused him to flush documents and diaries down a toilet of a New York hotel. He became a Class A war criminal for the Axis diplomacy and was sentenced to life imprisonment. After he was paroled, he remained silent. He died in 1975.

20. Oka Takazumi
Oka was born in the Yamaguchi Prefecture in 1890. He graduated from the Naval Academy and the Naval Staff College. He participated in the Conference on Disarmament in Geneva in 1932. He served as director-general of the Imperial Japanese Navy Affairs Bureau, assistant naval attaché, and the commander of the Chinkai Guard District. As the one in charge of the Japanese Navy during the Sino-Japan Wars and Pacific War, he collected numerous hard line staff and founded the second Division Military Affairs Bureau, which was responsible for the policy of national defense, and appointed Shingo Ishikawa, who advocated for wars, as the director. At the end of the third Konoe cabinet, at a critical period when Japan faced the selection of peace or war, he strongly declared war, regardless of the opposition from the Navy, and became the representative of hard line with the minister of the navy Shimada Shigetaro. He was sentenced to life imprisonment and died in 1973.

21. Sato Kenryo
Kenryo Sato was born in the Ishikawa Prefecture in 1895 and graduated from the Imperial Japanese Army Academy and Army Staff College. He served as chief of the 6th Heavy Artillery Regiment, instructor of Army Staff College and chief of the Military Affairs Bureau. In March 1938, he shouted "shut up" at the representatives who expressed objections when he explained the draft of the National General Mobilization law, in a conference of the House of Representatives. The "shut up incident" became a symbol of the Japanese army's hardline attitude. In 1941, he was appointed as director of the Military Affairs Bureau. The next year, he served as the chief of the Military Affairs Bureau in the Tojo cabinet. He was transferred to be vice chief of staff in the China Expeditionary Army in December 1944. He was sentenced to life imprisonment in the Tokyo Trials. He was released in 1956. In his late years, he insisted that the "Great Asia War" was sacred war. He died in 1975.

22. Shigemitsu Mamoru
Shigemitsu was born in the Ōita Prefecture. He graduated from the German Law School of Tokyo Imperial University and became a diplomat. In 1930, he became the ambassador to China. In 1932, while attending a celebration for the birthday of Emperor Hirohito in Shanghai, a Korean independence activist named Yoon Bong-Gil threw a bomb that wounded several people including Shigemitsu. However, Shigemitsu still attended and concluded a ceasefire agreement, which gave the Japanese army a favorable impression but simultaneously shaped a hawkish diplomat impression. In 1933, he became an ambassador to the Soviet Union, the United Kingdom and China. From 1943, he became the minister of foreign affairs in the Tojo cabinet, Koiso cabinet and Higashikuni cabinet. After Japan was defeated, Shigemitsu, as the representative of the Imperial Japanese government, signed the Japanese Instrument of Surrender aboard the USS Missouri. He was sentenced to seven years of imprisonment. After he was paroled, he simultaneously held the posts of Deputy Prime Minister of Japan and Foreign Minister. He advanced Japan's participation in the League of Nations. He died in 1957.

23. Shimada Shigetaro
Shimada was born in Tokyo in 1883. He graduated from the Imperial Naval Academy and the Naval Staff College. He was appointed as captain of the cruiser Tama and Battleship Hiei. He served as chief of staff

on the Japanese Grand Fleet in 1930 and served as Commandant of the Submarine School in 1931. He was appointed as commander of the IJN 3rd Fleet in the "January 28 incident" and became Vice Chief of the Naval General Staff in December 1935. Later he was appointed as commandant of the Kure Naval District and commander in chief of the IJN 2nd Fleet. In May 1940, he served as the commander of the China Area Fleet. In November of the same year, he was promoted to general admiral and commanding officer of the Yokosuka Naval District. Before the Japanese-US War, he was appointed as Minister of the Navy in the Tojo cabinet but spared no effort to assist Tojo. After the downfall of the Tojo cabinet, he was registered in the reserve service. He was sentenced to life imprisonment and was released in 1955. He died in 1976.

24. Shiratori Toshio
Shiratori was born in Chiba-ken Prefecture in 1887. He graduated from the School of Law at Tokyo Imperial University and then entered into Foreign Ministry. He worked in Hong Kong, the United States, mainland China and Germany. He served as Director of the Information Bureau under the Foreign Ministry in 1930. He kept a close touch with the army and the fascist scholars of Shunmei Okaw for a long time and advocated for jingoistic diplomacy to the United Kingdom and the United States. When the "September 18 incident" broke out, he, along with the reporter of the Mori Kaku cabinet and the Japanese army Suzuki Teiichi, jointly resisted condemnation from the League of Nations and tried to create a public opinion environment that Japan would escape the League of Nations. During the period he was appointed as the Japanese ambassador to Italy in 1938, he and Oshima Hiroshi actively promoted the triple alliance. Later, he was appointed as the representative of the House of Representatives, the minister of the Imperial Rule Assistance Association, and president of the alliance association. He was sentenced to life imprisonment and died in prison in 1949.

25. Suzuki Teiichi
Suzuki was born in the Chiba-ken Prefecture in 1888. He graduated from the Imperial Japanese Army Academy and the Army War College. After the "September 18 incident", he advocated for Japan escaping the League of Nations. From 1938, he served as Chief of Staff of the

3rd Army, Head of Political Affairs Bureau of the Asia Development Board, Minister of State, and Chief of the Cabinet Planning Board; he remained in office in the Tojo cabinet until October 1943. It was when he was appointed as Head of the Political Affairs Bureau of the Asia Development Board that Japan established a national defense system and the plan for strengthening their combat power. From October 1941 to December 1941, he reported an analysis of the Japanese economy and military forces, to advocate for a war with the United Kingdom and the United Nations and to occupy resources in the south. Before Japan was defeated, he was appointed as the president of Dai Nihon Sangyō Hōkokuka and tried to retain the production of Japanese military needs. He was sentenced to life imprisonment and was paroled in 1955. The convict was pardoned in 1958. After he was released from prison, he did not take any posts. He died at age 100 in 1989.

26. Togo Shigenori
Togo was born in the Kagoshima Prefecture in 1882. His family had descended from Korea. He graduated with a German major from Tokyo Imperial University. He served as director of the Bureau of North American Affairs, the first secretary of the Japanese Embassy in the United States, and Japanese ambassador to Germany. Togo assumed the post of director of the Bureau of North American Affairs in February 1932. In the June of the next year, he was appointed as director of the Bureau of European Asian Affairs. In 1937, he was appointed as a Japanese ambassador to Germany. He was reassigned as an ambassador to the Soviet Union due to a serious disagreement on the Japan-German alliance with Oshima Hiroshi. In October 1941, he was appointed as Japan's Minister of Foreign Affairs and Minister for Colonial Affairs. He had conflicts with Tojo Hideki due to his disagreement for establishing the Ministry of Greater East Asia, and therefore resigned his post as Foreign Minister. Togo was asked to return to his former position as Minister of Foreign Affairs in the Suzuki cabinet and he doubled as the minister of Greater East Asia which he had opposed establishing. He submitted an affidavit of 130 pages in the Tokyo Trials and defended himself, saying he was against the triple alliance, and he agreed to keep peaceful relations with the United Kingdom and the United States. Finally, he was sentenced to 20 years of imprisonment and died in prison in 1950.

27. Tojo Hideki
Tojo was born in the Iwate Prefecture in 1884. He graduated from the Imperial Japanese Army Academy and Army War College. He continuously served as Chief of the Personnel Department within the Army Ministry, chief of the military intelligence section, top command of the Kwantung Army Kenpeitai and chief of staff of the Kwangtung Army. When the Sino-Japanese War broke out, he was appointed as the chief staff of the Harbin Expeditionary Army. In May 1938, he served as the Vice-Minister of War. Two years later, he was appointed as Army Minister. In 1941, he was promoted to Prime Minister, Army Minister and Home Minister. Later, he doubled as the final Chief of the Imperial Japanese Army General Staff and then the "Tojo dictatorship" was formed. During his tenure, Japanese expansion upgraded. It was generally recognized that he took the highest responsibility for the war crimes of millions of civilians dying on Asian battlefields and the abused prisoners. Among the 55 causes charged by the prosecution in the Tokyo Trials, Tojo occupied 54 and was sentenced to be hanged.

28. Umezu Yoshijiro
Umezu was born in the Ōita Prefecture in 1882. He graduated from the Imperial Japanese Army Academy and Army War College. He served as the chief of the Imperial Japanese Army General Staff. In 1934, he served as commander of the Japan-China Garrison Army and commander of the IJA 2nd Division. The next year, he concluded the He Mei agreement with He Yingqin, which made China lose the whole sovereignty of Hebei. After the "February 26 incident", he supported the suppression of the rebellion. Shortly afterwards, he was appointed as Vice-Minister of War. During his tenure, he, along with the minister of the army Terauchi Hisaichi and the minister of education Suglyama Hajime, formed a new Control Faction of the Japanese Army. From September 1939 to October 1940, he was appointed as commander-in-chief of the Kwangtung Army. During his tenure, he suppressed the Northeast Anti-Japanese United Army and forced Chinese laborers to build fortifications at the border between China and the Soviet Union. In 1944, he served as the final Chief of the Imperial Japanese Army General Staff. After Japan was defeated, Umezu, as the representative of the Imperial Japanese government, signed the Japanese Instrument of Surrender aboard the USS Missouri. He was sentenced to life imprisonment and died on January 8, 1949.

Background Information

Legal Basis for the Tokyo Trials

Judgment of International Military Tribunal for the Far East (IMTFE Judgment) says in Chapter I, "The Tribunal was established in virtue of and to implement the Cairo Declaration of December 1, 1943, the Declaration of Potsdam of July 26, 1945, the Instrument of Surrender of September 2, 1945, and the Communique on the Moscow Conference of December 26, 1945." (IMTFE Judgment, translated by Zhang Xiaolin, Beijing: Masses Publishing House, 1986, p. 1) The establishment and operation of IMTFE is the result of a series of agreements and resolutions in from 1943 to 1945 among the United States, China, the United Kingdom and the Soviet Union, the last to officially declare war upon Japan. In late November, 1943, heads of China, the United States and the United Kingdom held a meeting in Cairo, Egypt, discussing strategies and post-war punitive measures against Japan. On December 1, Cairo Declaration was announced respectively in Chongqing, Washington and London, which stipulated that "The three great allies declared the war against Japan to restrain and punish the Japanese aggression." On July 26, 1945, the United States of America, the Republic of China, and Great Britain announced the Potsdam Declaration, urging unconditional surrender of the resisting Japan. In Article 8, "The terms of the Cairo Declaration shall be carried out" reiterated the tenet of the Cairo Declaration; in Article 6, "There must be eliminated for all time the authority and influence of those who have deceived and misled the people of Japan into embarking on world conquest" put forward the measures to settle Japanese militarism; In Article 10, "We do not intend that the Japanese shall be enslaved as a race nor destroyed as a nation, but stern justice will be meted out to all war criminals, including those who have visited cruelties upon our prisoners." explicitly stated punishment of war criminals through legal means. On August 15, Japan officially declared surrender; on September 2, Japan and the Allied Powers signed the Instrument of Surrender. On December 27, 1945, ministers of foreign affairs of the United States of America, Great Britain, and the Union of Soviet Socialist Republics announced the Communique on the Moscow Conference, which conferred rights to judge Japanese war criminals on General MacArthur, the Supreme Commander for the Allied Powers of the Far East. On

January 19, 1946, General MacArthur ratified the IMTFE Charter proposed by the International Procuration Section (IPS), and signed Special Proclamation of the Establishment of the IMTFE, thus the IMTFE was officially established. These documents are the most essential bases for the Tokyo Trials.

The Hague Convention No. IV

As one of the legal bases for the Tokyo Trials, the convention and its annex Regulations Concerning the Laws and Customs of War on Land were made at the second Hague Peace Conference in 1907, and the convention was also known as The Hague Convention No. IV. The convention includes fundamental principles and concrete norms of laws of war, and its content and wording were similar with The Hague Convention No. II and its annex in 1899. But some contracting states of the 1899 Convention did not sign and approve of the 1907 convention, so both the two conventions existed. The forewords of the two conventions specified an important clause: Though it is not stipulated in the Convention, civilians and soldiers are protected and governed by the principles of international law which "stems from conventions, humanitarianism laws and public conscience established among civilized countries". That is the famous "Martens clause", whose effect on laws of war was of great significance. Many later war treaties reiterated that.

Pact of Paris

As one of the legal bases for the Tokyo Trials, its full name is General Treaty for the Renunciation of War as an Instrument of National Policy or Kellogg-Briand Pact, signed in Paris on August 27, 1928. The Pact stipulated renunciation of war as an instrument of national policy and settlement of international disputes or conflicts in peace. The Pact was established on the basis of idealistic international relations theories, so it did not play practical roles, but it was the first time that war was renunciated as a foreign policy of nations. The pact was initiated by Briand, the then French Foreign Minister, and Kellogg, the then Secretary of United States in 1927, aiming at restraining Germany with the cooperation of France and the United States. The initial signatories were France, the United States, Canada, the United Kingdom, Ireland, Germany, Italy,

Belgium, Poland, Czechoslovakia, Japan, India, New Zealand, Australia and South Africa. China joined on May 8, 1929. On July 24, 1929, the Pact entered into force. Till May 1934, signatories amounted to 64.

Moscow Declaration

On October 1943, the United States, Britain and the Soviet Union held a meeting of foreign ministers in Moscow. After the meeting, the U.S. President Roosevelt, British Prime Minister Winston Churchill, the Soviet Union Marshal Stalin cosigned the Moscow Declaration on November 1. In accordance with the Declaration, the German war criminals and Nazi members should be sent to the places they committed crime and be punished according to the domestic laws of the victimized countries. The Declaration shows the same stance of the three countries in the punishment of the Axis war criminals. Although there was no specific content in the Declaration, it was of great significance to future international trials. At the proposal of the then US Secretary of State Hull, foreign ministers of the three countries agreed that the then Chinese ambassador to the Soviet Union Fu Bingchang signed the Moscow Declaration, thus the signatories of the declaration increased to four countries.

Cairo Declaration

The Declaration is one of the legal bases for the Tokyo Trials. From November 23 to November 27, 1943, the U.S. President Roosevelt, Chinese Supreme Commander Chiang Kai-shek and British Prime Minister Winston Churchill held a meeting in Cairo, the Egyptian capital. On December 1, 1943, they issued a general statement of fight against Japan. The main contents are as follows: the Republic of China, the United Kingdom and the United States shall persist in fighting against Japan until Japan surrenders unconditionally; Japan shall return all the occupied Pacific islands since World War I; all territories illegally obtained by Japan from China shall be returned to the Republic of China; North Korea shall be set free and independent. The Declaration, confirmed with the Potsdam Proclamation issued by the United States, the Republic of China and the United Kingdom on July 26, 1945 in Potsdam and the Japanese Instrument of Surrender signed on September 2, 1945 by the

Allied Nations and Japan on a battleship in Missouri, was a consensus on dealing with the post-war Japanese issues and an important document for dealing with the new post-war Asian order in the future.

Potsdam Proclamation

The Proclamation is one of the legal bases for the Tokyo Trials. At Potsdam Conference on July 26, 1945, the United States President Harry S. Truman, the Republic of China National Government Chairman Chiang Kai-shek (actually not present) and the United Kingdom Prime Minister Winston Churchill jointly issued the proclamation. Its main content is the statement that after defeating the Nazi Germany, the three countries would work together to defeat Japan and fulfill the Cairo Declaration and other decisions on post-war Japan. The Soviet Union joined the Declaration on August 8, 1945 after declaring war on Japan. The Japanese Emperor Showa delivered a note to China, the United States, Britain and the Soviet Union on August 10 that Japan accepted the Potsdam Proclamation. At 17:00 on August 15, 1945 (Chongqing time), the governments of China, the United States, Britain and the Soviet Union announced acceptance of the surrender of Japan and the end of World War II.

The London Agreement of August 8, 1945

On August 8, 1945, the United States, the United Kingdom, France and the Soviet Union signed the London Agreement, also known as the Agreement for the Prosecution and Punishment of the Major War Criminals of the European Axis. According to the articles of this Agreement, it shall come into force on the day of signature and shall remain in force for the period of one year and shall continue thereafter. Nineteen other countries including Australia, Belgium, Poland and Yugoslavia joined the Agreement later. The Agreement is comprised of a preface, seven articles and an annex, the IMTFE Charter. The Agreement stipulated that an IMTFE should be established for the trial of war criminals whose offenses have no particular geographical location; the constitution, jurisdiction and functions of the International Military Tribunal shall be those set in the Charter annexed to this Agreement; each of the Signatories shall take necessary steps to facilitate the investigation and trial of major war criminals; nothing in this Agreement shall prejudice the provisions established by the Moscow Declaration concerning the return of war criminals to the countries where they committed their crimes; and nothing in this Agreement shall prejudice the jurisdiction or the powers of any national or occupation court established or to be established in any allied territory or in Germany for the trial of war criminals. The London Agreement was one of the most important documents for the prosecution and punishment of war criminals after World War II. In the Charter annexed to it, crimes against humanity and crimes against peace were defined for the first time, which was significant to the development of the law of war and the international law. The Agreement and the Charter also became the basis for the trials thereafter as well as the establishment of the IMTFE.

Reports of Robert H. Jackson

Robert H. Jackson was one of the chief prosecutors of the Nuremberg Trials and the Representative of the United States at the London Conference of 1945. He made three reports in respect of the trials of war criminals. The first and most important one was submitted to the then U.S. President Harry S. Truman on June 6, 1945, concerning the preparation for the Nuremberg Trials. The report was approved by the President and became the official statement of the stance of the United States to the Nuremberg Trials as well as later a guidance document of the IPS in the Tokyo Trials. In this report, Jackson put forward a plan for conducting the trials. He also spared no efforts to find legal basis for crimes against peace in International Law, in which aggressive warfare was already deemed to be an international crime. The second report was filed on October 7, 1946, which stated the result of the Nuremberg Trials. The third report was conducted in December 15, 1947, concerning the deliberations of the London Conference and the development of the London Agreement.

The United Nations War Crimes Commission (UNWCC)

The announcement of the establishment of the United Nations War Crimes Commission (UNWCC) was made by the United Kingdom Lord Chancellor John Simon and the U.S. President Theodore Roosevelt on October 7, 1942. The announcement was approved by the United

Nations and the Commission was established in 1943, by a meeting in London of Government representatives of the Allied Nations, except the USSR. The first official meeting was held on January 18, 1944. Then the Far East Sub-Committee was established in Chongqing in May, and Wang Ch'ung-hui, the then Secretary General of the Chinese Supreme Defense Council was designated as Chairman. The Commission was primarily a fact-finding body of gathering and recording evidence, and formulate war criminal lists. It also performed valuable advisory functions in connection with laws and the governments concerned matters of a technical nature. However, the Commission had no power to investigate or prosecute criminals or conduct trials.

IMTFE Charter

The IMTFE Charter was published as an annex to the Special Proclamation of the Supreme Commander for the Allied Powers on January 19, 1946, and amended on April 26, 1946. The Charter, led by the U.S., was comprised of five Sections and seventeen Articles. As the basis for the IMTFE, the Charter stated the establishment and jurisdiction of the Tribunal, and that the criminal procedure used by the Tribunal was mainly based on Common Law. The Charter was modeled after the Charter of the International Military Tribunal (IMT), and these two Charters together added a number of important principles and provisions to the international law, especially those in respect of crimes against humanity and crimes against peace, which promoted the development of the law of war and the international law at large. However, it differed from the IMT Charter in certain ways due to the differences between the IMTFE and the IMT.

The Appointment of the Judges

The IMTFE Charter, published on January 19, 1946, stipulated that the number of the judges of the Tribunal shall be no less than five and no more than nine. On October 18, 1945, the United States Department of State informed the Allied Nations of the preparation for the IMTFE and invited each nation to send one judge and one prosecutor to attend the trials. On February 5, 1946, General Douglas MacArthur, the Supreme Commander of the Allied Powers designated the Australian judge William Webb as the President of the IMTFE, and appointed other eight judges. The nine judges were from the nations that signed the Japanese Instrument of Surrender. On April 26, the Charter of IMTFE was amended and two more judges respectively from India and the Philippines were appointed in order to balance the number of the judges with those of the nations which joined the Far Eastern Commission. The two judges arrived after the trials had begun.

International Prosecution Section (IPS)

The IPS was established by General Douglas MacArthur on December 8, 1945. Its main responsibilities were investigating Japanese war criminals, collecting evidence and prosecuting war criminals. The Director of the IPS was Joseph Berry Keenan, the chief prosecutor of the American prosecution team which arrived in Japan first. On January 2, 1946, the British prosecution team led by Arthur Comyns Carr was the second to arrive, followed by teams of other countries. The American prosecution team had already started to make a list of war criminals, but the work was not progressing smoothly until Arthur Comyns Carr intervened. By the year of 1947, the staff members of the IPS totaled 487, the majority of whom were from the U.S., while other countries' prosecution team only had two or three legal professionals and personnel. Meanwhile, the investigation on war criminals was led by two former FBI officers successively.

The Tribunal of Tokyo Trials

The Tribunal, also known as the Ichigaya Court, was based in the Imperial Japanese Army Headquarters building. The building was once the Imperial Japanese Army Academy, which became the Imperial Japanese Army Headquarters after the outbreak of the Pacific War. The building had three floors, and on the first floor, there was a courtroom, a lounge (for defendants, witnesses, defense lawyers, reporters, and observers), a lawyers' conference room and a reporters' telegraph room. The offices and an additional lounge (for court clerks, court stenographers, translators, printers, security guards, mailmen, and handymen) were also on the first floor. On the second floor, there were offices, lounges and conference rooms for the judges. The third floor had offices and conference rooms for IPS representatives.

The courtroom was the center point of the IMTFE. It was converted from an auditorium of the Imperial Japanese Army Academy, with the judge's bench at the head of the courtroom. The defendants' seats were located at the bottom of the courtroom, and in the middle, there were witness stands, and seats for the prosecution, the defense, and translators and the Language Arbitration Board. On either side of the courtroom, there was a VIP and press gallery. In front of the press gallery, there were recording studios and a public gallery, which could accommodate up to 700 people. Since the trials were widely anticipated by the Japanese public, it was hard to get public gallery tickets. Many of those who attended were relatives of the defendants.

Japanese Government's Approaches to Deal with the Trials

After its defeat in World War II, the Japanese government had three approaches to deal with the upcoming military trials. (1) As the General Headquarters started to arrest Class A war criminals, the Japanese government immediately convened a post-war meeting and a temporary cabinet meeting, resolving that "Japan will conduct the trial on their own in order to make the judgment as fair as possible", which was rejected by the General Headquarters. (2) Whether the emperor should held accountable for the war was of the most concern to the Japanese government. The cabinet soon passed through a document specifying war responsibility of the government and the army headquarters in a bid to exempt the emperor from any war responsibility. (3) At the post-war meeting held on November 23, 1945, defense policies were determined that the Japanese government should conduct defense in the interest of the nation, but the chief prosecutor pointed out that the Japanese government directly conducting the defense was against the Potsdam Proclamation; it could only provide materials to the defense team. Therefore the defense team for the Tokyo Trials was of non-governmental background, while ministries of the Japanese government including the Ministry of Foreign Affairs and the Ministry of War took an active part in material collection and investigation.

Defense for the Nation or for the Individuals

Three resolutions in respect of the supreme defense policies for the Tokyo Trials were made at the post-war meeting held on September 12, 1945: (1) exempt the emperor from any war responsibility; (2) defense for the nation; (3) defense for the individuals on the basis of the first two resolutions. On June 18, 1946, the basic defense policies put forward by Japanese defense team at its general meeting were consistent with the stand of the Japanese government, both prioritizing the defense for the nation. However, views differed within the defense team, with some defense counsels dissenting from the decision to put the nation before individuals in the defense, partly because some of them wished to defense for those defendants with whom they had personal connections, and partly due to the fact that some were critical of the nation and the government in the first place. As the trials proceeded, stands of the defendants were revealed and the inclination to defense for individuals began to get strengthened. Especially when it came to the rebuttal phase for defendants, their defense approaches differed markedly. A telling example was that when the trial regarding the attack on Pearl Harbor proceeded, the defenses for Shigenori Togo and Shigetaro Shimada went into a confrontation, reflecting the opposition between the Ministry of Foreign Affairs and the Ministry of War.

The Defense Team

Most of the members of the defense team were selected from branches of the Japanese government where those criminals belonged to (including the Ministry of Foreign Affairs, the Ministry of War) and some counsels' associations. On April 29, 1946, twenty-eight people were set as defendants, and soon after that, "IMTFE defense team" was built on May 4, with Somei Uzawa being the head of the team, and Ichiro Kiyose the deputy head. For the preparation of the Tokyo Trials defense, main defenders established a defense committee that contained six divisions responsible for collecting evidence, planning for the defense and contacting work. Different from the Nuremberg Trials, in the Tokyo Trials American counsels were allowed to defense for the accused. In the mid-May of 1946, first group of American counsels led by Captain Beverly M. Coleman arrived in Tokyo, and then two more defense counsels were appointed from the US forces in Japan. Their joining in the defense team was of great importance for Japanese defense counsels who were inexperienced and unfamiliar with the common law. During the trials, American counsels conducted the majority of the defenses while only a few Japanese counsels like Ichiro Kiyose were present.

Translation

Pursuant to the provisions of Article 9, Chapter III of the IMTFE Charter, the official languages of the Tokyo Trials were English and the parent language of the defendants. Both interpreting and written translation were required. During each court session, translators on duty would be in charge of the two-way translation between Japanese and English. If other languages like Chinese, Russian, German, French, and Mongolian were used by witnesses or counsels, those languages need to be translated into both English and Japanese. Documents and other papers presented to the court shall be translated into Japanese or English (or both) in advance. Most of the translators were Japanese who had a good command of English. The court would occasionally ask help from other sources. For example, when Chinese witnesses were present in court, most of their testimonies were translated by members of the China's military mission to Japan, with a small part covered by the private secretary of the Chinese Judge. The tribunal had a Language Arbitration Board of three people. The Board should settle matters of disputed translation in the trials and report to the court. Therefore the board members shall be on duty all the time during each trial. Translation had been an important and thorny issue since the start of the trials, because of a serious lack of translators, extreme difficulty of doing the English-Japanese two-way translation with accuracy, and the occurrence of translation work for other languages from time to time during the trials.

Indictment

The indictment was prepared and complied by the IPS. At 4 p.m. on April 29, 1946, the chief prosecutor Joseph B. Keenan submitted to the court the original document of the indictment signed by the prosecutors of all Allied Nations. A copy of the indictment and the IMTFE Charter were sent to each defendant under the order of the tribunal. The indictment consisted of three parts, namely the preface, counts and appendix. The indictment charged against all the individual defendants between January 1, 1928 and September 2, 1945, and unlike the Nuremberg Trials, "criminal organizations" were not charged against in the Tokyo Trials. The preface briefly introduced the defendants and the traits and political significance of crimes committed by the Japan's ruling clique. The second part, the body of the indictment, introduced fifty-five counts charging either all defendants or part of them with three groups of crimes, namely crimes against peace, murder, and conventional war crimes and crimes against humanity. The third part contained five appendixes, serving as important reference material for those counts. However, the indictment was too long and complex. As a result, the tribunal cut the fifty-five counts to ten in the written judgment.

The Counts Set Out in the Indictment for Tokyo Trials

The indictment against the defendants, prepared by the IPS, contained 55 counts under three Groups. Group One comprised 36 counts (from Count 1 to Count 36) of Crimes against Peace of all or part of the defendants participating in formulation or execution of a common plan or conspiracy to wage wars of aggression and wars in violation of international law, treaties, agreements, and assurances. Group Two was on murder, including 16 counts (from Count 37 to Count 52) of murder and conspiracy to murder of all defendants, part of whom, by unlawfully ordering, causing and permitting the armed forces of Japan to attack some cities and slaughter the inhabitants, unlawfully killed and murdered many thousands of civilians and disarmed soldiers. The counts under Group Three charged Conventional War Crimes and Crimes against Humanity of part of the defendants who participated in the formulation or execution of a common plan or conspiracy in violation of the laws of War, and ordering, authorizing and permitting their respective subordinates frequently and habitually to commit the breaches of the Laws and Customs of War, or deliberately and recklessly disregarding their legal duty to take adequate steps to secure the observance and prevent breaches. These three groups set forth in the indictment were not in line with the crimes as stated in the IMTFE Charter, namely, Crimes against Peace, Conventional War Crime, and Crimes against Humanity. Specifically, crimes of murder, part of the Conventional War Crimes, were highlighted as an independent group, while the counts under Group Three charged Conventional War Crime excluding murder, as well as Crimes against Humanity, which had been listed as an independent category of crimes in the Charter. All these led to a lack of logic and balance with the indictment as deemed by the tribunal, and the charges against individual defendants were cut to 10 counts in the judgment.

Trial Procedures

Pursuant to the provisions of Article 15 of the IMTFE Charter, the trial procedures were divided into the following eleven parts: (1) The prosecution read the indictment; (2) The court interrogated defendants about whether they confessed their crimes; (3) The chief prosecutor read the opening statement; (4) The prosecution presented witness and material evidence; (5) The defense presented witness and material evidence; (6) The prosecution made a rebuttal against the witness for the defense, and presented rebuttal evidence if possible; (7) The defense made a rebuttal against the witness for the prosecution, and presented rebuttal evidence if possible; (8) The prosecution presented a summation; (9) The defense presented a summation; (10) The chief prosecutor gave final statements; (11) The court entered a judgment and read the verdict. The rule of evidence in the Tokyo Trials is very complicated, as the establishment of the Charter and the Tribunal was based on the common law. During the two and a half years of the Tokyo Trials, more than half of the time was for the prosecution and the defense to submit evidence.

The Witness Ryukichi Tanaka

Ryukichi Tanaka, graduating from the Army Staff College, was a China hand in the Imperial Japanese Army. Tanaka attended the "China Class" in the Imperial Japanese Army General Staff in 1924 and started the work of collecting military intelligence in China since 1927. He waged the January 28 Incident in 1932 and the Suiyuan Event in 1936. In 1940, Tanaka, as Chief of Staff of the Japanese First Army, was sent to Taiyuan, a Chinese city, to get support from Chinese warlord Yen His-shan. In the same year, he was appointed Chief of the Military Administration Bureau of the Army Ministry. Due to holding a different stance on war from Hideki Tojo, Tanaka was later put in the reserve troops. In 1942, he was even sent to Kokuritsukokubudai hospital because of his "elderly depression". During the IMTFE, Tanaka testified several times for the prosecution, bearing witness against Hideki Tojo, Akira Muto, Heitaro Kimura, Yoshijiro Umezu, Seishiro Itagaki, Kingoro Hashimoto and other defendants, so he was regarded as "the Japanese Judas" in the public. He also testified for the defense, bearing testimonies in the case relating to the Changkufeng Incident in May and the defense for Shunroku Hata in September. Tanaka was once suspected of having a nervous breakdown after the trials and in 1949, he attempted suicide. He wrote in his testament that "As a Japanese warlord, I should have died in the Greater East Asia War...... I am one of the main criminals, especially considering my crimes committed in northern China and Manchuria. The absolution can't relieve me of my crimes." On June 5, 1972, he died of colorectal cancer at the age of seventy-eight.

The Witness Puyi

Puyi Aisin Gioro, the last emperor of Qing dynasty, was forced to abdicate after the Xinhai Revolution. In 1917, he was restored to the throne for twelve days. After the September 18 Incident, Puyi became the Kangde Emperor of Manchukuo with the Imperial Japan's support. After Japan's defeat in World War II, Puyi was imprisoned in the asylum in former Soviet Union's Khabarovsk. During the Tokyo Trials, with the joint efforts of Chinese delegates and others, Puyi arrived in Tokyo on August 16, 1946, as one of the IPS's most important witnesses. He testified in court for eight consecutive days, the longest recorded testifying in the IMTFE. Puyi mainly testified that Japan undermined China's sovereignty through military, economic and cultural invasion of northeastern China, and how he was oppressed and deprived of freedom by the Japanese side. However, the credibility of his testimonies was disputed at the time. In his autobiography *The First Half of My Life*, he wrote that he was frightened to be extradited to China as a war criminal for trials, so in the Tokyo Trials, he deliberately shifted all the war responsibility to the Japanese government, and hid some facts to escape punishment.

Judgment of the Tokyo Trials

The two-year Tokyo Trials ended on April 16, 1948. After six-month adjournment, the court reopened on November 4 of that year. The presiding president declared the judgment which was divided into ten parts, "Establishment and Proceedings of the Tribunal", "The Law", "Obligations Assumed and Rights Acquired by Japan", "The Military Domination of Japan and Preparations for War", "Japanese Aggression Against China", "Japanese Aggression Against the U.S.S.R.", "The Pacific War", "Conventional War Crimes (Atrocities)", "Findings on Counts of the Indictment", "Verdicts". All the twenty-eight defendants were convicted, except Yosuke Matsuoka and Osami Nagano who died of diseases, and Shūmei ōkawa who was found mentally unfit for trial, so the charges against him were dismissed. Seven of the defendants, the Kenji Dohihara, Koki Hirota, Seishiro Itagaki, Heitaro Kimura, Iwane Mutsui, Akira Muto, Hideki Tojo were sentenced to death by hanging. Sixteen of the defendants, Sadao Araki, Kingoro Hashimoto, Shunroku Hata, Kiichiro Hiranuma, Naoki Hoshino, Okinori Kaya, Koichi Kido, Kuniaki Koiso, Jiro Minami, Takasumi Oka, Hiroshi Oshima, Kenryo Sato,

Shigetaro Shimada, Toshio Shiratori, Teiichi Suzuki, Yoshijiro Umezu were sentenced to imprisonment for life. Shigenori Togo was sentenced to imprisonment for twenty years and Mamoru Shigemitsu seven years. The whole declaration of the judgment took seven days and the judgment was basically based on the majority opinion (United States, China, United Kingdom, Soviet Union, New Zealand, Philippines, Canada) of the court. Judges holding minority opinions submitted their minority opinion which was not read in court.

Majority Opinion and Minority Opinion

The judgment read out in the Tokyo Trials Tribunal is also called "Majority Opinion". Although the judges holding the minority opinion, including the justice of France and the justice of the Philippines, didn't participate in the discussion, they were involved in drafting the Majority Opinion, therefore the Tokyo Trials judgment was considered by all the judges. At the same time, the justice Bernard of France, the justice Pal of India and the justice Roling of the Netherlands produced a dissenting opinion and the justice of Philippines submitted a concurring opinion echoing such dissenting opinion. The presiding president, justice Webb of Australia, also submitted an individual opinion in which he disagreed with the majority on the legal basis for convicting the accused. These minority opinions were mainly regarding the jurisdiction, procedure, factual confirmation and judgment of the Tokyo Trials, which were not publicly presented at the time. In 1977, the justice Roling of Netherlands who was involved in the Tokyo Trials edited and published opinions of all the judges in the Tokyo Trials.

Presiding President's Individual Opinion

The president, justice Webb of Australia, also produced a judgment as he disagreed with the majority on the crimes the defendants were convicted of. He wrote a 20-page individual opinion, in which he doubted the application of the "Joint Conspiracy Crime" in the tribunal but defensed for it. About sentencing, Webb objected to sentencing the defendants convicted of the conventional war crime and the crime against humanity to death. He thought more suitable punishment should be lifelong overseas exile. He also pointed out another reason why death penalty was inappropriate was that Japanese Emperor was exempted from war responsibility. However, Webb insisted that Japanese Emperor should be put on trial.

The Philippine Judge's Concurring Opinion

The Philippines judge Jaranilla's 35-page concurring opinion (English) covered "Joint Conspiracy Crime", "Lack of cause of action concerning the planning and preparation of aggressive war", "Cause of action concerning murder and other atrocities", "Joint Conspiracies of Japan and Germany", "Objection to the Jurisdiction by the Defense", "Individual responsibilities", "Atomic Bombs Issues", "Dissenting opinions of the Indian justice", "Inappropriate penalty" and the conclusion. Jaranilla fully affirmed the Charter and the jurisdiction of the Tokyo Trials, including the legitimacy of America's use of atomic bomb. He thought that the verdicts of the Tokyo Trials were too lenient while all defendants should be sentenced to death. Jaranilla was one of the survivors in Bataan Death March by the Japanese Army in the Philippines.

The Dutch Judge's Minority Opinion

The justice Roling of the Netherlands submitted a 343-page minority opinion on the jurisdiction of the tribunal and penalties against the defendants. Roling thought that the tribunal should not be subject to the Charter in every aspect and the jurisdiction of the tribunal should be restricted in the Pacific War, so Japan-Russia border conflicts (the Changgufeng Event and the Nuomenkan Event) should be excluded. About sentencing, Roling held the same opinion with Sir Webb, more in view of the international law. He thought that "Joint Conspiracy Crime" is under the Common Law, and the defendants who only committed "Crime against Peace" should not be sentenced to death unless they also committed the conventional war crimes. He thought that it was inappropriate to convict the defendant Koki Hirota of the crime against peace and the conventional war crime and he should be exonerated and released; Takasumi Oka, Kenryo Sato and Shigetaro Shimada who were sentenced to imprisonment for life should be sentenced to death, and another four defendants Shunroku Hata, Koichi Kido, Mamoru Shigemitsu and Shigenori Togo should be exonerated and released.

The French Judge's Minority Opinion

The justice Bernard of France submitted a 23-page dissenting opinion (English) including, (1) judgment of the aggressive war's illegality should be based on the principles of the natural law rather than the Pact of Paris cited by the prosecution; (2) the confirmation of the responsibility of "Non-action" in "Conventional War Crimes" was inappropriate; (3) there were significant deficiencies in the trial proceedings of the IMTFE. For example, the conditions of defense for the defendants were not met, and the judgment was made by the simple majority; (4) the Japanese Emperor should be accused.

The Indian Judge's Dissenting Opinion

The justice Pal of India was the only one to exonerate all defendants. According to the trial records, his minority opinions were over one thousand pages, including main opinions as follows: (1) "Conspiracy Crime" doesn't exist; (2) Crime of aggression is illegal; (3) Crime against peace is the result of the ex post facto law in court; (4) Individuals don't bear the criminal responsibilities; (5) Omission should not constitute a crime; (6) Japanese attack on Pearl Harbor is self-defense rather than aggression. In Pal's judgment, he didn't deny the Japanese Army's atrocities. The reason why he had different opinions from other justices is possibly related to his experience of growing in colonies. The justice of the Netherlands thought, "Although it seems law-based when he (Pal) justified the Japanese criminals, what really guides him is the anti-imperialist political logic".

GHQ Trials

In October 1948, General Headquarters (GHQ) established the court in Marunouchi, Tokyo and put the former general admiral Soemu Toyoda and the former lieutenant general Hiroshi Tamura on trial, which was called "Marunouchi Trial" or "Ayoyama Trial" because of the trial place. This is the ad hoc tribunal for the defendants Toyoda and Tamura in the context that the United Nations gave up the second trial of war criminals, so it is regarded as "Quasi-Class A Trial". The indictment of the two defendants was submitted on October 19. The court first opened in the Mitsubishi Ichigokan Museum, Marunouchi, and on April 26, 1949, the trial of Toyoda was moved to Nippon Seinenkan located in Ayoyama. The trial lasted for over ten months, exonerating Toyoda and sentencing Tamura to imprisonment for eight years.

The Japanese Public Opinion on Judgments

After the sentence, the majority of the Japanese domestic public held positive opinions on the judgment of the Tokyo Trials, except the sentence of Koki Hirota which surprised the public. The editorial of Asahi Shimbun after the trial was typical. Although the editorial believed that judgment of war criminals should be based on written laws, it fully affirmed that: (1) The Tokyo Trials set a precedent that people responsible for wars should be judged by the international communities; (2) The trial was proceeded in a civilized way; (3) Fascisms must be punished; (4) War responsibility was ascribable not only to individuals but also to countries. World Peace is the common will of both victorious nations and defeated nations, which was generally corroborated by the analyses on the number and content of Japanese domestic media reports collected by American intelligence department during the three-year trial. However, as time went by, after the 1990s, the Japanese domestic public opinions had changed as the political atmosphere changed. The negative attitude to the trial has prevailed especially in recent years.

Execution on Gallows

On December 20, 1948, the Supreme Court of the United States announced that no appeals from the defendants in the Tokyo Trials would be accepted. On the next day, General MacArthur ordered the commander of the Eighth United States Army to execute the criminals. On December 23, the day to execute the seven criminals who were sentenced to death by hanging, the representatives of the four countries in the Allied Council against Japan and the penitentiary Shinsho Hanayama were present except the doctors and the guards of the Sugamo Prison. The corpses of the seven criminals weren't mugged as in the Nuremberg Trials. Their bone ashes were scattered by their families under the intense surveillance. But some ashes were taken out by the defense attorney Shohei Sammonji, buried on the top of Sangen Mountain in the tomb whose epitaph is "Tombstone for Seven Martyrs".

Names in Chinese and English

Chinese	*English*
莉莉·阿贝格	Abegg, Lily
约翰·M. 埃利森	Allison, John M.
托马斯·阿奎那	Aquinas, Thomas
老贝格尼诺·阿基诺	Aquino, Benigno Sr.
亚里士多德	Aristotle
昂山	Aung San
马哈穆德·谢里夫·巴西奥尼	Bassiouni, Mahmoud Cherif
麦纳·谢尔·贝茨	Bates, Miner Searle
亨利·贝尔纳	Bernard, Henri
弗朗西斯·比德尔	Biddle, Francis
本·布鲁斯·布莱克尼	Blakeney, Ben Bruce
W·G. 弗雷德里克·伯格霍夫·穆德	Borgerhoff Mulder, W. G. Frederick
詹姆斯·伯恩斯	Byrnes, James
本杰明·N. 卡尔多佐	Cardozo, Benjamin N.
阿尔瓦·C. 卡朋特	Carpenter, Alva C.
阿尔瓦·卡朋特	Carpenter, Alva
安东尼奥·卡塞斯	Cassese, Antonio
温斯顿·S. 丘吉尔	Churchill, Winston S.
马库斯·图留斯·西塞罗	Cicero, Marcus Tullius
大卫·科恩	Cohen, David
亚瑟·S. 柯明斯— 卡尔	Comyns Carr, Arthur. S.
查尔斯·考辛斯	Cousins, Charles
罗伯特·克雷吉	Craigie, Robert
密朗·C. 克拉默	Cramer, Myron C.
J·S. 辛宁·达姆斯特	Damste, J. S. Sinninghe
埃尔默·戴维斯	Davis, Elmer
詹姆斯·哈罗德·杜立特	Doolittle, James Harold
F. 提尔曼·德丁	Durdin, F. Tilman
博夫斯拉夫·艾切尔	Ečer, Bohuslav
罗伯特·安东尼·艾登	Eden, Robert Anthony
赫伯特·威尔·伊瓦特	Evatt, Herbert Vere
詹姆斯·福莱斯特	Forrestal, James
乔治·A.弗内斯	Furness, George A.
谢尔盖·亚历山德罗维奇·戈伦斯基	Golunsky, Sergei Alexandrovich
雨果·格劳秀斯	Grotius, Hugo
鲁道夫·赫斯	Hess, Rudolf Walter Richard
约翰·P. 希金斯	Higgins, John P.
阿道夫·希特勒	Hitler, Adolf
托马斯·霍布斯	Hobbes, Thomas
科德尔·赫尔	Hull, Cordell
塞西尔·赫斯特	Hurst, Cecil
弗雷德里克·埃弗森	Iverson, Frederick

Chinese	*English*
罗伯特·H. 杰克逊	Jackson, Robert H.
德尔芬·哈拉尼利亚	Jaranilla, Delfin
樊尚·奥里奥尔	Jules-Vincent Auriol
伊曼努尔·康德	Kant, Immanuel
约瑟夫·贝瑞·季南	Keenan, Joseph Berry
塞缪尔·G. 克雷曼	Kleiman, Samuel G.
许阁森	Knatchbull-Hugessen, H. M.
阿尔弗雷德·克雷奇默	Kretschmer, Alfred
威廉·洛根	Logan, William
佩特罗·佩兹	Lopez, Pedro
金良	Luang Wichitwathakan
阿兰·詹姆斯·曼斯菲尔德	Mansfield, Alan James
乔治·马歇尔	Marshall, George
詹姆斯·麦卡勒姆	McCallum, James
爱德华·斯图尔特·麦克杜格尔	McDougall, Edward Stuart
约瑟夫·阿尔伯特麦辛格	Meisinger, Josef Albert
P. P. 戈文达·麦农	Menon, P. P. Govinda
维亚切斯拉夫·莫洛托夫	Molotov, Vyacheslav
拉德纳·摩尔	Moore, Lardner
亨利·摩根索	Morgenthau, Henry
路易斯·蒙巴顿	Mountbatten, L. Louis
贝尼托·墨索里尼	Mussolini, Benito
亨利·格兰顿·诺兰	Nolan, Henry Grattan
艾瑞玛·哈维·诺斯克罗夫特	Northcroft, Erima Harvey
约翰·W. 奥布莱恩	O'Brien, John W.
罗伯特·L. 奥尼托	Oneto, Robert L.
拉萨·奥本海	Oppenheim, Lassa Francis Lawrence
拉达宾诺德·帕尔	Pal, Radhabinod
威廉·唐纳德·帕特里克	Patric, William Donald
帕特里克勋爵	Patrick, William Donald
赫伯特·佩尔	Pell, Herbert
约翰·博兰	Poland, John
马亨德拉·普拉塔普	Pratap, Mahendra
塞缪尔·普芬道夫	Pufendorf, Samuel
罗纳德·亨利·奎廉	Quilliam, Ronald Henry
约翰·拉贝	Rabe, John Rabe
埃德温·赖肖尔	Reischauer, Edwin O.
罗伯特·莱特	Robert Wright
伯纳德·维克多·A. 勒林	Röling, Bernard Victor A.
富兰克林·D. 罗斯福	Roosevelt, Franklin D.
哈特利·威廉·肖克洛斯	Shawcross, Hartley William
约翰·西蒙(第一代西蒙子爵)	Simon, John (1st Viscount Simon)
海因里希·施塔莫	Stahmer, Heinrich
约瑟夫·斯大林	Stalin, Joseph
亨利·L. 史汀生	Stimson, Henry L.
斯特里特	Streeter

Chinese	*English*
吴登茂	Thein Maung
埃利奥特·索普	Thorpe, Elliot R.
哈利·S. 杜鲁门	Trumen, Harry S.
约西亚斯·范·迪恩斯特	Van Dienst, Josias
乔奇·瓦尔加斯	Vargas, Jorge
卡尔·冯·克劳塞维茨	Von Clausewitz, Karl Philip Gottfried
皮特·冯·哈根巴赫	Von Hagenbach, Peter
威廉·弗拉德·韦伯	Webb, William Flood
约翰·M. 威尔	Weir, John M.
克里斯蒂安·沃尔夫	Wolff, Christian
罗伯特·赖特	Wright, Robert
伊万·米歇耶维奇·柴扬诺夫	Zaryanov, Ivan Mikheevich

List of Abbreviations

FEAC	Far Eastern Advisory Commission
FEC	Far Eastern Commission
GHQ	General Headquarters
IPS	International Prosecution Section
JCS	Joint Chiefs of Staff
SCAP	Supreme Commander for the Allied Powers
SFE	Subcommittee for the Far East
SWNCC	The State-War-Navy Coordinating Committee
UNWCC	The United Nations War Crimes Commission and the Development of the Laws of War
ALFSEA	Allied Land Force South East Asia

Postscript

When I was invited to write this book, I was not sure about its purpose, content and style. And due to my busy schedule, although the publisher often pressed for the manuscript, I was not able to put pencil to paper for a long time. After I realized that the publisher asked for an overview reading, the deadline was approaching. Thanks to Zhao Yuhui, Gong Zhiwei, and Zhang Suping, the three young people volunteered to help. Later on, Xu Chi also joined the team, so I eventually completed the book on time. This is what I feel sorry and grateful for.

After I drew up the framework, I assigned the work to the several young people according to their strengths and interests:

Part One (translated by HE Jun)
Chapter One: The Road to the Tokyo Trials (CHENG Zhaoqi)
Chapter Two: The Dispute Over Jurisdiction Prior to the Court Opening (CHENG Zhaoqi)
Chapter Three: The Trials (GONG Zhiwei)
Chapter Four: The Declaration of Judgment (ZHAO Yuhui)
Chapter Five: Other Asian Trials for Japanese War Crimes (ZHAO Yuhui)

Part Two (translated by YANG Fangbin)
Chapter Six: A Re-evaluation of the Tokyo Trial Argument (CHENG Zhaoqi)

Z. Cheng, *A History of War Crimes Trials in Post 1945 Asia-Pacific*,
https://doi.org/10.1007/978-981-13-6697-0

Chapter Seven: Evidence—Take Nanjing Massacre as Example (CHENG Zhaoqi)
Chapter Eight: Tokyo Trials and International Rules of Law (Xu Te)
Chapter Nine: Tokyo Trials and World Peace (ZHANG Suping)
Appendix (ZHAO Yuhui)—translated by HE Jun

After the first draft was completed, all of us did a cross-examination to avoid repetition and conflict. At the same time, we specially invited Mr. Cao Shuji to participate in reviewing the book. If the book is of some value, then besides the young people's efforts, I owe it mainly to Mr. Cao's work. However, due to my negligence during the draft and final review, if there is any error, the responsibility lies with me.

This book is not an academic work. As an overview reading, we thought that the illustrated text would increase the readers' interest. Li Bin, the painter who has been working on a huge epic scroll of "the Tokyo Trial", is very familiar with the relevant images. So we invited him to select the photos for this book (photos in this book have been taken from the National Archives of the United States, the National Public Libraries of Japan, the Second Historical Archives of China, the People's Court Newspaper, etc.). Here, I would like to show my warm thank to Mr. Li for generously offering us some of his unfinished paintings for publication.

I am also grateful to Wang Zongguang, Jiang Sixian, Lin Zhongqin, Cheng Tianquan, Yan Shuang, Peng Weiguo, Guo Xinli, Han Jianmin, Xiang Longwan, Mei Xiaokan, Wang Xiaoqiu, Li Anfang, Yang Qingcun, Liu Jianxin, Li Yushang, Liu Peiying, AWAYA Kentaro, NAKAZATO Nariaki, TOTANI Yuma, and editors Cui Xia, Jin Di, and Sun Min, all of whom have worked hard for this book.

Finally, I would like to express my special thanks to President Zhang Jie for his long-lasting support.

December 27, 2016 CHENG Zhaoqi

Zeitfracht Medien GmbH
Ferdinand-Jühlke-Straße 7
99095 Erfurt, Deutschland
produktsicherheit@kolibri360.de